Beth Shean Studies: Aspects of Religion, History, Art, and Archaeology in Hellenistic and Roman Nysa-Scythopolis

Beth Shean Studies: Aspects of Religion, History, Art, and Archaeology in Hellenistic and Roman Nysa-Scythopolis

Irene Bald Romano and Kyle W. Mahoney, with Appendix by Dimitris Tambakopoulos and Yannis Maniatis

American Philosophical Society Press
Philadelphia

Transactions of the
American Philosophical Society
Held at Philadelphia
for Promoting Useful Knowledge
Volume 112, Part 2

ISBN: 978-1-60618-124-9
ebook ISBN: 978-1-60618-129-4
U.S. ISSN: 0065-9746

Library of Congress Cataloging-in-Publication Data
Names: Romano, Irene Bald, author. | Mahoney, Kyle W., author. |
    Tambakopoulos, Dimitris, writer of supplementary text. | Maniatis, Yannis,
    writer of supplementary text.
Title: Beth Shean studies : aspects of religion, history, art, and archaeology in
    Hellenistic and Roman Nysa-Scythopolis / Irene Bald Romano and Kyle W.
    Mahoney ; with appendix by Dimitris Tambakopolous and Yannis Maniatis.
Description: Philadelphia : American Philosophical Society Press, 2023. | Series:
    Transactions of the American philosophical society, 00659746 ; 112, part 2 |
    Includes bibliographical references and index. | Summary: "The Hellenistic
    inscription and Roman marble portrait head of Alexander the Great that are
    the subjects of this monograph were discovered by the Palestine Expedition
    of the University Museum of the University of Pennsylvania (now the
    University of Pennsylvania Museum of Archaeology and Anthropology, in
    1925 as part of excavations that were conducted from 1921 to 1933 at Beth
    Shean in the British Mandate for Palestine with a permit from the Mandatory
    Department of Antiquities. The Beth Shean excavation was focused on the
    very important Bronze Age-Early Iron Age levels of the tel and the site's
    biblical connections, and not especially on its Hellenistic, Roman, Byzantine,
    or Islamic periods"—Provided by publisher.
Identifiers: LCCN 2023021313 (print) | LCCN 2023021314 (ebook) | ISBN
    9781606181249 (paperback) | ISBN 9781606181294 (mobi)
Subjects: LCSH: Excavations (Archaeology)—Israel—Bet She'an. | Art—Israel—
    Bet She'an. | Bet She'an (Israel)—Antiquities. | Bet She'an (Israel)—
    Antiquities, Roman. | Bet She'an (Israel)—History. | Bet She'an (Israel)—
    Religion—History. | Palestine Expedition of the University Museum of the
    University of Pennsylvania (1921-1933)
Classification: LCC DS110.B393 R65 2023 (print) | LCC DS110.B393 (ebook) |
    DDC 933—dc23/eng/20230509
LC record available at https://lccn.loc.gov/2023021313
LC ebook record available at https://lccn.loc.gov/2023021314

Cover design by Eugenia B. González.

Contents

Contributors..*vii*

Acknowledgments...*ix*

Illustrations...*xiii*

Abbreviations...*xxi*

Chapter 1   Introduction 1
    Irene Bald Romano and Kyle W. Mahoney

Chapter 2   The Hellenistic Catalogue of Priests from
Nysa-Scythopolis/Beth Shean: *Supplementum
Epigraphicum Graecum* 8 33....................................17
    Kyle W. Mahoney

Chapter 3   A Portrait of Alexander the Great from
Ancient Nysa-Scythopolis: An Object Biography 55
    Irene Bald Romano

Appendix   Marble Provenance Investigation of the Head
of Alexander the Great and a Hand Fragment from
Ancient Nysa-Scythopolis, Israel................................185
    Dimitris Tambakopoulos and Yannis Maniatis

Bibliography 197

Index *237*

Contributors

Irene Bald Romano, PhD, holds joint positions as Professor of Art History in the School of Art and Professor of Anthropology in the School of Anthropology at the University of Arizona; she is also Curator of Mediterranean Archaeology at the Arizona State Museum. Dr. Romano is an archaeologist with broad interests in research on Mediterranean archaeological objects, especially Greek and Roman sculpture.

Kyle W. Mahoney, PhD, teaches at Swarthmore College in the Department of Classics. He is an ancient historian and archaeologist specializing in the study of ancient Greek inscriptions and is engaged more broadly in the study of ancient Mediterranean religions.

Dimitris Tambakopoulos, PhD, is a former postdoctoral fellow and research associate at the Laboratory of Archaeometry of the National Centre for Scientific Research "Demokritos." His main research interests and expertise focus on the scientific determination of provenance and movement of marble in antiquity as well as statistical techniques.

Yannis Maniatis, PhD, is Research Director *Emeritus* at the National Centre for Scientific Research "Demokritos." He is an archaeological scientist, creator, and former Director of the Laboratory of Archaeometry. His main research interests and expertise are the provenance and movement of marble in antiquity, radiocarbon dating, and ceramic technology.

Acknowledgments

I am very grateful to the Israel Antiquities Authority and the Israel Museum, Jerusalem, for permission to study and publish the head of Alexander the Great. I owe special thanks to David Mevorach, Rachel Caine, and other colleagues at the Israel Museum for their assistance in 2016 with my research, and to Alegre Savariego for her assistance in the Rockefeller Museum. My immense gratitude is extended to Moshe and Greta Fischer for their warm hospitality in Israel and especially to my recently departed friend and colleague, Moshe Fischer, for his interest in this project and his invaluable scholarly assistance. I am also greatly indebted to Andrew F. Stewart for encouraging me, reading the manuscript, and providing his sage advice on all matters related to Alexander and sculpture. Sadly, both Moshe Fischer and Andy Stewart passed away before I was able to hand them a copy of this publication and thank them again. I am also grateful to colleagues at Hebrew University and at the Israel Antiquities Authority's storage facility at Beth Shemesh; to Lynn Makowsky, Katie Blanchard, Alexander Pezzati, Francine Sarin, and Jen Chiappardi for their assistance in the University of Pennsylvania Museum of Archaeology and Anthropology; to the staff of the Albright Institute of Archaeology, Jerusalem, the Blegen Library of the American School of Classical Studies at Athens, and the library of the Deutsches Archäologisches Institut in Berlin for facilitating my research; to Kimberly Mast in the Visual Resource Center in the School of Art at the University of Arizona for her assistance with the images; and to Benjamin Arubas, Yael Barschak, Gabi Laron, Amihai Mazar, David Milson, Gabriel Mazor, the American Numismatic Society, the Israel Antiquities Authority, the Israel Museum, Jerusalem, the Rockefeller Museum, Jerusalem, and the Penn Museum for image permissions; and to Hans Goette for traveling to Jerusalem to take professional photographs of the head of Alexander for me. For scholarly advice I also owe my thanks and assign none of the blame for any of my errors to Carmen Arnold Biucchi, Benjamin

Arubas, Marianne Bergmann, Amelia Brown, Getzel Cohen, Elise
Friedland, Hans Rupprecht Goette, David Henlin, Ralf von den Hoff,
Sascha Kansteiner, Detlev Kreikenbom, Ingrid Laube, Kyle Mahoney,
Martin Dorka Moreno, Scott Pike, John Pollini, David Gilman Romano,
Tali Sharvit, Beatrice St. Laurent, Mary Sturgeon, Elena Stolyarik, and
Tobias Wild. I am grateful to Yannis Maniatis and Dimitris Tambakopoulos from the Laboratory of Archaeometry, Institute of Nanoscience
and Nanotechnology, National Centre for Scientific Research "Demokritos," Aghia Paraskevi, Greece, for their analysis of the marble of the
head of Alexander and a hand from the same context; to Scott Pike of
Willamette University for conducting the marble analysis of the colossal
fingers from Beth Shean in the University of Pennsylvania Museum; to
my colleague Kyle Mahoney for undertaking the study of the Hellenistic
inscription from Beth Shean; and to Yannis Nakas, who worked with me
to create drawings of the head of Alexander and reconstructions of its
possible setting. I am deeply appreciative of the financial support for
this project provided by the W. F. Albright Institute of Archaeology,
Jerusalem; the American Philosophical Society, Philadelphia; 1984 Foundation; School of Art and College of Fine Arts, University of Arizona;
and School of Social and Behavioral Sciences, University of Arizona.
We owe our thanks to the American Philosophical Society for their
interest in publishing this monograph, and to Pamela Lankas for her
editorial work.

                                                    —**Irene Bald Romano**

I extend my warmest thanks to Irene Bald Romano for giving me the
opportunity to study this inscription and publish the results with her in
the present volume. I thank Katy Blanchard, Keeper of the Near East
Collections at the University of Pennsylvania Museum of Archaeology
and Anthropology, for her kind permission to study the stele, as well as
Alessandro Pezzati for help with the acquisition of photographs and
permission for their publication. General thanks are due to the Penn
Museum for support of this research, especially with respect to the permission to study the stone upon which *Supplementum Epigraphicum Graecum*
8 33 is inscribed. Of course, my deepest thanks go to the American
Philosophical Society and our excellent editor, Pamela Lankas. I am also
most grateful to Julia Wilker for discussing issues of late Seleucid history
with me and to Jake Nabel for carefully reading and commenting on the
manuscript. Angelos Chaniotis and Jeremy McInerney are also due thanks,
as are all the participants at Epigraphic Friday, held at the Institute for

Advanced Study in Princeton on March 6, 2020, where I presented this inscription. Any errors are, of course, my own.

—**Kyle W. Mahoney**

Illustrations

Cover and Figure 1.1 Tel of Beth Shean and lower city from the theater.
Photo: I. B. Romano.

Figure 1.2 Beth Shean lower city and tel, February 1996.
Photo: Gabi Laron, The Hebrew University of Jerusalem. Reproduced with permission of Gabi Laron. Photo: https://www.biblicalarchaeology.org/wp-content/uploads/2012/02/beth-shean1.jpg (accessed January 23, 2023).

Figure 1.3 Map of Roman Palestine.
Map: David Milson. Image: Hezser, C., ed. *The Oxford Handbook of Jewish Daily Life in Roman Palestine.* Oxford: Oxford University Press, 2010, fig. xvii; online edition, Oxford Academic, September 18, 2012: https://doi.org/10.1093/oxfordhb/9780199216437.001.0001 (accessed January 11, 2023). Reproduced with permission of David Milson.

Figure 1.4 General plan of area of Beth Shean and Tel Iztabba.
Plan: Benjamin Arubas, 2021. Reproduced courtesy of Benjamin Arubas, the Hebrew University Expedition to Bet Shean-Scythopolis.

Figure 1.5 Map of Decapolis cities.
Image: Licensed under Creative Commons, https://commons.wikimedia.org/wiki/File:Thedecapolis.png (accessed January 9, 2023).

Figure 2.1 *SEG* 8 33, general view.
University of Pennsylvania Museum of Archaeology and Anthropology 29-107-961. Photo: Penn Museum, reproduced with permission.

Figure 2.2 *SEG* 8 33, detailed view of inscribed lines.
University of Pennsylvania Museum of Archaeology and Anthropology 29-107-961. Photo: Penn Museum, reproduced with permission.

Figure 2.3 *SEG* 8 96, catalogue of priests from Samaria.
Photo: Reisner, G.A., C.S. Fisher, and D. G. Lyon. *Harvard Excavations at Samaria 1908–1910.* Cambridge, MA: Harvard University Press, 1924, pl. 59a. Permission of the Harvard University Museum of the Ancient Near East: https://curiosity.lib.harvard.edu/expeditions-and-discoveries/catalog/38-990021305790203941 (accessed August 22, 2020).

Figure 2.4 *SEG* **19 904/20 413, private dedication from Ptolemais in honor of Antiochos IX Kyzikenos.**
Photo: Landau, Y. H. "A Greek Inscription from Acre." *IEJ* 11 (1961): pl. 28a. Permission of *Israel Exploration Journal.*

Figure 3.1 Portrait of Alexander the Great, Beth Shean.
Israel Museum, IAA 1931-7. On display in the Israel Museum, Jerusalem, with the Knesset building in background. Photo: I. B. Romano. Collection of Israel Antiquities Authority, with permission.

Figure 3.2. Map of Alexander's route.
Image: http://upload.wikimedia.org/wikipedia/commons/4/40/Macedon Empire.jpg (accessed August 20, 2020).

Figure 3.3 Plan of the city center of Nysa-Scythopolis.
Plan: Benjamin Arubas. Courtesy of Benjamin Arubas, the Hebrew University Expedition to Bet Shean-Scythopolis.

Figure 3.4 View of the lower city of Beth Shean from tel.
Photo: I. B. Romano.

Figure 3.5 Plan of the temple and cistern on the tel of Beth Shean by E. Davies, dated 09-14-1925.
Plan: Archives of University of Pennsylvania Museum of Archaeology and Anthropology. Courtesy of Penn Museum, image #134793.

Figure 3.6 Columns drums for Roman temple on tel, Beth Shean.
Photo: I. B. Romano.

Figure 3.7 Limestone Corinthian column capital from temple on the tel, Beth Shean.
Photo: I. B. Romano.

Figure 3.8 Plan of Round Church with outlines of the temple and cistern, Beth Shean.
Plan: Beth Shean Archives of University of Pennsylvania Museum of Archaeology and Anthropology. Reproduced courtesy of Penn Museum.

Figure 3.9 Bronze coin of Gordian III, mint of Nysa-Scythopolis. *A (Obverse)*: **Laureate head of Antoninus Pius facing right.** *B (Reverse)*: **Dionysos standing to left with his thyrsus and panther at his feet.**
Photos: American Numismatic Society, http://numismatics.org/collection/ 2012.71.187 (accessed August 21, 2020).

Figure 3.10 *A:* **Altar dedicated by Seleukos, son of Ariston, to Dionysos, the founder, Beth Shean.** *B:* **Detail of altar.**
Israel Museum, IAA 1991-2104. Photos: I. B. Romano. Collection of Israel Antiquities Authority. Reproduced with permission.

Figure 3.11 Statue of Dionysos from Silvanus Hall, Beth Shean. *A:* **Frontal view.** *B:* **Back view.** *C:* **Detail of damage to face of Dionysos.**
Israel Museum, IAA 1990-821. Photos: I. B. Romano. Collection of Israel Antiquities Authority. Reproduced with permission.

Figure 3.12 Double-herm of Dionysos and Ariadne, Beth Shean.
Israel Museum, IAA 1932-36. Photo: I. B. Romano. Collection of Israel Antiquities Authority. Reproduced with permission.

Figure 3.13 Bronze coin of Caracalla, mint of Nysa-Scythopolis, 216 CE. *A* (*Obverse*)**: Laureate bust of Caracalla to right.** *B* (*Reverse*)**: Zeus enthroned to left.**
Photos: American Numismatic Society, http://numismatics.org/collection/ 2012.71.188 (accessed August 21, 2020).

Figure 3.14 "Peopled" scroll frieze from Severan Theater, Beth Shean.
Photo: I. B. Romano.

Figure 3.15 Torso of an emperor wearing a cuirass, reused in a pier south of the colonnade of the Silvanus Hall, Beth Shean, second century CE.
Israel Museum, IAA 1991-2106. Photo: I. B. Romano. Collection of Israel Antiquities Authority. Reproduced with permission.

Figure 3.16 Statue of Tyche/Fortuna from Severan Theater, Beth Shean.
Israel Museum, IAA 1991-2093. Photo: I. B. Romano. Collection of Israel Antiquities Authority. Reproduced with permission.

Figure 3.17 Statue of Aphrodite with Eros, from Eastern Bathhouse, Beth Shean.
Israel Museum, IAA 2001-2987. Photo: ©The Israel Museum, Jerusalem. Collection of Israel Antiquities Authority. Reproduced with permission.

Figure 3.18 Statue of a nymph with a shell, from Eastern Bathhouse, Beth Shean.
Israel Museum, IAA 2001-2986. Photo: I. B. Romano. Collection of Israel Antiquities Authority. Reproduced with permission.

Figure 3.19 Head of Athena, Tel Naharon, in vicinity of Beth Shean.
Israel Museum, IAA 1978-505. Photo: I. B. Romano. Collection of Israel Antiquities Authority. Reproduced with permission.

Figure 3.20 Limestone funerary bust, North Cemetery, Beth Shean.
University of Pennsylvania Museum of Archaeology and Anthropology 29-107-921. Photo: F. Sarin and J. Chiappardi. Reproduced courtesy of Penn Museum.

Figure 3.21 Dionysos/Bacchus or a satyr head from a figured Corinthian capital, Beth Shean.
University of Pennsylvania Museum of Archaeology and Anthropology 29-107-919. Photo: F. Sarin and J. Chiappardi. Reproduced courtesy of Penn Museum.

Figure 3.22 *A:* **Figured capitals on Palladius Street, Beth Shean.** *B:* **Figured capital with head of Dionysos.** *C:* **Detail of figured capital.**
Photos: A, C, I. B. Romano; B, courtesy of Moshe Fischer.

Figure 3.23 Marble left hand, Beth Shean. *A:* **Back of hand.** *B:* **Inside of hand.** *C:* **Detail of wrist.**
Rockefeller Archaeological Museum, Jerusalem S.968. Photos: I. B. Romano. Collection of Israel Antiquities Authority. Reproduced with permission.

Figure 3.24 Colossal marble right hand fragment, Beth Shean. *A:* **Top view.** *B:* **Side view.**
University of Pennsylvania Museum 29-107-924b. Photo: F. Sarin and J. Chiappardi. Reproduced courtesy of Penn Museum.

Figure 3.25 Marble left thumb(?), Beth Shean.
Rockefeller Archaeological Museum, Jerusalem S.851. Photo: I. B. Romano. Collection of Israel Antiquities Authority. Reproduced with permission.

Figure 3.26 Colossal finger, Beth Shean.
University of Pennsylvania Museum 29-107-924a. Photo: F. Sarin and J. Chiappardi. Reproduced courtesy of Penn Museum.

Figure 3.27 Colossal finger, Beth Shean.
University of Pennsylvania Museum 29-107-924f. Photo: F. Sarin and J. Chiappardi. Reproduced courtesy of Penn Museum.

Figure 3.28 Colossal finger, Beth Shean. *A:* **Frontal view.** *B:* **Back view.**
University of Pennsylvania Museum 29-107-924d. Photo: F. Sarin and J. Chiappardi. Reproduced courtesy of Penn Museum.

Figure 3.29 Portrait of Alexander the Great, Beth Shean. Frontal view.
Israel Museum, IAA 1931-7. Photo: Hans Rupprecht Goette. Collection of Israel Antiquities Authority. Reproduced with permission.

Figure 3.30 Portrait of Alexander the Great, Beth Shean. Right profile view.
Israel Museum, IAA 1931-7. Photo: Hans Rupprecht Goette. Collection of Israel Antiquities Authority. Reproduced with permission.

Figure 3.31 Portrait of Alexander the Great, Beth Shean. Detail of right side of face.
Israel Museum, IAA 1931-7. Photo: Hans Rupprecht Goette. Collection of Israel Antiquities Authority. Reproduced with permission.

Figure 3.32 Portrait of Alexander the Great, Beth Shean. Left profile view.
Israel Museum, IAA 1931-7. Photo: Hans Rupprecht Goette. Collection of Israel Antiquities Authority. Reproduced with permission.

Figure 3.33 Portrait of Alexander the Great, Beth Shean. Detail of feature on left side below hair.
Israel Museum, IAA 1931-7. Photo: I. B. Romano. Collection of Israel Antiquities Authority. Reproduced with permission.

Figure 3.34 Portrait of Alexander the Great, Beth Shean. Back view.
Israel Museum, IAA 1931-7. Photo: Hans Rupprecht Goette. Collection of Israel Antiquities Authority. Reproduced with permission.

Figure 3.35 Portrait of Alexander the Great, Beth Shean. Bottom of neck.
Israel Museum, IAA 1931-7. Photo: I. B. Romano. Collection of Israel Antiquities Authority. Reproduced with permission.

Figure 3.36 Portrait of Alexander the Great, Beth Shean. View of top of head.
Israel Museum, IAA 1931-7. Photo: ©The Israel Museum, Jerusalem, by Elie Posner. Collection of Israel Antiquities Authority. Reproduced with permission.

Figure 3.37 Portrait of Alexander the Great, Beth Shean. View of top of head with hole for attribute.
Israel Museum, IAA 1931-7. Photo: ©The Israel Museum, Jerusalem, by Elie Posner. Collection of Israel Antiquities Authority. Reproduced with permission.

Figure 3.38 Portrait of Alexander the Great, Beth Shean. Detail of hole for attribute.
Israel Museum, IAA 1931-7. Photo: I. B. Romano. Collection of Israel Antiquities Authority. Reproduced with permission.

Figure 3.39 Reconstruction drawing of top of head of Alexander the Great (IAA 1931-7) with locks of hair around hole.
Drawing: Yannis Nakas.

Figure 3.40 Azara herm. *A:* **Three-quarter frontal view.** *B:* **Right profile view.**
Musée du Louvre, Paris Ma 436 (MR 405). Photos: Wikimedia.org, in public domain, https://commons.wikimedia.org/wiki/File:Azara_herm_Louvre_Ma436.jpg and https://upload.wikimedia.org/wikipedia/commons/c/c8/Azara_herm_Louvre_Ma436_n3.jpg (accessed January 9, 2023).

Figure 3.41 Gold medallion with image of Alexander, Aboukir, Egypt, ca. 215–243 CE.
Walters Art Gallery, Baltimore, 59.1. Photo: Licensed under Creative Commons, https://art.thewalters.org/detail/21555/medallion-with-alexander-the-great/ (accessed August, 21, 2020).

Figure 3.42 Hypothetical reconstruction of the standing statue of Alexander, Beth Shean.
Drawing: Yannis Nakas.

Figure 3.43 Roman statue of Alexander from Severan theater of Perge.
Archaeological Museum, Antalya. Photo: https://commons.wikimedia.org/wiki/File:Perge_Theater_-_Alexander_1.jpg (accessed January 9, 2023).

Figure 3.44 Bronze coin of Gerasa, minted under Elagabalus (r. 218–222 CE). *A (Obverse)*: **Elagabalus.** *B (Reverse)*: **Diademed bust of Alexander and the legend "Alexander of Macedon."**
Photos: American Numismatic Society, New York, of coin in the Sofaer Collection, Israel Museum, Jerusalem. Collection of Israel Antiquities Authority. Reproduced with permission.

Figure 3.45 Gold medallion with image of Caracalla, Aboukir, Egypt, ca. 215–243 CE.
Walters Art Gallery, Baltimore, 59.3. Photo: Licensed under Creative Commons, https://art.thewalters.org/detail/3501/medallion-with-roman-emperor-caracalla/ (accessed August 21, 2020).

Figure 3.46 Reconstruction of portrait head of Alexander the Great, Beth Shean (IAA 1931-7) with a star attribute.
Drawing: Yannis Nakas.

Figure 3.47 Interior of the temple on tel of Beth Shean with hypothetical cult statue of Zeus, flanked by Alexander the Great and Dionysos.
Drawing: Yannis Nakas.

Figure 3.48 Portrait of Alexander the Great, Beth Shean. Detail of face.
Israel Museum, IAA 1931-7. Photo: Hans Rupprecht Goette. Collection of Israel Antiquities Authority. Reproduced with permission.

Figure 3.49 Rockefeller Archaeological Museum, Jerusalem.
Photo: I. B. Romano, 2016.

Figure 3.50 Rockefeller Archaeological Museum, Jerusalem, inner courtyard.
Photo: I. B. Romano, 2016.

Figure 3.51 Head of Alexander the Great, Beth Shean, IAA 1931-7 in an old mount in Rockefeller Archaeological Museum, Jerusalem, date unknown.
Photo: ©The Israel Museum, Jerusalem. Collection of Israel Antiquities Authority. Reproduced with permission.

Figure A.1 Marble left hand, Tel Beth Shean. Rockefeller Archaeological Museum, Jerusalem S.968 (sample 1).
Photo: I. B. Romano. Collection of Israel Antiquities Authority. Reproduced with permission.

Figure A.2 Over-life-sized male head from Tel Beth Shean, IAA 1931-7 (sample 2).
Photo: Hans Rupprecht Goette. Collection of Israel Antiquities Authority. Reproduced with permission.

Figure A.3 Diagram of natural logarithm of manganese (Mn^{2+}) versus the natural logarithm of the maximum grain size (MGS) for the two samples from ancient Nysa-Scythopolis and the ancient marble quarries of Dokimeion/Afyon (AF), Penteli (PE), Altintas (ALT-1, ALT-2), Carrara (CA), Hymettos (HY), Doliana (DOL), Aphrodisias (APHR), Ephesos (EPH), Miletos (MIL), Proconnesos (PR-1, PR-2), Paros (PA-LK, PA-L, PA-M), Thasos (THA), and Naxos (NX-AP, NX-ML).
Diagram: Tambakopoulos and Maniatis.

Figure A.4 Diagram of $\delta^{13}C‰$ versus $\delta^{18}O‰$ for the two samples from ancient Nysa-Scythopolis and the ancient marble quarries of Dokimeion/Afyon (AF), Penteli (PE), Altintas (ALT-1, ALT-2), Carrara (CA), Hymettos (HY), Doliana (DOL), Aphrodisias (APHR), Ephesos (EPH-1, EPH-2), Miletos (MIL), Proconnesos (PR-1, PR-2), Paros (PA-LK, PA-L, PA-M), Thasos (TH-AL, TH-AF), Naxos (NX-AP, NX-ML), Kos and Hierapolis (HIE).
Diagram: Tambakopoulos and Maniatis.

Figure A.5 Diagram of variables derived from discriminant analysis for sample 1 and its three possible quarries: Penteli, Afyon, and Altintas.
Diagram: Tambakopoulos and Maniatis.

Figure A.6 Diagram of variables derived from discriminant analysis for sample 2 and its three possible quarries: Aphrodisias, Miletos, and Proconnesos.
Diagram: Tambakopoulos and Maniatis.

Abbreviations

Standard abbreviations employed by the *American Journal of Archaeology* (*AJA*: https://www.ajaonline.org/submissions/abbreviations) and the *Supplementum Epigraphicum Graecum* (*SEG*: https://referenceworks .brillonline.com/entries/supplementum-epigraphicum-graecum/ abbreviations-aabbr) are used throughout this volume.

BNJ	*Brill's New Jacoby* (Worthington 2006–23)
P. Dura.	*Papyrus from Dura Europos* (Welles, Fink, and Gilliam 1959)
P. Fam. Tebt.	*Papyrus Family Archive from Tebtunis* (van Groningen 1950)

Greek spellings are used throughout the text.

OTHER ABBREVIATIONS

Abb.	Fig. (in German)
cm	Centimeters
D.	Depth
H.	Height
m	Meters
P.	Preserved
r.u.	Relative units
Taf.	Pl. (in German)
Th.	Thickness
W.	Width

Chapter 1

Introduction

Irene Bald Romano and Kyle W. Mahoney

The Hellenistic inscription and Roman marble portrait head of Alexander the Great that are the subjects of this monograph were discovered by the Palestine Expedition of the University Museum of the University of Pennsylvania (now the University of Pennsylvania Museum of Archaeology and Anthropology, hereafter "Penn Museum") in 1925 as part of excavations that were conducted from 1921 to 1933 at Beth Shean in the British Mandate for Palestine with a permit from

Figure 1.1 Tel of Beth Shean and lower city from the theater.

Photo: I. B. Romano.

the Mandatory Department of Antiquities (Figures 1.1 and 1.2).[1] Though the Penn Museum's Beth Shean excavations were a model of rigorous methodology for their time, the focus of the excavators—and of the museum and its donors—was on the very important Bronze Age–Early Iron Age levels of the tel and the site's biblical connections, and not especially on its Hellenistic, Roman, Byzantine, or Islamic periods. All the excavation directors were primarily Late Bronze Age–Early Iron Age/ biblical archaeology specialists. Clarence Fisher (1921–23), the first field director of the site, was dismissed in 1923, with Alan Rowe (1925–29) named as his successor, and later Gerald M. Fitzgerald (also spelled FitzGerald; 1930–33), leaving some discontinuities in interpretations and in the publication of finds. A generous division of the finds allowed a large quantity of archaeological material from these excavations to be shipped to Philadelphia for the Penn Museum's collections, including

---

[1] Publications of the Penn Museum's excavation campaigns include Rowe (1928, 1930, 1940) and Fitzgerald (1930, 1931, 1932, 1934). See Pickett (2013) for a discussion of the history and context of these Penn excavations. For the later history of excavations at the site see Mazar et al. (2008).

Figure 1.2 Beth Shean lower city and tel, February 1996.

Photo: Gabi Laron, The Hebrew University of Jerusalem. Reproduced with permission of Gabi Laron. Photo: https://www.biblicalarchaeology.org/wp-content/uploads/2012/02/beth-shean1.jpg (accessed January 23, 2023).

the inscription that is the subject of Kyle Mahoney's contribution (Chapter 2), while the Alexander head, the focus of Chapter 3, remained in the Mandate.[2]

Scythopolis, or Nysa-Scythopolis (hereafter "Scythopolis"), as Beth Shean was called during the Hellenistic and Roman periods,[3] is located on the western bank of the Jordan River in a strategic position at the confluence of key north–south and east–west routes and in a fertile valley suitable for abundant agricultural production (Figure 1.3). Pliny (*NH* 5.16) and Solinus (36.1–2; cf. Diod. Sic., *Bibliotheke* 1.15.6) record that the site was founded by Dionysos when he stopped there to bury his nursemaid, the nymph Nysa. This aetiological myth establishes Dionysos

---

[2] See Chapter 3, pp. 174–82, for its modern museum history.

[3] See pp. 9–10, this chapter and Chapter 2, pp. 28–30 for discussion of the history and significance of these names. Beth Shean is the site's ancient Semitic name as well as its modern name. The transliteration is variously recorded as Beisan, Baysan, Beit She'an, or Bet Shean. Tel el-Husan or Tell Hössn is its Arabic name.

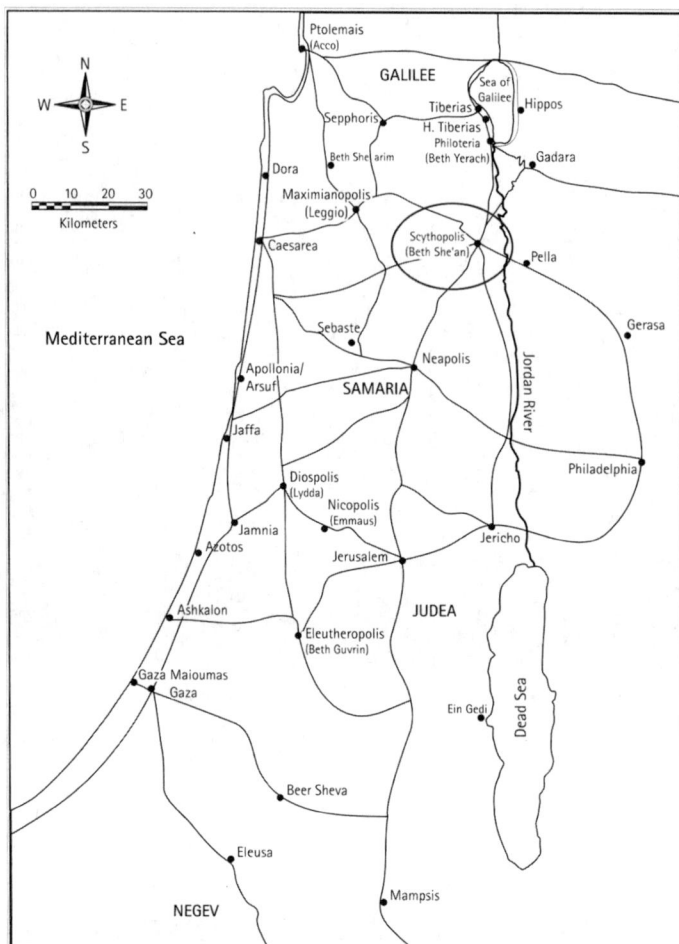

Figure 1.3 Map of Roman Palestine.

Map: David Milson. Image: Hezser, C., ed. *The Oxford Handbook of Jewish Daily Life in Roman Palestine*. Oxford: Oxford University Press, 2010, fig. xvii; online edition, Oxford Academic, September 18, 2012: https://doi.org/10.1093/oxfordhb/9780199216437.001.0001 (accessed January 11, 2023).

as the patron deity of the city, a god whose presence is well attested iconographically and epigraphically at the site.[4]

Beth Shean's history is a long and complicated one, beginning in the Neolithic period (fifth millennium BCE). It especially enjoyed great prosperity during the Bronze Age, in the fifteenth to the mid-twelfth centuries BCE, when the site served as a key center for the Egyptian

---

[4] See pp. 9–10, this chapter and, for a more extensive account, see Chapter 3, pp. 59–60, 74–82.

imperial administration in northern Canaan.[5] In the Early Iron Age, Beth Shean became an important Canaanite city and was destroyed in the early tenth century, possibly by the biblical King David. It subsequently became an Israelite city, and Beth Shean is mentioned in many Old Testament passages. Joshua (17:11–12, 16) and Judges (1:27; cf. also 1 Chronicles 7:29) maintain that, although Beth Shean belonged to the tribe of Manasseh, Canaanites nevertheless continued to inhabit the area. The first book of Samuel (31:8–12) implies that Beth Shean belonged to the Philistines. The same source may imply the existence of a temple of Astarte in Beth Shean where Saul's armor was deposited. The corpses of Saul and his sons were said to have been affixed to the walls of Beth Shean, whereas 1 Chronicles (10:10) says his head was placed in the temple of Dagon (cf. 2 Samuel 21:12). 1 Kings (4:12) includes Beth Shean as a part of Solomon's kingdom, whereas 2 Kings (15:29) implies that Tiglath-Pilaser III (r. 745–727 BCE) ravaged the area and sent the inhabitants to Assyria in 732 BCE. Very little is understood about Scythopolis's Classical and early Hellenistic history.[6] The presence of Alexander the Great in the region is much disputed, as is discussed in the following text,[7] and it seems activity at Beth Shean essentially ceased until the third century BCE.[8] The site flourished especially during the Roman and Byzantine periods (Figure 1.4).[9]

HELLENISTIC SCYTHOPOLIS

After the death of Alexander, the region initially fell under the control of the Ptolemies (Diod. Sic., *Bibliotheke* 18.43; *Marmor Parium BNJ* 239 F b12), who ruled Palestine for about a century. Tel Beth Shean may have served as the site of a Macedonian garrison under Ptolemy II

---

[5] A topographic list at Karnak from the reign of Thutmose III (r. 1479–1425 BCE), who first conquered the area for Egypt, is the oldest secure reference to the place and name (Mazar 2011, 153). The name appears as *bit ša-a-ni* on the Amarna tablet EA 289, a letter from Abdi-Heba of Jerusalem to the Pharaoh (probably Akhenaten, r. 1352–1336 BCE).

[6] See Lifshitz (1977) for a summary of the Hellenistic (and Roman) history.

[7] See Chapter 3, pp. 64–66.

[8] Mazar (2006, 37).

[9] See pp. 5–14, this chapter, and for the history of the site, excavations, and monuments, see Tsafrir and Foerster (1997), and Mazar et al. (2008) and Mazar (2010) for the Bronze Age and Iron Age remains. Panitz-Cohn (2014) also provides an account of all excavations and includes a full bibliography. Publication of excavation campaigns after those of the Penn Museum include Foerster and Tsafrir (1987–88, 1988–89, 1993); Tsafrir and Foerster (1989–90, 1997); Mazar and Amitai-Preiss (2006); Mazar and Mullins (2007); Mazor and Najjar (2007); Mazor (2008); Panitz-Cohn and Mazar (2009); Bar-Nathan and Atrash (2011); Mazar (2012); Mazor and Atrash (2015); Mazor, Atrash, and Finkielsztejn (2018).

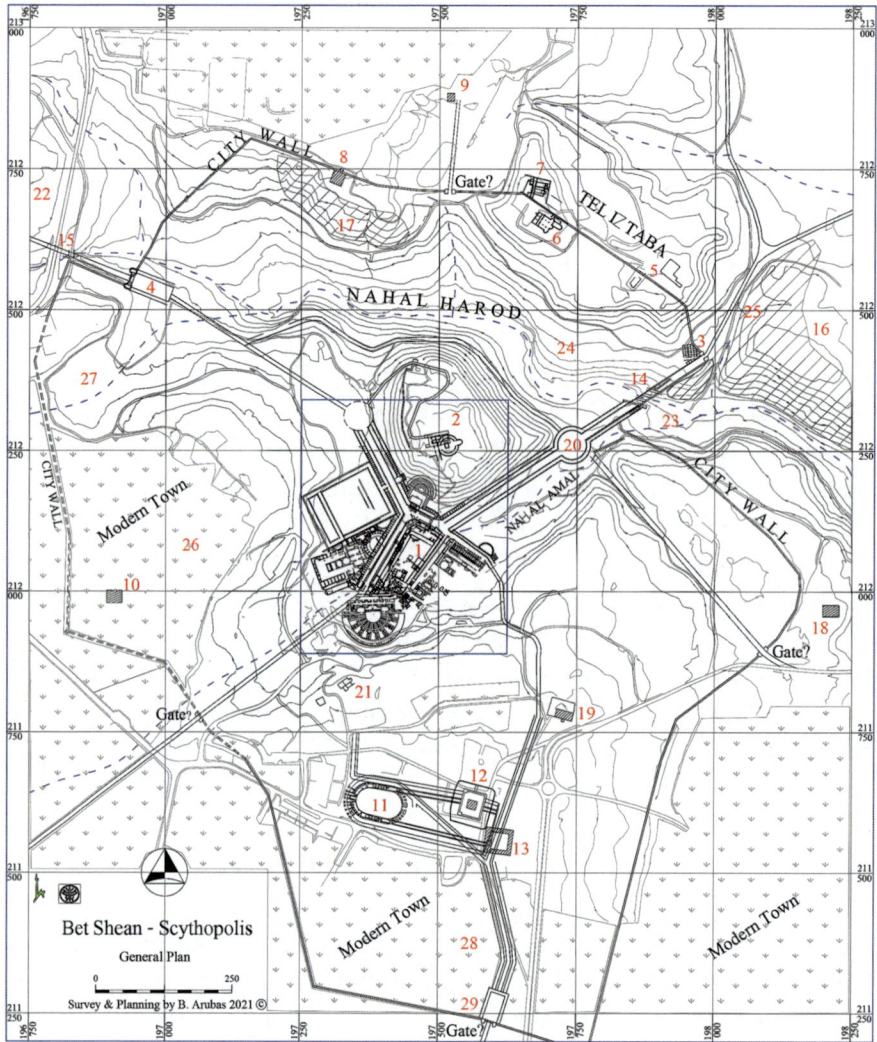

Figure 1.4 General plan of area of Beth Shean and Tel Iztabba.

Plan: Benjamin Arubas (2021). Reproduced courtesy of Benjamin Arubas, the Hebrew University Expedition to Bet Shean-Scythopolis.

(r. 285–246 BCE), with a Ptolemaic hoard of twenty silver tetradrachms, eleven dating to 259/258–249/248 BCE, found on its southern edge.[10] It would certainly make sense for there to have been some Macedonian military presence in this strategically important location, and the name Scythopolis most probably originated with the creation of this installation.[11] Josephus (*Antiquities* 12.183) attests to a settlement with some sort of hierarchy when he tells of the tax collector Joseph, son of Tobias, who executed the leading citizens (τοὺς πρώτους) of Scythopolis upon their refusal to pay taxes, sometime between 240–220 BCE.

To the north of the ancient Tel Beth Shean, extensive Hellenistic remains have come to light beyond the Nahal Ḥarod on Tel Iztabba, a significant settlement of ca. 225,000 square meters, which has been proposed as the main site of the Hellenistic settlement. Stamped Rhodian and Knidian transport amphoras of the third to first centuries BCE discovered there, as well as on Tel Beth Shean, imply trade with the Aegean world, although the actual settlement of Tel Iztabba seems to have been founded around 170 BCE and destroyed in a conflagration associated with the Hasmonean takeover in 108/107 BCE.[12] A new campaign of

---

[10] See Fisher (1923, 239, 242), Fitzgerald (1931, 51–57), Fuks (1976, 59–73; 1983, 44–51), Mazar and Amitai-Preiss (2006, 37–40), Lichtenberger and Tal (2020, 45). In addition, during the course of the Hebrew University's renewed excavations on Tel Beth Shean, other Hellenistic coins were found, the earliest (two) from the time of Ptolemy II (r. 285–246 BCE), ten Seleucid (Antiochos IV Epiphanes [r. 175–164 BCE] to Antiochos IX [r. 115–95 BCE]), four Hasmonean, and two Tyrian shekels (Amitai-Preiss 2006; Mazor and Atrash 2018a, 1–2). See Chapter 2, pp. 38–39, 42–43 on the significance of the Seleucid coins with respect to the Hellenistic inscription from the tel. The presence of over 30 stamped amphora handles of the 3rd century BCE on the tel also suggests some limited activity, perhaps for defensive purposes (Finkielsztejn 2018, 18; Mazor and Atrash 2018a, 1).

[11] On the name Scythopolis, see Tcherikover (1927, 71–72), Abel (1952, 57), Avi-Yonah (1962), Jones (1971, 240–41), Lifshitz (1977, 262–67), D. Graf (1992, 10–11), Lichtenberger (2003, 128–30), Cohen (2006, 290–91). The meaning of the name is unclear, but it has been connected to settler-soldiers. The idea that Scythopolis refers to a Scythian invasion in the seventh century BCE can probably be discarded (Hdt. 1.105; Syncellus 405 (ed. Dindorf): Σκύθαι τὴν Παλαιστίνην κατέδραμον καὶ τὴν Βασὰν κατέσχον τὴν ἐξ αὐτῶν κληθεῖσαν Σκυθόπολιν; see, however, Lifshitz (1977, 263–64), who connects this invasion with Jeremiah 1:14). It is possible that Scythian mercenaries (or even simply units of horse-archers so designated) were settled here as cleruchs under Ptolemy II, as Avi-Yonah (1962) suggests. Indeed, Youtie and Bonner (1937, 49–52) published a *defixio* from Beth Shean that includes the names Sarmation and Sarmanna, which could indicate Scythian origin. Finally, some suggest a Semitic origin in the name of the nearby town of Sukkot (although this seems to have been on the other side of the Jordan), the god Sikkuth, or Beth Sheqet, a proposed alternative for Beth Shean; these interpretations are possible but otherwise unsupported by direct evidence. We should also not exclude the idea that *Scythian* is essentially synonymous with *barbarian*.

[12] Applebaum (1989, 6–8), Cohen (2006, 290–92). On the handles from Tel Beth Shean, see Ariel (2006); for those from Tel Iztabba: *Supplementum Epigraphicum Graecum (SEG)* 29 1614, see Finkielsztejn (2018). These handles (roughly fifty) mostly date to the third quarter of the third century BCE and support the idea of a military settlement in the Ptolemaic period. For a similar situation at nearby Philoteria, see Tal (2019) who suggests significant Ptolemaic activity in this area during the middle of the third century BCE. According to Tal, this included the refoundation (accompanied at times by changing of names) of Beth Shean/Scythopolis, Bet Yeraḥ/Philoteria, Acco/ʿkh/Ptolemais, Joppa/ypy/Iope, and ʿzh/Gaza.

excavations on Tel Iztabba begun in 2019, led by Oren Tal and Achim
Lichtenberger, will certainly reveal more about the relationship between
these neighboring tels.[13] It appears that the main Seleucid settlement was
located on Tel Iztabba, whose layers are thus typically uppermost and
often isolated.[14] Already the team has identified four areas on the eastern
side of the tel (A, B, C, and D).[15] Area A revealed evidence of Byzantine
occupation,[16] whereas Areas B and C yielded primarily Seleucid material.
In Areas B and C, the team excavated walls with primarily basalt foundations (at times intersected by limestone blocks) that belonged to domestic
structures. Some of the rooms were decorated with First Pompeian Style
or Masonry Style red-, yellow-, and black-colored stucco, and the structures show clear evidence of violent destruction. A particularly exciting
discovery from Area D is a hoard of ten copper-alloy coins of Seleucid
date, which were wrapped in white-colored linen. All date to the reign
of Alexander II Zabinas, and the hoard was deposited in the 120s BCE
during the struggles that pitted Zabinas first against Demetrios II and
later against Antiochos VIII Grypos and Kleopatra Thea.[17]

In the struggles among the Diadochi for control of Alexander's
empire, the Seleucids, under Antiochos III (r. 222–187 BCE), defeated
Ptolemy V at the beginning of the second century BCE and took full
control of this part of the Near East. In 218 BCE, Scythopolis surrendered
to Antiochos III (Polyb. 5.70.4–5), and shortly after the Fifth Syrian War
(202–198/194 BCE), the city became subject to the Seleucids.[18] Recent
excavations on Tel Beth Shean recovered ten Seleucid coins, which thus
provide further material evidence for a Seleucid presence on the tel in
the second century BCE; the earliest coin was minted at Ptolemais during
the reign of Antiochos IV.[19] An inscription found in the valley about
seven kilometers northwest of the site indicates that a Seleucid garrison
was stationed here at the same time.[20] In light of this evidence, supported
by the interpretation of the inscription discussed by Mahoney, we might

---

[13] See, for example, Lichtenberger et al. (2020), Lichtenberger and Tal (2020), Ebeling et al. (2020, 2021).

[14] Lichtenberger et al. (2020, 49).

[15] Lichtenberger and Tal (2020, 46–47).

[16] Ebeling et al. (2020, 181–82).

[17] Lichtenberger and Tal (2020), Edrey et al. (2022). See Chapter 2, pp. 30–43 for the greater significance of this find with respect to the Hellenistic inscriptions.

[18] As Cohen (2006, 290) notes, Polybius says that the combined territories of Scythopolis and Philoteria were large enough to support the army of Antiochos: "the implication is that the territories of the two cities were rich and/or extensive."

[19] Amitai-Preiss (2006, 608, no. 3).

[20] *SEG* 29 1613; Landau (1966), L. Hannestad (2011, 253–54), Aperghis (2004, 104, 269–73, 318–20).

consider the possibility that Seleucid Nysa was originally on Tel Iztabba, while its earlier, Ptolemaic "twin city" Scythopolis was across the Nahal Ḥarod on Tel Beth Shean, the latter made fully Seleucid by the implantation of a dynastic cult.[21]

Initially, cordial relations with and religious freedom for the Jews were fostered, but Antiochos IV Epiphanes (r. 175–164 BCE) shifted this dynamic, and his persecutions of the Jews in Judaea and Samaria precipitated turmoil in Palestine and the Maccabean Revolt of 167–160 BCE (Joseph., *Jewish War* 1.31–33; 2 Macc. 5:11–14).[22] The inscription analyzed in full by Mahoney in Chapter 2 dates to the third quarter of the second century BCE and attests to the existence of Seleucid cults of Zeus Olympios, *Theoi Soteres*, the ancestors of the Seleucid king, and the king himself on Tel Beth Shean.

Antiochos IV is most probably responsible for renaming the site Nysa after his daughter or niece, although this is a matter of some debate, as others wish to connect Nysa with the nurse of Dionysos, an important dynastic god of the Ptolemies.[23] The name Nysa appears first on coins dating to the 50s BCE, where it is found alongside Gabinia, a name given to honor the governor responsible for the city's restoration at that time.[24] At some point the name was certainly connected with the nurse of Dionysos, who was allegedly buried at Scythopolis. According to these traditions, Dionysos founded the city and peopled it with Scythians. The prevalence of Dionysiac imagery and evidence for the worship of both Dionysos and Nysa (sometimes as Tyche) in the imperial period at Beth Shean, discussed further by Romano,[25] have led to the conclusion that the association goes back to the Ptolemies, who fostered this link with their dynastic god. It is likely, however, that the myth about the city's

[21] See Chapter 2, pp. 27–30 and Lichtenberger and Tal (2020, 46).

[22] See Gruen (2016) and Bernhardt (2017, including summaries of previous scholarship on the subject and various models of interpretation of the persecution of the Jews by Antiochos IV and the Maccabean Revolt).

[23] Jones (1971, 250), Rigsby (1980, 238–42), Di Segni (1997, 145–46), Lichtenberger (2003, 129–30). Some good support for the former idea is found in the fact that Nysa on the Maiandros was also named for a Seleucid royal lady (Lichtenberger 2003, 130). In this Carian Nysa, whose chief gods were Demeter, Kore, and Pluto, a later link with the Dionysos mythos was forged based on the name. Similarly, Nikaia was named after the wife of Lysimachos and was only later associated with a nymph. The lady Nysa in question appears on an inscription from Delos (*Orientis Graeci Inscriptiones Selectae [OGIS]* 771), where she is called daughter of king Antiochos and wife of Pharnaces I of Pontos. The king is probably Antiochos IV, who had married his sister Laodike and had thus become stepfather of Nysa, who was the daughter of Laodike and Antiochos, the firstborn son of Antiochos III. It has also been argued that she was the true daughter of Antiochos IV (Habicht 2006, 169n74).

[24] Barkay (2003, 157–159), Lichtenberger (2003, 129).

[25] See Chapter 3, pp. 60, 74, 82, 86–87, 146–147n312, and Figure 3.16.

name of Nysa and its connection to Dionysos's nurse arose later to obscure any connection with a Seleucid princess.[26] Indeed, Antiochos IV re-founded and renamed other cities in this area after Seleucid figures: Gerasa became Antiocheia-by-the-Chrysorrhoas, Hippos became Antiocheia Hippos, and Gadara became Antiocheia and Seleukeia Gadara.[27] Similarly, Abila was called *Seleukeia*.[28]

The inscription discovered by the Penn Museum excavations, the subject of Chapter 2 in this volume, provides the clearest historical view of Scythopolis during the Hellenistic period, in part because it can be tied to other archaeological and textual data.[29] This fragmentary limestone stele, which dates to the reigns of Demetrios II Nikator (r. 145–138 BCE and 129–125 BCE), was found in the same cistern (*the Byzantine reservoir*, as it was called by the excavators) as the Alexander head and some other sculpture fragments (see Figure 3.5). After the death of Antiochos IV (d. 164 BCE), a series of civil wars was fought among legitimate and illegitimate holders of the Seleucid throne. Scythopolis had a role to play in these wars, and during this turbulent era the Seleucid royal cult became an instrument with which an aspiring king and his supporters could acquire and maintain legitimacy or strip it from a rival. A Seleucid precursor to the Roman imperial tradition of *damnatio memoriae* can thus be detected in this region, as Mahoney discusses.[30]

The Jewish Hasmoneans brought an end to Seleucid control in Judaea ca. 108/107 BCE, expelling the Greek inhabitants, according to Josephus (*Antiquities* 13.275–81, 14.88; *Jewish War* 1.64–66), and re-establishing Jewish control and religious freedom for a brief period from

---

[26] Rigsby (1980, 240–42). See Chapter 3, esp. pp. 74–82, 146–50 for a full treatment of Dionysos at Scythopolis. The names Nysa and Scythopolis were subsequently reinterpreted in the Byzantine period: John Malalas derived the name from the myth of Iphigenia among the Taurians. After escaping from the Taurians, Iphigenia, Pylades, and Orestes came to this region, which was at that time called *Trikomia/ Trikomis*. After building a temple to Artemis, the natives deemed Iphigenia worthy to be priestess, and they had her sacrifice a local girl named Nysa. After the sacrifice, they set up an altar with an inscription that named the place Nysa and honored the sacrificed girl as a goddess. Orestes, Iphigenia, and Pylades departed, but the place was settled by the pursuing Scythians, whence came the second name (Malalas 5.35–36; Kedrenos, vol. 1, 236–37 [Bekker 1838]; see also Steph. Byz., s.v. Σκυθόπολις and Νῦσαι). These Iphigenian stories demonstrate how the place names encouraged speculation and reinterpretation at different times.

[27] Lichtenberger (2008, 134–35, 146–50).

[28] Lichtenberger (2003, 279–80).

[29] See Chapter 2, pp. 17–49. The inscription is reported in the excavation notebooks and photo albums in the University of Pennsylvania Museum to be from the "foundations of the Byzantine reservoir," whereas the excavators describe the find spot of the Alexander head and marble hand as "the Hellenistic reservoir, west of room 1064." See Chapter 3, pp. 94–95 for a discussion of the chronology of the cistern/reservoir, and Chapter 2, pp. 20–21n7 for bibliography and previous editions of the inscription.

[30] Chapter 2, pp. 36–43.

108/107 until 63 BCE.[31] The Hasmonean takeover was brought about through the betrayal of the city to John Hyrkanos by the Seleucid governor Epikrates, who was a general of Antiochos IX Kyzikenos (r. 115–95 BCE). Hyrkanos's sons Aristoboulos and Antigonos subsequently ravaged the area. It has been argued that pagan sanctuaries were destroyed at this time, but there is no archaeological evidence for such a destruction on Tel Beth Shean.[32] There is, however, an extensive burnt layer covering the site on Tel Iztabba, which has been associated with the destruction of the Seleucid-era settlement.[33] There is some indication that during the reign of Alexander Jannaeus (103–76 BCE) the inhabitants were expelled or forced to change religion (Joseph., *Antiquities* 13.395–397; cf. also Strabo 16.2.40).[34] In any case, Josephus (*Antiquities* 13.355) tells us that Kleopatra III of Egypt and Alexander Jannaeus met at Scythopolis in 102 BCE in order to make an alliance.

In sum, the textual, epigraphic, numismatic, and other archaeological evidence for the Hellenistic period at Beth Shean is spotty and variously interpreted. There are some simple Hellenistic dwellings on the tel,[35] as well as the Ptolemaic coin hoard[36] and some Seleucid coins, as mentioned previously, stamped transport amphora fragments,[37] other third and second century BCE ceramic fragments,[38] and the important inscription discussed in Chapter 2.[39] Yet, to our knowledge, no significant Hellenistic architectural remains have been discovered there or in the area below the tel, which seems not to have been developed until the Roman period.[40] During the Hellenistic period, Tel Beth Shean was probably a small settlement, with a defensive purpose and simple dwellings, located mainly on the northern lower part of the mound, whereas the more substantial Hellenistic settlement was on Tel Iztabba, Scythopolis's "twin city,"

---

[31] See Fuks (1982) for a discussion of the Jews of Scythopolis.

[32] Bar-Kochva (1997, 132).

[33] Lichtenberger et al. (2020, 52).

[34] Four coins of Alexander Jannaeus were discovered in the more recent excavations on the tel (Amitai-Preiss 2006, 610, nos. 17–20).

[35] Mazar (2006, 38–40).

[36] See Barkay (2003, 20–22) for the numismatic evidence for the city in the first century BCE.

[37] Some of the stamped amphoras were found on the lower terraces of the tel in houses (Ariel 2006, 595). See also Finkielsztejn (2018, 15–20) for a discussion and comparison of the stamped amphora handles from Tel Beth Shean and Tel Iztabba. Stamped amphoras, the majority Rhodian of the third and second centuries BCE, were also found on Tel Iztabba (Ariel 1988, Ariel 2004, Finkielsztejn 2018).

[38] Fitzgerald (1931, 32, 39) records fragments of Hellenistic and Roman pottery found under the floor of the central area of the Round Church; see also Mazor and Atrash (2018a, 1–2).

[39] Chapter 2, pp. 17–43.

[40] See Chapter 3, pp. 69–73 for the discussion of the temple on the tel. Mazor and Atrash (2018a, 1) suggest that any Hellenistic remains would have been cleared away in preparation for the building of the Roman temple podium.

which, as previously mentioned, was founded ca. 170 BCE.[41] Although no archaeological evidence for a Hellenistic temple has survived, the Greek inscription implies the existence of some sacred space dedicated to Zeus on Tel Beth Shean. This may have been as simple as an open-air temenos or a shrine.

ROMAN AND BYZANTINE SCYTHOPOLIS

With Pompey's conquest of Koilē-Syria, including Judaea, in 63 BCE and the reorganization of the region by Gabinius (as proconsul in Syria), Scythopolis was re-Hellenized and re-founded (Joseph., *Jewish War* 1.166) and became an important center of the Decapolis, the largest in the league of ten Graeco-Roman cities. Though the number and inclusion of these cities varied, Pliny (*NH* 5.16) identifies them, along with Scythopolis, as Hippos-Sussita, Gadara, Pella, Dion, Philadelphia (modern Amman, Jordan), Damascus, Rhaphana, Galasa (Gerasa), and Canatha; Kapitolias and Abila are mentioned in other lists (Figure 1.5).[42] During the Roman period, Scythopolis was mainly a commercial and administrative center, famous for its production of flax grown in the fertile Jordan Valley and for the processing of high-quality, widely exported, expensive linen textiles.[43]

Roman Scythopolis was a cosmopolitan city with a complex mix of languages, religions, and ethnicities. Aramaic; Hebrew; Greek, the lingua franca of the Roman Near East; and Latin, the "language of power" primarily spoken by the administrative/ruling class,[44] were the tongues of Roman Palestine. Roman Scythopolis was a self-styled Greek city, though certainly not the only Hellenized urban center in the Roman Near East.[45] Scythopolis, however, seems to have taken special pride in its classical heritage and preserved the memory of its Hellenic foundations throughout the Roman period.[46] Civic titles like *Hellenis polis* appear on

---

[41] Mazar and Amitai-Preiss (2006, 38–39). See also Fitzgerald (1930, 16; 1931, 44–46), Ariel (2006, 595–97), Mazor and Atrash (2018a), and Finkielsztejn (2018, 15–18).

[42] See Lichtenberger (2003) for a discussion of the numismatic, archaeological, and epigraphical evidence for each of these cities.

[43] Talmud, *Pe'ah* 7:4, 20a (linen); Bietenhard (1977), Fuks (1983, 119), Lichtenberger (2003, 132n1105), Butcher (2003, 211), Ben-Yehuda (2005), Kislev et al. (2011). Linen was also an important product of Gerasa, as attested by the inscription for the linen workers on the theater seats (Retzleff and Majeed Mjely 2004, 40–41).

[44] See Eck (2003; 2009, 20, 34–38) for the small number of Latin inscriptions from Judaea/Syria; compared to Caesarea (Isaac 2009).

[45] See Belayche (2009b) for an excellent summary of the issues of language and religion as markers of culture in the Roman Near East, especially in the province of Palaestina. See also Chrubasik and King (2017) for the complexities and varying ways in which Hellenism is expressed in the eastern Mediterranean.

[46] Fuks (1976, 1983), Foerster and Tsafrir (1992), Tsafrir and Foerster (1997, 90–91), Belayche (2001, 257–67).

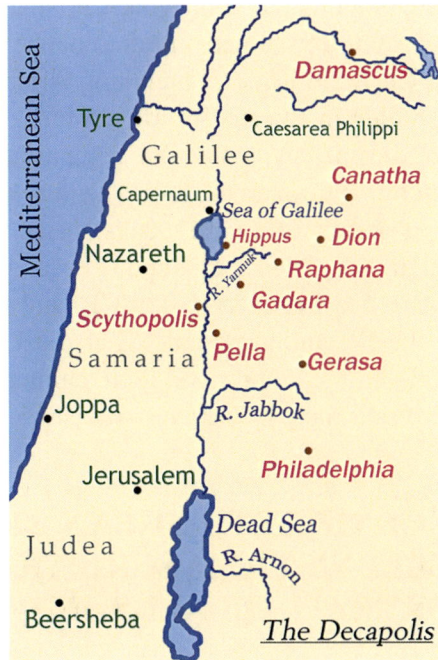

Figure 1.5 Map of Decapolis cities.

Image: Licensed under Creative Commons, https://commons.wikimedia.org/wiki/File:Thedecapolis.png (accessed January 9, 2023).

a coin issue of 175/176 CE and on an inscribed base for a statue of Marcus Aurelius Antoninus (Marcus Aurelius on the occasion of the emperor's visit in 175 CE? or Caracalla or Elagabalus?). In the inscription on the statue base the city is identified as that "of the Nysaeans, also called Scythopolitans," emphasizing its origins as the mythical place where Dionysos buried his nurse Nysa, and that it was among the Ἑλληνίδων πόλεων.[47] The inscriptions of Scythopolis are uniformly Greek, including those on locally made limestone funerary busts of local people, giving a strong indication of the preference for the language (see Figure 3.20).[48]

A well-documented earthquake that occurred on May 19, 363, partially destroyed the site and ushered in major renovations of the Early

---

[47] Foerster and Tsafrir (1986–87), Tsafrir and Foerster (1997, 90, 97), Barkay (2003, 162–65, fig. 26), Belayche (2001, 263). See Heyden (2010) for a discussion of the Late Roman/Early Byzantine life of this monument, which survived until the earthquake of 749 CE vis-à-vis the attitudes toward pagan monuments by Christians.

[48] Skupinska-Løvset (1983, 117–20). The Latin inscription from a monument, probably an arch, at Tel Shalem near Scythopolis is an exception. See Chapter 3, pp. 84–85.

Byzantine period. Scythopolis had a thriving Christian community even before the period of Constantine and the dominance of Christianity in the East. Prominent Christian leaders (including Arian Christians), such as the bishop Patrophilus in the mid-fourth century, made Scythopolis their home. Despite anti-pagan legislation beginning in the period of Constantine and continuing through the fourth century and very early fifth century,[49] worship of polytheistic Greek cults seems to have continued in Scythopolis through this period. Scythopolis became the capital of the new province of Palaestina Secunda in 409 CE, and the city continued to prosper through the Byzantine period. After the Umayyad conquest of Scythopolis in 634 CE, the city thrived until another major earthquake struck in 749 CE, leaving the city center in ruins.[50]

IMPORTANCE OF BETH SHEAN STUDIES ON THE HELLENISTIC INSCRIPTION AND PORTRAIT OF ALEXANDER

Although both the Hellenistic inscription and the portrait of Alexander the Great from Beth Shean have been known to scholars since their discovery in 1925, neither object has received the attention it deserves as important evidence for the Hellenistic and Roman history of Scythopolis and the region, as well as for cult activities at Scythopolis. The inscription allows for the most detailed historical narrative of Hellenistic Scythopolis that can be written, and it demonstrates that the city played an important role in the complex dialogue that linked king, polis, and the gods during the late Seleucid era. From a wider view, the "condemnation of memory" exhibited by an erasure on the inscription allows for a discussion of the pre-imperial history of this phenomenon, whose roots are at least in part to be found in the Hellenistic East.

Although there are divergent opinions concerning the date of the marble portrait of Alexander, both published and informally expressed to Romano, the results of this in-depth analysis suggest that this enigmatic and important head should be dated to the Roman period. In addition, it is the only large-scale sculptural portrait of Alexander from the Roman Near East, and it is one of his few portraits from a secure archaeological context, although a secondary one in this case. It is intriguing to consider

---

[49] For a summary of various anti-pagan laws, see Saradi-Mendelovici (1990, 48–49).
[50] See Tsafrir and Foerster (1997, esp. 112, 99–135) for a summary of the vibrant life of this multicultural city from the mid-fourth to sixth centuries CE, especially in the late fourth and early fifth centuries.

that it may have been an object of veneration in a Roman revival of a cult of Alexander in the temple on the acropolis of Scythopolis, provoking questions of why the Macedonian ruler/hero would have been of such keen interest in Roman Palestine some 500 years after his death. The head was deliberately mutilated, adding to the plentiful evidence for Christian iconoclasm at Scythopolis and inviting a closer look at the motivations for the damaging of pagan images in the Late Roman/Early Byzantine period. The modern transfers and settings of the Alexander head are also explored with consideration of the reception of the ancient image across its "life" span to the present day. Analysis of all the sculptural fragments from the cistern on the tel, combined with the historical, epigraphical, and archaeological background of Beth Shean, provides compelling, albeit hypothetical, evidence for a reconstruction of the images housed within the temple on the Roman acropolis. Finally, much has been written about archaeologically and historically rich Beth Shean, and we hope that this contribution adds significantly to our knowledge of the site and its history.

Chapter 2

The Hellenistic Catalogue of Priests from Nysa-Scythopolis/ Beth Shean: *Supplementum Epigraphicum Graecum* 8 33

Kyle W. Mahoney

Supplementum Epigraphicum Graecum (SEG) 8 33—a catalogue of the priests of Zeus Olympios, the *Theoi Soteres*, the royal ancestors of the Seleucid king, and King Demetrios II Nikator—is the only Hellenistic inscription documenting the religious life of Scythopolis (Fig-

Figure 2.1 *SEG* **8 33, general view.**

University of Pennsylvania Museum of Archaeology and Anthropology 29-107-961. Photo: Penn Museum, reproduced with permission.

ure 2.1). The inscription is, moreover, one of only two Hellenistic stone stelai recovered from Tel Beth Shean, and it also constitutes the oldest reference to Zeus in the Decapolis.[1] Although other stone inscriptions have been recovered in the lower city, *SEG* 8 33 remains the only one discovered on the tel. In this chapter, I present a new edition of the text and provide an exhaustive historical commentary that accounts for the stone's original Hellenistic display context as well as its *Nachleben* during the Roman imperial era. The Appendix contains a chronologically ordered

---

[1] Lichtenberger (2003, 279).

list of the published or noted Greek inscriptions from Scythopolis, which is intended to aid further epigraphic research.

SEG 8 33 has, for the most part, been analyzed with reference to the local religious history of Scythopolis, particularly as it regards the debate over which god was worshiped in the temple on Tel Beth Shean.[2] Although this is an important issue that I shall address in due course, the greater historical significance of the text has yet to be fully realized. The primary aim of my commentary is to fill this gap and to suggest that we must place this inscription in the context of the struggles that pitted Demetrios II Nikator first against Alexander Balas and Diodotos Tryphon for supremacy in the region from 145 to 138 BCE, and subsequently against his brother, Antiochos VII Sidetes, and the pretender Alexander Zabinas from 129–125 BCE. These struggles had originated when the Treaty of Apameia (188 BCE) required Antiochos III to send hostages to Rome.[3] With crown princes and even reigning kings held in captivity at Rome and among the Parthians, other contenders were able to make claims on the Seleucid throne, and for more than a generation the descendants of Seleukos IV and Antiochos IV—as well as their supporters—fought for supremacy and legitimacy on battlefields, in poleis, and in temples.[4] Eventually, the intertwined families of the brothers

---

[2] See Thiersch (1932, 52, 65–66), who thought it certain that the priests on this inscription had to do with the temple on Tel Beth Shean; Watzinger (1935, 20), who indicates that the inscription implies the existence of a cult of Zeus Olympios; Lifshitz (1961, 188), who discusses Zeus Olympios and Zeus Akraios at Scythopolis; Seyrig (1962, 207–11), who suggests a triad of Zeus, Tyche, and Dionysos corresponding more generally to Syrian triads of thunder god, Astarte, and a child deity (on which see also Kasher 1990, 46–48); Ovadiah (1975, 116–17, 120), who supports the idea of a Hellenistic temple of Zeus Olympios later dedicated to Zeus Akraios (see the English abstract on 122); Lifshitz (1977, 274), who identifies Zeus Olympios with Zeus Akraios; Fuks (1983, 81–83), who argues that the temple was also used for worship of the Seleucid king and his ancestors; Applebaum (1989, 5), who argues that the inscription proves the existence of a temple in the second century BCE; Barkay (2003, 142–43), who suggests a temple of Zeus Olympios/Akraios; Thiel (2007, 145–48), who argues that Zeus Olympios was merged with Zeus Akraios in the imperial period, and that the Hellenistic predecessor to the second-century CE temple was the most important sanctuary in Hellenistic Scythopolis; L. Hannestad (2011, 270), who notes that the inscription demonstrates the existence of a cult of Zeus and Seleucid monarchs; Tal (2011, 250), who thinks the inscription probably belonged to a temple of Olympian Zeus; Mazor (2015, 358), who discusses the early origins of the Zeus cult; Belayche (2017, 14) supports Zeus Olympios as the god of the Hellenistic city, and Belayche (2019, 142–43) places Zeus Olympios in the temple and connects him with Zeus Akraios.

[3] Polyb. 21.42; App., *Syr.* 39. The treaty demanded twenty hostages between the ages of 18 and 40 to be replaced every three years. On Seleucid hostages at Rome and in Parthia, see Nabel (2017).

[4] See Chrubasik (2016, chap. 3). The quotes on 125–26 ("The presence of more than one contender for the kingship, and the transformation of local groups into politicized agents, therefore enables us to analyse the phenomenon of local politicization more fully. Yet it is precisely the local politicization that – in return – also offers insight into kings and usurpers' behavior, and thus into the limits of Seleukid kingship and its defining characteristics") and 126 ("[K]ingship in the Seleukid kingdom was neither legitimate nor illegitimate, but rather it depended on acceptance by the political agents within the empire") are particularly illuminating for the present study.

Demetrios II and Antiochos VII—who were both married to Kleopatra Thea, who had children with both brothers—resulted in further rivalry that pitted Antiochos VIII Grypos, son of Demetrios II, against Antiochos IX Kyzikenos, son of Antiochos VII. In these seemingly incessant civil wars, Seleucid monarchs and their supporters recognized that manipulation of the royal cult offered both a path to acceptance as ruler and a means to deprive rivals of such acceptance. The erasure and (perhaps) subsequent replacement of royal names in inscriptions of this era from this region thus exhibit a kind of Seleucid *damnatio memoriae*, not unlike what is seen in the Roman imperial period, if on a lesser scale. The importance and significance of this phenomenon is addressed in the present chapter.

At the close of the chapter, I switch gears to discuss the later life of the inscription, which became a historical artifact that documented the Hellenic past of what had become the Roman city of Scythopolis. As Irene Romano notes in Chapter 3, Scythopolitans of the imperial era took great pride in the Hellenic origins of their city, and the text of *SEG* 8 33—the only Greek stone inscription that we have from Tel Beth Shean and the oldest from Scythopolis—stimulated the historical imagination of Roman Scythopolis.[5] I conclude this chapter by suggesting that, along with sculptural material studied by Romano, this inscription played a part in the maintenance of this Greek identity and the active construction of the past in Roman Scythopolis.[6]

TEXT AND EPIGRAPHICAL NOTES[7]

145–125 BCE

['Έτους - -]
['Ιερεῖς Διὸς] Ὀλυμπ[ίου]

---

[5] See Cohen (2006, 292–93). As noted in the Introduction (p. 13), *SEG* 37 1531, a dedicatory inscription on a statue base for Marcus Aurelius (or perhaps Caracalla or Elagabalus), places Scythopolis among the Ἑλληνίδες πόλεις: Ἀγαθῆι Τύχηι | Αὐτοκράτορα Καίσαρα | Μ. Αὐρήλιον Ἀντωνῖνον | Σεβ. τὸν κύριον Νυσαέων | τῶν καὶ Σκυθοπολιτῶν | τῆς ἱερᾶς καὶ ἀσύλου τῶν | κατὰ Κοίλην Συρίαν Ἑλλη- | νίδων πόλεων ἡ πόλις | διὰ ἐπιμελητοῦ Θεοδώ- | ρου Τίτου. Coins advertise the same status (Barkay 2003, 162–163; Andrade 2013, 111).

[6] On Hellenistic ruler cults under the Roman Empire, see Chankowski (2011) and Noreña (2016).

[7] Penn Museum, Near Eastern Section, accession number 29-107-961. Fragment of a stele of gray-brown limestone, broken on top, bottom, left, and right sides, with part of the right edge and finished back preserved. H. 0.28 m, W. 0.21 m, Th. 0.075 m, Letter H. 0.007–0.013 m. List of the priests of Zeus Olympios, the *Theoi Soteres*, the Royal Ancestors, and King Demetrios II Nikator. Securely restored, completely inscribed lines include seventeen to twenty characters. Photographs: Rowe (1930, pl. 53, 1), Ovadiah (1975, pl. 1). Rowe (with Abel and Vincent, 1930, 45), Thiersch (1932, 53, 65–66), Mouterde (1933, 180–82), Rostovtzeff (1935, 60–61), Watzinger (1935, 20), Bikerman (1938, 242–45), Lifshitz (1961, 188), Avi-Yonah (1962, 129), Seyrig (1962, 207–11), Ovadiah (1975, 116–17), Lifshitz (1977,

[καὶ Θεῶν Σωτή]ρων

[. . . . .]ννννννν Ἐπ[. . . .]

5   [προγόν]ων τοῦ βασιλέως

[. . . . .]υλος Ἐπικράτου,

[βασιλ]έως ⟦Δ[ημητ]ρίου⟧

[Ἡρακλ]είδης Σαραπίωνος.

[- - -]

Apparatus Criticus[8]

Line 1 was supplemented first by Mouterde: [Ἔτους . . . .], [ἔτους . . .] Rostovtzeff, Lichtenberger, [Ἔτους . .] Ovadiah. 2 [Διὸ]ς *SEG*, Ovadiah, Ὀλυμπ[ίου] Rowe, Abel, and Vincent, Mouterde, Lichtenberger, Ὀλυμπ[ίου καὶ] *SEG*, Ovadiah. 3 [θεῶν Σωτή]ρων *SEG*, [Θεῶν Σωτή]ρων Ovadiah, [καὶ θεῶν σωτή]ρων Mouterde, [καὶ θεῶν σωτή]ρων [ὁ δεῖνα] Ἐπ . . . Rostovtzeff, [καὶ θεῶν σωτή]ρων [ὁ δεῖνα] Ἐπ[. . .] Lichtenberger. 4 Ἔτ[ους . . .] Rowe, Abel, and Vincent, [ὁ δεῖνα] Ἐπ? . . . . . Mouterde, [ὁ δεῖνα] Ἐπ[- - *SEG*, [ὁ δεῖνα] Ἐπ[. .] Ovadiah, [ὁ δεῖνα] Ἐπ[- -] Thiel. 5 [. . . . . . .]ων Rowe, Abel, and Vincent, [τῶν δὲ προγόν]ων *SEG*, Ovadiah. 6 [v.g. Εὔβο]υλος Mouterde, [. . . .]υλος Rostovtzeff, [- -βο]υλος *SEG*, [. .βο]υλος Ovadiah, [. . .]υλος Lichtenberger. 7 . . . . ΣΩΣ . . . . .ΟΥ Rowe, Abel, and Vincent, [τοῦ δὲ βασιλ]έως *SEG*, Ovadiah, Δ[ημητ]ρίου Mouterde, Rostovtzeff, Ovadiah, Lichtenberger, ⟦Δ[ημητ]ρίου⟧ *SEG*. 8 [Ἡρακλ]είδης Rowe, Abel, and Vincent, *SEG*, Ovadiah, [Ἡρακλ]είδης (?) Mouterde, [Ἡρακλ]είδης (?) Σαραπίωνος . . . . . . Rostovtzeff, [Ἡρακλ]είδης (?) Σαραπίωνος [. . .] Lichtenberger.

Notes on Readings

Line 2: Only the left half of pi is preserved.

Line 4: Through study of the stone in the Penn Museum, I have been able to produce a more accurate text, but unfortunately this has

---

273–75), Fuks (1978), Rigsby (1980, 235n9, 241), Fuks (1983, 81–82), Applebaum (1989, 5), Kasher (1990, 46–47), Bar-Kochva (1997, 132), Di Segni (1997, 146), Belayche (2001, 262), Barkay (2003, 142–44), Debord (2003, 285, 300), Lichtenberger (2003, 153–55, 279–81), Van Nuffelen (2004, 292, 298), Cohen (2006, 291–92), Mazar (2006, 38), Thiel (2007, 145–48), Lichtenberger (2008, 148), Savalli-Lestrade (2009, 148–49), Dirven (2011, 145–46), L. Hannestad (2011, 270), Tal (2011, 250), Mazor (2015, 358, 373), Belayche (2017, 14), R. Parker (2017, 209n24), Mazor and Atrash (2018a, 1), and Belayche (2019, 142–43).

[8] I have largely left out the edition of Thiel (2007, 146), except where his lines match those of other editions. The text found in his article has confused the lines. Line 5 has been split in two, reading ([τῶν δὲ πργόν]ων (*sic*) τοῦ | βασιλέως). Thus, our line 6 has become line 7 in his text. Our line 7 has also been split in two, so that it reads [— τοῦ δὲ βασιλ]έως | ⟦Δ[ημητ]ρίου⟧. Line 8 has thus become line 10 in his text.

Figure 2.2 *SEG* **8 33, detailed view of inscribed lines.**

University of Pennsylvania Museum of Archaeology and Anthropology 29-107-961. Photo: Penn Museum, reproduced with permission.

resulted in a new problem. Only the original publication of Rowe, Abel, and Vincent and the edition of Thiel give some idea of the condition of the stone, where there is a large gap prior to the epsilon (Figure 2.2). Although the letters are not written *stoichedon*, they are consistent enough to estimate a genuine gap of eight letters preceded by a space for six more about which we cannot be certain. The final pi is preserved by a 0.009-m upright stroke, which could conceivably be part of a pi or tau. The former seems more likely, given what may be the bottom of the right vertical stroke of a pi immediately to the right, but I could not be certain. We need a name of the priest of Zeus Olympios and the *Theoi Soteres*, so a short name in the nominative followed by the *vacat* followed by a short father's name in the genitive makes most sense, but it is strange that such a sizeable gap has been left in what otherwise seems to be a perfectly inscribable area.[9]

---

[9] Thiel (2007, 146) suggests an invocation of some sort with a title of the king: "Ep[iphanes?]." This is not a known title of Demetrios II, however, and there does not seem to be enough space for a title of this length.

Line 7: Of the iota, only a 0.005-m vertical stroke is legible. Of the upsilon, only a 0.007-m vertical stroke and 0.004 m of the right diagonal stroke are legible.

Line 8: Of the epsilon, only 0.007 m of the top horizontal stroke is legible.

EPIGRAPHICAL AND ARCHAEOLOGICAL ANALYSIS

SEG 8 33 was originally published by Rowe with Vincent and Abel in 1930. The fragmentary text is cut onto a gray-brown limestone block that is now broken on all four sides. Part of the right margin, however, is preserved. *SEG* 8 96 from Samaria (Figure 2.3), which similarly lists priests of Zeus Olympios and the *Theoi Soteres*, the ancestors of the king, and King Demetrios, may indicate that a handful of lines are missing after line 8, but this need not be the case.[10] The stone, which measures 28 cm × 21 cm, with a thickness of 7.5 cm, was discovered in a cistern on the tel,[11] where a marble head of Alexander (see Figure 3.29), which has been dated by various scholars from the third century BCE to the late second or early third century CE,[12] a life-sized marble hand (see Figure 3.23),[13] eight marble finger or hand fragments (see Figures 3.24-3.28) from a colossal acrolithic statue that probably dates between the mid-second and first quarter of the third centuries CE,[14] and a limestone capital decorated with a head or mask of Dionysos or a satyr of Severan date (see Figure 3.21) were also found.[15] It is interesting that the stele does not seem to be made of the local soft, white limestone from Mt. Gilboa, whose quarries were not exploited until the later first century CE.[16]

---

[10] For the text of *SEG* 8 96, see p. 32, this chapter.

[11] Rowe (1930, 45n79): "The stone bearing this inscription was discovered, in 1925, in the debris of the base of the Byzantine reservoir which was sunk in the east end of the southern temple of Rameses II. Below the reservoir was another reservoir of the Hellenistic period." On the confused interpretation of this area, see Chapter 3, pp. 94–95. The excavators thought that the cistern was Hellenistic and that it had been filled in over the years, but that the southern part was partitioned off in the Byzantine period. It was in this Byzantine section of the cistern that *SEG* 8 33 was discovered, which should indicate that it was not considered debris in the Hellenistic and imperial periods; rather, its characterization as trash ought to have been made in the Byzantine period. Romano's careful review of the notebooks, however, has demonstrated that there is no coherence to the debris, some of which was misdated by the original excavators. I follow her conclusion that the deposits represent a clearing of the tel prior to the construction of the Round Church.

[12] See Chapter 3, pp. 108–84.

[13] See Chapter 3, pp. 99–101.

[14] Romano (2006, 191–93), Chapter 3, pp. 101–8.

[15] Romano (2006, 194–95), Chapter 3, pp. 96–99.

[16] Tsafrir and Foerster (1997, 89).

Although we cannot be certain about the provenance of the limestone, the stele must have been brought in from elsewhere and erected on the tel. The restorations and estimation of missing characters can be accepted as secure, given the fact that line 8—the longest inscribed—certainly included twenty characters. This fact makes *SEG*'s restoration of lines 5 ([τῶν δὲ προγόν]ων) and 7 ([τοῦ δὲ βασιλ]έως) less likely, as they would require twenty-four and twenty-two characters, respectively, even though these two lines are a letter or two shorter than line 8. Similarly, the restoration of line 2 found in *SEG* ([Ἱερεῖς Διὸ]ς Ὀλυμπ[ίου καὶ]) seems to allow for too few letters in line 3, where the nu of [Σωτή]ρων is below the lambda and upsilon of Ὀλυμπ[ίου] in line 2. Moving leftward from this point, line 2 includes thirteen letters. Placing the [καὶ] at the beginning of line 3 results in fourteen characters, which is close enough to what we should expect.

As Romano discusses in detail in Chapter 3, a temple was located on the tel during imperial times, whose basalt foundations measured 37.05 m × 22.08 m.[17] Architectural remains include a partial Corinthian capital (1.27 m in diameter at base) and column drums that are 1.2 to 1.3 m in diameter. The building materials included limestone, granite, and marble, the last of which implies a date between 150 and 250 CE for at least one phase.[18] Relying on the evidence of the Ptolemaic coin hoard mentioned in the Introduction, the excavators suggested that the temple was originally built during the third century BCE, although other scholars have raised doubts about this conclusion, and the oldest architectural remains seem to date to the later first or second century CE.[19] Coins from the time of Antoninus Pius and Lucius Verus depict a temple with a tetrastyle façade, Corinthian columns, and an arched gable of Syrian type, which Barkay argues indicates a second-century CE remodeling.[20] The possibility of a Hellenistic temenos or shrine must be left open, but no archaeological evidence exists to confirm the idea. We could imagine, for instance, a small *naiskos*, which has left no trace, or perhaps an open-air shrine of some sort. In the second half of the fifth or early sixth century CE, the Round Church was built upon the foundations of the earlier temple, parts of which were used in the construction of the church.[21]

---

[17] Rowe (1930, 44).

[18] Chapter 3, pp. 69–71.

[19] See Vincent (1924, 424–25), James (1970, 71), and M. L. Fischer (1990, 61–62), who gives the date based on a Corinthian capital from the temple; Barkay (2003, 143–44), Lichtenberger (2003, 166–67), Romano (2006, 192–93), Chapter 3, pp. 69–71; a Flavian date has been suggested by Arubas (personal communication with Romano, June 15, 2016 and December 4, 2019).

[20] Barkay (2003, 143, 143n66). The coins in question are Barkay's nos. 14 and 26.

[21] Tsafrir (1998, 212–13) and Barkay (2003, 144).

Presumably, at this same time the material associated with the pagan cult—including our inscription—was dumped into the cistern.

GODS, PEOPLE, AND THE PLACEMENT OF *SEG* 8 33

As mentioned earlier, the identification of the deity or deities worshiped in this Roman temple is disputed.[22] Rowe argued that the two principal deities of the Hellenistic city were Dionysos and Astarte-Atargatis, and that the former was most probably the inhabitant of the temple during imperial times.[23] Ovadiah, however, has argued convincingly that during the imperial era the temple was dedicated to Zeus Akraios ("of the summit"),[24] basing his conclusion largely on an octagonal limestone altar dedicated to Zeus Akraios in the second century CE and found at the foot of the tel,[25] as well as a second dedication to Zeus Akraios Soter discovered reused in the Arab settlement of Beth Shean and originally dating to 138/139 CE.[26] It has also been noted that Akraios suggests "the god located on high," and it therefore should be significant that the tel constitutes the highest point in the area.[27]

The ancestors of the king need little comment. The fuller lists from Seleukeia-in-Pieria (*OGIS* 245/*SEG* 35 1521) account for all the kings back to Seleukos I Nikator, and we can be confident that a similar catalogue is implied behind [προγόν]ων τοῦ βασιλέως.[28] It should be

---

[22] Attested cults (based on numismatic, epigraphic, artistic, and archaeological evidence) of Scythopolis include ones for the following figures: Gabinius, Nike, Dionysos, Nysa, Pan, Zeus, Demeter, Kore, Pluto, Tyche, the Nymphs, Sarapis, Isis, Azeizos, the Di Manes, Hermes, Aphrodite, Athena, Herakles, perhaps Hera, a fertility goddess, Artemis, Thea Poa Nyssa, and the imperial cult; an equestrian statuette may also be indicative of a local cult, as similar statuettes have been found in other cities of the Decapolis; see Lichtenberger (2003, 134–64).

[23] Rowe (1930, 44–45). Thiersch (1932) suggested a cult of Dionysos/Zeus Olympios/Antiochos IV, but he based his conclusion on the sculpted marble head, which almost certainly represents Alexander; see Chapter 3, pp. 57–58, 108–74.

[24] Ovadiah (1975, 120).

[25] *SEG* 37 1529 (Tsafrir 1989, 76–78): Ἀγαθῆι | Τύχηι | Διὶ Ἀκραίωι | Θεογένη | Τωβίου | ἀνέθη- | κεν. See also Barkay (2003, 142).

[26] Lifshitz (1961, 186–89), *SEG* 20 456: Ἔτους γσ´, | Λούκιος Οὐάριος Κυ- | ρείναι Πρόκλος Δὶ | Ἀκρα[ί]ωι [Σ]ω[τ]ῆρι | μετ᾽ εὐχαριστίας | ἀνέθηκε[ν]. See also Barkay (2003, 142). Zeus Olympios Soter was worshipped with Tyche at Gerasa in the mid-second century CE (Welles 1938, no. 13; Lichtenberger 2008, 136, 148). Nevertheless, the [Σ]ω[τ]ῆρι in the Scythopolitan inscription is probably meant to indicate that the dedicator, after having been saved in some way, was now making a thanksgiving offering (μετ᾽ εὐχαριστίας). I thank Angelos Chaniotis for pointing this out to me.

[27] Barkay (2003, 144). Barkay (2003, 140–45) also gathers the numismatic evidence in favor of a temple to Zeus, which lasts through Gordian III (240/241 CE).

[28] Van Nuffelen (2004, 292). Lists A and B from Seleukeia-in-Pieria: Seleukos Zeus Nikator, Antiochos Apollo Soter, Antiochos Theos, Seleukos Kallinikos, Seleukos Soter, Antiochos, Antiochos Megalos. The king at this time (187–185 BCE) was Seleukos IV.

noted that at Scythopolis, Samaria, and Seleukeia-in-Pieria, there are separate priests for the ancestors, on the one hand, and the king, on the other, whereas in Antiocheia-in-Persis (*OGIS* 233) there is only one priest for both the ancestors and the reigning kings. Other lists of priests for the cult of the Seleucid kings and their ancestors are known from Seleu-keia-on-the-Tigris, Dura Europos, and perhaps also Teos.[29] All texts documenting the royal cult date during or after the reign of Antiochos III, and any attempt to standardize the worship of the Seleucid kings seems to have been ultimately ineffective prior to the reign of Antiochos IV, to whom we shall return shortly. Even in the later second century BCE, however, the local nature of these cults should be stressed, as we find variations among different sites that highlight the civic nature of this worship.[30]

The identity of the *Theoi Soteres* is disputed. Rostovtzeff favored Apollo and Artemis,[31] whereas Seyrig and Lifshitz identify them with the Dioscuri.[32] They may simply represent the guardian gods of the Seleucid dynasty.[33] In addition to Samaria and Scythopolis, we find them inscribed on a small altar of imperial date in another city of the Decapolis, Kanatha, where a Roman temple with inscriptions to Zeus Megistos is located.[34] In this case, however, the dedication is a thanksgiving offering for salvation, and a connection with earlier Seleucid traditions is difficult to establish.

Returning now to Zeus, the available data allow for two inter-pretations of his epithets at Scythopolis.[35] Either Zeus Akraios and Zeus Olympios are essentially identical, with the latter originally connected to

---

[29] *P. Dura* 23 similarly has separate priests for Seleukos I and the royal ancestors (see pp. 45–46, this chapter). The inscription from Seleukeia-on-the-Tigris dates from the reign of Antiochos III (or possibly after) and may list individual priests for each deceased king, with perhaps a priest for the reigning king as well (McDowell 1935, 258–59, see also Van Nuffelen 2001). The inscription from Teos (*OGIS* 246) includes names of Seleucid kings in the genitive, one of whom may be Demetrios II. There are also references to Ptolemies, which Piejko (1982) understandably associates with Ptolemy VI, who was offered the Seleucid crown (see p. 33, this chapter).

[30] On these lists, see Van Nuffelen (2004, 291–93, 298–300), R. Parker (2017, 209), Erickson (2019, 143–44, 151–52).

[31] Rostovtzeff (1935, 60n12).

[32] Seyrig (1962, 207), Lifshitz (1977, 273–74).

[33] On the category of *Theoi Soteres*, see F. Graf (2017).

[34] Waddington (1870, no. 2343), Prentice (1908, no. 417a), and, most recently, Sartre-Fauriat and Sartre (2020, no. 160: Τὸν ἅγι- | ον βωμὸν | ἠγήρθη | Κεναθηνὸς | ΕΚΡΑΙΛΙΙ σ- | ωθεὶς Θεοῖ- | ς Σωτῆρσι | νοσῶν <ῥύ>σ- | ιν Ροῦφος. For the imperial era dedications to Zeus Megistos, see Waddington (1870, nos. 2339 and 2340), Prentice (1908, nos. 413–413a), Sartre-Fauriat and Sartre (2020, nos. 154 and 155, and no. 279). On these texts, see Schürer, Vermes, Millar, and Black (1973, 37–38).

[35] Lichtenberger (2003, 153–55).

the Seleucid royal cult, or an earlier Baal was replaced by Zeus via *interpretatio Graeca*.[36] If the latter solution is correct, we cannot know whether this *interpretatio* occurred in the Hellenistic period, with Baal becoming Zeus Olympios, who later became Zeus Akraios, or whether Zeus Akraios was identified with Baal, while Zeus Olympios is to be associated solely with the Seleucids. That Zeus Olympios and Zeus Akraios were closely associated may be supported by the list of annual priests from Seleukeia-in-Pieria dating to 187–185 BCE, where the priest of Zeus Olympios is identical with the priest of Zeus Koryphaios ("of the peak"; *OGIS* 245/*SEG* 35 1521) on one catalogue, whereas on another the same man is the priest of Zeus Olympios, Zeus Koryphaios, Zeus Kasios, and the *Theoi Soteres*. It must be admitted, however, that no such inscription from Scythopolis links cults or priesthoods of Zeus Olympios and Zeus Akraios directly.[37]

Regardless of the relationship (or lack thereof) linking the epithets Olympios and Akraios, it can be asserted confidently that the introduction of the cult of Zeus Olympios at Scythopolis was due to Antiochos IV, whose interest in the god is abundantly clear.[38] Earlier scholars attributed Antiochos's enthusiasm for Zeus Olympios to a greater sense of Hellenism or a desire to link all of the diverse sky gods of his empire through one name, but neither of these ideas is particularly convincing.[39] Rigsby argued that Antiochos's focus on this god must be connected with Zeus Olympios's role as the civic deity of Seleukeia-in-Pieria, the first city founded by Seleukos I Nikator and also the site of his burial.[40] Zeus Olympios was, of course, an important deity for the Macedonians, who worshiped him at Dion after Archelaos reorganized the cult.[41] Rigsby argued further that Antiochos's youth spent in Rome and his accompany-

---

[36] For the Baal theory, see Seyrig (1962, 207–8) and Lichtenberger (2003, 154–55).

[37] See also Rigsby (1980, 235–36). Another issue is, of course, that these cults of Seleukeia-in-Pieria existed together at the same time, whereas we have no evidence for a cult of Zeus Akraios at Scythopolis before the imperial period.

[38] He famously ordered that the temple of Yahweh in Jerusalem be called the temple of Zeus Olympios (2 Macc. 6:2; see also 1 Macc. 1:41–50); see Thiersch (1932, 65–66), Rigsby (1980, 235n9), and Lichtenberger (2008, 134–36). Indeed, in one interpretation of the events, to maintain Hellenic control Antiochos IV established Zeus as the supreme god in the region (2 Macc 6:1–12). See Gruen (2016, 344–55), who is against the argument that Antiochos IV promoted worship of himself as Zeus Olympios.

[39] For an overview of the theories, see Rigsby (1980, 233–34). The second idea was proposed by Newell (1918, 23) and is supported by Thiersch (1932, 65–66). Philhellenism is acknowledged by Mørkholm (1966, 62).

[40] For the importance of Zeus to Seleukos I, who sought a personal connection with the god, see Erickson (2013). Libanius of Antioch (*Orationes* 11.91) traces Seleukos back to Temenos and thus the Argead dynasty, Heracles, and Zeus himself.

[41] See Rigsby (1980, 233–38). Indeed, the name Pieria refers to the landscape around Dion and Olympos.

ing familiarity with Jupiter Capitolinus—who had a shrine in every Roman colony—influenced the policy.[42] It may also be significant that Antiochos was residing in Athens in 175 BCE when his brother, Seleukos IV, was assassinated.[43] It was thus from Athens that he set out to claim the royal title, which he successfully acquired with the help of Eumenes II of Pergamon. The Athenians promptly thanked Eumenes (*OGIS* 248), and already by 174 BCE Antiochos had undertaken the completion of the temple of Zeus Olympios at Athens, for which project he hired the Roman architect Cossutius.[44] Thus, in addition to fostering a connection with his ancestral traditions, Antiochos IV made Zeus Olympios a significant part of his personal history as well. Accordingly, if—as seems most plausible[45]—Scythopolis was renamed Nysa by Antiochos IV, it would make good sense to associate the implantation of the cult of Zeus Olympios, the *Theoi Soteres*, the royal ancestors, and the reigning king with this king's activity in the area. More will be said about this subject shortly.

A related issue that needs to be addressed concerns the findspot of *SEG* 8 33. This matter is, in turn, tied up with the larger problem surrounding the status of the settlement on Tel Beth Shean. The meager archaeological evidence recovered for the third century BCE seems to indicate a military outpost, whereas the extensive remains on Tel Iztabba that belong to a settlement founded around 170 BCE are far more impressive. It is, unfortunately, unclear when exactly Scythopolis acquired the status of *polis*. Applebaum argued that Ptolemy III made Scythopolis a polis between 240 and 220 BCE,[46] whereas Avi-Yonah attributed the grant to Antiochos IV, who ruled from 175–164 BCE.[47] Mazar has suggested that it is unlikely that Scythopolis was formally a polis in the Hellenistic period.[48]

Our inscription may very well help to solve this problem. Cults of Zeus Olympios are known in the Decapolis at Scythopolis, Gerasa, Hippos, Gadara, and Kapitolias. Of these cities, we know that four had

---

[42] Rigsby (1980, 238). According to Livy 41.20.9, he built a temple to Jupiter Capitolinus in Antioch.

[43] See the inscription published by Tracy in *Hesperia* 51 (1982), 61–62, no. 3, which demonstrates that Antiochos was in Athens in 178/177 BCE. See also Appian, *Syr.* 45.

[44] Habicht (1997, 233–34). Ammianus Marcellinus 22.13 tells us that Antiochos IV had a copy of Pheidias's statue of Zeus Olympios made for the park of Daphne, located south of Antioch. For the relations between Athens and the Seleucids, see also Habicht (2006, 155–73).

[45] Chapter 1, pp. 9–10.

[46] See Applebaum (1989, 1–8). He bases his conclusion primarily on Josephus's account of the tax collector Joseph, son of Tobias, who executed the leading citizens of Scythopolis when they refused to pay up (*Antiquities* 12.183).

[47] Avi-Yonah (1962, 129).

[48] Mazar (2006, 38–39).

been given Seleucid dynastic names (Nysa-Scythopolis, Antiocheia-Hippos, Antiocheia/Seleukeia-Gadara, and Antiocheia-Gerasa).[49] Lichtenberger has argued convincingly that the cities with (a) cults of Zeus Olympios and (b) Seleucid dynastic names were also given the right of *asylia* by the Seleucids, whereas those in the Decapolis that kept their Ptolemaic names (Philadelphia and Pella/Berenike) had neither cults of Zeus Olympios nor the right of *asylia*. In addition, a direct connection between sanctuaries of Zeus Olympios and *asylia* is supported by evidence from Gerasa, Hippos, and Gadara.[50] And other cults of Zeus Olympios are known in the wider region at Samaria, Mt. Gerizim, Seleukeia-in-Pieria, Jerusalem, and Dura Europos. Taken all together, this evidence suggests that the implantation of the cult in this area during the second century BCE was—at least to some degree—both organized and intentional.[51]

What we have here is Seleucid interest in the status of particular settlements; it seems most reasonable to suggest that recognition of these places as poleis accompanied their renaming, the implantation of Zeus Olympios, and the grant of *asylia*. Given the fact that the larger settlement on Tel Iztabba belongs to the years around 170 BCE, Avi-Yonah's argument that Antiochos IV acknowledged Scythopolis as a polis becomes more plausible. At Scythopolis, we have evidence for (a) an archaeologically documented settlement founded during the reign of Antiochos IV, (b) a cult of Zeus Olympios, (c) the change of name in honor of a Seleucid princess, and (d) the right of *asylia*.

To my mind, it makes most sense to associate all four of these points and conclude that the inauguration of the dynastic cult of Zeus Olympios, the *Theoi Soteres*, the royal ancestors, and the king was concomitant with the foundation of the settlement on Tel Iztabba. After this new city on Tel Iztabba had been established, the earlier, Ptolemaic outpost on Tel Beth Shean had to be fully "Seleucized." I suggest that this is why we find the Seleucid cults implanted here rather than on Tel

---

[49] Although we do not know the earlier, pre-Roman name of Kapitolias, it likely had a Seleucid past, whereas Abila was renamed Seleukeia-Abila and had the right of *asylia*, but no cult of Zeus Olympios has been discovered. It would not be surprising, however, if such evidence came to light sometime in the future. See Lichtenberger (2008, 149–50).

[50] Lichtenberger (2003, 279–81; 2008, 146–50).

[51] Debord (2003, 205) notes that the similarity of *SEG* 8 33 to *SEG* 8 96 may imply political coherence, which is otherwise difficult to observe in Seleucid royal cults. On the Seleucid royal cult, see Bikerman (1938, chap. 7) and Van Nuffelen (2004). With respect to the area of Koilē Syria and Phoinikē, we know from a letter of Seleukos IV to Heliodoros in 178 BCE that a man named Olympiodoros was appointed high priest of all sanctuaries in the area, which should imply a degree of central organization (Cotton and Wörrle 2007).

Iztabba. Any previous associations with the Ptolemies could thus be thoroughly eradicated, and the space once utilized by the Ptolemaic military was now an inviolable zone dedicated to the worship of the Seleucid kings and their dynastic gods. That Antiochos IV would make a statement in this way is entirely plausible, given what we know of how he implanted the cult of Zeus Olympios elsewhere. Indeed, the earliest Seleucid coin discovered on Tel Beth Shean is of Antiochos IV.[52] We may also wonder whether the double name (Nysa-Scythopolis) dates to this period: Scythopolis would have been the earlier, Ptolemaic name for Tel Beth Shean, whereas the name Nysa was originally given to the new settlement on Tel Iztabba. Whatever the case, this reconstruction of events adequately accounts for the findspot of *SEG* 8 33.

As far as the humans named on *SEG* 8 33, Epikrates, the father of the priest of the royal ancestors, may have been the ancestor of the Epikrates who as general for Antiochos IX Kyzikenos betrayed Scytho-polis to John Hyrkanos sometime between 111 and 107 BCE (Joseph., *Antiquities* 13.279–80).[53] The priest of King Demetrios, Herakleides, son of Sarapion, has a relatively common Greek-Egyptian name that reflects the earlier Ptolemaic presence in the area.[54] The most famous Herakleides, son of Sarapion, was the scholar also known as *Herakleides Lembos*, whom different traditions call a native of Kallatis, Alexandria, or Oxyr-hynchos. A diplomat of Ptolemy VI, he brokered the peace between his king and Antiochos IV after the Battle of Pelusion in 169 BCE (Diogenes Laertius 5.94, 8.44; *Suda* H 462, s.v. Ἡρακλείδης).[55]

HISTORICAL ANALYSIS

The King Demetrios of line 7 can be none other than Demetrios II Nikator, the son of Demetrios I Soter and grandson of Seleukos IV.[56] Demetrios II ruled as the Seleucid monarch twice (Table 2.1), first from 145–138 BCE and again from 129–125. We are fortunate to have the second

[52] Amitai-Preiss (2006, 608, no. 3).
[53] See Thiersch (1932, 66) and Mouterde (1933, 182).
[54] See Avi-Yonah (1962, 129).
[55] On the names, see also Avi-Yonah (1962, 129), Ovadiah (1975). On the identity of Epikrates, see Thiersch (1932, 66), Mouterde (1933, 182), Grainger (1997, 89). For men with the name Herakleides, son of Sarapion: see *Les graffites grecs du Memnonion d'Abydos* 23; a Herakleides, son of Sarapion, son of Herakleides is mentioned in a dispute in the Arsinoite nome documented on *P. Fam. Tebt.* 20 (Alexandria, 120/121 CE). On Herakleides Lembos, see *RE* VIII, 1, 1912, s.v. Herakleides (51), 488–91 (Daebritz 1912). Cf. also Polyb. 28.1.1, 22.2.
[56] See Grainger (1997, 42–44).

Table 2.1 The Late Seleucids

Name	Reign	Rival(s)	Successor(s)
Alexander Balas	150–145 BCE	1. Demetrios I Soter 2. Demetrios II Nikator	1. Demetrios II Nikator 2. Antiochos VI Dionysos
Demetrios II Nikator	145–138 BCE (first reign)	1. Alexander Balas 2. Diodotos Tryphon 3. Antiochos VI Dionysos	1. Antiochos VII Sidetes
Antiochos VI Dionysos	145/144–142/141 BCE	1. Demetrios II Nikator	1. Diodotos Tryphon
Diodotos Tryphon	142/141–138 BCE	1. Demetrios II Nikator 2. Antiochos VII Sidetes	1. Antiochos VII Sidetes
Antiochos VII Sidetes	138–129 BCE	1. Diodotos Tryphon 2. Demetrios II Nikator	1. Demetrios II Nikator
Demetrios II Nikator	129–125 BCE (second reign)	1. Alexander Zabinas	1. Alexander Zabinas
Alexander Zabinas	128–123 BCE	1. Demetrios II Nikator 2. Antiochos VIII Grypos	1. Antiochos VIII Grypos
Antiochos VIII Grypos	125–121 BCE (with Kleopatra Thea), 121–96 BCE	1. Alexander Zabinas 2. Antiochos IX Kyzikenos	1. Seleukos VI Epiphanes
Antiochos IX Kyzikenos	ca. 115–95 BCE	1. Antiochos VIII Grypos 2. Seleukos VI Epiphanes	1. Seleukos VI Epiphanes

inscription from Samaria, similarly listing priests of Zeus Olympios and the *Theoi Soteres*, the ancestors of the king, and King Demetrios, but in this case the name of Demetrios has been inserted into a recessed area created by the erasure of a name inscribed earlier (Figure 2.3).[57] The text reads as follows (note that the brackets implying an erasure do not indicate the removal of Demetrios's name but rather whatever was inscribed in the *rasura* before ΔHM[) (*SEG* 8 96, with *SEG* 33 1295):

> ['Έτους . . . ']
> ['Ἱερεῖς]
> [Διὸς Ὀλυμπίου]
> [καὶ Θεῶν Σωτήρων]
> 5   Διφιλίδης Ἑρμ[- - -],
> τῶν δὲ προγόνων τ[οῦ βασιλέως]
> Νικόδημος Νικο[δήμου?],
> βασιλέως [[Δημ[ητρίου]]]
> Ἀν[τίπα]τρος Ἀμ[μωνίου?],
> 10   ἱερ[ομνήμω]ν? Διόδο[τος?]
> [- - -]χομ[- - -]
> [- - -]
> λ[- - -]μιος [- - -],
> Ἡγ[ήσ]ανδρος [- - -],
> 15   ὁ γραμματεὺ[ς τοῦ ἱεροῦ?]
> Νικίας Νικίο[υ].

The erasures on both inscriptions undoubtedly have to do with the dynastic struggles that erupted during the reigns of Demetrios II, Alexander Balas, Diodotos Tryphon, Antiochos VI Dionysos, Antiochos VII Sidetes, Alexander Zabinas, Antiochos VIII Grypos, and Antiochos IX Kyzikenos.[58]

---

[57] See Reisner, Fisher, and Lyon (1924, pl. 59a), Mouterde (1933, 181–82). Joseph., *Antiquities* 12.257–264 says that the Samaritans had requested to locate Zeus Hellenios in their temple on Mt. Gerizim, whereas 2 Macc. 6:2 calls the god on Mt. Gerizim "Zeus Xenios." Mouterde (1933, 182) allows for the possibility that Demetrios's name has been restored here, but he is cautious about the idea. The photograph makes it clear that this is the case. Mouterde suggested, plausibly, that the name Demetrios was erased then reinscribed when Demetrios returned from Parthia.

[58] For excellent narratives of this period, see Ehling (2008, 154–216) and Chrubasik (2016, 123–45, with 154–61 on Tryphon, 161–69 on Alexander Balas, and 169–72 on Zabinas). A briefer but still penetrating account up through the death of Antiochos VII is found in Habicht (2006, 215–27). The ancient literary sources include the following: Polyb. 33.18; 1 Macc. 10–15; 2 Macc. 1:7; Livy, *Per.* 52.9–13, 55.11, 57.8, 59.13, 60.11; *Epit. Oxyrh.* 213–14; Diod. Sic., *Bibliotheke* 31.32a, 32.9c–d, 10, 33.3, 4, 4a, 9, 20, 28, 28a, 34/35.1, 15–18, 22, 28, 34, 40.1a; Strabo 14.5.2, 16.2.10; Joseph., *Antiquities* 13.35–369, 14.38, 249, *Jewish War* 1.48–52, 61–65; Plutarch, *Moralia* 184d-e; Frontin., *Strat.* 2.13.2; Appian, *Syr.* 67–69; Aelian, *NA* 10.34; Athenaeus 4.38, 153a–b (= Poseidonios *BNJ* 87 F 12 [Dowden]), 4.38, 153b–c (= Poseidonios *BNJ* 87 F 24 [Dowden]), 5.46, 210c–d (= Poseidonios *BNJ* 87 F 9b [Dowden]), 5.46, 210d–e (= Poseidonios *BNJ* 87 F 21b [Dowden]), 5.47, 211a–d, 6.49, 246d (= Poseidonios *BNJ* 87 F 23 [Dowden]), 8.7, 333b–d (= Poseidonios *BNJ* 87 F 29 [Dowden]), 10.53, 439d–e (= Poseidonios *BNJ* 87 F 11 [Dowden]), 12.56, 540a–b (= Poseidonios *BNJ* 87 F 21a [Dowden]), 12.56, 540b–c (= Poseidonios *BNJ* 87 F 9a [Dowden]); Just., *Epit.* 35.1–2, 36.1, 38.9-10, 39.1-4, 40.2, 42.1; Euseb., *Chron.*

Through the support of Attalos II, Balas[59]—of obscure origins from Smyrna—had been recognized as the son of Antiochos IV Epiphanes, and Rome granted him the right to reclaim his father's throne from Demetrios I Soter, which he accomplished in 150 BCE with the support of the Ptolemies and Attalids. Demetrios II, the teen-aged son of Demetrios I, ascended the throne with the help of an army of Cretan and Aegean mercenaries commanded by Lasthenes, with whom he had landed in Phoenicia in 147 BCE. The support of Ptolemy VI, the erstwhile ally and father-in-law of Alexander Balas, was key. Although offered the Seleucid crown by Balas's supporters in Antioch, Ptolemy VI declined and instead gave Demetrios his daughter, Kleopatra Thea,[60] the one-time wife of Balas. Together Ptolemy and Demetrios defeated Balas in battle near Antioch in 145 BCE (see *SEG* 13 585),[61] and Balas was subsequently murdered by his officers. Ptolemy VI died of his wounds, and Demetrios quickly expelled all Egyptian forces from Seleucid territory and reneged on his agreement to cede Koilē Syria to the Ptolemies.

A rebellion at Antioch was dealt with harshly by Demetrios's mercenaries, and a force of 3,000 troops was sent to Demetrios by Jonathan, the High Priest in Jerusalem. Diodotos Tryphon,[62] a former minister of Balas and probably responsible for the offer of the crown to Ptolemy VI, became guardian of Balas's son Antiochos VI[63] and went into open revolt against Demetrios, whose dismissed troops he acquired in Antioch. Tryphon took Apameia and then Antioch, and, while not claiming the throne for himself, seems to have been widely recognized as on par with the boy king.[64] Demetrios, who was still in control of Laodikeia and Seleukeia-in-Pieria, was initially allied with the High Priest Jonathan and had promised to withdraw the Seleucid garrison from Jerusalem. After Demetrios failed to honor this promise, Jonathan and his brother Simon joined Tryphon.[65] Simon was made satrap of the coastal zone between Egypt and Tyre, and the brothers successfully campaigned against Demetrios in this region, Galilee, and southern Judaea. Jonathan, after acquiring

---

117.1–124.5 [Karst] (= Porphyrios of Tyre *BNJ* 260 F 32 [Toye]); Jer., *Commentary on Daniel* 11.20 (= Porphyrios of Tyre *BNJ* 260 F 48 [Toye]); Jer., *Chron.* 157.2-3, 159.4, 160.1, 160.3-4, 162.1, 163.1, 167.1, 171.3; Oros. 5.10.8. For the Babylonian sources, see Shayegan (2003), Ehling (2008, 76–77). An astronomical diary (Sachs and Hunger 1996, 167, no. 137, line 10) dates the capture of Demetrios II by the Parthians to 138 BCE, whereas the entry for the year 130 mentions the retaking of Babylon by Antiochos VII. Babylonian King List 6 ends with the name of Demetrios II.

[59] Grainger (1997, 6–7).

[60] Grainger (1997, 45–47).

[61] Also, perhaps, *OGIS* 246, with Piejko (1982).

[62] Grainger (1997, 69–70).

[63] Grainger (1997, 28–29).

[64] Chrubasik (2016, 154).

[65] Grainger (1997, 97–98 [Jonathan] and 116–18 [Simon]).

Figure 2.3 *SEG* **8 96, catalogue of priests from Samaria.**

Photo: Reisner, G. A., C. S. Fisher, and D. G. Lyon. *Harvard Excavations at Samaria 1908–1910*. Cambridge, MA: Harvard University Press, 1924, pl. 59a. Permission of the Harvard Museum of the Ancient Near East: https://curiosity.lib.harvard.edu/expeditions-and-discoveries/catalog/38-990021305790203941 (accessed August 22, 2020).

Joppa and fortifying Jerusalem, made overtures to Rome and Sparta, and in 143/142 BCE, Tryphon—now fearful of Jonathan's growing power—invited the latter to Scythopolis (1 Macc. 12:40–48; Joseph., *Antiquities* 13.187–193). When Jonathan arrived with a large army, Tryphon flattered him and convinced him to come to Ptolemais. After dismissing most of his forces, Jonathan arrived at Ptolemais, where Tryphon took him captive. Tryphon soon executed Jonathan, whose brother Simon—now High Priest himself—joined with Demetrios.

Tryphon murdered the young Antiochos in 142/141 BCE and declared himself king and *Autokrator*, but—despite sending the Senate a golden statue of Victory—he was not recognized by Rome.[66] Demetrios proceeded to grant liberties to Simon and Judaea, and in 139/138 BCE he campaigned against the Parthians but was taken captive in July or August of 138.[67] Justin (36.1) tells us that this occurred during peace talks, and that Demetrios was subsequently paraded around the cities of Parthia and displayed mockingly to those who had flattered him. At this point, Demetrios's younger brother Antiochos VII Sidetes arrived as a contender after being invited by his brother's wife Kleopatra Thea, who subsequently married him.[68] After Antiochos drove Tryphon from Upper Syria, the latter took refuge in Dor, located on the coast, west-northwest of Scythopolis. After besieging the place (1 Macc. 15:10–14, 25; Joseph., *Antiquities* 13.222–224), Antiochos VII was able to expel Tryphon, who fled to Apameia where he either committed suicide or was executed. 1 Maccabees (15:37–41) tells us that at this point Antiochos, who had earlier made concessions to Simon, turned his sights toward Judaea. After settling affairs in this region, Antiochos made great preparations for a campaign against the Parthians, which he commenced in 131 BCE. After a series of initial successes by Antiochos, Phraates II, king of Parthia, became nervous.

Demetrios II had meanwhile been sent to Hyrcania, where he married a Parthian princess, Rhodogune, with whom he had several children.

---

[66] On the date of the death of Antiochos VI, which is disputed, see Ehling (2008, 178–79). The last coins of Antiochos VI date to 141/140 BCE, but Josephus and Appian imply that his death came after Demetrios II's capture by the Parthians. The earlier date is probably to be preferred, but note that Shayegan (2003, 88) argues that the cuneiform sources imply that he was alive in January 140 BCE. Grainger (1997, 28) is not convinced that Tryphon had him murdered.

[67] On the Parthian campaign and captivity of Demetrios II, see Shayegan (2003) and Nabel (2017, 31–34). In the literature, one will find different dates for these events, since 1 Macc. 14:1 implies that Demetrios II had left for the East in 141/140 BCE, whereas Porphyrios/Eusebios implies that he left in 139/138 BCE. The publication of the cuneiform sources, however, has made it clear that Demetrios was captured in 138, and here I follow the chronology outlined in Shayegan (2003, 84–87) and Nabel (2017, 31–34).

[68] Grainger (1997, 29–31).

After two failed attempts at escape, in 129 BCE he was dispatched to fight his brother Antiochos VII, who was killed in battle against the Parthians before ever meeting Demetrios. King once more, Demetrios unsuccessfully invaded Egypt in a campaign against Ptolemy VIII Physkon and Kleopatra III made on behalf of his mother-in-law, Kleopatra II. It is fascinating that this struggle between Ptolemy VIII and Kleopatra III, on the one hand, and Kleopatra II, on the other, also included erasure of inscriptions and papyri and damage to sculpture.[69] Ptolemy VIII subsequently sponsored the pretender Alexander Zabinas,[70] who defeated Demetrios at Damascus in 125 BCE, and shortly thereafter Demetrios was killed near Tyre. After plundering a temple of Zeus in Antioch, Zabinas was in turn defeated and executed by Demetrios's son Antiochos VIII Grypos in 123.[71]

It is in this context of interminable civil war that we must place the defacement of *SEG* 8 33. Savalli-Lestrade has discussed the use of *damnatio memoriae* by Hellenistic monarchs, which, intriguingly, was most concentrated in Ptolemaic circles from the period 179–108 BCE.[72] *Damnatio memoriae* first affected Ptolemaic dignitaries and officers who had fallen out of favor, but, as mentioned earlier, from 132–127 BCE statues, portraits, inscriptions, and papyri of Ptolemy VIII Physkon and Kleopatra III were defaced by Kleopatra II, while from 130–127 and 115–112 Kleopatra III did the same to papyri and inscriptions of Kleopatra II.[73] Given the close relationships—sometimes hostile and at other times cooperative—that linked members of the Ptolemaic and Seleucid courts at this same time, it seems reasonable to surmise that strategies of *damnatio memoriae* were learned by the Seleucids from the Ptolemies. Indeed, Ptolemy VI, during whose reign we see some of the earliest examples of the phenomenon, was the father-in-law of both Alexander Balas and Demetrios II, and Ptolemy VIII was responsible for the rise of Alexander Zabinas.

In any case, while we are in the dark about many of the topographic details, we can place Tryphon in Scythopolis in 143/142 BCE and in Dor in 138,[74] and it is reasonable to suggest that during this time Demetri-

---

[69] Savalli-Lestrade (2009, 146–48).

[70] Grainger (1997, 7).

[71] Grainger (1997, 31–32). Euseb., *Chron.* 117.1–124.5 [Karst] (= Porphyrios of Tyre *BNJ* 260 F 32 [Toye]) says that Zabinas committed suicide.

[72] See Savalli-Lestrade (2009), where she first outlines the place of *damnatio memoriae* in democratic city-states, where the practice seems to have originated. Typically, a city-state would not employ such measures unless circumstances were particularly dire, such as impending destruction by a hostile monarch or the need for redemption after siding with a losing king.

[73] For the ancient sources, see Savalli-Lestrade (2009, 155–56, table B; 157–58, table C).

[74] For an inscribed sling bullet from the siege, see T. Fischer (1992).

os's name was erased by partisans of Tryphon. Alternatively, we could surmise that the erasure occurred after Zabinas's victory over Demetrios, or perhaps even during the reign of Antiochos VII. *SEG* 8 96 has a slightly different story to tell. Here three possibilities present themselves: (1) supporters of Demetrios may have erased the name of Antiochos VI or Antiochos VII and inserted the name of Demetrios; (2) Demetrios's name may have been erased by followers of Tryphon or his brother Antiochos VII and then reinscribed during his second reign; or (3) partisans of Zabinas erased his name, which was subsequently replaced by supporters of his son Antiochos VIII Grypos after Zabinas's death. The depth of the affected area on the stone may, moreover, indicate more than one erasure—and thus perhaps more than one replacement of royal names. Savalli-Lestrade argues that we must be dealing with the erasure of Demetrios's name and its subsequent reinscription, since the document lists annual priests.[75] This is a fair point and may very well be correct. We should avoid being too doctrinaire, however, because we do not know exactly when these erasures occurred, nor do we know what the precise focus of those performing the erasure and/or reinscribing was. The ultimate desire was certainly to erase the godhood of the king, and we cannot exclude the possibility that one king's name was replaced with another's, even if this perpetrated a lie with respect to the holder of the priesthood on *SEG* 8 96. If we imagine that these decisions were made at the level of the city-state, it is also possible that one king's name was replaced with another's to avoid embarrassment (or even reprisals) after a rival had taken power.

In this connection, it is certainly noteworthy that a marble head that may represent Tryphon crowned with a diadem was found in Larisa-on-the-Orontes or Apameia in Syria. According to T. Fischer, the forehead was intentionally damaged after Tryphon's fall from power, and the head was inscribed with a dedication to Artemis by a certain Panderos, who had presumably fought against Tryphon.[76] An image of the usurper Tryphon thereby became an offering to a divine relative of the Seleucids.[77] The inscription reads as follows (*SEG* 44 1332):

---

[75] Savalli-Lestrade (2009, 149). Compare the excellent analysis of *OGIS* 105 that Savalli-Lestrade presents (144–145). The text is an inscribed statue base of Ptolemy VI, which had been dedicated at Paphos by Ptolemaios Makron, the Ptolemaic governor of Cyprus. In 168 BCE Makron had defected to Antiochos IV, who made him governor of Koilē Syria. His name and patronymic were accordingly erased from the base, but the ethnic Ἀλεξανδρεύς was left, either because it was assumed that the next governor would be from the same city, or because the locals wanted to highlight the fact that the traitor was not a Cypriot.

[76] T. Fischer (1971), Habicht (2006, 221n163).

[77] According to Just., *Epit.* 15.4, Seleukos's mother Laodike had dreamt that Apollo impregnated her and gave her a ring engraved with an anchor, which she was supposed to give to the child when he was born. This ring was found in her bed the next morning, and, after Seleukos was born, it was noted that

Πανδέρως
δὶς [σωθ]εὶς ἐγ με-
γάλων κινδύνων
κατ’ ὄ[ναρ] τῆι Ἀρτέ-
5   μιδι

In this same vein, it is intriguing that Tryphon had attempted to break with Seleucid tradition in a number of ways. Diodoros (*Bibliotheke* 33.3) says that Diodotos and Hierax were placed in charge of Antioch by Balas, and it is reasonable to surmise that this Diodotos is the same as Diodotos Tryphon, and that he and Hierax offered the crown to Ptolemy VI.[78] A clearer break with the Seleucid dynasty would be difficult to devise. The addition of "Dionysos" to the name of Antiochos VI, Tryphon's ward, may have aimed at highlighting the Ptolemaic side of the young king's ancestry.[79] Nevertheless, his other epithet, Epiphanes, recalled his purported grandfather, Antiochos IV. Similarly, coins of Antiochos VI, although in some ways hearkening back to his Seleucid ancestors, reveal novelties. The latter include reverses featuring the Dioscuri, the Boiotian helmet, and the panther.[80] The last is obviously a reference to Dionysos. After murdering Antiochos, Tryphon changed his name from Diodotos to the unique *Basileus Tryphon Autokrator*, which seems to draw on Ptolemaic traditions.[81] Tryphon also instituted a new chronological scheme that followed his own regnal years instead of the Seleucid era. This clearly meant to distinguish his reign from those of his predecessors.[82] His coinage, too, was innovative, as it combined references to Alexander the Great, military prowess, and τρυφή – that luxury from which he took his name.[83] Yet he also minted posthumous coins of Antiochos IV.[84] If Tryphon and his supporters were responsible for the defacement of *SEG* 8 33 and 96, we can read the erasures in a similar way. Although connection with the immediate Seleucid past was actively

---

he had a birthmark in the shape of an anchor on his thigh. When he left for the East with Alexander, Laodike gave him the ring and told him the truth, and, after he had acquired power, he founded the city of Antioch in honor of his mortal father Antiochos, but the area around was dedicated to his true father, Apollo. His descendants were said to have possessed the same birthmark. Artemis was, accordingly, the divine aunt of the Seleucid dynasty; see Hadley (1974).

[78] Habicht (2006, 219).
[79] On Dionysos and the Ptolemies, see Pfeiffer (2016).
[80] Chrubasik (2016, 155).
[81] Ehling (2008, 180).
[82] Chrubasik (2016, 157).
[83] Chrubasik (2016, 159): "Thus, his royal imagery not only tried to underline military success and prowess, it also promised wealth and splendour."
[84] Habicht (2006, 219n156).

suppressed, no damage was done to the Seleucid ancestors inscribed on the catalogues.

We may also wonder whether, if both inscriptions featured erasure of Demetrios's name, this was not due to his capture by the Parthians and subsequent marriage into the enemy royal family. Although he attempted to escape twice, he nevertheless fathered children with Rhodogune. It is even possible that the Antiochene revolt from Demetrios and his final desertion were due to his real or imagined Parthianism (Just., *Epit.* 39.1; Joseph., *Antiquities* 13.267–69).[85] He had been given the name of Seripides or Siripides, which is either a corruption of Σιδηρίτης—referring to chains—or a diminutive of Aramaic *'swr*, which would mean something like "bound little prisoner."[86] If the name was originally Σιδηρίτης, moreover, the similarity in form would have invited a direct comparison with the nickname of his brother and rival, Σιδήτης. Coins dating to his second reign feature a beard, which may very well have been inspired by Parthian custom.[87] Hoover has noted that Tyre—the site of Demetrios's demise—immediately removed Demetrios's portrait from its coinage and minted coins that featured the local hero Herakles-Melqart. The king's name and titles were removed and replaced with legends that named the city as holy and inviolate.[88] All of this begs the question: Could one remain a dynastic god in such a state, when one has literally slept with a foreign enemy?[89]

---

[85] Ehling (2008, 207–8) attributes the hostile attitude toward Demetrios II that we find in the ancient sources to his (possible) Parthian flare. See especially Just., *Epit.* 39.1.3: *Sed dum aliena adfectat, ut adsolet fieri, propria per defectionem Syriae amisit, siquidem Antiochenses primi duce Tryphone, execrantes superbiam regis, quae conversatione Parthicae crudelitatis intolerabilis facta erat, mox Apameni ceteraeque civitates exemplum secutae per absentiam regis a Demetrio defecere.*

[86] Euseb., *Chron.* 117.1–124.5 [Karst] (= Porphyrios of Tyre *BNJ* 260 F 32 [Toye]); Moses Khorenats'i 2.2 (= Thompson 1978, 131–32). On the name, see Nabel (2017, 33). On the Aramaic etymology, see Kosmin (2014, 173); Toye's commentary in *BNJ* provides the Greek derivation; see also Thompson (1978, 132n8).

[87] Ehling (2008, 206–8), who suggests that, in addition to the Parthian-style beard, Demetrios may also have taken on Parthian dress, eating habits, and etiquette; see also Canepa (2017, 212–213) and Nabel (2017, 32–33).

[88] Hoover (2004, 495).

[89] A similar disdain was felt for Vonones I when he returned from Rome to rule over the Parthians: Tac. *Ann.* 2.2: *Post finem Phraatis et sequentium regum ob internas caedis venere in urbem legati a primoribus Parthis, qui Vononem vetustissimum liberorum eius accirent. magnificum id sibi credidit Caesar auxitque opibus. et accepere barbari laetantes, ut ferme ad nova imperia. mox subiit pudor degeneravisse Parthos: petitum alio ex orbe regem, hostium artibus infectum; iam inter provincias Romanas solium Arsacidarum haberi darique. ubi illam gloriam trucidantium Crassum, exturbantium Antonium, si mancipium Caesaris, tot per annos servitutem perpessum, Parthis imperitet? accendebat dedignantis et ipse diversus a maiorum institutis, raro venatu, segni equorum cura; quotiens per urbes incederet, lecticae gestamine fastuque erga patrias epulas. inridebantur et Graeci comites ac vilissima utensilium anulo clausa. sed prompti aditus, obvia comitas, ignotae Parthis virtutes, nova vitia; et quia ipsorum moribus aliena perinde odium pravis et honestis.* I thank Professor Elizabeth Meyer for directing me to this passage.

The reign of Demetrios's brother Antiochos VII—who had also married Kleopatra Thea, the former wife of Demetrios—had created a great deal of awkwardness. This awkwardness was certainly recognized by the Parthian king, Phraates II, when he released Demetrios in order to foment war between the two brothers (Just., *Epit.* 38.9–10). It is therefore possible that the erasure of Demetrios's godhood was accomplished by supporters of Antiochos VII. One of the stated reasons for Antiochos's anabasis was the recovery of his captured brother (App., *Syr.* 68). Presumably, he wanted to rid himself of the rival to his throne and marriage bed. There appears to have been little love lost between Demetrios and Kleopatra Thea, who shut the gates of Ptolemais to her husband after his defeat by Zabinas. She thus sealed his fate—and Appian says this was due to his Parthian marriage (*Syr.* 68). Her hatred for Demetrios is underscored by the fact that she killed her elder son by him, Seleukos V (Livy, *Per.* 60.11; App., *Syr.* 69; Just., *Epit.* 39.1.9), and she subsequently tried to kill the second son, Antiochos VIII Grypos. Indeed, Savalli-Lestrade has even argued that the erasure of Demetrios's name was ordered by Kleopatra Thea after his capture or death.[90] Hostility between Antiochos VII and Demetrios may also be implied by the treatment of the former's remains. Justin (*Epit.* 39.1.6) informs us that the body of Antiochos was sent back to Syria in a silver coffin, which was received with great enthusiasm by the cities and Alexander Zabinas. Justin attributes the latter's enthusiasm to his desire for legitimacy and acceptance as the adopted son of Antiochos, which he subsequently received due to this counterfeit piety.

Although it is difficult to choose among these various options, the bigger picture is the same no matter which ones are correct: *we have here good evidence for rivalries played out on the level of local dynastic cults, where the living ruler was both literally and epigraphically demoted from or promoted—or most probably repromoted—to divinity in a way that mirrored the vicissitudes of fortune.*

It is fascinating that a private dedication from Ptolemais may exhibit the same tendency (*SEG* 19 904/20 413; Figure 2.4). The text reads as follows:

---

[90] Savalli-Lestrade (2009, 149), where Demetrios II's death is incorrectly placed in 129 BCE. Savalli-Lestrade suggests that Grypos had his father's name reinscribed on *SEG* 8 96 after his mother's death. This is plausible, but I find it more likely that these decisions were made by the officials of the cities. Cf. Van Nuffelen (2004, 300) on the cults of the Seleucid kings and ancestors: "les cultes municipaux étaient créés par la volonté autonome des cités, sans ordonnance royale." The quote from Chrubasik (2016, 126) is especially relevant here: "[K]ingship in the Seleukid kingdom was neither legitimate nor illegitimate, but rather it depended on acceptance by the political agents within the empire."

Figure 2.4 *SEG* 19 904/20 413, private dedication from Ptolemais in honor of Antiochos IX Kyzikenos.

Photo: Landau, Y. H. "A Greek Inscription from Acre." *IEJ* 11 (1961): pl. 28a. Permission of *Israel Exploration Journal.*

  Ὑπὲ<ρ> βασιλέως μεγάλου Ἀντιό⟦χου⟧ Σω⟦τῆρος(?)⟧
  Εὐεργέτου Καλλινίκου τοῦ ἐγ βασιλέ⟦ως⟧
  ⟦Ἀντιόχ⟧ου Σωτῆρος μεγίστου καὶ βασιλίσσης
  ⟦Κλεοπά⟧τ⟦ρ⟧ας Θεᾶς {ε.ς} Εὐετηρίας [καὶ] τῶγ παιδίων
5 ⟦. . .ε.⟧ς τῶν πρώτων φίλων καὶ
  [ἀρ]χιγραμματεὺς τῶν δυνάμεων,
  ἀπολελειμμένος δὲ καὶ ἐπὶ τῶν τόπων,
                    Διὶ Σωτῆρι.

Landau dated the inscription to 130/129 BCE and thought the king referred to in line 1 was Antiochos VII, as he read ⟦Δημητρ⟧ίου Σωτῆρος at the beginning of line 3. Nevertheless, Ehling is probably correct that line 1 references Antiochos IX Kyzikenos.[91] The Greek implies that the Antiochos in question was the son of Kleopatra Thea rather than her husband, as Landau thought. Around 115 BCE, Antiochos IX had risen as counter-king to his half-brother Antiochos VIII Grypos, son of Demetrios II. Grypos had apparently tried to poison Kyzikenos at an earlier date. The erasures are very irregular, however, and this prompted Schwartz to suggest that they were the result of damage that accompanied later reuse

---

[91] Grainger (1997, 32–33). On the inscription and Antiochos IX, see Ehling (2008, 78–79).

of the stone.[92] Landau agreed, and this may be the correct interpretation, especially if we take the irregularity of the erasures into account. We should leave open the possibility, however, that they were intentional, given the fact that we find erasure of royal names in *SEG* 8 33 and *SEG* 8 96. Indeed, although the erasure of *SEG* 8 96 was thorough, that of *SEG* 8 33 is rather more haphazard, as we can still read parts of Demetrios's name. Even without the erasure, the emphasis on the children of king Antiochos VII and Kleopatra Thea underscores the rivalry between the two sides of this complex family.[93]

Finally, a few words about the Seleucid coins recovered by the more recent excavations are in order. These include: two bronze coins of Antiochos VII, one dating to 136/135 BCE and the other to 132 BCE or a few years later;[94] three bronze coins of Alexander Zabinas, all dating 128–122 BCE and one of which was minted at Antioch;[95] one bronze coin of Demetrios II from his second reign of 129–125 BCE, minted at Antioch and inscribed ΒΑΣΙΛΕΩΕΣ ΔΗΜΗΤΡΙΟΥ [ΘΕΟΥ ΝΙΚΑ]ΤΟΡΟΣ;[96] one bronze coin of Ptolemais;[97] and two bronze coins of Antiochos IX, one from his first reign (114/113–112/111 BCE) and the other from his second (96–95 BCE).[98] Furthermore, the recent campaign of excavations at Tel Iztabba has recovered approximately twenty-five Seleucid coins, including a hoard of ten copper-alloy specimens dating to the reign of Alexander Zabinas (128–123 BCE). The earlier excavations conducted by the Israeli Antiquities Authority recovered around 350 Seleucid coins, of which around forty date to the reign of Zabinas.[99] The presence of the Zabinas hoard could—but need not necessarily—suggest that, after Zabinas took Koilē Syria and with it

---

[92] J. Schwartz (1962). On this text, see also Lifshitz (1963), whose restorations are rejected by Robert and Robert (1963, 180–81). All published texts subsequent to the *editio princeps* have removed the double brackets that indicate erasure. I include them here only to suggest that perhaps Landau was correct when he first saw some defacement of the stone.

[93] Indeed, Kleopatra Thea had died while attempting to poison her son Antiochos VIII Grypos, who made her drink first from the tainted cup; Just., *Epit.* 39.2. We have a very similar inscription from Delos. *IDelos* 1550 (116/115 BCE) is a dedication made by Antiochos VIII Grypos in honor of the proconsul Gnaeus Papirius Carbo: βασιλεὺ[ς Ἀντίοχος Ἐ]πιφανὴς | Φιλομήτωρ [Καλλίνικος ὁ ἐγ] βασιλέως | Δημητρίου [καὶ βασιλίσσης] Κλεοπάτρας | Γναῖον Παπ[ίριον Γαίου Κά]ρβωνα | στρατη[γὸν ἀνθύπατον? Ῥωμαίω]ν ἀρετῆς | ἕνεκ[εν καὶ εὐνοίας τῆς εἰς ἑαυ]τόν. For two similar dedications from Delos that mention Antiochos IX Kyzikenos as son of Antiochos VII and Kleopatra Thea, see *OGIS* 255–56.

[94] Amitai-Preiss (2006, 608, nos. 4–5).

[95] Amitai-Preiss (2006, 608–609, nos. 6–8).

[96] Amitai-Preiss (2006, 609, no. 9).

[97] Amitai-Preiss (2006, 609, no. 10).

[98] Amitai-Preiss (2006, 609, nos. 11–12).

[99] Lichtenberger and Tal (2020).

Scythopolis in 126/125–124/123 BC,[100] his partisans effaced the inscription of his defeated enemy Demetrios II. As mentioned earlier, the only other Seleucid coin discovered was of Antiochos IV, and it is interesting that the coins cluster around the same time period under discussion in the present study.

THE *NACHLEBEN* OF *SEG* 8 33 IN BETH SHEAN

We must comment on the possible implications of the inscription's depositional history and *Nachleben* in Roman Scythopolis. To prepare for the construction of the Round Church, early Christians probably dumped the stele into the cistern with other debris from the temple and its surrounding precinct on the tel, among which was the head of Alexander that had been intentionally damaged.[101] Because this material was probably all deposited at the same time—in the late fifth or early sixth century CE—we can reasonably argue that it was formerly part of the same use context—in this case most probably inside or near the temple on the tel.[102] Altogether, this included the head of Alexander (probably from a statue, see Figure 3.29), fragments of a colossal acrolithic statue (see Figures 3.24-3.28), a life-sized hand from a third statue (see Figure 3.23), and our Seleucid inscription. The Severan-period figured capital with a representation of Dionysos or a satyr (see Figure 3.21) was probably part of the temple precinct, though it is not certain where precisely, and the column drums deposited in the cistern were certainly from the temple. The fragmentary nature of this material underscores the fact that we are dealing with only the tip of the iceberg, but what we have is nevertheless intriguing. Romano suggests that the sculptures can all be dated between the second half of the second or the early third centuries CE. Historical considerations support Romano's conclusions as regards the date of the posthumous portrait head of Alexander, for it seems most unlikely that late Seleucid or Hasmonean rulers fostered such a link with Alexander. In the case of the Seleucids, since the time of Seleukos I there was an

---

[100] Lichtenberger and Tal (2020, 52–53).

[101] Chapter 3, pp. 94–95, 166–74.

[102] Tsafrir (1998, 212–13) notes that we have no good evidence for the date of the abandonment of the temple and destruction of its walls prior to the construction of the church. It is possible that the temple went out of use sometime around 391 CE, when Theodosius shut the pagan sanctuaries. The church seems to date to late fifth or early sixth century CE, so the temple may have remained standing and unused for quite some time, although we should not exclude the idea that the earthquake had damaged the structure.

attempt to forge a direct link with Zeus,[103] and, by the middle and late second century BCE, emphasis was placed on the royal cult. We have already seen that the dynastic lists associated with this royal cult begin with Seleukos I and do not make any references to Alexander. For the Jewish Hasmoneans, an image of the Macedonian Alexander would have been anathema, and furthermore, the site was unoccupied for most of the first half of the first century BCE. The redevelopment of the area that took place under Gabinius in the 50s BCE has left very little trace in the archaeological record. Tel Beth Shean itself was probably characterized by ruins for the remainder of the first century BCE, and this makes a late-first century BCE date for the Alexander head untenable.

In any case, Romano proposes that a colossal acrolithic statue whose fingers survive may have represented a seated Zeus, who was accompanied by his son Alexander as the new Dionysos.[104] Romano further suggests that Alexander could have been worshipped alongside Zeus and Dionysos as a σύνναος θεός, perhaps in a context of a ruler cult that included the Roman emperor.[105] How would the defaced Seleucid inscription fit in here?

Before answering this question, several caveats are in order. Obviously, we do not know the original display context for *SEG* 8 33. We can quite confidently conclude, however, that the stele was present on the tel during the Roman period, for it makes little sense to argue that someone would have lugged it up the hill in the fifth or sixth century CE in order to discard it in the cistern.[106] Thiel's suggestion that it was set up somewhere near a small Hellenistic naos is acceptable, but, as we have noted, there is no clear archaeological evidence for an earlier temple or shrine.[107] Several events could have affected the life of the stele. The first is the capture of Scythopolis by John Hyrkanos, which may have been accompanied by destruction of the pagan sanctuaries.[108] Archaeological evidence for such a destruction at Beth Shean is, however, lacking. The refoundation of the city by Gabinius in the 50s BCE would presumably have brought changes, but once again we have very little evidence con-

---

[103] Erickson (2013).

[104] Chapter 3, pp. 161–63. The coins with Dionysos's birth from Zeus's thigh, which date to the reigns of Septimius Severus (Barkay 2003, no. 39), Elagabalus (Barkay 2003, nos. 59 and 65), and Gordian III (Barkay 2003, no. 93), dovetail nicely with this idea.

[105] As Dirven (2011, 148–49) points out, inscriptions from Gerasa associate the priests and cult of the Roman emperors with Zeus Olympios; Welles (1938, nos. 2–5, 10, 14).

[106] Chapter 3, pp. 94–95 notes the same for the sculpture found in the cistern.

[107] Thiel (2007, 145).

[108] Thiel (2007, 149) suggests that a small Hellenistic naos of Zeus Olympios was destroyed at this time.

cerning what happened on the tel. Similarly, the Jewish insurgents who struck the city in 66 CE left no significant mark on the tel (Joseph., *Jewish War* 2.457–460).[109] Construction of the temple in the later first or second century CE certainly would have had an effect on the monument landscape. The earthquake of May 19, 363, was a watershed moment, as the next several decades saw major renovations, and some pagan inscriptions have been found in secondary-use contexts associated with this reconstruction.[110] The closing of pagan sanctuaries at the end of the fourth century CE is another event that needs to be taken into consideration. Finally, the clearing of the tel and the construction of the Round Church inalterably changed the character of the area. This clearing provides the one firm point of our chronology, as this is the only occasion on which we can say for certain that *SEG* 8 33 was moved, and it is possible that most of the damage to the stone occurred at this same time.

As noted previously, it is significant that the more recent excavations have found pagan inscriptions in secondary-use contexts. Some of these inscriptions were found reused in structures that were rebuilt after the earthquake of 363 CE (*SEG* 63 1589–1590).[111] This was expressly not the case for *SEG* 8 33, which was found among the debris in the cistern on the tel. Although we cannot be certain, this opens up the possibility that the inscription continued to be a part of the monument landscape of the tel from the second century BCE through the fourth century CE.

Elsewhere in the Eastern Roman Empire and even further east in Parthian territory, cults of Hellenistic kings continued to be observed.[112] In some cases, such cults may very well have been reactivated to reestablish links with the Greek past. A contract from Dura Europos, which had been founded by Nikanor, an official of Seleukos I Nikator,[113] indicates that Seleukos I and the royal ancestors of the Seleucid kings were still being worshiped in the late second century CE.[114] It is difficult to deny that in this case traces of the royal cult of the Seleucids survived well into the Parthian era. Rostovtzeff suggested that the cult was revived

---

[109] Arubas's appendix in Di Segni and Arubas (2009, 119–22), however, suggests that renovation of the city began after the suppression of the Jewish Revolt.

[110] For the epigraphic evidence attesting to major renovations, see Di Segni and Arubas (2009).

[111] See Belayche (2009a, 176n65). *SEG* 20 456 and 457 were found reused in Arab houses (Lifshitz 1961, 186). The same is reported for *SEG* 37 1529 (Tsafrir 1989, 76).

[112] See Chankowski (2011) and Noreña (2016).

[113] See Cohen (2006, 156–69) for an overview of Dura Europos.

[114] See Rostovtzeff (1935, 56). The text in question is *P. Dura* 23 (180 CE): ἐν Εὐρώπωι τῆι πρὸς | Ἀραβίαι ἐπὶ | ἱερέων Διὸς μὲν Λυσανίου τοῦ Ζηνοδότου τοῦ Ἡλιοδώρου | Ἀπόλλωνος δὲ Θεοδώρου τοῦ Ἀθηνοδότου τοῦ | Ἀρτεμιδώρου, τῶν δὲ προγόνων Ἡλιοδώρου τοῦ Διοκλέους τοῦ Ἡλιοδώρου, βασιλέως δὲ Σελεύκου Νικ[ά]- | τορος Δανύμου τοῦ Σελεύκου τοῦ Δανύμου.

during this time "as a kind of romantic reaction on the part of the Macedonian colonists of Europos against the pretensions of the Parthian kings to be the legitimate successors of the Seleucids."[115] A bas-relief from the same city dated to 158 CE depicts the *Gad* ("Fortune") of Dura Europos—Zeus Olympios—being crowned by Seleukos I, who is himself identified by a Palmyrene inscription.[116] It is probable that Seleukos was worshiped as the founder at Antioch,[117] and there was certainly a cult of Seleukos I at Seleukeia-in-Pieria, where his tomb, with a temple and temenos called the Nikatoreion, had been established by his son Antiochos.[118] The fact that this Nikatoreion was mentioned by Appian (*Syr.* 63) implies that it was still a feature of the city in the first half of the second century CE.[119] Similarly, an inscription from Apollonia in Pisidia implies the existence of a cult of Seleukos in the second century CE (*MAMA* 4 226).

What did this inscription mean to the citizens of Scythopolis when it was deposited in or around the Roman temple? Along with Alexander, Dionysos, and Zeus, the inscription points toward the Hellenistic past of this Greek city, which proudly called itself a *Hellenis polis* on its coins and on the statue base of Marcus Aurelius,[120] which was still standing in 749 CE when another earthquake struck the city.[121] *SEG* 49 2076, the dedication of a statue for the empress Eudoxia (400–404 CE), includes a quotation from Homer's *Odyssey* (1.426, 10.211), which must have aimed to underscore the city's Hellenism in the eyes of local and visiting literati.[122] We know from (1) *SEG* 8 46 (21/22 CE), a sarcophagus of Antiochos, son of Phallion;[123] (2) *SEG* 46 2047, the dedication of Seleukos, son of Ariston, to Dionysos Ktistes (141/142 CE);[124] and (3) *SEG* 63 1589, an altar with a metrical inscription dedicated to Sarapis by

---

[115] See Rostovtzeff (1935, 58–59) and Cohen (2006, 157).

[116] Rostovtzeff (1935, 66 and 64, fig. 1) and Chankowski (2011, fig. 1).

[117] Chankowski (2011).

[118] Kosmin (2014, 103–5).

[119] Noreña (2016, 92).

[120] The inscription may refer not to Marcus Aurelius but to Caracalla or Elagabalus.

[121] See Tsafrir and Foerster (1997, 127) and Heyden (2010, 301–2). Note the remarks of Chankowski (2011) concerning the broader context of Hellenistic ruler cults in the imperial era: "[O]n notera la présence de l'héritage hellénistique dans la conscience historique locale."

[122] Ἀρτεμίδωρος ἄνασ- | σαν ὅλης χθονὸς | Εὐδοξίαν χρυσεί- | ην ἔστησε περισκέ- | πτωι ἐν χώρωι.

[123] On the date and identification of the deceased as a pagan of Scythopolis, see Fuks (1981), who notes that very few Jews were given the name Antiochos, as it was reminiscent of the hated Antiochos IV. This last point underscores the importance of personal names as evidence for expression of identity in this area.

[124] This same Seleukos dedicated the other hexagonal altar to Dionysos and Zeus Soter as founders (Cohen 2006, 297n18; Belayche 2017, 14).

another Seleukos, son of Ariston (third century CE)[125] that the inhabitants of Scythopolis—and perhaps in particular the elite[126]—continued to give their children Seleucid dynastic names well into the imperial period.[127] Di Segni has suggested that at least some of these elite families owed their status to Seleucid patronage.[128] Such locals would have preserved family memories and traditions about their Hellenistic forebearers. Zeus, the dynastic god of their ancient Seleucid kings from the time of Antiochos IV, was still an active part of their religious life. Even if we cannot be certain that Zeus Olympios was directly equated with Zeus Akraios, it must be admitted that this argument makes the most sense of the available evidence. An interest in the Hellenistic past of the city is palpable in the inscriptions that call Dionysos and Zeus "founders,"[129] which must be read as an attempt to harmonize with the Hellenism that arrived in the fourth, third, and second centuries BCE.[130]

SEG 8 33—and probably other similar inscriptions that have not survived—provided a tangible link with the Scythopolitan πρόγονοι, the

---

[125] Clearly the descendant of the Seleukos from *SEG* 46 2047. This younger Seleukos appears in two other inscriptions, one on a statue base and the other on an altar dedicated to multiple deities (239/240 CE and 235/236, respectively; Di Segni 1997, 142–43).

[126] See Di Segni (1997, 140–43).

[127] *SEG* 8 32 is the dedication of a man named Seleukos to Ares Hoplophoros from the third century CE. This Seleukos, however, seems to have been a soldier stationed in or moving through the area (Belayche 2009a, 176n65). Ovadiah (1975, English abstract, 122), however, seems to accept the presence of the cult at Scythopolis, in which case this could be another Scythopolitan Seleukos. Di Segni (1997, 143n12) suggests that this Seleukos is the same as the younger Seleukos, son of Ariston. Yet another Seleukos can be read in the final legible line of the photograph of an inscription found in situ in the sanctuary of Demeter and Kore, which presumably is the same as the altar to multiple deities mentioned in n. 125 (Belayche 2017, 12, fig. 1.2B).

[128] See Di Segni (1997, 141–42).

[129] The altar to Dionysos κτίστης is dated to 141/142 CE: *SEG* 46 2047: Ἀγαθῆι τύχηι· | Θεῶι Διονύσωι | κτίστηι τῶι κυ- | ρίωι Σέλευκος | Ἀρίστονος χα- | ριστήριον ἔτει εσ' (see Figure 3.10B). Cohen (2006, 297n8); Belayche (2017, 14) provides a summary of the second inscription: "An unpublished inscription (just listed by the excavators in a preliminary report), was engraved on a hexagonal altar offered by the same Seleukos son of Ariston, who paid homage to Θεῶι Διονύσωι κτίστηι τῶι κυρίωι. Thus its date might correspond to the same years, the fourth decade of the second century. This altar honours two deities, both praised as founders (*ktistais* in the plural). Dionysos is listed second, with no epithet. The name of the first deity is, alas, missing, because the stone is broken, but his epiclesis is preserved: ΣΩΤΗΡΙ. It recalls *Zeus Akraios sôter*, well known in Scythopolis where he received a thanksgiving dedication in 138/39."

[130] Mazor (2015, 372) suggests that the head of Alexander represents him as Lord Dionysos, and that "[b]oth share the founding (*ktistes*) narrative of Scythopolis and presumably its syncretism into the Hellenistic ruler cult." There is even an inscription documenting a man named Diodotos—the original name of Tryphon—at Scythopolis, although in this case we probably should not read too much into the name (*SEG* 20 458; third century CE); Lifshitz (1962, 80–81, with pl. 7B). The inscription is on a small altar, but unfortunately the god to whom it was dedicated has been obliterated. It should be noted that the tau is restored. Similarly, *SEG* 8 44 ([Ἀ]μφόδ[ου] | Δήμητρ[ος] (vel Δημητρ[ίου])) is generally thought to refer to Demeter, but, if instead we are dealing with a district of Demetrios, we have some evidence for the use of another Seleucid dynastic name.

Seleucids, and the defaced name of the king served as a reminder that the divinity of a ruler was—and always had been—dependent on the responsible stewardship of his people. As Carlos Noreña has put it:[131]

> The figure of the Roman emperor was not a static or monolithic symbol. It was highly variable, and could be constructed in many different ways, and to many different ends. These different constructions of the emperor were significant. For most of the first two centuries AD the emperor was systematically represented, both by the central state and by local communities, as a paradigm of personal virtues and as a model benefactor. This conceptual convergence of personal ethics and material benefaction was the defining feature of Roman imperial ideology during the early and middle Empire. It was also, of course, an almost direct inheritance from Hellenistic kingship theory, and as such, would have cast the "good" emperor in terms very familiar to the provincial subjects in the Roman East.

For Noreña, Hellenistic ruler cults in the cities of the Eastern Roman Empire were essentially meant to activate historical memories—however distant—of local communities. The heritage of Alexander and his successors provided the necessary framework for these memories. As Romano poignantly notes, the portrait of Alexander from Scythopolis is certainly in dialogue with the tradition of "Alexander as a mythical founder of Near Eastern cities and a role model for emperors in a vital period of Roman history."[132] I suggest that *SEG* 8 33 had a role to play in this dialogue: Next to Alexander, the ideal, divine Hellenistic monarch, there was also a record of the opposite—that king whose failures deprived him of godhood, life, and memory. The audience need not have known the particulars of Demetrios II's reign to appreciate the message. The erasure next to ΒΑΣΙΛΕΩΣ spoke for itself and invited reflection upon good and bad rulers. Erasure of imperial monuments—that *damnatio memoriae* we see exhibited on *SEG* 8 33—had become a widely recognized Roman imperial tradition, and the meaning of the stele would have been instantly decipherable: A ruler can be divine only in so far as his actions toward the people warrant divinity. Given the lack of detail in the excavation records, my reconstruction of the stele's *Nachleben* must remain hypothetical. It is nevertheless quite imaginable that this antique inscription would have been appreciated by Scythopolitans of the Late Antonine and Severan

---

[131] Noreña (2016, 97).

[132] On the imperial cult at Scythopolis, see Mazor (2015), and, in the greater region, A. Segal (2022); see also Chapter 3, p. 64.

eras, which saw the condemnation of Commodus, Clodius Albinus, Geta, Macrinus, Diadumenian, Elagabalus, and Severus Alexander.

APPENDIX I: GREEK INSCRIPTIONS FROM SCYTHOPOLIS[133]

1. *SEG* 8 57–82 (stamped Rhodian amphora handles, Hellenistic period)
2. *SEG* 29 1614 (stamped Rhodian amphora handles from Tel Iztabba, Hellenistic period)
3. *SEG* 55 1746 (stamped Rhodian amphora handles, Hellenistic period)
4. Ebeling et al. (2020, 187–88), with Taf. 30, 1–8 (selection of epigraphic finds from Tel Iztabba, including a graffito on the base of an Eastern Terra Sigillata bowl, stamped Rhodian amphora handles, a stamped Knidian amphora handle, graffiti on amphora bodies, and a fragmentary inscription on a stone slab, second century BCE).
5. Ebeling et al. (2021, 70; stamped Rhodian amphora handles from Tel Iztabba, second century BCE)
6. *SEG* 29 1613 (with *SEG* 29 1808, *SEG* 39 1636, *SEG* 40 1508, *SEG* 41 1574, and *SEG* 57 1851, stele with dossier of Antiochos III and his general Ptolemy, 199–195 BCE)
7. *SEG* 61 1455/1459 (inscribed lead weight, 163/162 BCE)
8. *SEG* 8 33 (catalogue of priests of Zeus Olympios, the *Theoi Soteres*, the Royal Ancestors, and Demetrios II, 145–125 BCE)
9. *SEG* 28 1451 (inscribed lead weight, 117/116 BCE)
10. *SEG* 52 1683 (inscription on a square lead weight, 117/116 BCE)
11. *SEG* 38 1644 (stamped Rhodian amphora handles, ca. 100 BCE)
12. *SEG* 64 1807 (base for Aischylos, a successful local wrestler, imperial period)
13. *SEG* 8 46 (with *SEG* 31 1424 and *SEG* 48 1898, sarcophagus with epitaph of Antiochos, son of Phallion, 21/22 CE)
14. *SEG* 32 1490/1529 (milestones with distance from Scythopolis, 69–324/326 CE)
15. Mazor (2015, 375) reports that "[a]n inscription discovered on a round pedestal next to the agora's western temple and dated to the early first century CE mentions Cassiodoros the *agoranomos*, head

---

[133] I do not claim this list to be exhaustive; it simply represents the inscriptions I have been able to assemble during the course of my research, and I hope that others find it a useful reference.

of the gymnasium, the temple builder (*ieroktistes*), and priest of the emperor (ἱερασάμενος θεοῦ Σεβαστοῦ Καίσαρος)."

16. Mazor (2015, 375) continues that "Cassiodoros is mentioned again in two other inscriptions dedicated by the city *boulé* and *demos* to his daughter Lusida."

17. *SEG* 8 43 (inscribed limestone column capital referring to a local product, first century CE)

18. *SEG* 8 44 (inscribed column, perhaps referring to the district of Demeter, first century CE)

19. *SEG* 20 457 (limestone base from a temple to Zeus, first century CE)

20. *SEG* 43 1069/1073bis (epitaph of Theodora, daughter of Herakleites, perhaps from Scythopolis, first–third century CE)

21. *SEG* 46 2048 (limestone bust inscribed with a name, 100–250 CE)

22. Di Segni and Arubas (2009, 118n9, citing Mazor 2007, 4) report an unpublished inscription that confirms a visit by Hadrian in 130 CE. Cf. Mazor (2015, 375): "Within the vault constructed under the staircase leading to the temple of Demeter and Kore-Persephone, an inscription dedicated to Hadrian (Τραιανοῦ Ἀδριανοῦ Σεβαστοῦ) was discovered along with several dedicatory inscriptions to Tinius Rufus, the governor of the province, his wife, and daughter. They most probably are connected to the emperor's visit to the city around 130 CE."

23. *SEG* 20 456 (limestone base dedicated to Zeus Akraios Soter by Lucius Varius Proclus, 138/139 CE)

24. Belayche (2017, 14) provides a summary of the following inscription: "An unpublished inscription (just listed by the excavators in a preliminary report), was engraved on a hexagonal altar offered by the same Seleukos son of Ariston, who paid homage to Θεῶι Διονύσωι κτίστηι τῶι κυρίωι. Thus its date might correspond to the same years, the fourth decade of the second century. This altar honours two deities, both praised as founders (*ktistais* in the plural). Dionysos is listed second, with no epithet. The name of the first deity is, alas, missing, because the stone is broken, but his epiclesis is preserved: ΣΩΤΗΡΙ. It recalls Zeus *Akraios sôter*, well known in Scythopolis where he received a thanksgiving dedication in 138/ 39."

25. *SEG* 46 2047 (hexagonal limestone altar found in front of the apse of the Roman basilica and dedicated to Dionysos Ktistes by Seleukos, son of Ariston, 141/142 CE)

26. *SEG* 41 1575 (hexagonal altar, possibly dedicated to Zeus Akraios, 144/145 CE)
27. *SEG* 37 1531 (with *SEG* 40 1509, statue base dedicated to Marcus Aurelius, Caracalla, or Elagabalus, 161–180 CE, 198–217 CE, 218–222 CE)
28. *SEG* 37 1529 (octagonal altar dedicated to Zeus Akraios by Theogene, daughter of Tobias, second century CE)
29. Mazor (2015, 375): "Two other inscriptions which were found in the agora dedicated statues to Septimius Severus (193–211 CE) and Caracalla (211–218 CE), and both of them start with the same formula (Ὑπὲρ σωτηρίας Αὐτοκράτορος θεοῦ)."
30. *SEG* 28 1446 (polygonal pedestal or altar dedicated by Abselamos, Severan era)
31. *SEG* 33 1296 (inscriptions on funerary portraiture, early second–mid-third century CE)
32. *SEG* 47 2057 (inscribed gold phylactery, second–third century CE)
33. *SEG* 62 1695 (circular carnelian amulet against stomach ache, second–third century CE)
34. Ebeling et al. (2021, 69–70; mason's marks on columns reused in the "Podium Building" on Tel Iztabba, second–third century CE)
35. *SEG* 37 1530 (basalt block dedicated to Azeizos, late second–third century CE)
36. *SEG* 63 1590 (hexagonal limestone altar dedicated to Dionysos by Germanos and found in secondary use in fifth–sixth century CE context, late second–early third century CE)
37. *SEG* 39 1637 (milestone, 210/211 CE)
38. *SEG* 8 32 (dedication to Ares Hoplophoros by a man named Seleukos, third century CE)
39. *SEG* 8 53 (inscribed distaff, third century CE)
40. *SEG* 20 458 (limestone altar dedicated by Megalos, the freedman of the widow of Diodotos, third century CE)
41. *SEG* 63 1589 (dedication of an altar to Sarapis by Seleukos, son of Ariston, found in secondary-use context, third century CE)
42. Di Segni (1997, 142–43) reports that "[t]wo additional dedications by Seleucus son of Ariston the ἀλίπτης were discovered by the Antiquities Authority team: one on a statue base bearing the date 303 of the city era, namely, 239/40 CE, the other on an altar dedicated to several deities and bearing the date 299, corresponding to 235/6 CE." Cf. Belayche (2017, 11–12, 14, with fig. 1.2B) who summarizes and provides a partial photo of an inscription from the

sanctuary of Demeter, Kore, and, perhaps, Pluto. One can read "good fortune," "lady (κυρία) Kore," "for Pluto," "and also the Moirai," "Hermes" (?), and the name Seleukos (third century CE)

43.   *SEG* 35 1566 (*defixio*, fourth century CE: for the full text of the two *defixiones* from Beth Shean, see Youtie and Bonner (1937); they date them to the late third–early fourth century CE and the fourth century CE)

44.   *SEG* 20 455 (with *SEG* 43 1073, limestone column honoring Galerius with Latin and Greek inscriptions, 305–311 CE)

45.   *SEG* 8 48 (tomb door inscribed with the name Apolinarios (*sic*), fourth century CE)

46.   *SEG* 8 52 (inscribed vessel, fourth century CE)

47.   *SEG* 38 1643 (with *SEG* 39 1638, *SEG* 40 1511, and *SEG* 49 2081, mosaic with building inscription in the stoa, fourth century CE)

48.   *SEG* 59 1718 (building inscription commemorating the renovation of the city, late fourth century CE)

49.   Di Segni and Arubas (2009, 116) report an unpublished inscription that refers to a governor named Beryllos (late fouth century CE)

50.   *SEG* 49 2079 (building inscription on a stone lintel in secondary use, before 400 CE)

51.   *SEG* 49 2080 (building inscription recording the renovation of the city on a limestone slab found near the theater, before 400 CE)

52.   *SEG* 8 45 (white marble plaque inscribed with epitaph, fourth–fifth century CE)

53.   *SEG* 8 54–56 (lamps, fourth–fifth century CE)

54.   *SEG* 54 1678 (sidewalk mosaic with inscription in favor of the Blues, fourth–fifth century CE)

55.   *SEG* 44 1367bis (with *SEG* 49 2077, limestone lintel with building inscription recording the restoration of the nymphaeum after the earthquake of 363 CE, 400–404 CE)

56.   *SEG* 49 2076 (statue for Eudoxia, wife of emperor Arcadius, 400–404 CE)

57.   *SEG* 49 2078 (mosaic with building inscription from the south entrance of the bathhouse, 400–404 CE)

58.   *SEG* 50 1515 (with *SEG* 53 1838 and 1873, and especially *SEG* 63 1591 for the full text, mosaic inscriptions in the "House of Leontis," ca. 450 CE)

59.   *SEG* 54 1679 (donation of Nonnos from Kyzikos to the synagogue, ca. 450 CE)

60.   *SEG* 8 47 (column inscribed with the name Agathokles, fifth century CE)

61. *SEG* 8 50 (inscribed marble tablet, fifth century CE)
62. *SEG* 52 1684–1688 (inscriptions on amulets and weights, fifth–early sixth century CE)
63. *SEG* 56 1906 (eulogia token inscribed with the name of Solomon, late fifth–early sixth century CE)
64. *SEG* 49 2084 (with *SEG* 55 1745, epigram and building inscription for a basilica on a block found in secondary use, 500/501 or 515/516 CE)
65. *SEG* 49 2082 (building inscription recording the construction of a piazza with shops found in secondary use, 506/507 CE)
66. *SEG* 52 1681 (rectangular, decorated stone block in the street with building inscription recording pavement with new water channel, 521/522 CE)
67. *SEG* 8 37 (mosaic documenting the foundation of a monastery, before 522 CE)
68. *SEG* 49 2083 (two white limestone slabs with building inscriptions found in the pavement of a new road with water channel beneath, 522 CE)
69. *SEG* 28 1447 (building inscription of Eustathios from the apse of the church in the monastery, 522 CE)
70. *SEG* 28 1448 (building inscription of Eustathios, ca. 522 CE)
71. *SEG* 8 34–35 (inscribed limestone blocks recording the renovation of walls, before 529 CE)
72. *SEG* 20 459 (superseded by *SEG* 52 1682, limestone building inscription, ca. 530 CE)
73. *SEG* 49 2085 (building inscription recording building or renovation of city walls, 530/531 CE)
74. *SEG* 42 1471 (building inscription, 534/535 CE)
75. *SEG* 38 1642 (with *SEG* 39 1639, mosaic with building inscription from the north stoa of the palaestra, 550 CE)
76. *SEG* 58 1765 (mosaic inscription honoring Theodoros, founder of a palaestra, ca. 550 CE)
77. *SEG* 49 2086 (inscription commemorating the renovation of the lepers' bath, 558/559 CE)
78. *SEG* 8 36 (fragmentary inscribed marble plaque, sixth century CE)
79. *SEG* 8 38 (mosaic with building inscription, sixth century CE)
80. *SEG* 8 39–40 (mosaic in the monastery of Lady Mary with epitaphs, sixth century CE)
81. *SEG* 8 41 (mosaic with months listed and represented symbolically, sixth century CE)

82. *SEG* 8 42 (mosaic with months listed, similar to item 81, sixth century CE)
83. *SEG* 8 49 (inscription on tomb door implying purchase by Amos, sixth century CE)
84. *SEG* 8 51 (inscribed glass weight, sixth century CE)
85. *SEG* 26 1683 (with *SEG* 37 1532 and *SEG* 53 1836, mosaic with inscription from the synagogue, sixth century CE)
86. *SEG* 45 1980 (offerings for Zosimos and others from the monastery, sixth century CE)
87. *SEG* 52 1689 (fragment of a marble plaque inscribed on both sides and found reused in a Byzantine winepress southeast of the ancient city, sixth century CE)
88. *SEG* 28 1450 (with *SEG* 61 1456, mosaic inscriptions from the synagogue north of the city, 600–624 CE)
89. *SEG* 54 1680 (dedication of the mosaics of a church, 725 CE)
90. *SEG* 32 1530 (epitaph, Byzantine period)
91. *SEG* 37 1533 (mosaics with inscriptions from a monastery, Byzantine period)
92. *SEG* 40 1510 (epitaph on a limestone sarcophagus for Immidous, Byzantine period)
93. *SEG* 64 1808 (Christian dipinto, Byzantine period)
94. *SEG* 28 1449 (with *SEG* 65 1774, building inscription of Eulogios now located in the Roman theater, Byzantine period)
95. Edrey et al. (2022, 8; report of the discovery of a fragmentary stone inscription at Tel Iztabba)
96. *SEG* 65 1775 (building inscription, Byzantine period)
97. *SEG* 65 1776 (fragment of a marble slab, Byzantine period)
98. *SEG* 65 1777 (seat markers, Byzantine period)
99. *SEG* 65 1778 (Christian graffito, Byzantine period)

Chapter 3

A Portrait of Alexander the Great from Ancient Nysa-Scythopolis: An Object Biography

Irene Bald Romano

INTRODUCTION AND PREVIOUS SCHOLARSHIP

The focus of this chapter is an over-life-sized marble head from Tel Beth Shean, currently on display in the Israel Museum, Jerusalem (Figure 3.1).[1] This author argues that it is a Roman portrait of Alexander the

---

[1] Field Number 25-11-158; Beisan Find Number 1925, no. 213; Israel Antiquities Authority (IAA) no. 1931-7, in the Israel Museum, Jerusalem; Rowe (1930, 44–45, pl. 55); Thiersch (1932); Watzinger (1935, 21, Abb. 54–55, Taf. 23); Schwarzenberg (1967, 108n92, 111n124); Avi-Yonah (1973, 44); Lifshitz (1977, 275); Vermeule and Anderson (1981, 8–9, figs. 13, 14); Wenning (1983, 108–11, pl. 16, 3); Fuks (1983, 78); R. R. R. Smith (1988, 181, no. 16; 1991a, 224, fig. 264); Kreikenbom (1992, 15–16, 118, Kat. Nr. I.6); Stewart (1993, 169, 338n46); Tsafrir and Foerster (1997, fig. 41); M. L. Fischer (1998, 38, 255n343, pl. 1a, 1b); Lichtenberger (2003, 147); *The Israel Museum* (2005, 244–45); Thiel (2007, 140–45); Erlich (2009, 10–11); Trofimova (2012, 90, 96–97, fig. 94); Dayagi-Mendels and Rozenberg (2013, 95, fig. 1); Mazor (2015, 372, 374, fig. 14.14); Romano (2020, 946–48); Cadario (2020, 244, fig. 12); Romano et al. (2020–21); Kreikenbom and Sharvit (2023, 405–06); and Friedland (2022, 54).

Figure 3.1 Portrait of Alexander the Great, Beth Shean.

Israel Museum, IAA 1931-7. On display in the Israel Museum, Jerusalem, with the Knesset building in background. Photo: I. B. Romano. Collection of Israel Antiquities Authority, with permission.

Great. This head is being published here in the context of Beth Shean in its entirety, although it has been referenced without complete analysis or close clinical observation by a number of scholars since its discovery in 1925, resulting in varying opinions concerning its date and identification. None of these scholars considered questions of its relevance to the scholarship of posthumous Alexander portraiture, especially Roman portraits. Most scholars have assigned it a date in the Hellenistic period, in part relying on the excavators' reports and the inadequate evidence for dating the temple on Tel Beth Shean to the Hellenistic period, discussed further in the text that follows, and their assessment of the date of the head as belonging to the same period.[2] Soon after the discovery of the head the excavators sought the expertise of H. B. Walters, then Keeper of the Department of Greek and Roman Antiquities at the British Museum, who, using photographs, dated it to the Hellenistic period, probably the

---

[2] Rowe (1930, 44–45, pl. 55, fig. 9; temple plan), Fitzgerald (1931, 33, 44, pl. XXV, 1).

third century BCE.[3] The excavators suggested the head belonged to a statue of Dionysos and assigned it to the cult image for the temple on the acropolis.[4] In 1932 Thiersch published a long article using this object as his main focus, in which he accepts the conclusions of Rowe and Fitzgerald concerning its Hellenistic date and its assignment to the cult statue in the temple.[5] Yet, Thiersch presents a complex and largely implausible argument for the head representing Antiochos IV Epiphanes as Dionysos-Alexander-Zeus.[6] In 1935 Watzinger rejected Thiersch's complicated view and was the first scholar to label this head a portrait of Alexander; he dated it to the second century BCE, but his analysis was limited to a brief discussion.[7]

There is a gap in the scholarship concerning this head until the post-World War II period. In his 1967 discussion of the Lysippan Alexander, Schwarzenberg cited Thiersch's analysis of the Beth Shean head, especially the rising locks (*anastolé* motif) of Alexander, and argues for a conflation of the imagery of Dionysos with Alexander, but did not present any in-depth analysis.[8] In 1973 Avi-Yonah accepted that the head should be identified as a portrait of Alexander of the Hellenistic period.[9] Lifshitz made a brief reference to this head in 1977, assuming it belonged to a colossal Hellenistic statue of Dionysos and recalling the role of Dionysos in the Ptolemaic pantheon.[10] In 1981 Vermeule and Anderson called the head "the most important Hellenistic sculpture in the Holy Land."[11] They accepted the plausibility of Walters's third century BCE date, but posited that a date into the time of Mark Anthony could also be possible; they called the head a *Dionysus-Alexander*, but presented little discussion as their purpose in that publication was not to engage with a detailed analysis of specific sculptural works.

Into the 1980s the head was more consistently accepted by scholars as a portrait of Alexander,[12] but there were still some divergent views

---

[3] Alan Rowe records in his Field Diary (Beth Shean archives, Penn Museum) for December 18, 1925 (141) that after sending photos of the head to H. B. Walters, he received a letter stating that the head "surely belongs to the Hellenistic Age, i.e., 3rd c. B.C." Walters continues, "But I am not prepared to say whether it should be regarded as a work of the Alexandrine, Rhodian, or any other School of the period. It is not sufficiently characteristic."

[4] Rowe (1930, 44–45).

[5] Thiersch (1932).

[6] See Chapter 2, p. 19n2 for Thiersch's conclusions about the Hellenistic inscription.

[7] Watzinger (1935, 20–21, Abb. 54–55, Taf. 23).

[8] Schwarzenberg (1967, 108n92, 111n124). For the origins of the *anastolé* in fourth century BCE images of heroes, see Dorka Moreno (2019b, 62–64).

[9] Avi-Yonah (1973, 44).

[10] Lifshitz (1977, 275).

[11] Vermeule and Anderson (1981, 8–9).

[12] Fuks (1983, 78), for example, labeled the head Alexander.

about its identity and date. In a 1983 article on Hellenistic sculpture in Israel, Wenning argued that the head from Beth Shean is a Lysippan-type Alexander of the second century BCE (ca. 170–150 BCE), the oldest Hellenistic sculpture in Palestine, and possibly a product of southeastern Asia Minor.[13] He questioned its identification with the cult statue of the temple, pointing to the first-century CE lamp found in the cistern below the temple's foundations as evidence that the temple is not earlier Hellenistic as the excavators had posited, but suggests the possibility of an earlier shrine.[14] He used the head as evidence of the veneration of Alexander in Seleucid Scythopolis and of ancient Tel Beth Shean as a Hellenistic city with cults and monuments. Depending on the earlier scholarship on the head, R. R. R. Smith, in both his 1988 book on Hellenistic royal portraits and his 1991 handbook of Hellenistic sculpture, dated it to the Hellenistic period (second century BCE), but was uncertain about its identity, labeling it as either a posthumous portrait of Alexander or an image of a god or a Seleucid king ("Possibly from a (cult?) statue of a Hellenistic king, based on images of Dionysos and later Alexander types").[15]

In his 1992 article on colossal ruler portraits of Alexander, Kreikenbom discusses this head, erroneously conflating it with the colossal marble fingers found in the same context; we show in the following text that the fingers do not belong to the same sculptural image as the head.[16] The head from Beth Shean is certainly over-life-sized, but not colossal. Citing its shaggy and full hair framing the face with free-hanging curls, its asymmetrical but calm features, and the slight turn of the head to the right, Kreikenbom compares it to Hellenistic portraits of Alexander from Alexandria and one from Kos, and puts its date close to the statue of Alexander from Magnesia by Sipylos, now in Istanbul and generally dated to the second century BCE.[17] In a 2023 compendium of sculpture in Roman Syria, Kreikenbom dates the head to the Late Hellenistic period or the beginning of imperial times, ca. first century BCE, based on stylistic grounds, especially citing the hair, but recognizing the complex issues associated with this date.[18]

In 1997 Tsafrir and Foerster labeled the photograph of the head a portrait of Alexander of the Hellenistic period.[19] In 1998 Moshe Fischer

---

[13] Wenning (1983, 108–11, pl. 16.3).
[14] See pp. 61, 94–95, this chapter, for a discussion of the lamp.
[15] R. R. R. Smith (1988, 181, no. 16; 1991a, 224, fig. 264).
[16] Kreikenbom (1992, 15–16, 118, Kat. Nr. I.6). See pp. 101–8, this chapter.
[17] See, for example, Stewart (1993, 334, 502, fig. 133: 175–150 BCE).
[18] Kreikenbom and Sharvit (2023, 405–06, Skyth-16, pl. 237 A–D).
[19] Tsafrir and Foerster (1997, fig. 41).

also accepted a Hellenistic date for this head of Alexander (or Dionysos/ Alexander), though it stands nearly alone as a Hellenistic (mid- to second half of the second century BCE) example in his corpus of marble sculpture from Israel; Fischer shows how very rare Hellenistic sculpture in marble is in this region.[20] One of the most important contributions of Fischer's volume is a focus on the sources of the marbles used for the sculptural and architectural finds. In the case of the head of Alexander the analysis by Ze'ev Pearl indicated an Asia Minor source for the marble at Afyon or Aphrodisias.[21] Using more data points and multiple testing strategies, the source of the marble is now confirmed in the analysis discussed here in the Appendix by Tambakopoulos and Maniatis as very likely to be Aphrodisias.[22]

In his 2003 publication Lichtenberger makes only a brief reference to this head, but firmly asserts it is not Dionysos but likely a Hellenistic ruler such as Alexander, dating it to the Hellenistic period.[23] In 2009 Erlich discusses this head as an example among the very few Hellenistic sculptures from Palestine.[24] Erlich is firm in an appraisal of its identification as Alexander and in assigning it a second-century BCE date before the Hasmonean takeover (who, Erlich suggested, mutilated it), agreeing with Wenning that it was created and used by Seleucid rulers to legitimize their rule. Although there is archaeological evidence in ancient Palestine for Hasmonean destruction of Hellenistic sites, including on Tel Iztabba,[25] and corroborating literary descriptions, there is no clear evidence that the Hasmoneans engaged in iconoclastic behavior and the deliberate mutilation of pagan sculptures, which is much more characteristic of the Early Christian period, including deliberate defacing of certain features followed by beheading, as we see in this portrait of Alexander, discussed later in the text.[26]

In his 2015 article addressing imperial cults in the Decapolis, Gabriel Mazor calls this head a Hellenistic representation of a divinized Alexander as Dionysos, two gods who shared the founding narrative of Scythopolis

---

[20] M. L. Fischer (1998, 38, 255n343, pls. 1a, 1b). See Erlich (2009, 9–13) for a summary of the known marble sculptures from the region.

[21] M. L. Fischer (1998, 255n343).

[22] See p. 120, this chapter, and Appendix by Tambakopoulos and Maniatis.

[23] Lichtenberger (2003, 147).

[24] Erlich (2009, 10–11).

[25] See Chapter 1, pp. 7, 11.

[26] At Tel Dor, for example, column fragments and a limestone Nike acroterion of the third to early second century BCE from a Hellenistic temple or propylon were dumped into a pit during the mid- to late second century BCE; the Nike is battered and worn but there is no clear evidence of deliberate mutilation of the pagan image (Stewart and Martin 2003).

as *ktistes*.[27] Mazor points to a series of Hellenistic (second half of second century BCE) clay bullae from Beth Shean with representations of Nysa nursing the infant Dionysos as evidence of the Hellenistic (third century BCE) origins of the founding narrative of Dionysos, though it is not clear this has any bearing on the identity of the sculpture in question.[28] The curators in the Israel Museum, likewise, have accepted a Hellenistic date for the head, but have not linked it with Dionysos. On its display label it is identified as a portrait of Alexander the Great of the Hellenistic period with the range of dates from the third to first centuries BCE, encompassing the varying dating arguments presented by most scholars (see Figure 3.1).[29]

In 1993 Stewart was the first scholar to question the Hellenistic date of the Beth Shean head in print, briefly pointing out in a footnote some of the problems of assigning it to the Hellenistic period and calling attention to the undercut locks along the brow and cheeks, which recall Severan works.[30] Among the dating issues are also the lack of local marble sources in this region, requiring marble—the raw material, finished or semi-finished sculptures, as well as architectural decoration—to be imported. It is important to note that marble sculpture or architectural elements were very rarely imported to the region of ancient Palestine before the middle of the second century CE.[31] Trofimova followed Stewart's lead and suggested a date in the Roman period (second century/Severan period), though she misunderstood the context and the relationship of the head to other sculptural fragments.[32] Her contribution, now superseded by Dorka Moreno's comprehensive 2019 monograph on *Imitatio Alexandri?*,[33] is a discussion of gods and heroes in the guise of Alexander or the divinized Alexander with attributes of gods or heroes, discussed further in the following text.

In his 2007 article devoted to the sanctuary of Zeus Akraios at Scythopolis, Thiel is among the few scholars to provide a cogent analysis

---

[27] Mazor (2015, 372, 374, fig. 14.14).

[28] Mazor (2015, 358).

[29] Dayagi-Mendels and Rozenberg (2013, 95, fig. 1) summarize the current label information in the Israel Museum. The museum's website records the information from the 2005 Abrams Inc. publication of highlights of IMJ (The Israel Museum 2005) in which the date given for the head is second century BCE, https://www.imj.org.il/en/collections/222840 (accessed December 3, 2018).

[30] Stewart (1993, 338n46).

[31] See pp. 82–83, this chapter.

[32] Trofimova (2012, 90 [fig. 94], 96–97). She says the head was found near (rather than in) Scythopolis and seems to relate it to large statue fragments (probably referring to the colossal fingers) that she assumes belong to Dionysos. She accepts Stewart's suggestion that a uraeus was inserted in the hole in the top of the head, thus concluding it has Ptolemaic connections, though she also accepts a probable Roman date.

[33] Dorka Moreno (2019b).

of the context of this head.[34] He rightly questioned the Hellenistic date of the temple, pointing to local parallels for similar peripteral temples of the Roman period (including in the two Decapolis cities of Gerasa and Philadelphia, both dated around or after the middle of the second century CE) and suggested that the temple on Tel Beth Shean was renovated or monumentalized in the Antonine period. He cited Fischer's work on Corinthian column capitals from the region, which dated the partial capital for this temple no earlier than the mid-second century CE.[35] Thiel asserted that the head is a Roman copy of the early first century CE (associating it with the date of the Herodian lamp in the fill, which he used as a *terminus post quem* for the temple), modeled generally on well-known images of Alexander of the Hellenistic period; he suggested that the statue might have been erected in the colonnade of the temple as a Hellenic hero and *ktistes*. He rejected the head as part of the cult image of the temple, and instead accepted the colossal marble fingers as more likely fragments to be associated with the cult image of the second century CE temple dedicated to Zeus Akraios.

I recently published a brief discussion about this head in relation to the colossal fingers from the same context,[36] and in 2020–21, in collaboration with Tambakopoulos and Maniatis, who presented the marble analysis, I published a summary article about the Beth Shean Alexander in the *Israel Museum Studies in Archaeology*.[37] After Stewart's 1993 magnum opus on Alexander's portraiture,[38] the most important recent scholarship on the subject is by Martin Kovacs, whose 2017 *Habilitationsschrift* remains unpublished, but who traced the development of Alexander portraiture and its iconography,[39] and the previously mentioned 2019 volume by Martin Dorka Moreno on Alexander *in imitatione*, which does not mention this head from Beth Shean.[40] The identification, functions, changing iconography of presumed Alexander portraits and the origins of Hellenistic ruler portraits in the earliest portraits of Alexander, the similarities of images of rulers, heroes, and gods are significant topics that are taken up by these two German scholars and presented here, insofar as they are relevant to this head from Beth Shean.

---

[34] Thiel (2007).

[35] M. L. Fischer (1990, 61). See also pp. 69–70, 72, and Figure 3.7, this chapter.

[36] Romano (2020, 946–48).

[37] Romano et al. (2020–21). In response to incisive comments from peer reviewers of the manuscript for this current publication, I have modified and certainly expanded upon some of the views presented in the *IMSA* article.

[38] Stewart (1993).

[39] Kovacs (2017). See also Kovacs (2015).

[40] Dorka Moreno (2019b). See especially 19–27 for a discussion of the history of scholarship on the portraiture of Alexander the Great, vis-à-vis portraits of gods and heroes.

Though portraits identified as Alexander have been discovered in Greece, Egypt, Cyrenaica, and Asia Minor, this head represents, to my knowledge, the only surviving large-scale sculpted portrait of Alexander from the Near East.[41] This portrait's probable primary context in the temple on the acropolis of Scythopolis triggers consideration of the possible existence of a cult to, or at least veneration of Alexander in the Roman East and provides a springboard from which to reconsider, in a general way, Roman engagement with Alexander vis-à-vis social memory in this part of the Roman Empire. Issues of its identification are explored in this chapter, but if we accept that this head is an image of Alexander the Great, it is important in the large corpus of his portraiture because it would be among a relatively small number found in a controlled archaeological context, although a secondary one in this case. As with most of the marble images of Alexander, only the head is preserved, leaving us to speculate about whether it was part of a full-scale statue and with what body type, or a bust or, less likely, a herm. Crucial for its interpretation, but ignored by most scholars until Stewart, is the identification of the missing attribute that was once inserted into a hole in the top of its head, a subject that introduces questions about Alexander *in imitatione*—gods, heroes, or rulers in the guise of Alexander or bearing a likeness to Alexander—or Alexander conflated with them. Also of importance is an understanding of the reception of the portrait in the Late Roman/Early Byzantine period when it was subjected to deliberate mutilation before being dumped into a cistern on the citadel. It and other sculptural fragments from the same context provide evidence for the sculptural landscape on the acropolis of Scythopolis in the Roman to Early Byzantine period. And, finally, the modern reception of the head from the time of its discovery in 1925 to the present day is considered as a part of its complete biography. The head of Alexander is on display today in The Israel Museum, the most important museum devoted to the history, art, and archaeology of the state of Israel, where it is presented as a portrait of a key figure in Israel's past.

The object biography approach employed in this study is a methodology that arose from the field of anthropology and entails an examination of a work of art or cultural object in all aspects of its life cycle—its manufacturing technique, time and place, and its use(s) and inter-

---

[41] Although there is a colossal marble portrait of Alexander from Cyrene, several portraits from Greece and Asia Minor (Pergamon, Aphrodisias, Perge, Magnesia-by-Sipylos, and possibly from Cibyratis [Bubon] in northern Lycia; see pp. 81–82n97, this chapter), there is only this one from the Roman Near East. A Hellenistic or Roman bronze equestrian statuette of Alexander comes from much farther east, from Begram in Afghanistan (Stewart 1993, 45, 172–173, 423, fig. 52).

pretation(s) throughout its history in changing sociocultural–political contexts, as well as in modern museum settings.[42] Other art historians have used this approach to study "the lives and afterlives" of ancient sculpture but their interests have focused primarily on the use and history of specific works in their ancient past, for the most part neglecting their modern history, contemporary questions, and contexts.[43] Presenting the full biography of ancient objects when it is possible to reconstruct the complete information, as is the case with this Alexander head, opens up interesting questions about uses, appropriation, and reception of works of art across the span of their "lives," both in their ancient and post-ancient contexts, shedding light on human and institutional (including political, civic, and religious) relationships with cultural objects across temporal and cultural boundaries. Such studies can show how ancient works of art resonate in post-ancient times, broadening our perspectives of the complex role of sculpture in evoking political, patriotic, or religious responses; establishing cultural identity; or bringing about a shared under-standing of a historical past or present. This approach can also inform current museum practice, highlighting transcultural relationships and soci-ocultural entanglements that are part of the biographies of objects—topics that resonate with museum visitors and allow them to draw links to their own experiences, identities, or histories.

Alexander the Great—the man, the myth, the hero, the conqueror, the ruler-turned-god, his accomplishments, and his images in various media—has held an enduring fascination since his death in 323 BCE. Alexander has been the subject of a myriad of ancient biographies;[44] literary and artistic depictions of his legendary exploits in various lan-guages and formats, including in stories of "The Alexander Romance," his transformation as Iskander in Persian miniature paintings, and as a Byzantine emperor in fourteenth-century miniatures;[45] in popular modern literature;[46] and in a challenging mountain of modern scholarship.[47] He

---

[42] Kopytoff (1986), Schiffer and Miller (1999), Gosden and Marshall (1999), Joy (2009), and Fogelin and Schiffer (2015).

[43] For example, Kristensen and Stirling (2016).

[44] See also pp. 64–66, this chapter, for ancient biographies of Alexander.

[45] See Stoneman (2008), Zuwiyya (2011), Stoneman and Erickson (2012), and Stoneman et al. (2018). For the Trebizond "Alexander Romance" (Venice Hellenic Institute Codex Gr. 5), see also Kastritsis (2011). For a recent commentary, see Nawotka (2017).

[46] For example, see Mary Renault, *Fire from Heaven* (1969), *The Persian Boy* (1972), *Funeral Games* (1981), regarding his successors.

[47] The latest biographies are a religious portrait of Alexander by Naiden (2018) and Boardman (2019) on his portraiture and legacy to the present day.

has inspired a series of prints by Andy Warhol[48] and a recent comparison with twenty-first-century male hairstyles,[49] and he has been used as a political pawn in the high-stakes politics of national identity in the Balkans.[50] It would seem there is little more to be said about Alexander, yet this marble portrait from Scythopolis has barely been considered as a part of the tapestry of Alexander's historical legacy. Its details are fully published here for the first time and provide key information about an important ancient site—its monument landscape and cultic associations in the Roman period—and about Alexander as a mythical founder of Near Eastern cities and a role model for emperors in a vital period of Roman history.

ALEXANDER IN SCYTHOPOLIS?

Alexander probably never visited inland Judaea or Scythopolis. In 333 BCE he and his troops marched down the Phoenician and Syrian coast, laying siege to and capturing the coastal towns of Tyre and Gaza. He then moved to Egypt, making sacrifices to Zeus-Ammon at the Siwa oasis and founding the city of Alexandria. In 331, he left Egypt and retraced his steps along the coast, traveling inland into Syria toward Damascus (Figure 3.2). We are told by one source, Q. Curtius Rufus in the first century CE (4.8.9), that Alexander sacked inland Samaria in 331 BCE after the inhabitants murdered the Macedonian governor; this is not confirmed by other sources.

A reconstruction of the life, deeds, and physical appearance of Alexander the Great is hampered by the fact that his historical biographies were all written long after his death, with the oldest surviving account that of Diodorus (*Bibliotheke* 17), written 300 years after his death, and the most reliable account by Arrian (*Anabasis*) written during the second century CE,[51] 500 years after Alexander's lifetime. A kind of "romantic tapestry" about him was created, and mythologies of his life and deeds

---

[48] Commissioned by Alexander Iolas in 1982 when a bronze head of Alexander was touring in the "The Search for Alexander" exhibition (Nygard and Tomasso 2016).

[49] Issawi (2021).

[50] For Alexander and Balkan identity, see Danforth (2003). For the controversial statue of Alexander on horseback in the central square of Skopje, Macedonia, see H. Smith (2011). Another statue was set up in the airport that was named for a time after Alexander and was recently removed. The statues to the Macedonian-Greek hero and the implied claims of Macedonia, the former Republic of North Macedonia (and former Yugoslav Republic of Macedonia [FYROM] to the Greeks), continue to be a source of discussion and a lightning rod as diplomatic or political solutions were/are being sought for the name of the country on Greece's northern border. See also Plantzos (2023).

[51] For a recent assessment of Arrian, the historian, see Leon (2021) and see Djurslev (2023), for a review of Leon (2021).

Figure 3.2 Map of Alexander's route.

Image: http://upload.wikimedia.org/wikipedia/commons/4/40/MacedonEmpire.jpg (accessed August 20, 2020).

were embellished over the centuries. As Shane Wallace summarizes, "Alexander, as we have him, is mostly a construct of the Roman world."[52]

Writing from Rome some 400 years after the events, Flavius Josephus records that after the sieges of Tyre and Gaza, Alexander went to Jerusalem and made sacrifices to the god of the Jews in the temple there. Josephus also recounts that after a request from the high priest, Alexander allowed the Jews to continue their religious laws, and he exempted them from paying tribute to him. Josephus also claims that some Jews joined Alexander's army and accompanied him on his eastward campaign (*Antiquities* 11.304–339). No other Greek or Roman historical sources record this event, although the Talmud (Yoma 69b) recounts a similar story.[53] The accuracy of Josephus's and the Talmudic accounts on the matter of

---

[52] Wallace (2018, 162).

[53] Cohen (2012) points out that the context of both Josephus's statement and the Talmudic reference to this event should be viewed within the framework of Jewish animosity toward the Samaritans. (I am grateful to Sheila Cohen for sharing with me Getzel Cohen's unpublished lecture notes.) See also Ben Shahar (2018). An upper register on a floor mosaic discovered in 2014 in a fifth-century CE synagogue at the site of Huqoq in the southern Galilee has been tentatively interpreted by the excavator Jodi Magness as a depiction of the meeting, described in the Talmud, at the gates of Jerusalem between Alexander (accompanied by his troops with elephants, and appearing bearded with blond hair and a diadem, wearing a cuirass and a purple cloak) and the high priest Simon the Just, depicted as an older bearded man. Others have suggested that the scene should be interpreted as a depiction of Antiochos VII, who led the Seleucid attack on Jerusalem in 132 BCE, and the Judaean leader and high priest John Hyrcanus (Williams 2016, Britt and Boustan 2017). Erlich (2018) evaluates the various interpretations and argues that the scene on the mosaic depicts Caracalla as the "new Alexander" with his Macedonian phalanx and elephants, in conversation with the Rabbi Judah the Patriarch (Nasi, who died in 220 CE), with whom Caracalla is reported to have had a close relationship.

Alexander in Jerusalem has been questioned, and it is generally agreed that Alexander's visit to the high priest of Jerusalem—and his diversions inland—are fiction.[54]

Scythopolis's Hellenistic history, following Alexander's death in 323 BCE and the breakup of his widespread kingdom, is murky and complicated, with limited and disputed archaeological and epigraphical evidence. These details are elucidated in Chapter 1[55] and in Mahoney's reappraisal in Chapter 2 of a second-century BCE inscription found in the cistern to the south of the temple at Scythopolis, listing priests of Zeus Olympios and the *Theoi Soteres*, the ancestors of the king, and the king (Demetrios II). The fraught relationships during this period are highlighted by this unusual case of Hellenistic *damnatio memoriae* or "condemnation of memory" with the erasure of the name of a king.[56]

ROMAN SCYTHOPOLIS

The area at the foot of Tel Beth Shean began to be developed during the late first century CE, and Scythopolis grew to one of the largest urban centers of the region, a grand Roman metropolis (Figures 3.3 and 3.4; see also Figures 1.1, 1.2, and 1.4). The architectural development of the city has recently been reassessed by Benjamin Arubas, who concludes that the lower city began to be developed under the Flavians and expanded in the Trajanic and Hadrianic periods.[57] The city, however, also certainly experienced a major transformation in the periods of Antoninus Pius and Marcus Aurelius, during the peak of the Pax Romana in the East, and was expanded again during the Severan period at the end of the second and beginning of the third centuries, though this expansion is called into question by Arubas in favor of an earlier flourishing. In general, however, the Severan period was indeed a period of intense urban development and economic prosperity in the eastern provinces, with corroborating archaeological evidence in other cities of Transjordan, including Philadel-

---

[54] See Stewart (1993, 309–10nn58–59), Schäfer (2003, 5–7), Gruen (2003, 264), Cohen (2012), and Wallace (2018, 166–67) for the fictional account that served to emphasize Jerusalem's importance; Ben Shahar (2018, 403–08).

[55] See Chapter 1, pp. 5–12, and Chapter 2.

[56] For the complicated history of Hellenistic Beth Shean and the region, I refer the reader to Mahoney's discussion in Chapter 2, pp. 30–43.

[57] Arubas recently completed his doctoral dissertation on this subject and it has not yet been published. This information comes from a personal communication with the author on December 4, 2019. See also Atrash and Overman (2022) for a recent assessment of the monumentalization of the city in the first and second centuries CE.

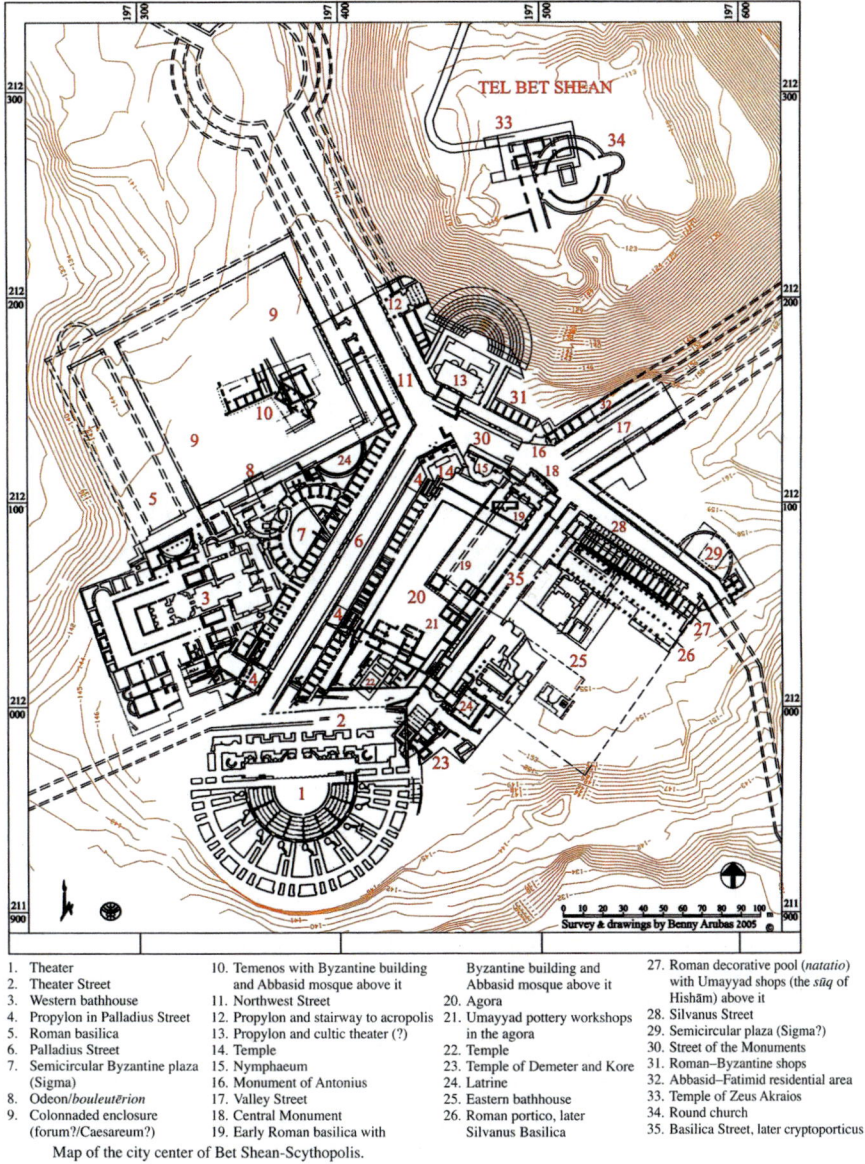

1. Theater
2. Theater Street
3. Western bathhouse
4. Propylon in Palladius Street
5. Roman basilica
6. Palladius Street
7. Semicircular Byzantine plaza (Sigma)
8. Odeon/*bouleutērion*
9. Colonnaded enclosure (forum?/Caesareum?)
10. Temenos with Byzantine building and Abbasid mosque above it
11. Northwest Street
12. Propylon and stairway to acropolis
13. Propylon and cultic theater (?)
14. Temple
15. Nymphaeum
16. Monument of Antonius
17. Valley Street
18. Central Monument
19. Early Roman basilica with Byzantine building and Abbasid mosque above it
20. Agora
21. Umayyad pottery workshops in the agora
22. Temple
23. Temple of Demeter and Kore
24. Latrine
25. Eastern bathhouse
26. Roman portico, later Silvanus Basilica
27. Roman decorative pool (*natatio*) with Umayyad shops (the *sūq* of Hishām) above it
28. Silvanus Street
29. Semicircular plaza (Sigma?)
30. Street of the Monuments
31. Roman–Byzantine shops
32. Abbasid–Fatimid residential area
33. Temple of Zeus Akraios
34. Round church
35. Basilica Street, later cryptoporticus

Map of the city center of Bet Shean-Scythopolis.

Figure 3.3 Plan of the city center of Nysa-Scythopolis.

Plan: Benjamin Arubas. Courtesy of Benjamin Arubas, the Hebrew University Expedition to Bet Shean-Scythopolis.

Figure 3.4 View of the lower city of Beth Shean from tel.

Photo: I. B. Romano.

phia and Gerasa.[58] At Scythopolis, the southern theater (the so-called Severan Theater) was rebuilt in grand style with marble "peopled scroll" friezes, ca. 200 CE, whereas the Northern Theater and a hippodrome (converted to an amphitheater, ca. 300 CE) were built anew sometime in the second century.[59]

The lower city and the tel were connected to one another by an impressive staircase with a propylon facing onto the so-called Northern Street, with another propylon on the opposite side of the street giving access to a large quadriporticus, which has been questionably identified as a caesareum, with an odeum built along its southern porticus (see Figure 3.3, no. 9).[60] No matter the interpretation of the complex, the date

---

[58] M. L. Fischer (1990, 34–37, esp. n310). See also Mango (2003) for the Severan development of the city of Byzantion.

[59] Northern theater: Mazar et al. (2008, 1641), amphitheater/hippodrome: Foerster and Tsafrir (1987–88, 35–38), Tsafrir and Foerster (1997, 99, 105, 133–135, figs. E, 2, 45, 46), and Mazar et al. (2008, 1641). Arubas argues that the "Severan Theater" was remodeled in the Severan period but the main remodeling of an earlier theater was done in Hadrianic times (Benjamin Arubas, personal communication, December 4, 2019).

[60] Mazor and Najjar (2007).

of that propylon and stairway must be the same as the monumental complex, giving us a clue to the date when access to the acropolis and, therefore, the acropolis itself were monumentalized in the Roman period. Unfortunately, there is no agreement on this date. In 2007 Mazor and Najjar dated the first phase of the odeum to the first half of the second century and the "caesareum" to the Hadrianic period (130–150 CE), and in a later publication Mazor and Atrash suggested that the odeum was part of a Severan monumentalization of the city.[61] Arubas dates the quadriporticus complex to the time of the layout of the city at the beginning of the second century CE.[62]

TEMPLE ON THE ROMAN ACROPOLIS
OF BETH SHEAN

The only major structure on the tel in the post-Early Iron Age period was a large Roman temple whose general plan can be restored from some 22 architectural fragments (Figure 3.5). The excavators reconstructed a peripteral temple with an entrance on the west, though this orientation is dubious,[63] measuring 37.05 by 22.8 meters with column drums of between 1.25 and 1.32 meters in diameter and columns rising some 10 meters (Figure 3.6).[64] Judging from fragmentary remains on the tel, some of the superstructure of the temple was executed in marble.[65] This suggests a date for at least one phase of the temple within the floruit of marble importation to the region from ca. 150 to 250 CE.[66] A large limestone Corinthian capital (restored height of 1.7 m), manufactured in two parts,

---

[61] Mazor and Najjar (2007), Mazor and Atrash (2015, 5). Benjamin Arubas has argued that the urban plan of Scythopolis was executed late in the rule of Hadrian after the Bar Kokhba revolt, between 130 and 140 CE, and he redates—or questions the dating of—some of the major Roman monuments of Scythopolis, including the theater and its *scaenae frons* (Di Segni and Arubas 2009, 119–22).

[62] Benjamin Arubas, personal communication, December 4, 2019.

[63] See Thiel (2007, 137).

[64] Rowe (1930, 43–44). Benjamin Arubas has reconstructed the column height at 15.2 meters, with a Corinthian capital of 1.7 meters high (personal communication, December 4, 2019). Vincent (1924, 425) estimated the interior height of the temple at around 18 meters.

[65] Vincent (1924, 425).

[66] M. L. Fischer (1998, 231–47), Lichtenberger (2003, 166–67), and Romano and Fischer (2009). See pp. 59–60, 82–83, this chapter. In the Beth Shean object register for 1923 there are references to Roman red wares on the summit (tel), but these are not described or used for any dating evidence (Object Register, Beth Shean Excavation Records, Penn Museum Archives). Barkay uses coins from Scythopolis of Antoninus Pius and Lucius Verus that show a tetrastyle Corinthian temple with an arched gable as evidence of a second-century CE remodeling of this temple (Barkay 2003, 143n66 and coins nos. 14 and 26), but it is more likely to be the tetrastyle temple in the lower city (see pp. 75–76 and Figure 3.3, no. 14, this chapter).

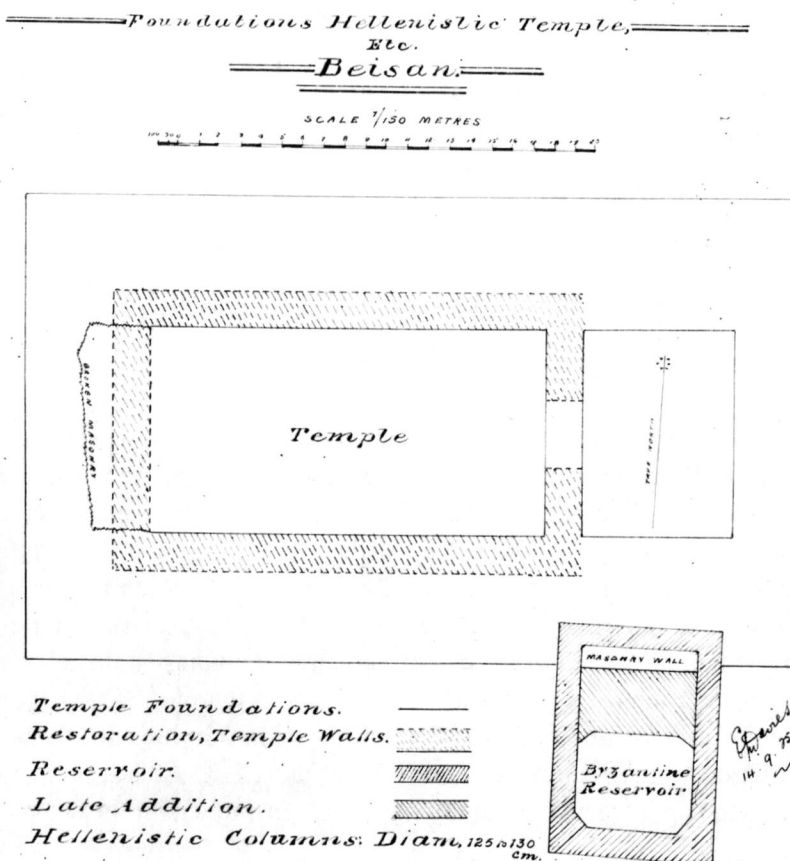

Figure 3.5 Plan of the temple and cistern on the tel of Beth Shean by E. Davies, dated 09-14-1925.

Plan: Archives of University of Pennsylvania Museum of Archaeology and Anthropology. Courtesy of Penn Museum, image #134793.

was found on the tel and must be from the temple. In his thorough study of Corinthian capitals from this region, M. L. Fischer indicates the capital can be dated to the mid-second century CE at the earliest (Figure 3.7).[67]

---

[67] M. L. Fischer (1990, 61–62, Nr. 229). Benjamin Arubas prefers a date for this capital in the later first century CE, perhaps the Flavian period (personal communications June 15, 2016 and December 4, 2019), though an analysis of his arguments must wait for his publication.

Figure 3.6 Columns drums for Roman temple on tel, Beth Shean.

Photo: I. B. Romano.

The excavators proposed a Hellenistic date for the temple of around the third century BCE,[68] but there are no architectural remains that can be dated to the Hellenistic period. That there was some kind of Hellenistic shrine to Zeus on the tel, possibly a sacred place as simple as an open-air temenos or a *naiskos*, is likely based on the content of the second-century BCE inscription that is the subject of Chapter 2.[69]

   A restoration of the propylon in the lower city leading to the staircase to the acropolis can be archaeologically documented in the late fourth century CE, suggesting that there continued to be activity to and from the acropolis during this period and that the temple was probably still in

---

[68] Rowe (1930, 44–45) and Fitzgerald (1931, 33). This is largely conjectural and probably based on the Hellenistic date they assigned to the head of Alexander.

[69] See Chapter 2, esp. pp. 23–25. The head of Alexander, the marble hand, and most of the colossal marble fingers were all found in what Rowe (1930, 44–45) describes as debris in the large reservoir to the south of the temple, and the 1925 Object Register, Beth Shean Excavation Records, Penn Museum Archives identifies the findspot as the Byzantine addition to the cistern (the southern section). See also pp. 71, 94–95, Figure 3.5, this chapter, for the description of the cistern. One of the fingers in the Rockefeller Museum (S.851), found in 1923, came from the "large cistern w. end inner circle" according to the Finds Registry in the Rockefeller Museum. It is not clear to what exactly the "inner circle" refers.

Figure 3.7 Limestone Corinthian column capital from temple on the tel, Beth Shean.

Photo: I. B. Romano.

use in the late fourth century.[70] The only other significant post-Early Iron Age structure on the tel of which there are architectural remains is the so-called Round Church, built over the eastern area of the temple in the second half of the fifth or beginning of the sixth centuries CE (Figure 3.8).[71] The construction of this church would most likely have been the final occasion when the sculptural fragments, discussed in the text that follows, as well as the inscription and column drums from the temple, were cleared away and deposited in a cistern that lay beneath the approximate center of the church, though the sculptures may have been earlier victims of the Christian desecration of demons, idols, and symbols of classical polytheism. The Roman temple must have already been out of use by the time of the building of the Byzantine Round Church, perhaps for some 50 to 100 years,[72] prompting us to consider what became, in

[70] Tsafrir and Foerster (1997, 112).

[71] Arav (1989), Tsafrir and Foerster (1997, 109), Mazar et al. (2008, 1634), Nocera (2013). See also M. L. Fischer and Tepper (2021) for the same types of capitals used in the Round Church.

[72] Tsafrir and Foerster (1997, 111), Tsafrir (1998, 213), Mazar et al. (2008, 1634), Kristensen (2013, 218–32).

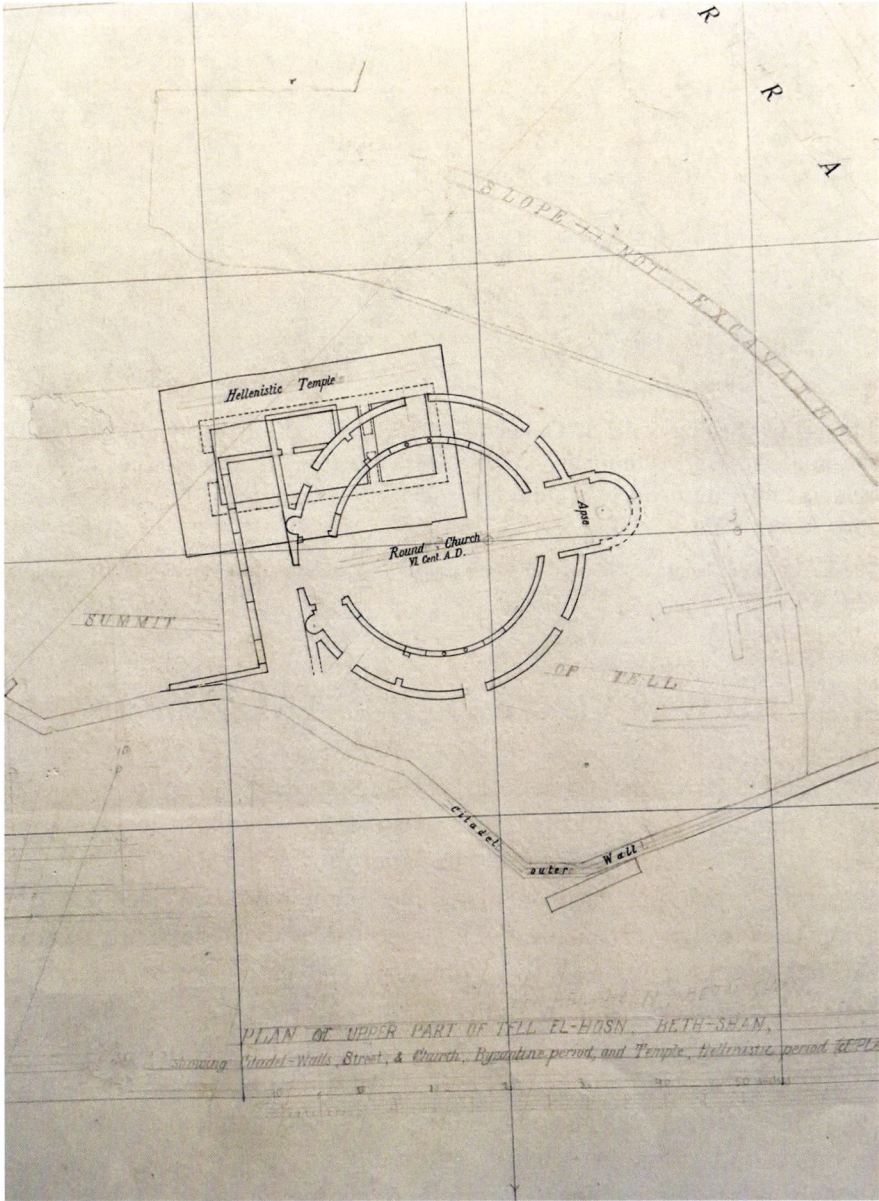

Figure 3.8 Plan of Round Church with outlines of the temple and cistern, Beth Shean.

Plan: Beth Shean Archives of University of Pennsylvania Museum of Archaeology and Anthropology. Reproduced courtesy of Penn Museum.

the interim, of the cult statue and other pagan images that might have been in or around the temple.[73]

---

[73] See pp. 166–74, this chapter.

Figure 3.9 Bronze coin of Gordian III, mint of Nysa-Scythopolis. *A (Obverse):* Laureate head of Antoninus Pius facing right. *B (Reverse):* **Dionysos standing to left with his thyrsus and panther at his feet.**

Photos: American Numismatic Society, http://numismatics.org/collection/2012.71.187 (accessed August 21, 2020).

WHO WAS VENERATED IN THE TEMPLE?

We cannot be certain to whom the Roman temple on the acropolis, of Scythopolis was dedicated. The excavators assigned it to Dionysos/ Bacchus or Astarte-Atargatis.[74] The latter attribution does not hold up to scrutiny, but that the Roman temple might have been dedicated to Dionysos is not unreasonable and is supported by the general prominence of Dionysos as the patron god of the city and its purported "founder." Scythopolis was a major center of Dionysiac worship in the region.[75] The god appears on the coinage of Scythopolis, especially from the period of Antoninus Pius (138–161 CE) to Gordian III (238–240/241 CE; Figure 3.9). He is variously depicted standing, both nude and draped, advancing or processing, riding in a chariot, and with Zeus and Nysa (as Tyche),[76] though none of the images definitively represents a statue and none

---

[74] Rowe (1930, 44). The first book of Samuel (31:8–10) attests to an Iron Age temple of Astarte in Beth Shean.

[75] Gitler (1991, 28n34). Raphia, in southern Palestine, also had a connection with Dionysos, for its very name suggests the place where Zeus's thigh was sewn up with the baby Dionysos, and its coinage features the baby Dionysos, as well as the youthful god (Belayche 2001, 266). See also Ovadiah and Mucznik (2015), Eisenberg-Degen et al. (2019, esp. 109–10). Neto-Ibáñez (1999) has proposed that a sacred grove (ἄλσος) of Dionysos existed at Scythopolis in the first century CE, based on a passage in Josephus (*Jewish War* 2.466–471).

[76] Barkay (2003, 111–137), Lichtenberger (2003, 135–141), Gitler (1991), Ovadiah and Mucznik (2015, 388–90).

Figure 3.10*A*: Altar dedicated by Seleukos, son of Ariston, to Dionysos, the founder, Beth Shean.

***B:* Detail of altar.**

Israel Museum, IAA 1991–2104. Photos: I. B. Romano. Collection of Israel Antiquities Authority. Reproduced with permission.

shows him inside a temple.[77] An inscribed second-century (141/142 CE) limestone (probably locally made) hexagonal altar found in the basilica in the lower city was dedicated by one Seleukos, son of Ariston (a Greek descended from the Hellenistic settlers or named in memory of a founding Greek who served with Alexander?), to the mythical "founder" Dionysos, reflecting the tradition recorded by Pliny (*NH* 5.16) and Solinus (36.1–2; cf. Diod. Sic., *Bibliotheke* 1.15.6) that at this place Dionysos's nurse-maid Nysa was buried. The altar was decorated with relief masks of Dionysos, Pan and Silenos and their attributes (Figure 3.10). Although the inscription and relief masks were left intact, the upper part of the altar, the surface on which offerings would have been made to Dionysos, was removed, probably in the Early Byzantine period.[78] Dionysos, possibly with Nysa, is also thought to have been worshiped in the city center

---

[77] See Lichtenberger (2003, 141).

[78] *SEG* 46 2047: Ἀγαθῆι τύχηι· | Θεῶι Διονύσωι | κτίστηι τῶι κυ- | ρίωι Σέλευκος | Ἀρίστονος χα- | ριστήριον ἔτει εσ'; Foerster and Tsafrir (1988, 31), Foerster and Tsafrir (1992, 122), Di Segni et al. (1996, 336–40), Di Segni (1997), Di Segni et al. (1999, 64–75), and Belayche (2001, 264).

in the tetrastyle prostyle temple with a circular cella and a spiral staircase to underground vaults. That temple was built in the first century CE, renovated in the second century (before 180 CE), and largely destroyed and dismantled before 400–404, probably ca. 369–395 CE.[79]

A free-standing statue of Dionysos found buried under the floor of the Silvanus Hall[80] and another fragmentary torso that has been identified as Dionysos on the basis of the lock of hair on the left shoulder and the diagonally arranged goat's skin[81] are also evidence of an interest in Dionysos in the Roman period at Scythopolis (Figure 3.11). In addition, two archaizing, second-century CE double-headed herms representing Dionysos wearing a *taenia* and abundant grape clusters (and the horns of Pan on top of one) with a facing Ariadne, were found at Beth Shean, probably originally set up in a Roman villa, showing private reverence for the local god (Figure 3.12).[82] Figurines of Dionysos were found in the northern cemetery, further attesting to the popular veneration of this god.[83] A fragment of a head or mask of Dionysos/Bacchus or a satyr from a locally made figured Corinthian capital from the cistern on the tel, discussed later in the text (see Figure 3.21),[84] may be assigned to the temple precinct, adding more weight to the possible identification of the temple as that of Dionysos.

The case is even stronger, however, for identifying the temple as that of Zeus. On the basis of epigraphical evidence it has been argued that the temple on the acropolis was dedicated to Zeus Akraios or Zeus Olympios,[85] possibly one and the same god.[86] A second-century (144/145 CE) Greek inscription to Zeus Akraios on an octagonal limestone altar dedicated by Theogene was found at the foot of the tel, not far from the stairway leading to the height.[87] Another second-century (139/140 CE) inscription dedicated to Zeus Akraios was found reused in the Arab

---

[79] Tsafrir and Foerster (1997, 97), Tsafrir (1998, 215–18).

[80] See pp. 85–86, 166–67, 174, and Figure 3.11, this chapter.

[81] Gersht (1996, 440, fig. 12).

[82] One is on display in the Israel Museum, Jerusalem, IAA 1932-36; H. head 0.332 m; Turnheim and Ovadiah (1994, 107), Gersht (1996, 439), Lichtenberger (2003, 147), Ovadiah and Mucznik (2015, 391, figs. 10–11), Kreikenbom and Sharvit (2023, 398–99, Skyth-9, pl. 234 A–B). It has a slot in the top of the head for the addition of another attribute. The comparable herm head (H. 0.18 m), found in the 1930s, had been in an English collection, and was sold on the London art market in 2008 (https://www.bonhams.com/auctions/15940/lot/221/, accessed November 7, 2018). The specific findspots of these herms are not recorded; Kreikenbom and Sharvit (2023, 398, Skyth-8, pl. 233 A–D [Antonine-Severan period]).

[83] Rowe (1930, 44).

[84] See pp. 95–99, this chapter.

[85] Tsafrir and Foerster (1997, 95, 98), Ovadiah (1975, 117).

[86] Lichtenberger (2003, 154–55); see also Chapter 2, pp. 17, 19n2, 26–29, on the cult of Zeus Olympios.

[87] Ovadiah (1975, 120), Tsafrir (1989).

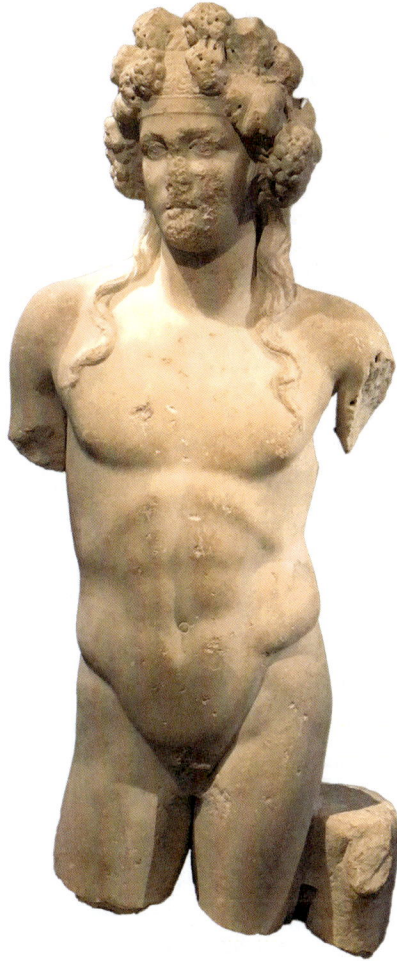

Figure 3.11 Statue of Dionysos from Silvanus Hall, Beth Shean. *A*: Frontal view.

Israel Museum, IAA 1990–821. Photos: I. B. Romano. Collection of Israel Antiquities Authority. Reproduced with permission.

town of Tell Hössn.[88] The epithet *akraios* suggests a god of the heights and refers to the acropolis (tel) or to another high place in the vicinity of Scythopolis or to Zeus's natural home on mountaintops. The Greek inscription found in the cistern on the tel, mentioned earlier and discussed in full in Chapter 2,[89] includes the partly restored word *Olymp(ios)*,

---

[88] Lifshitz (1961, 186–90).
[89] See Chapter 2, pp. 17–48.

Figure 3.11 *(continued) B:* **Back view.**

showing a connection with Zeus, and a list of priests, implying that in the second-century BCE there was some cult place for Zeus in Beth Shean. The numismatic corpus from Scythopolis also indicates a prominent role for Zeus in the city. On coins from the period of Antoninus Pius to Gordian III the god is shown seated on a throne in the traditional guise of Olympian Zeus, including within a temple on several issues (Figure 3.13).[90] Lichtenberger makes the compelling suggestion that the temple on the tel was dedicated to Zeus as the father of the founding god Dionysos.[91]

If both Dionysos and Zeus were worshiped at Scythopolis, we should recall the close association of Zeus and his "twice-born" son Dionysos to whom, in various versions of the myth, Semele gave birth and was reborn from the thigh of Zeus. The union of these two gods may be recognized in a dedication to Zeus Bacchus on a limestone base, found reused in the Arab town of Tell Hössn and dated to the turn of the first to second century CE, though the reading is not secure.[92] A second altar was dedicated at Beth Shean by Seleukos, son of Ariston, to a god whose epiklesis is ΣΩΤΗΡΙ, likely Zeus Akraios Soter, and to Θεῶι Διονύσωι

---

[90] Barkay (2003, 140–45, nos. 14 [Antoninus Pius] and 26 [Lucius Verus]).

[91] Lichtenberger (2003, 144).

[92] Lifshitz (1961, 189–90, pl. 8B). *SEG* 20 457: [Ἀγαθῆι τύ]χηι, ἔτους γ. . | - - - - - - - - - ωι Διὶ Βακ/ | - - - - - - - - - Αἴας Νικο. . | - - - - - - - - - | λίνου κατ᾽[εὐχ]- | [ἣν τὸν] ναὸν ἐκ τ[ῶν] | [ἰδίων] ἀνέθηκ[εν]. For doubts on the reading, see Seyrig (1962, 208–10), Robert and Robert (1962). The merging of an earlier cult of Dionysos with that of Zeus Olympios of the Seleucids was proposed by Thiersch (1932, 64–65).

Figure 3.11 *(continued)* **C: Detail of damage to face of Dionysos.**

κτίστηι τῶι κυρίωι.[93] This inscription further supports an imperial association of Zeus and Dionysos, which we also know existed thanks to coins of Scythopolis from the period of Septimius Severus, Elagabalus, and Gordian III that feature Dionysos being born from Zeus's thigh, with Tyche-Nysa to the left receiving the baby Dionysos.[94]

There is no epigraphical, numismatic, or archaeological evidence that Scythopolis was awarded the much-coveted civic title of *neokoros*

---

[93] Cohen (2006, 297n18) and Belayche (2017, 14). Another dedication (late second–third century) to Dionysos on a hexagonal altar from the Roman theater is by a man named Germanos (*SEG* 63 1590): [Θ]εῶι Διονύσωι Γερμανός (Ovadiah and Mucznik 2015, 393).

[94] Barkay (2003, 141, no. 39 [Septimius Severus], nos. 59 and 65 [Elagabalus], no. 93 [Gordian III]).

Figure 3.12 Double-herm of Dionysos and Ariadne, Beth Shean.

Israel Museum, IAA 1932–36. Photo: I. B. Romano. Collection of Israel Antiquities Authority. Reproduced with permission.

(temple warden). Thus, it would be difficult to claim that the temple was dedicated to the imperial cult.[95] The presence of the portrait of Alexander among the sculptures dumped into the cistern to the south of the temple, and arguably once erected in the temple, however, suggests that the temple could have been the locus of a cult to Alexander or religious veneration of his image. There is ample numismatic and epigraphical evidence for such Greek ruler cults in the Roman East with sanctuaries,

---

[95] Neapolis is the only known *neokoros* in Roman Palestine (Burrell 2004, 260–65). The identification of the building in the lower city of Scythopolis as the *caesareum* is in doubt (Mazor and Najjar 2007: see the critical comments on its identification in reviews by Trümper 2009, Weber 2009, and Fischer 2010). See also Mazor (2015) for a discussion of the imperial cult in the lower city of Scythopolis. For the imperial cult in the Decapolis and Caesarea Maritima, see Dirven (2011) and Segal (2022).

Figure 3.13 Bronze coin of Caracalla, mint of Nysa-Scythopolis, 216 CE.
A (Obverse): **Laureate bust of Caracalla to right.**

B (Reverse): **Zeus enthroned to left.**

Photos: American Numismatic Society, http://numismatics.org/collection/2012.71.188 (accessed August 21, 2020).

priests, games held in honor of the ruler, and statues erected as cult images in their honor.[96] Priesthoods for Alexander in the Roman period, for example, are known at Bargylia (Caria), Ephesos, Erythrai, Thessalonike, and Alexandria. The Alexandreia games in his honor were held in Rhodes and by the *koinon* of the Ionians, and statues to Alexander as a god are known from inscribed statue bases in Thessalonike and Bargylia. In no case, however, has a temple or a cult statue of Alexander been securely identified for a *Roman* cult of Alexander. A group of bronze portraits in the Sebasteion at Cibyratis (Bubon) in Lycia of emperors and members of the imperial family included Marcus Aurelius, Lucius Verus, Septimius Severus, two of Caracalla, and possibly one of Alexander, but conclusions about this group are frustratingly hampered by the illicit excavations and dispersal of the finds.[97] This portrait head from Scytho-

---

[96] Stewart (1993, Appendix 3, 419–20), Chankowski (2011), and Noreña (2016).

[97] See İnan (1979, 1993). For a recent summary of the Sebasteion and the sculptural program, see Kokkinia (2021). There is no inscribed base for a statue of Alexander in the Sebasteion, but a statue of the Greco-Macedonian ruler would make sense in a display of Severan emperors (see Vermeule 1980, 189–90). Two bronze heads of Alexander have been said to be from Bubon. One is an over–life-sized head that was/is in a private collection in Switzerland, was exhibited in Basel, and in the 1980s *Search for Alexander* exhibition, and was on loan from 2012 to 2018 from a private collection to the Metropolitan Museum of Art, where it is dated on the label from 150 BCE to 138 CE (L.2012.4.1; Berger 1971: first half of third century CE; İnan 1979, 274, pl. 79,1.2; Yalouris et al. 1980, 102–3, no. 9, color pl. 4; Price

polis may be a rare instance of the survival of a Roman statue of Alexander in association with a temple. In the end, the evidence strongly suggests that the main deity to whom the temple on Tel Beth Shean was dedicated was probably Zeus as the father of both Dionysos and Alexander. This supreme god may have shared honors and rituals with both Alexander and Dionysos as *theoi synnaoi*, as will be discussed in the text that follows.[98]

SCULPTURE FROM THE LOWER CITY OF SCYTHOPOLIS AND VICINITY

Scythopolis was one of the major centers of Roman Palestine, where a great deal of the architectural ornament and architectural sculpture, as well as free-standing sculpture, was made of imported marble—imported both as finished or partly-finished items.[99] Because there were no marble sources in the region, marble was imported from Greece and Asia Minor (but rarely from Italy[100]), especially in the second half of the second century and first half of the third century CE.[101] There are only a few well-dated exceptions to this mid-second century *terminus post quem* for marble imports to the immediate region, including an over-life-sized cuirass statue of the Augustan period from Samaria Sebaste made of Carrara marble.[102]

1984, 162, 263–64; Stewart 1993, 419; Dorka Moreno 2019a shows it is a probable forgery). This head was the inspiration for the commission by Alexander Iolas of a series of prints by Andy Warhol in 1982 when the head was in the touring exhibition (Nygard and Tomasso 2015). A Severan period bronze head of Alexander(?) in the Santa Barbara Museum of Art (2002.31.2) is also associated with the Bubon group; it is a bequest of Suzette Morton Davidson (*Search for Alexander Supplement to the Catalogue* 1981, no S-4; 1982, no. S-3, "private collection"; Del Chiaro 1984, 82–83, 107, no. 32). The comparison to the marble head from Beth Shean is not close, however.

[98] See pp. 160–66, this chapter.

[99] M. L. Fischer (1998), Romano and Fischer (2009). See Friedland (2022) for a summary of the sculpture from Beth Shean that takes into account some previously unpublished finds from the Hebrew University of Jerusalem and Israel Antiquities Authority's (IAA) campaigns at Beth Shean in the 1990s.

[100] This seems to be, for the most part, consistent with other sites in Roman Syria-Palestine (Friedland 2012, 60–61).

[101] M. L. Fischer and Grossmark (1996) and M. L. Fischer (1998, 231–47).

[102] IAA 36-2185; P.H. 2.40; restored H. ca. 3 m; displayed at the Hebrew University, Jerusalem (Reisner et al. 1924, 176, pl. 79e and f; M. L. Fischer 1998, 159, no. 182; Fittschen 2002; Laube 2006, 135–36, no. 59, Taf. 60; Weber 2008, 258–62, figs. 8–11; and Kropp 2013, 319). It was found in 1908 east of the altar of the temple of Augustus and Roma, in debris in front of the stairway to the Severan temple (see Reisner et al. 1924, vol. II, pl. 17a and 18 for excavation photos of the area of the altar). The source of the marble of this statue as Carrara (Luna) has recently been confirmed by scientific testing by Yannis Maniatis and Moshe Fischer, but remains unpublished (personal communication, Moshe Fischer, January 2018). For another Carrara sculpture from the region see the fragmentary marble satyr carrying the infant Dionysos from the Eastern Baths at Gerasa, dated to the end of the second century CE (Weber-Karyotakis 2017, cat. no. 6, 17–21, figs. IV, 31–35: "probably an import piece from Asia Minor [Aphrodisias]"); recent scientific analysis has identified the marble as Luna/Carrara (Al-Bashaireh 2018, no. 40). See also Erlich (2009, 10–13) for a handful of other marble sculpture examples in the region, and Bar-

The materials available for the foundations and basic architectural elements at Scythopolis were a local basalt, a soft local limestone, and another higher quality limestone originating in the quarries of Mount Gilboa (ca. 10 km to the west), exploited no earlier than the end of first century CE.[103] As indicated, much of the sculptural and architectural decoration in Roman Scythopolis was of imported marble.[104] Scythopolis was located some 80 kilometers from the main importation harbor cities of the Mediterranean. Thus, marble must have been a relatively expensive commodity in this inland area with significant transport costs associated with getting the product by ship to the nearest port (probably Caesarea, in this case) and then overland to Scythopolis.

Although the architectural sculpture from Scythopolis is remarkable, including the "peopled scroll" friezes from the Severan Theater (Figure 3.14),[105] it is worth briefly reviewing some of the published examples of free-standing sculpture from Scythopolis as a background against which to evaluate the head of Alexander the Great. First, no sculpture that can be firmly dated to the Hellenistic period has been confirmed at the site. Second, virtually all the free-standing marble sculpture has been found in secondary contexts, mostly mutilated and redeposited, making this corpus extremely important for understanding the phenomenon of iconoclasm,[106] while at the same time presenting challenges for reconstructing the primary sculptural settings.

A very high-quality, larger-than-life-sized marble torso of an emperor wearing a cuirass, reused as a building stone in a pier south of the colonnade of the Silvanus Hall, is one of the few and best preserved imperial portrait sculptures that survives from Scythopolis (Figure 3.15).[107] The head is missing and the decoration on the cuirass of a Medusa, griffins, and eagle has been defaced. This torso can be dated by comparison to the well-studied corpus of cuirassed Roman statues to the Antonine period and is probably of the emperor Antoninus Pius or Marcus Aurelius. The back is unfinished, suggesting it was displayed in

---

Nathan and Snyder (2019) for colored marbles imported for *opus sectile* floors in the Herodian period at Banias and Jericho. Further north along the Phoenician coast, marble (likely Parian) sarcophagi are found in the necropolis of Sidon and at nearby sites. For a recent summary of marble sculpture in Roman Syria, see Koçak and Kreikenbom (2023, XIII–XVI).

[103] For the use of the limestone from Mt. Gilboa in the late first or second century CE, see Tsafrir and Foerster (1997, 89), Segal (2006).

[104] Tsafrir and Foerster (1997, 89–90), Romano and Fischer (2009).

[105] Ovadiah and Turnheim (1994).

[106] Kristensen (2013, 218–32).

[107] IAA (1991–2106); Foerster and Tsafrir (1987–1988, 33), Tsafrir and Foerster (1994, 101), Tsafrir and Foerster (1997, fig. 39), Fischer (1998, 160–61, 200, no. 188), Kreikenbom and Sharvit (2023, 406–7, Skyth-17, pl. 238 A–B [Early to Middle Antonine, ca. 140–180 CE]). See also Friedland (2022, 52) for reference to two other cuirassed sculpture fragments from Beth Shean.

Figure 3.14 "Peopled" scroll frieze from Severan Theater, Beth Shean.

Photo: I. B. Romano.

a position where the back would not have been seen. Two unpublished inscriptions are also evidence that (sculptural?) monuments were dedicated at the site to the emperors Septimius Severus and Caracalla.[108]

There are no known traces in Scythopolis itself of any portraits (or bases for portrait statues) of Hadrian or any monuments commemorating the brutal quelling of the Jewish revolt or the reorganization of Judaea into the new province of Syria-Palaestina. At Tel Shalem, 12 kilometers south of Scythopolis, however, a cuirassed bronze torso of Hadrian was discovered at a Roman fort where a detachment of the Legio VI Ferrata of the Roman imperial army was stationed. The statue may have been set up in a shrine at the military fort following Hadrian's second visit to Judaea in 135 CE.[109] Also, blocks reused in the Byzantine period near

---

[108] Mazor (2015, 375).

[109] On display in the Israel Museum, Jerusalem, IAA 1975–763; H. 0.89 m (Foerster 1980, 1985). Gergel (1991) proposed that the Hadrian head and torso are a pastiche of an imported head, an official portrait of the emperor, fitted to the cuirassed body that was originally a *tropaion* of local provenience and of late Hellenistic date. A fragmentary bronze head of a youth was found in the same context with the bronze statue of Hadrian and may be part of the same statue group, representing a captive crouching at the emperor's side or beneath his foot.

Figure 3.15 Torso of an emperor wearing a cuirass, reused in a pier south of the colonnade of the Silvanus Hall, Beth Shean, second century CE.

Israel Museum, IAA 1991–2106. Photo: I. B. Romano. Collection of Israel Antiquities Authority. Reproduced with permission.

Tel Shalem bear a very large Latin inscription honoring Hadrian, believed to have been displayed on an arch erected near one of the army camps and commemorating the quelling of the Bar Kokhba Revolt in 135 CE.[110]

There are many free-standing sculptures of pagan divinities from Scythopolis, several of the founding god of Scythopolis, Dionysos. These include a life-sized standing Antonine example of the god in his youthful

---

[110] Eck (1999: H. of letters in first line: 0.41 m, restored length of inscription: 10 m).

effeminate guise, found buried under the floor of the so-called Silvanus Hall, a 56-meter-long stoa with an ornamental stepped pool in front (see Figure 3.11).[111] The torso, though not the head, is a replica of the Apollo Centocelle type.[112] A *mitra* is worn across Dionysos's forehead, and a wreath of large bunches of grape and ivy leaves decorates his head. The top and back of the head are only summarily finished. The genitalia, eyes, nose, and mouth are mutilated, presumably an act of selective Christian iconoclasm.

In the 1986–1988 excavations of the Severan Theater by Mazor and Bar-Nathan several marble statues were found, including one of a youthful nude male with a chlamys around his neck and forearm and a seated animal, probably a ram, next to his right leg. It has been variously identified as a possible Hermes Psychopompos type, an Apollo, or a Dionysos. Pointing to the fleecy ram next to him and the caduceus with snakes wrapped around his left arm, Sharvit, however, identifies the statue as a Hermes of the Shepherd type.[113] The body and head types are inspired by different Greek sculptural sources and are combined in this Roman version. The statue may have been displayed on the *scaenae frons* of the theater, but was broken and deposited in a pit outside the theater, after having been decapitated and its nose, mouth, and genitalia broken, probably by early Christian zealots.[114] The marble was scientifically tested in the late 1980s and was identified as deriving from the quarries of Proconnesos in northwest Asia Minor.[115] Retesting may provide other possibilities, especially among Asia Minor quarries, many of which have recently been scientifically identified.

Found in a stratum of rubble from the 749 CE earthquake at the theater is a fragmentary statue of Tyche/Fortuna, wearing a chiton and himation and holding a cornucopia in her left hand, probably dating to the late second or early third century CE (Figure 3.16).[116] There may have been a rudder at her right side. The head was separately made and attached, as the cutting in the neck and traces of lead show, and we cannot rule out the possibility that a portrait head was added. The marble is described as white/light gray but has not been scientifically tested.

---

[111] IAA 1990-821; Foerster and Tsafrir (1990, 1992, 122–23, fig. 12), Gersht (1996, 439–40, fig. 11), Tsafrir and Foerster (1997, 129, fig. 40), M. L. Fischer (1998, 161, 201, no. 190), Kristensen (2013, 222–25, no. 117, fig. 3.12), Kreikenbom and Sharvit (2023, 396–97, Skyth-6, pl. 232 A–C, Early Antonine period, ca. 140–160 CE).

[112] See Kansteiner (2016, 43, 43n98) for further bibliography.

[113] IAA 1961-528; Foerster and Tsafrir (1992, 122, fig. 14), Tsafrir and Foerster (1997, 129), M. L. Fischer (1998, 189, 199, no. 187), Sharvit (2015, 613–17, H. 1.92 m), Kreikenbom and Sharvit (2023, 400–01, Skyth-11, pl. 235 A–B).

[114] Kristensen (2013, 229n135).

Figure 3.16 Statue of Tyche/Fortuna from Severan Theater, Beth Shean.

Israel Museum, IAA 1991–2093. Photo: I. B. Romano. Collection of Israel Antiquities Authority. Reproduced with permission.

A nude torso of Aphrodite in white/light-gray marble was also found in the Severan Theater, under a Byzantine I pavement, and it appears to have been intentionally mutilated with her breasts partly gouged out.[117]

---

[115] Pearl (1989, 50–51).

[116] IAA 1991-2093; Sharvit (2015, 619–20, H. 0.73; Restored H. ca. 1.80; W. 0.46; Depth 0.29 m), Kreikenbom and Sharvit (2023, 401–02, Skyth-12, pl. 235 C).

[117] Sharvit (2015, 617–19, H. 0.60; W. 0.44; D. 0.22 m), Kreikenbom and Sharvit (2023, 392–93, Skyth-2, pl. 220 C–D [second century CE]), Friedland (2022, 49, fig. 1).

This is a replica of the Venus Pudica type with her head turned to her left, and the body is leaning forward. There are remains of two long curls on the shoulders, and at the back of her head is a neck support, just as on the Hermes. Around each upper arm is a bracelet.

Excavations in the 1990s by the Hebrew University in the Eastern Bathhouse revealed 13 life-sized marble sculptures that were mutilated and deposited in a sealed layer datable to 515/516 CE, giving a *terminus ante quem* for their deposition. Among the finds was a nude life-sized statue of Aphrodite/Venus Pudica with an Eros on a dolphin as a support (Figure 3.17).[118] It seems to have been mutilated before it was dumped in the hypocaust after the baths were abandoned. The head has not been found, and it is possible that the statue was beheaded before its deposition, an act of Christian iconoclasm.[119] The statue is remarkable for the excellent preservation of its painted surfaces—on the hair, nipples, navel, pubic area, bracelets of the Aphrodite, as well as on the hair, eyebrows, and wings of Eros. The marble is from Asia Minor, probably from the quarries of Aphrodisias.[120]

A headless, semi-nude statuette of a nymph holding a shell supported by a decorated column was also found dumped into the hypocaust of the Eastern Bathhouse (Figure 3.18). The shell is cut through for a pipe for use as a fountain piece, an appropriate sculpture for the bath setting.[121] A number of such statues, statuettes or reliefs of nymphs in the guise of Aphrodite (semi-nude with her hairstyle and stance) holding a shell have been found in various locales in the Roman Empire from the second century CE on, especially in bath or fountain contexts.[122] For example, a battered, headless nymph statue was found in the west supply tunnel of the fountain of Peirene in Corinth, once on display in the fountain house but cut up for reuse and dumped into the reservoir in the Late Antique period.[123]

A second-century CE helmeted head of Athena from an almost twice life-sized statue was found in a Byzantine context on the northwest edge of Scythopolis at Tel Naharon in a fifth-century CE refuse pit where it was buried without its body and with its nose removed, almost certainly

---

[118] Israel Museum, Jerusalem, IAA 2001-2987, H. 1.63 m; Tsafrir and Foerster (1994, 99–101), Tsafrir and Foerster (1997, 129 and fig. 37), Foerster (2005), Kreikenbom and Sharvit (2023, 391–92, Skyth-1, pl. 229 A–B [Antonine adaptation, ca. 150–190 CE of an early Hellenistic model, ca. 300 BCE]).

[119] Kristensen (2013, 222–30).

[120] Foerster (2005, Appendix A by A. Nissenbaum,16–17; Appendix B by N. Porat, 18–21).

[121] IAA 2001-2986; Tsafrir and Foerster (1997, fig. 38), Kreikenbom and Sharvit (2023, 403, Skyth-13, pl. 235 D [second half of second century CE]).

[122] See examples in Laflı and Christof (2018).

[123] Corinth S-1024; Robinson (2011, 215–16, fig. 116), Brown (2016, 167–68; 2018, 85, fig. 5.1).

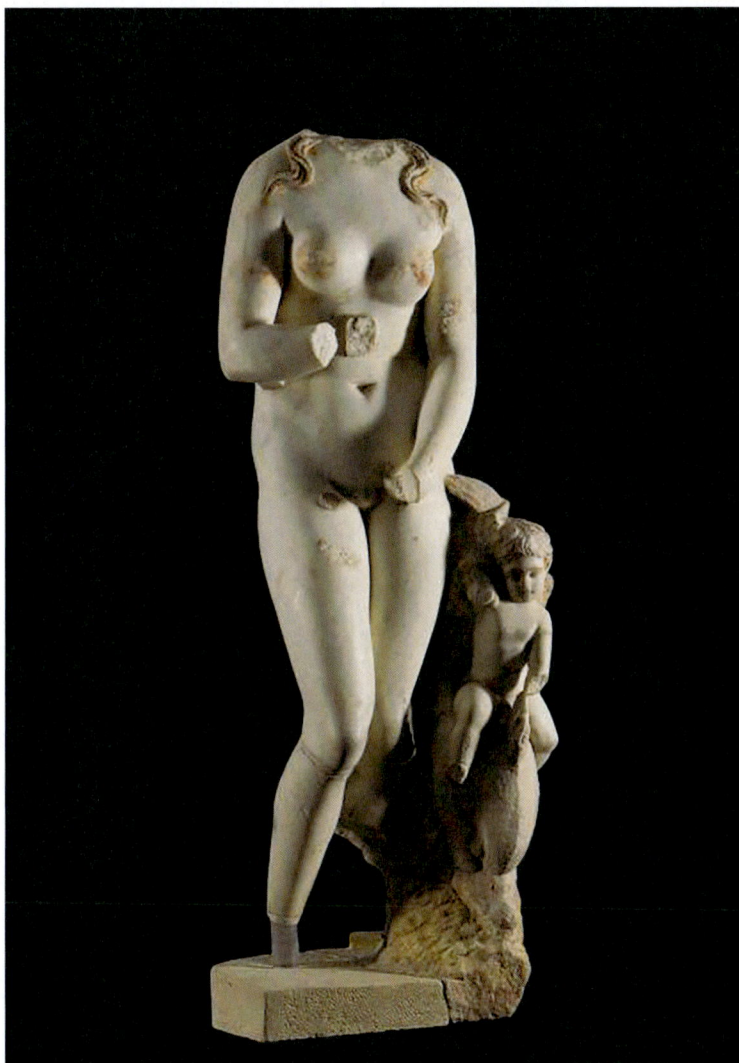

Figure 3.17 Statue of Aphrodite with Eros, from Eastern Bathhouse, Beth Shean.

Israel Museum, IAA 2001–2987. Photo: ©The Israel Museum, Jerusalem. Collection of Israel Antiquities Authority. Reproduced with permission.

the result of Christian iconoclastic practices (Figure 3.19). It is made of dolomitic marble from Thasos in the northern Aegean.[124] Athena wears

[124] IAA 1978-505; P.H. 0.55 m; Vitto (1991, H. 0.55; restored H. ca. 2.45 m), Gersht (1996, 436–37, fig. 6), M. L. Fischer (1998, 161, 201, 249, no. 191), Friedland (2008, 343, no. 3), Kristensen (2013, 230–31), Kreikenbom and Sharvit (2023, 395–96, Skyth-5, pl. 231 B–D [first half of 2nd c. CE]). This head was damaged in an attack on October 5, 2023, by an American tourist, possibly motivated by

Figure 3.18 Statue of a nymph with a shell, from Eastern Bathhouse, Beth Shean.

Israel Museum, IAA 2001–2986. Photo: I. B. Romano. Collection of Israel Antiquities Authority. Reproduced with permission.

a Corinthian helmet, typical of Athenas of the Ince type that are often found in Roman bath buildings.[125] The highly polished face contrasts with the roughened and painted red hair, like the Alexander head, and use of the drill is strikingly evident in the rendering of the hair. The back of the head has been left unfinished. Vitto stresses that the oddly rendered

religious fanaticism, as reported in various news outlets, e.g., https://apnews.com/article/israel-museum-roman-statues-damaged-tourist-arrested-c1f793f1df00d477adac3e651e5751a7 (accessed 7 October 2023).

[125] Marvin (1983, 372), Waywell (1971, 376–77).

Figure 3.19 Head of Athena, Tel Naharon, in vicinity of Beth Shean.

Israel Museum, IAA 1978–505. Photo: I. B. Romano. Collection of Israel Antiquities Authority. Reproduced with permission.

helmet probably points to a local interpretation and workmanship, though we have very little evidence of local sculptors/workshops who worked in marble at Scythopolis.[126] A second female head wearing a chignon

---

[126] Romano and Fischer (2009, 392–95.) Some of the theater friezes are carved in limestone (Ovadiah and Turnheim 1994, 122, 160n22: recent excavations in the lower city have uncovered cruder limestone blocks with "peopled" scroll friezes that are not yet unpublished); the preserved Corinthian capital and figured-capital fragment (see Figure 3.7, pp. 69–72, Figure 3.21, and pp. 95–99, this chapter) from the temple are limestone; and the funerary busts from the nearby cemeteries are limestone (see Figure 3.20 and pp. 93–94, this chapter). It is very likely that all of these were made by local sculptors, but there is little evidence of local craftsmen who worked in marble. See Peleg (2006, photo 20.2) for a fragmentary plaster cast of a human head from Beth Shean, probably from the Roman period, showing that there was probably some local sculptural activity, such as copying, at the site involving the use of casts.

hairdo, found in the same context, probably represents Aphrodite or Artemis and is of second-century date; it is of remarkable quality with a fine polish and is also of Thasian marble.[127]

In summary, the majority of the sculptures preserved from the lower city of Scythopolis and its environs are dated on the basis of context, technique, typology or style to the second or early third century CE, especially during the Antonine or Severan periods.[128] The surviving marble sculptures are made of imported marble from some of the major Greek and Asia Minor quarries—Mt. Pentelikon, Thasos (Cape Vathy), Aphrodisias, Marmara (Proconnesos), and possibly other quarries in Asia Minor.[129] Some of these sculptures preserve abundant traces of pigment, especially the Aphrodite with Eros from the Eastern Bathhouse, and are made of marble from Aphrodisias, like the Alexander head, as discussed in the text that follows.[130] There is little evidence for local workshops of marble sculptors, so we must presume that the marble sculptures came to Scythopolis in a finished or mostly finished state and were commissioned or purchased for specific purposes and contexts. One of the common characteristics of the marble sculptures from Scythopolis is the summarily worked or unfinished backs, suggesting that they were mostly positioned where the backs were not intended to be seen or that the finishing work was supposed to have been undertaken on site, if that would have been desirable, by hired sculptors or craftsmen who may have traveled with the commissioned works. We can identify marble sculptures from the lower city of Scythopolis that would have decorated the *scaenae frons* of the theater, bath structures, and probably a private villa, as well as those that would have been erected in important civic contexts in the center of the city. Almost all, however, were found in secondary contexts. The large number of marble sculptures from Scytho-polis that suffered some intentional damage is remarkable, and it is highly likely that this destruction was undertaken by Christian zealots of

---

[127] IAA 1978-506; P.H. 0.21 m; Vitto (1991, 36–39, figs. 5–9), Pearl and Magaritz (1991), M. L. Fischer (1998, 161, 201, fig. 192), Kreikenbom and Sharvit (2023, 393–4, Skyth-3, pl. 230 A–D [Artemis, first half second century CE]).

[128] There is a body of marble sculpture from the 1990s' excavations at Beth Shean that has yet to receive their final publication, for example, a statue group of Leda and the swan mentioned in Foerster (2008, 77 n47).

[129] For a summary of the marble varieties found in Roman Palestine, see Fischer and Pearl, Excursus III in M. L. Fischer (1998, 247–61). For Scythopolis, see Romano and Fischer (2009). There are other marble sculptures from the region that have not been scientifically tested, but whose marble origins are linked to the quarries from Aphrodisias by virtue of their high-quality carving and general appearance, e.g., the Late Antique flying Daidalos found on the southeast slope of the citadel of Amman (Hannestad 2001; Weber 2015, 574, 577–78, fig. 5.7.2).

[130] See the Appendix.

Figure 3.20 Limestone funerary bust, North Cemetery, Beth Shean.

University of Pennsylvania Museum of Archaeology and Anthropology 29-107-921. Photo: F. Sarin and J. Chiappardi. Reproduced courtesy of Penn Museum.

Scythopolis, who became more religiously conservative and demonstrative in the later fifth and sixth centuries.[131]

The sculptural corpus of Roman Scythopolis is largely composed of *Idealplastik*—sculptures representing classical mythological subjects. Sculptural works related to Dionysos as the patron god of Scythopolis and his circle (including nymphs, Pan, satyrs) are especially common, though images of other deities or personifications, such as Athena, Aphrodite, Hermes, and Tyche, are also identified. There are no obvious sculptural representations of Zeus from the site, though I argue later in this chapter that the colossal fingers found in the cistern are very likely from a seated statue of Zeus.[132] Official imperial portrait statues were

---

[131] See pp. 166–74, this chapter.
[132] See pp. 101–8, this chapter.

erected at Scythopolis, for we know of at least one statue base with an inscription honoring Marcus Aurelius Antoninus (but which Marcus?)[133] (and two possible other sculpture(?) monuments known from unpublished inscriptions),[134] but there is only one marble sculpture that can be identified as an imperial portrait—a cuirassed Roman emperor, probably Antoninus Pius or Marcus Aurelius (see Figure 3.15). There are, in fact, few official, imperial marble portraits identified in the sculptural corpus of the entire ancient Near East.[135] There is, finally, a very interesting corpus of funerary portraits in limestone from the region,[136] including from the cemetery of Scythopolis, especially of the second and third centuries CE (Figure 3.20). These are locally made and represent local Scythopolitans, some inscribed with the names of the deceased.[137] There are no sculptor or workshop signatures on any of the sculptures from Scythopolis, neither those of limestone, nor of marble.[138]

SCULPTURE FROM THE CISTERN ON THE ACROPOLIS OF SCYTHOPOLIS

Fragments of four separate sculptural works were found on Tel Beth Shean, all excavated in the 1920s in the reservoir or cistern to the south of the temple by the University Museum's Palestine Expedition (see Figure 3.5). The cistern was partially cut by the foundations of the temple, and was believed by the excavators to have been originally constructed in the Hellenistic period, along with the temple; they argued that after the cistern was filled in over the centuries the southern section was partitioned off in the Byzantine period.[139] That the cistern was built, at least in part, before the temple (which is not Hellenistic but Roman,

---

[133] See Chapter 1, p. 13.

[134] Mazor (2015, 375).

[135] Foerster (2008, 77–78), Kristensen (2013, 202), Weber (2015, 577–79). See Eck (2014) for an exploration of honorific statues of notable individuals in first- and second-century CE Syria Palaestina (Caesarea and Askelon) through surviving inscribed bases.

[136] Similar funerary sculptures are found in Samaria (Skupinska-Løvset 1999, 238–39).

[137] Skupinska-Løvset (1983), Romano (2006, 195–202), Romano and Fischer (2009, 398–99).

[138] See Friedland (2022, 48, 52–53, figs. 8, 9) for other limestone sculptures from Beth Shean.

[139] Rowe (1930 n79); A. Rowe, Field Diary (November 19 and 24, 1925, 109, 111, 116, "Big Hellenistic Reservoir" with the Byzantine addition to the south, in Beth Shean Excavation Records, Penn Museum Archives). "It now appears that there were three reservoirs at different times in this place, two being inside the others" (November 24, 1925, 116). Fitzgerald (1931, 32n28) indicates that the foundations of the "Hellenistic temple" were laid over an earlier cistern. Yet, in the notebook Rowe noted (September 13, 1925) that the masonry style of the cistern, at least its northernmost wall, is the same as that of the temple.

based on the architectural fragments) seems clear, but there is no coherent archaeological evidence presented for the phases of the cistern, though there are interior walls. A single ceramic lamp that the excavators dated to the second century BCE was used to "fix the date" of the reservoir to the Hellenistic period.[140] Yet, the date for this lamp is questioned and is more likely first century CE,[141] and it is certainly not the latest object in the fill and cannot be used to date the cistern or the fill. In fact, the contents of the cistern were a jumble of debris, including large column drums from the temple, as well as earlier Iron Age objects, with no real stratigraphy. It seems evident that the cistern deposit represents a clearing of the tel in preparation for the construction of the Round Church in the second half of the fifth or beginning of the sixth centuries CE.

The sculptures found in the cistern are as follows: a limestone architectural fragment with a head or mask of Dionysos or a satyr with grape clusters, possibly from a figured capital of the Severan period, in the Penn Museum in Philadelphia;[142] a life-sized marble hand, now in the Rockefeller Archaeological Museum, Jerusalem;[143] eight marble finger and hand fragments from a colossal acrolith, seven housed in the Penn Museum and one in the Rockefeller Museum;[144] and the marble head of Alexander the Great, now in the Israel Museum, Jerusalem. These fragments or groups of fragments represent four distinct sculptural works, as they are of different scales, techniques, or materials.[145] As a group they invite us to envision the monument landscape on the acropolis of Scythopolis in the Roman period, for we can assume it would be very unlikely that the sculptures would originally have been set up in the lower city, then carried up the steep slopes of the tel to be redeposited in the cistern.[146]

---

[140] Alan Rowe, Field Diary, December 9, 1925, 133. University of Pennsylvania Museum 29-102-264 (field no. 25-11-432); L. 0.073; W. 0.05 m; light-brown clay, blackened on nozzle.

[141] For example, see Thiel (2007, 141, 141n46).

[142] Philadelphia, University of Pennsylvania Museum of Archaeology and Anthropology Acc. no. 29-107-91 (see Figure 3.21). See n147 for references.

[143] Rockefeller Museum S.968.

[144] University of Pennsylvania Museum of Archaeology and Anthropology Acc. no. 29-107-924a–g; and Rockefeller Museum S.851, found in January 1923 in the large cistern ("w. end, inner circle," according to the finds registry in the Rockefeller Museum), broken in two pieces; C. S. Fisher (1923, 239), Rowe (1930, 45, fig. 9 [temple plan], pl. 45), Fitzgerald (1931, 33, 44, pl. XXV, 1), Romano (2006, 191–93, no. 93), Romano and Fischer (2009, 507–8), and Romano (2020).

[145] It has been assumed by some scholars (e.g., Kreikenbom 1992, 118, Kat. Nr. I.6) that the fingers belong with the head of Alexander, but the difference in scale and technique make that impossible. The excavator thought the marble hand and large marble head, found in the same context, belonged to the same statue (Alan Rowe, Field Diary, November 19, 1925, in archives of Penn Museum). In addition, a fragment of a marble statuette preserving the head of a ram was found in the same context, possibly an attribute for a statue (Romano 2006, 202, no. 101; Kreibenbom and Sharvit 2023, 407, Skyth-18).

[146] See pp. 72–73, this chapter.

Figure 3.21 Dionysos/Bacchus or a satyr head from a figured Corinthian capital, Beth Shean.

University of Pennsylvania Museum of Archaeology and Anthropology 29-107-919. Photo: F. Sarin and J. Chiappardi. Reproduced courtesy of Penn Museum.

LIMESTONE FIGURED-CAPITAL FRAGMENT

An over-life-sized (P.H. 0.25, P.W. 0.245, P.Th. 0.11 m) frontal limestone head or mask of Dionysos/Bacchus or a satyr with large grape clusters surrounding his head is probably from a local type of figured Corinthian capital in which an anthropomorphic head is carved at the center of the abacus (Figure 3.21).[147] Other limestone examples of this type of capital have been found at Scythopolis and elsewhere in Palestine,[148] whereas

[147] See Romano (2006, 194–95, no. 94) for further previous bibliography; Romano and Fischer (2009, 394–95, fig. 4).
[148] See Fischer M. L. (1990, 36, 64–65) and M. L. Fischer (1991) for figured capitals in Roman Palestine, especially 133, no. 7 from nearby Scythopolis (H. of heads on either side 0.16 and 0.20 m); 133 for masks on such capitals; 136 for the common types of Dionysos and his circle.

Figure 3.22 *A*: Figured capitals on Palladius Street, Beth Shean.

Photos: A, C, I. B. Romano; B, courtesy of Moshe Fischer.

Figure 3.22 *(continued) B:* Figured capital with head of Dionysos.

similar figured capitals from Caesarea and Ascalon are made of marble.[149] The heads on these capitals from Scythopolis represent Dionysos or his

---

[149] M. L. Fischer (1991, 125–32).

Figure 3.22 *(continued)* **C: Detail of figured capital.**

followers, such as Pan[150] and satyrs. A well-preserved figured capital of local limestone with a bust of Dionysos was found in the city center, now erected on the western edge of Palladius Street at a propylon building (Figure 3.22).[151]

    With its exaggerated, rounded features and bulbous nose, the style of the example from the cistern on the acropolis of Scythopolis (see Figure 3.21) is certainly local and is comparable to some of the figures on the "peopled scroll" friezes for the Severan Theater, where local

---

[150] Tsafrir and Foerster (1989–90, 122, fig. 110).

[151] M. L. Fischer (1991, 141n135), Foerster and Tsafrir (1992, 122, 134, fig. 11), Romano and Fischer (2009, 394–95, fig. 3).

sculptors worked in limestone.[152] The date of this capital fragment is probably Severan, the same date as the other examples from Scythopolis and the marble capitals from Caesarea.

Because so little of the superstructure of the temple has survived, it is difficult to assign this capital fragment to a specific position on the temple (in a Severan reconstruction?), though the large size of the head/ mask is compatible with the scale of the large limestone Corinthian column capital fragment (restored H. 1.7 m[153]) from the temple. It certainly must come from somewhere in the temple complex.[154] That Dionysiac iconography is employed in a locally manufactured column capital from the tel gives weight to the popularity and worship of Dionysos at Scythopolis.[155]

LIFE-SIZED MARBLE HAND

Also found in the debris of the cistern on the tel, on the day before the discovery of the Alexander head, was a single fragment of a life-sized left hand (P.L. 0.175; Max. W. 0.11; Th. 0.078 m), broken off below the wrist and with all the fingers broken off to the metacarpals (Figure 3.23).[156] The back of the hand and sides of the fingers are finely polished, whereas the inside of the hand is unpolished, suggesting that the palm of the hand and underside of the fingers would not have been visible to viewers of the statue. At the base of the middle finger on the underside is a shallow depression (L. 0.013; W. 0.008; Depth 0.003 m), the purpose of which is unclear but may relate to some object held in the hand. On the inside of the thumb is a yellowish-brown discoloration, and near the break of the thumb on the inside is a blackened area, possibly from contact with carbon; on the break at the wrist is a brown discoloration.

---

[152] Ovadiah and Turnheim (1994, 122, 160, no. 22), Romano and Fischer (2009, 395).

[153] Benjamin Arubas, personal communication, December 4, 2019.

[154] Vincent (1924, 425): Vincent mentions that the entablature of the temple included a rinceau and masks from the Dionysiac circle, but I believe he may have interpreted this figured-capital fragment as a frieze fragment. I cannot confirm fragments that could be associated with a decorated entablature.

[155] See M. L. Fischer (1991, 141) for the importance of symbolism in the locally made figured capitals. See Chapter 2, pp. 19, 25–30; pp. 74–82, this chapter, for the deity to whom the temple was dedicated.

[156] Rockefeller Museum, S.968 (inventory number from the Palestine Archaeological Museum is retained as its current number); Excavation Field Number 25-11-159. It was found in the cistern on November 18, 1925, and sent to Jerusalem in December 1926, where it remained in the care of the Mandate Department of Antiquities. The hand was recorded in the excavation notebook and sketched (Beth Shean archives, Penn Museum). Romano et al. (2020–21, 4n13), Kreikenbom and Sharvit (2023, 408, Skyth-20, pl. 238 E–F).

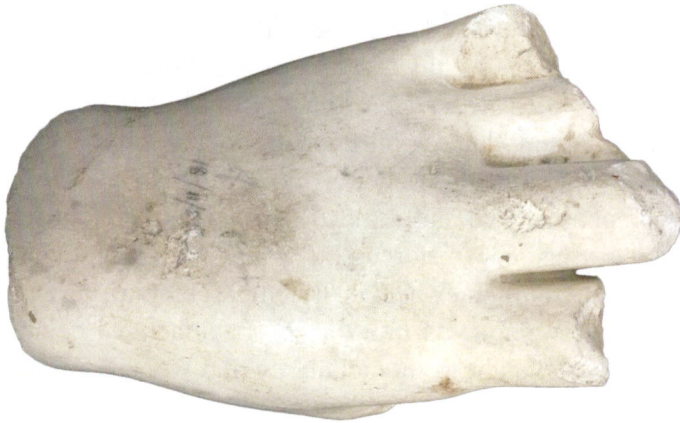

Figure 3.23 Marble left hand, Beth Shean. *A:* **Back of hand.**

Rockefeller Archaeological Museum, Jerusalem S.968. Photos: I. B. Romano. Collection of Israel Antiquities Authority. Reproduced with permission.

Figure 3.23 *(continued) B:* **Inside of hand.**

The hand is curled slightly with the thumb turned inward; the long middle finger is curving slightly, whereas the other fingers are straight to the break of the metacarpal joint. The index finger is separated from the middle finger by a deep groove and completely detached at the break. The other three fingers are touching one another with shallow grooves separating them.

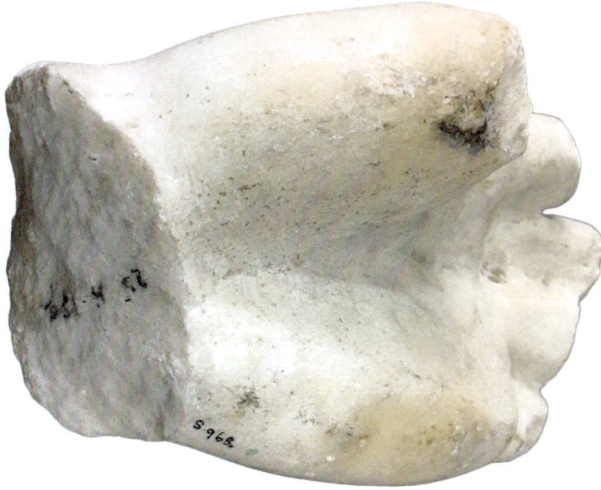

Figure 3.23 *(continued) C:* **Detail of wrist.**

The marble is fine-grained with grayish veins running diagonally from the fingers to the wrist. Scientific analysis conducted by Dimitris Tambakopoulos and Yannis Maniatis in 2016 at the Demokritos Laboratory in Athens resulted in the identification of the marble as originating in the quarries on Mt. Pentelikon, north of Athens.[157] The difference in the origins of the marbles (Pentelikon for the hand versus Aphrodisias for the Alexander head, as discussed in the following text and in the Appendix), and the smaller scale of this hand compared to the over-life-sized head of Alexander disqualify this hand from an association with the Alexander image. It is certainly not related to the colossal marble fingers, discussed in the following text, which are considerably larger. There are no other sculpture fragments from Scythopolis that can be associated with this hand, and thus there are few conclusions that can be drawn about whether this life-sized statue on the acropolis was completely of marble or a composite, acrolithic image, or whom the statue represented.

COLOSSAL ACROLITHIC STATUE

Eight highly polished marble finger and hand fragments (Figures 3.24–3.28), seven in Philadelphia (29-107-924a-g; see Figures 3.24, 3.26–3.28)

---

[157] See Appendix this volume, for results of the marble analysis.

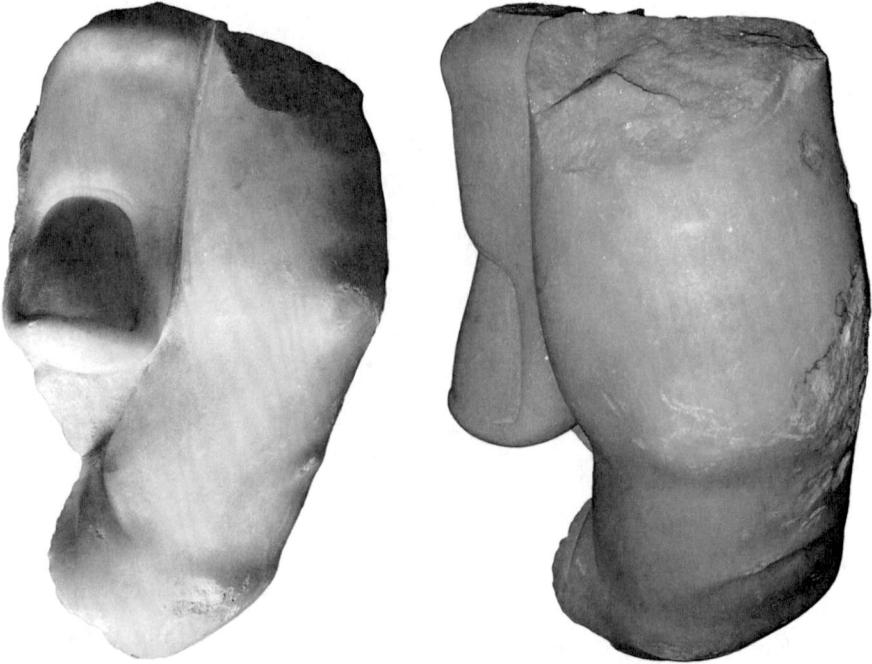

Figure 3.24 Colossal marble right   *B:* **Side view.**
hand fragment, Beth Shean. *A:* **Top**
view.

University of Pennsylvania Museum 29-107-924b. Photo: F. Sarin and J. Chiappardi. Reproduced courtesy of Penn Museum.

and one in Jerusalem (S.851; see Figure 3.25) come from a colossal
acrolith that was set up on the acropolis of Scythopolis in the Roman
period, most likely in the second half of the second century or early third
century CE.[158] All of the fragments were found in the cistern on the tel.

---

[158] Since these fragments have been discussed in Romano (2006, 191–93) and in greater detail in Romano
(2020), they will only be summarized here. In 2016 I examined one additional colossal finger in the
storage rooms in the Rockefeller Museum (S.851). In 1921 or 1922 it was found broken in two pieces
in the large cistern ("west end, inner circle"); excavation find no. 695 (this same field number was
assigned to another finger in the Penn Museum, 29-107-924a); P.L. 0.25; W. 0.11; Max.Th. at raised
joint 0.088 m. This finger is recorded in the objects' register in the Rockefeller Museum as being in
the Palestine Archaeological Museum (PAM) in January 1923, but construction of that museum did not
begin until 1930 and opened in 1935 (St. Laurent 2013, 38), so it must have been taken with the other
finds from those early seasons to its forerunner, the Palestine Museum of Antiquities, which was founded
in 1921 (see p. 175, this chapter). The rest of the colossal fingers were found in various excavation
seasons, in 1921, 1923, 1925, and 1927. This one was not linked with the others, possibly because of
a confusion with the field numbers and the precise number of fragments, and it remained in the British
Mandate for Palestine, while the other seven fragments were sent to Philadelphia as part of the division
of finds.

Figure 3.25 Marble left thumb(?), Beth Shean.

Rockefeller Archaeological Museum, Jerusalem S.851. Photo: I. B. Romano. Collection of Israel Antiquities Authority. Reproduced with permission.

Some of the fragments in the Penn Museum were previously identified as toes, but that conclusion is unlikely.[159] The largest fragment (b: P.L. 0 375; P.W. 0.245; P.Th. 0.215 m; see Figure 3.24) is of the right thumb with a bent index finger that has pronounced knobby joints and a raised vein along the index finger. It may have been positioned either in a downward pose with the thumb facing forward, masking the disproportionately thick index finger, or horizontally where the curved fingers could have grasped an object. Two fragments (Penn Museum 29-107-924d and g) have circular dowel holes, used for the attachment of the fingers to the hand of the statue (see Figure 3.28B).[160] One interesting

---

[159] Rowe (1930, 45), Fitzgerald (1931, 44). The identification of only one (c: P.L. 0.22; P.W. 0.115; P. Th. 0.125 m) is questionable, but it is unlikely to be part of a toe.

[160] On fragment 29-107-924d (see Figure 3.28B) P.L. 0.020; P.W. 0.10; P.Th. 0.09 m): there is a hole in the back (Diam. 0.022, Depth 0.04 m) as well as one in the finished end (Diam. 0.02, Depth 0.05m).

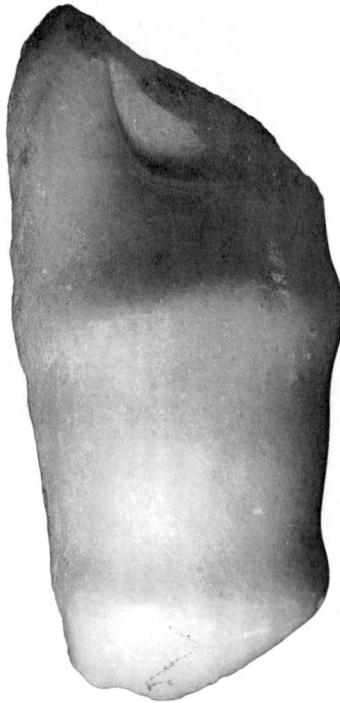

Figure 3.26 Colossal finger, Beth Shean.

University of Pennsylvania Museum 29-107-924a. Photo: F. Sarin and J. Chiappardi. Reproduced courtesy of Penn Museum.

aspect of the newly rediscovered finger in the storage rooms of the Rockefeller Museum is a concretion on its upper back that may be ancient plaster/stucco or an adhesive (see Figure 3.25). The stone of all the fingers is a calcitic white marble with gray veins. Stable isotopic analysis carried out in 2007 by Scott Pike indicates that the marble of the fingers and hand fragments in the Penn Museum is probably from an Asia Minor quarry, possibly Aphrodisias.[161]

---

[161] Average grain size: 1 mm. Stable isotopic analysis of samples from three of these fragments by Scott Pike of Willamette University using the Stable Isotopic Laboratory at the University of Georgia's Department of Geology in 2007 produced the following results: 29-107-924a: $\delta^{13}C$ 2,14, $\delta^{18}O$ -3,41; 29-107-924b: $\delta^{13}C$ 2,02, $\delta^{18}O$ -3,60; 29-107-924d: $\delta^{13}C$ 2,09, $\delta^{18}O$ -3,23. A least-squares statistical program used to show the likelihood of each sample coming from the quarries in the database indicates that several Asia Minor sources are possible. Visual analysis of the marble, combined with historical information about the quarries, suggests a possible identification of the marble as Aphrodisian, though recent work in Turkey has produced new information about previously unknown quarries (see Appendix, pp. 193–95). In addition, multipronged approaches to marble analysis using electron paramagnetic resonance petrographic and chemical analyses have refined the science of marble provenance studies. With further testing it may now be possible to pinpoint the specific quarry.

Figure 3.27 Colossal finger, Beth Shean.

University of Pennsylvania Museum 29-107-924f. Photo: F. Sarin and J. Chiappardi. Reproduced courtesy of Penn Museum.

This statue was clearly executed in a technique compatible with acrolithic sculpture in which the head and other exposed flesh parts would have been fashioned of marble, while the rest of the statue would have been made of a lighter material such as wood or stucco, covered with metal (including gold) sheeting, and painted and/or gilded. That the fingers were separately constructed rather than carved as part of the entire hand or hand and arm is not common for acrolithic sculpture, though we do not have a large sample of acrolithic hand and arm fragments.[162] These large fingers would have been attached to an internal wooden support for the rest of the hand and arm[163] or attached to the marble hand that was, in turn, attached in a more substantial way to the arm.

Examples of Roman acrolithic colossi, of deities and emperors or members of the imperial family, come from various parts of the Roman world and were used in various contexts; the most famous of these is the marble Constantine the Great, found in the Basilica of Maxentius in Rome.[164] As opposed to Roman Asia Minor, acrolithic statues in the

---

[162] For the Scythopolis colossus, we have only the small dowel holes on two fragments (Penn Museum 29-107-924d [Figure 3.28*A, B*] and g) that survive. In general, other examples of acrolithic sculpture have large swallowtail cuttings for attached parts or hollowed-out slots for supporting members, in keeping with wooden construction (Despinis 2012).

[163] Despinis (2012, figs. 8, 10, 15).

[164] See Pensabene et al. (2002) for scientific testing of the marble fragments with the results showing the head and major fragments are of Paros I marble, while the right hand and neck are later additions in Luna marble. See Romano (2020) for other examples of Roman acroliths.

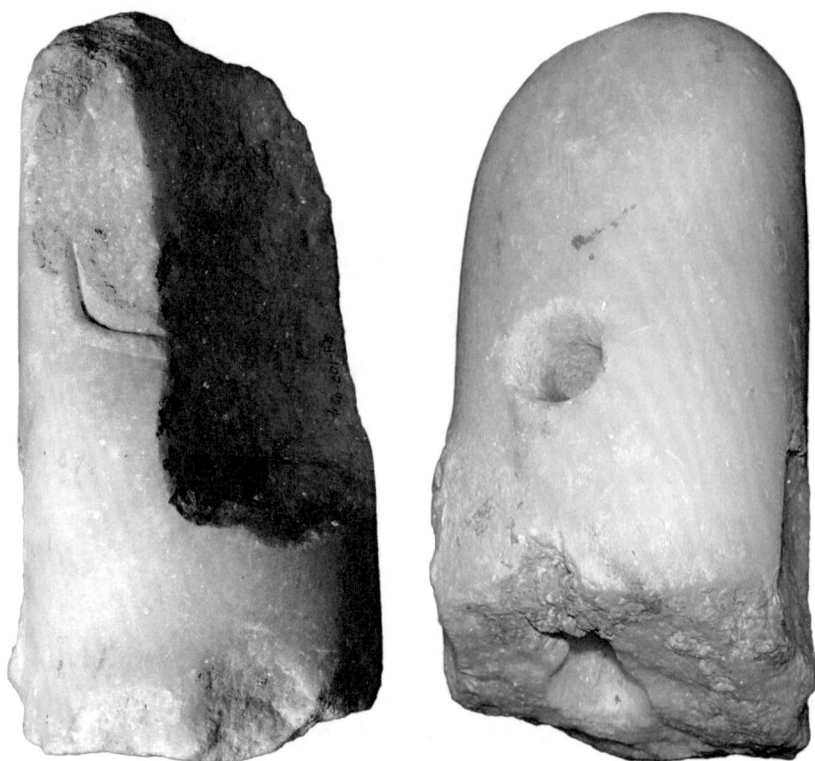

Figure 3.28 Colossal finger, Beth   *B:* **Back view.**
Shean. *A:* **Frontal view.**

University of Pennsylvania Museum 29-107-924d. Photo: F. Sarin and J. Chiappardi. Reproduced courtesy of Penn Museum.

Roman Near East, especially Syria-Palestine, are very rare or remain unpublished, thus there is only a small corpus to examine for local comparisons.[165] The high polish on the fragments generally indicates a date in the Roman period, but there is no specific stylistic or technical evidence for chronology. The best criterion for assigning a general date

---

[165] For example, a colossal right foot in marble, probably from a seated male acrolith from Caesarea (M. L. Fischer 1998, 150, 184, no. 153; Kropp 2013, 324–25n638; Weber 2008, 253–58; see also Gersht 2008, 513, 515 for votive feet from a shrine at the eastern circus) and marble fragments of a colossal acrolith (restored H. ca. 12–13 m) from ancient Philadelphia (Amman), including the left fist with three fingers and a fragment of the bent right elbow with part of the upper and lower arm, found, in part, in the temenos of the so-called Temple of Herakles on the citadel (Jordan Archaeological Museum, Amman; P.L. arm 0.91, H. arm 0.715, H. hand 0.54, W. hand 0.54 m; El Fakharani 1975, 548; Kanellopoulos 1994, 82, 100–03; Najjar 2002, 94, 96, Abb. 139; Weber 2002, 511–12, no. D 12, figs. 132–33, pl. 154 A–F [see 512 for complete bibliography]; Kristensen 2013, 203–04).

to the acrolithic statue from around the mid-second century through the first third of the third century CE is the level of activity at Scythopolis during that period, contemporaneous with the main period of marble importations to the region.[166]

Because of the nature of their composite construction, acroliths that included wood would not long survive outside some enclosed space, so we must assume that this colossal image was housed inside the temple on the acropolis. The scale of the fingers indicates a truly enormous statue, around eight- to ten-times life-sized, and suggests the likelihood that this statue was an important image in the temple, possibly its main cult image.

The Dionysiac elements of the architectural decoration of the temple and the prominence of the "founder" Dionysos at Scythopolis initially suggest the possibility that this colossus represents Dionysos. Coins from Scythopolis of the Antonine and Early Severan period show a standing Dionysos pouring wine with his right hand for a panther at his feet, with his thyrsos at his left side, and, in some, he wears a short, pleated tunic, boots, and a wreath on his head (see Figure 3.9*B*). A locally made fragmentary limestone relief (H. 0.51 m) from Beth Shean, now in a private collection in Jerusalem, also depicts a standing Dionysos that closely matches the coin images of the god. The god wears a wreath; an elbow-length, sleeved tunic that falls just above his knees; a panther skin fastened at his left shoulder and across his body; and boots; in his raised left hand he holds a thyrsos, and in his lowered right is a vessel; a panther is seated behind him.[167]

Yet, this acrolithic statue would have to have been seated and draped since a standing statue of eight- to ten-times life-sized, rising some 16 to 20 meters, would certainly have exceeded the height of the interior of this 37-meter-long temple. Moreover, acroliths need drapery to disguise their internal structure.[168] Dionysos is rarely shown draped and in a seated pose appropriate to a cult image after the Archaic and Classical periods.[169] If there was a standing, clothed statue of Dionysos in the temple on the acropolis that matched the coin depiction and the limestone relief, it was not likely to be the one to which these colossal fingers belong. As

---

[166] M. L. Fischer (1998, 231–65).

[167] Barkay (2003, 131–32, fig. 18), Lichtenberger (2003, 148), Kreikenbom and Sharvit (2023, 389–90, fig. 2).

[168] Based on twenty-two extant architectural fragments, Benjamin Arubas has estimated the height of the temple to the entablature at 15.8 meters (personal communication, December 4, 2019).

[169] See Gasparri and Veneri (1986, 437–39). For example, see Romano (1982) for the Archaic seated statue of Dionysos from the Attic deme site of Ikarion.

mentioned, the single, life-sized fragment of a marble left hand (see Figure 3.23) also does not allow us to suggest with any degree of certainty that it belonged to a statue of Dionysos, as much as one would like to see physical evidence for a conjectured Dionysos statue in this temple.

A draped seated statue suggests only two likely possibilities: the acrolithic image reconstructed from these fingers is of a partly clothed Zeus or a Roman emperor. It is unlikely to be Zeus Bacchus, whose appearance in sculpture is not attested.[170] There is, as mentioned, no specific evidence that an imperial cult was established at Scythopolis within the temple on the height. If this impressive acrolith was an imperial portrait statue, one would have to argue that it would not have been *the* statue to which honors and cult activities were directed, but a representation of a *theos synnaos*, a cult partner to the main deity,[171] or an honorary statue, given a place of great importance alongside the cult statue of the deity—but overshadowing it by its sheer size. Although these are possible scenarios, the most likely conclusion is that the colossal fingers belong to an acrolithic cult image of a seated Zeus Akraios or Zeus Olympios, perhaps one and the same—the god in whose honor this temple was likely erected.

HEAD OF ALEXANDER THE GREAT

The marble head found in the cistern on Tel Beth Shean is over-life-sized with a maximum preserved height of 0.40 to 0.42 meters (H. face 0.189; W. face 0.19; H. crown of head to bottom of chin 0.285; P.H. neck 0.14; W. front of neck 0.14; Max. W. 0.27–0.28; Max. Th. 0.28; Th. at neck 0.17 m).[172]

Condition

The head is preserved in a single piece from the crown to the bottom of the neck. In general, the preservation is excellent, with the most serious

---

[170] Coin images showing the infant Dionysos emerging from the thigh of Zeus date to the reigns of Septimius Severus (Barkay 2003, no. 39), Elagabalus (Barkay 2003, nos. 59 and 65), and Gordian III (Barkay 2003, no. 93).

[171] Burrell (2004, 317–28), see 56, 157, 311 for cult partners, especially in the period of Caracalla and Elagabalus. For example, see Rose (1997, 182–84, no. 125), for the temple at Leptis Magna with two cellas for acroliths of Augustus and Roma and with statues of Tiberius and Livia in the pronaos. Or consider the case in Sardis where Zeus and Hera were probably the deities being worshiped, but Antoninus Pius, Faustina the Elder, and probably Marcus Aurelius, Faustina the Younger, Lucius Verus, and Lucilla were placed inside and around the *neokoros* temple (Burrell 2004, 320–21).

[172] IAA 1931-7. See n3, this chapter, for bibliography.

damage appearing to be deliberate. The low degree of wear and the especially good preservation of the paint suggest that the head was displayed in a protected location for the duration of its primary use.

The surfaces of some locks of hair are broken, for example, the *anastolé* lock to the proper right of the central part, a large lock in the second row on the right side above the *anastolé*, a vertical lock beside the right eye, and locks along the left side of the face. The surfaces of some of the eight locks arranged around the hole on top of the head are broken and others are worn with little paint or incised details remaining. Small undercut locks of hair are broken off around the face where knobs remain: two on the right and left sides of the forehead, one at the temple on each side, one on each side at mid-cheek, and one on the right side of the neck (Figures 3.29 to 3.32).

There is damage on the right eyebrow; on the left side of the forehead above the bridge of the nose and left eye; and on the left eyebrow, eyelid, and eyeball. The nose and medial cleft are removed, with a gouge across the nose from left to lower right. A deep hole is cut into and below the mouth, especially on the right side, possibly with a pickaxe, leaving just a trace of the left edge of the mouth. The left jawline and chin are chiseled in an irregular pattern; an oval area on the surface of the "Adam's apple" is damaged, and it is not clear whether this has been chiseled or accidentally damaged. Much of the damage to the face, however, seems clearly deliberate, especially to the nose and mouth, probably done by early Christian zealots; there is plentiful evidence of damage caused by Christian zealots at Scythopolis, as is described in the text that follows (see also Figure 3.48).[173]

The neckline is irregular, with some jagged edges and surface chips. In back, the upper neck is barely visible beneath the long hair; the lower neck surface broadens, especially visible on the back left side. At the proper left side, the lower neck juts forward and to the side, ending in a ledge overlapping the side of the neck and separated from it by a drilled channel, with a finished surface above and a break at the front of the neck. This is likely the upper edge of a garment or cuirass, discussed later (Figures 3.33 and 3.34). The underside of the neck has a rough, irregular, and broken surface with a slight convexity visible at the left edge; on the underside at the proper front right is a leveled surface with traces of claw chisel marks, directed diagonally from the edge inward (Figure 3.35). These chisel marks cut into the broken surface of the neck

---

[173] Kristensen (2013, 218–32). See pp. 166–74, this chapter.

Figure 3.29 Portrait of Alexander the Great, Beth Shean. Frontal view.

Israel Museum, IAA 1931-7. Photo: Hans Rupprecht Goette. Collection of Israel Antiquities Authority. Reproduced with permission.

and make little sense as having been created in ancient times; they are likely evidence that a very broken and damaged underside was leveled in order to create a clean surface to allow mounting of the head in the Rockefeller Museum in the 1930s or later. (See Figure 3.51 for the head on its earliest known mount.) A more recent hole has been drilled in the bottom of the neck for its current museum mount. There is no evidence of an ancient dowel hole, and little evidence remains of a tenon for the mounting the head to the torso.

Because of the irregular damage to the lower edges and underside of the head, it is not completely clear whether the head was originally

Figure 3.30 Portrait of Alexander the Great, Beth Shean. Right profile view.

Israel Museum, IAA 1931-7. Photo: Hans Rupprecht Goette. Collection of Israel Antiquities Authority. Reproduced with permission.

made separately from the torso, in one piece with the upper torso, or in one piece with an entire statue. If the head was made separately, a normal technique used to set it into a cavity between the shoulders would be to fashion a tenon of a convex bowl or a truncated cone at the bottom of the neck.[174] In this case, the head would join the cavity at an approximately fifteen-degree angle, with an incline from a higher back to a lower front. In this scenario, we would have to suppose that the tenon, as well as

---

[174] For examples of this type of bowl neck treatment for separately made heads, see Stewart (1993, figs. 124–25, 141–43). See also Claridge (1990, 143–45, fig. 11, esp. k–l) for examples of these kinds of joins and their general chronology.

Figure 3.31 Portrait of Alexander the Great, Beth Shean. Detail of right side of face.

Israel Museum, IAA 1931-7. Photo: Hans Rupprecht Goette. Collection of Israel Antiquities Authority. Reproduced with permission.

possibly the transition to the shoulders and chest, were cut away. This would have been an act of deliberate destruction, probably by Christian iconoclasts attempting to remove the head from the body of the statue. It is difficult to understand, however, why Christian iconoclasts would have bothered to brutally hack at the underside of the head if it were made separately and, thus, relatively easily decapitated. We can suggest, therefore, that the head may have been carved in one piece at least with

Figure 3.32 Portrait of Alexander the Great, Beth Shean. Left profile view.

Israel Museum, IAA 1931-7. Photo: Hans Rupprecht Goette. Collection of Israel Antiquities Authority. Reproduced with permission.

the upper body, presuming in this case that a garment might have been wrapped around the waist to hide the join between the head-cum-torso and lower body, as shown in the treatment of the Alexander images in Brooklyn, Magnesia-by-Sipylos, and Priene, or perhaps the entire portrait was carved in one piece.[175]

---

[175] Stewart (1993, figs. 132–35). See pp. 121–22, 129–30, this chapter, for a discussion of the evidence for drapery and the question whether this head is from a full statue, a bust or, less likely, a herm; see pp. 166–74, this chapter, for iconoclastic behavior.

Figure 3.33 Portrait of Alexander the Great, Beth Shean. Detail of feature on left side below hair.

Israel Museum, IAA 1931-7. Photo: I. B. Romano. Collection of Israel Antiquities Authority. Reproduced with permission.

Description

The beardless male head is inclined to his right and tipped slightly upward. The long hair is divided by a central groove above the forehead, to the right and left of which are thick arching *anastolé* locks that rise above the forehead, with light incisions to indicate individual strands, better differentiated and preserved than those on the proper left side. The hair falls on both sides of the face to the mid-neck in layers of thick sausage-like clumps, more fully worked on the right side than the left and completely covering the ears, which do not appear at all. There is a drilled

Figure 3.34 Portrait of Alexander the Great, Beth Shean. Back view.

Israel Museum, IAA 1931-7. Photo: Hans Rupprecht Goette. Collection of Israel Antiquities Authority.
Reproduced with permission.

channel along the hairline on the right and left sides of the brow and face, requiring bridges or struts for the tips of the undercut locks of hair to attach to the skin of the brow, cheeks, and neck; three of these struts survive intact on the right and left side of the cheeks and neck and one on either side of the forehead (see Figures 3.29–3.32).

On top of the head, above the central part and behind the rising front locks, is a circular hole (Diam. 0.015; Max. Depth [at back] 0.03 m) for the attachment of an attribute, probably of bronze, interpreted in the text that follows; a brownish discoloration appears around the inside the hole (Figures 3.36–3.39). In front of the hole is a shallow channel that is hidden behind the *anastolé* frontal locks but merges with the drilled central hair part above the forehead. Around the hole are eight raised

Figure 3.35 Portrait of Alexander the Great, Beth Shean. Bottom of neck.

Israel Museum, IAA 1931-7. Photo: I. B. Romano. Collection of Israel Antiquities Authority. Reproduced with permission.

locks of hair in a petal-like arrangement, clearly planned and carved in relation to the hole. From a birds-eye view with the front of the head at the six-o'clock position, two smaller locks are at the five- and seven-o'clock positions in front of the hole, and three larger are at the back of the hole, with the largest and highest at the back, in the twelve-o'clock position. There is no evidence of the use of the drill on these, and there are traces of light incisions on them, with some worn and some broken-off surfaces. Behind the hole and surrounding locks, the hair on the crown is shallowly carved and in an irregular arrangement, with comma-shaped locks, brushed forward in areas, sideways and back in others. At the back, the carving is executed with less attention to detail, and the hair is arranged in three layers with comma-shaped curls; a groove separates the middle layer of short curls from the lower, elongated sausage-shaped locks that end in spiral or loose-upturned curls on the back of the neck. These locks are tooled with narrow, light incisions with no evidence of a deep drill. There is no evidence of the addition of a crown, diadem, or

Figure 3.36 Portrait of Alexander the Great, Beth Shean. View of top of head.

Israel Museum, IAA 1931-7. Photo: ©The Israel Museum, Jerusalem, by Elie Posner. Collection of Israel Antiquities Authority. Reproduced with permission.

taenia in the hair, as there are no holes or grooves that are continuous around the head.[176]

The face is rectangular with full, broad cheeks, turning subtly at the jaw to the neckline. The forehead is low with a pronounced concavity above the right eye (see Figure 3.29). The brow line describes a gentle convex curve, set more or less horizontally, with no tooling for eyebrow hairs; this detail may have been executed in paint. The axes of the eyes and mouth converge toward the proper right, mimicking the slight turn of the head to the right. The eyes are set wide apart beneath the brow;

---

[176] On the label for the sculpture on its pedestal and in the discussion of the Alexander head on the Israel Museum's website, quoting the 2005 Abrams publication of highlights from the museum (*The Israel Museum* 2005, 245), it is recorded that there are drill holes in the hair that indicate it was crowned by a golden wreath (https://www.imj.org.il/en/collections/222840, accessed December 3, 2018). In fact, there is only one hole—the one on the top of the head.

Figure 3.37 Portrait of Alexander the Great, Beth Shean. View of top of head with hole for attribute.

Israel Museum, IAA 1931-7. Photo: ©The Israel Museum, Jerusalem, by Elie Posner. Collection of Israel Antiquities Authority. Reproduced with permission.

the upper lid is a thickened rolled ridge, overlapping the lower lid at the outer edge. The lachrymal glands are delineated with a drill, more pronounced on the withdrawn right eye than the left. There is no evidence of incised circles or semi-circles for the irises or drilled pupils, but in certain light the ghost of a painted semi-circular iris rolled under the upper eyelid is detectable, especially on the better-preserved right eye. Both the area below the eyes over the lower eye socket, especially below the right eye, and the naso-labial area are finely modeled and executed with subtle indentations. The mouth is small with a deep depression visible at the outer left corner. The thick, sturdy neck swells in the center at the "Adam's apple" and is squared off on the sides with strong platysma muscles defined on the right and left sides to mimic the slight inclination of the head to the right and up.

Figure 3.38 Portrait of Alexander the Great, Beth Shean. Detail of hole for attribute.

Israel Museum, IAA 1931-7. Photo: I. B. Romano. Collection of Israel Antiquities Authority. Reproduced with permission.

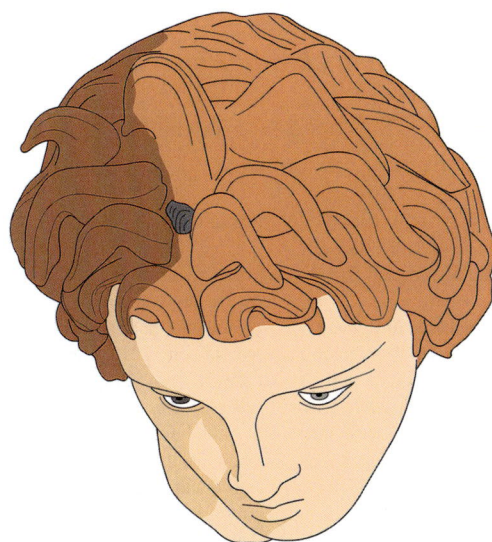

Figure 3.39 Reconstruction drawing of top of head of Alexander the Great (IAA 1931-7) with locks of hair around hole.

Drawing: Yannis Nakas.

Marble Analysis

In the late 1980s stable isotopic testing was conducted by Ze'ev Pearl on a sample from the head to determine the ancient marble quarry. Moshe Fischer reported that the results showed that the marble is probably from an Asia Minor quarry at Afyon or Aphrodisias.[177] The field of marble studies has progressed greatly since the late 1980s with new white marble quarries identified and studied, especially in Turkey, and new analytical techniques (electron paramagnetic resonance [EPR], petrographic analysis) which, in a combined approach, allow for more certain results than the sole use of stable isotopes. With permission from the Israel Antiquities Authority, the marble of the Alexander head was retested in 2016 to confirm the ancient quarry. That work was carried out by Drs. Yannis Maniatis and Dimitris Tambakopoulos at the Demokritos Laboratory in Athens, with results that confirm that the marble is very probably from one of the white marble quarries of Aphrodisias.[178] We know that the Aphrodisias quarries were used locally to a limited extent in the Late Hellenistic period and were not fully exploited until the later first century BCE, with the height of their use in the Roman imperial period, especially from the Antonine period on, in the second and third centuries.[179] Thus, the marble analysis provides supporting evidence for a likely Roman date for the head, further discussed in the following text.

Polish and Pigment

The face and neck of the head are polished to a medium, porcelain finish,[180] whereas the hair, in contrast, is unpolished, allowing the red

---

[177] M. L. Fischer (1998, 255n343), Pearl (1989, sample nos. 109–10).

[178] See Appendix for the results, pp. 193–95.

[179] "Aphrodisias Excavations Project" 2019, "Quarries." Long (2012; 2017, 65–74) suggests that from the evidence at the quarry sites around Aphrodisias the large amounts of marble quarried would meet just the local architectural demands in the Roman period and that the Aphrodisian export trade paled in comparison to the role of Aphrodisian marble sculptors (Long 2012, 165, 167). Van Voorhis examines a sculptors' workshop at Aphrodisias active from the Severan period into Late Antiquity; she agrees with Long that the non-Göktepe marble was utilized primarily locally (2018, 37). However, based on the number of high-quality works of sculpture that have been identified in the eastern Mediterranean made of Aphrodisian marble, including some at Scythopolis, it seems there was, indeed, an export market for the white marble, beyond the extraordinarily high-quality white and gray Göktepe marble (see pp. 124, 137–39, this chapter). This issue bears further investigation. See also Toma (2018) for a discussion of an Aphrodisian architectural ensemble at Nysa (Turkey) and Attanasio et al. (2012) regarding Roman sculpture of Aphrodisian (and Carian, in general, including Göktepe marble) white marble at Cherchel (Algeria). Bruno et al. (2012, 564) reports the large size of these quarries indicate an export market was viable, especially from the Antonine period on.

[180] The faces of the Athena and other female head from Tel Naharon (see Figure 3.19 and pp. 88–92, this chapter) are more highly polished than the Alexander head.

pigment to adhere better (see Figures 3.29 to 3.32). Traces of thick white ground are preserved in a few spots on the hair, on top of which is a ruddy red-brown pigment, especially well preserved on the front of the head. Thinner pigment appears on the back, although there are only faint traces on top of the head. There are also traces of red on the eyebrows, eyelids, right and left eyes, and left edge of the lip. There are faint traces of yellow-orange pigment on the feature below the locks of hair at the bottom of the neck on the left side (see Figure 3.33), interpreted as a remnant of a garment or cuirass, discussed later in the text.

The presence of so much preserved red color on this head, especially on the hair, is of much interest. Thanks to recent research we know a great deal about the techniques of polychromy and gilding of ancient marble statuary,[181] though on this head no traces of gold are visible with the naked eye. Future scientific analysis of the composition of the pigment(s) might provide a clue to the original appearance of the ancient image and confirm whether the reddish color (red ochre?) is a *bol*, a preparation coat for another pigment or for gilding, or whether this is the bottom layer of the final polychrome agent, probably somewhat faded or transformed from its original vibrancy and subtlety. The fact that red appears on the eyelids and eyes suggests that the red may not represent the final coloration.

Portraits of Alexander of the Hellenistic period, especially from Egypt, have been identified with red pigment on the hair (and on the skin), used as a ground coat for gold leaf, including on a third–second century BCE marble portrait from Hermopolis, now in the Princeton Art Museum.[182] Ancient sources, writing hundreds of years after Alexander's death, record that the Macedonian ruler had a golden or tawny leonine mane of hair (Aelian, *Varia historia* 12.14; Pseudo-Kallisthenes, *Bios Alexandrou tou Makedonos* 1.13.3; Julius Valerius, *Res gestae Alexandri Macedonis* 1.7). We should interpret these comments as romantic views of what Alexander, the heroic warrior ruler-turned god, *should* have looked like. His golden hair was a feature perpetuated in some posthumous idealized portraits of him. In the Alexander mosaic from the House of

---

[181] See Bourgeois and Jockey (2005), Abbe (2010, 2015), Blume (2015, esp. 104–9) for gilding of statues of gods, heroes, and rulers, especially in Ptolemaic Egypt (Powers et al. 2018, esp. 787–89): In the case of this second-century marble Antinoos statue, the gold leaf was applied directly to the surface of the ivy wreath without a preparation layer. Many exhibition catalogues and articles by Vinzenz Brinkmann and Ulrike Koch-Brinkmann have also documented the history of polychromy on both marble and bronze sculpture, including Brinkmann et al. (2017).

[182] Princeton Art Museum 2008-330, formerly in the private collection of Wilhelm Horn: Parian marble; H. 0.184 (Gebauer 1938/1939, 85, K5; Yfantidis 1984, 294, Nr. 164; Bianchi 2010; Blume 2015, Kat. 80, 271-2, pl. 80.11).

the Faun in Pompeii, ca. 100 BCE, however, the Macedonian ruler is depicted with straight, dark-brown hair with auburn streaks.

The possibility that gold leaf or a golden-yellow pigment might have been applied to the feature at the lower left edge of the neck (a Macedonian garment that should be "royal purple" or a cuirass of gleaming gold?) and on the hair of this Alexander portrait from Scythopolis would be of great interest, and the hope is that there will be an opportunity in the future to conduct scientific analysis of its polychromy. Analysis might also tell us whether there were several applications of pigments to renew the vibrancy of the color over the long life of the statue— something that might be expected for a sculpture that may have been on display for some 200 years or more.[183]

STATUE, HERM, OR BUST?

If this portrait head of Alexander was made in one piece with at least the upper torso or with a full statue or a herm, what are each of these possibilities? First, that the head is from a herm and made in one piece with the upper chest for insertion into a shaft is a remote possibility. The inclination of the Scythopolis head to the right does not immediately speak against its possible identification as part of a herm, since portrait herms of rulers, gods, or other individuals are not required to be strictly frontal, as is shown by the head position of various bronze and marble herms from the villas around the Bay of Naples, especially from the Villa of the Papyri at Herculaneum and those from the Athenian *gymnasia*, mostly with larger-than-life-sized heads (0.29–0.32 m).[184] Yet, none of these herm heads exudes the sense of dynamic movement as that of the Beth Shean head. The presence of the edge of a garment or cuirass at the left side of the Beth Shean portrait would, likewise, not automatically eliminate the possibility of a herm since a garment sometimes appears on the left shoulder in the Roman *kosmetai* from Athens, for example.

The scale of the Alexander head (H. 0.40–42 m) finds good parallels in the separately made heads-cum-busts for herms from a room for the display of Claudian portraits in the Sanctuary of Diana at Lake Nemi.[185] For example, the marble herm head of Fundilia Rufa, the patroness of

---

[183] See pp. 129–30, this chapter, for the garment or cuirass.

[184] See Mattusch 2008, 199–200, no. 89 (Genzano Herakles herm, from Oplontis, Villa of Poppaea), 220, no. 99 (Menander herm from Torre Annunziata in Boston); Daehner and Lapatin 2015, 119, figs. 8.7, 8.8; 296–97 (Doryphoros herms). See Vlachogianni (2018, 163): The Athenian *kosmetai* herms can be either strictly frontal or with their heads turned slightly to the right.

[185] Fejfer (2008, 285–306).

the actor Fundilius Doctus, whose portrait is also displayed in the room, measures 0.43 meters in height, while that of Lucius Aninius Rufus is 0.40 meters, and of Staia Quinta is 0.44 meters, with the heights of the herm shafts between 1 and 1.12 meters.[186] These all have a pronounced convexity to the underside or a large square boss for insertion into the herm, the evidence for which on the Alexander head, as discussed previously, has been damaged almost beyond recognition.[187] The bowl-shaped underside of the neck of the Schwarzenberg Alexander from Tivoli, now in Munich (H. 0.48 m), suggests it was made for insertion into such a herm.[188] The first- or second-century CE Azara herm from a villa at Tivoli provides the only more or less completely preserved parallel for a herm of Alexander the Great, though the head is reworked (Figure 3.40).[189] In this case the head and herm shaft are made in one piece. The total height of the Azara herm is 0.68 meters, including the preserved part of the herm shaft, with the head ca. 0.22 meters high, about half the size of the Scythopolis head. The shaft of the Azara herm is short, making it a suitable portrait for table-top display.

With the exception of the Roman herms of *kosmetai* or other officials of the gymnasia of Athens, the aforementioned examples of herms all come from Italian contexts. Fejfer points out that in the Roman East, such portrait herms are found extensively only on the Greek mainland from the second century onward.[190] As far as we know, the herm form for portraits did not find particular favor in Roman Palestine.[191]

Is it possible that the head belongs to a half-figure bust (with an upper body and both arms)[192] or a free-standing bust, both of which were especially popular portrait formats in the late second and third centuries CE for portraits of private individuals, members of the imperial family, philosophers, poets, and other notable historical figures?[193] The possible settings for such busts are many, including on tables (for smaller ones) or on low or high pillars or columns, in private, public, funerary, and religious settings, such as the ones of Marcus Aurelius and Antoninus Pius found near the Temple of Demeter in the Agora of Cyrene.[194] In

---

[186] Guldager Bilde and Moltesen (1997, 142–144, nos. 21, 23, 24).

[187] Fejfer (2008, 232, fig. 152).

[188] Stewart (2014, 46–47).

[189] See pp. 132–33, this chapter.

[190] Fejfer (2008, 229n5).

[191] Though, see p. 76 and Figure 3.12, this chapter, for two herms from Scythopolis, not for portraits but of Dionysos and Ariadne.

[192] See, for example, Fejfer (2008, fig. 164): first to second quarter of third century CE.

[193] Fejfer (2008, 236–61).

[194] Rosenbaum (1960, nos. 47 and 50); see also nos. 104–05. Fejfer (2008, 248–49, fig. 168, 483n82) suggests the latter were placed on a bench in a cult building with statues of Demeter and Kore.

Figure 3.40 Azara herm. *A*: **Three-quar-**   *B*: **Right profile view.**
ter frontal view.

Musée du Louvre, Paris Ma 436 (MR 405). Photos: Wikimedia.org, in public domain, https://commons
.wikimedia.org/wiki/File:Azara_herm_Louvre_Ma436.jpg and https://upload.wikimedia.org/wikipedia/
commons/c/c8/Azara_herm_Louvre_Ma436_n3.jpg (accessed January 9, 2023).

general, free-standing busts took over the function of honorific statues
in the later second and early third centuries CE, especially in the later
Severan period.[195]

The free-standing marble half-bust of Commodus as Hercules from
the Horti Lamiani on the Esquiline Hill, made of very fine, polished
Göktepe marble from quarries near Aphrodisias,[196] is perhaps the best
known of the free-standing imperial busts of the same general period
(180–193 CE) proposed for the Scythopolis Alexander.[197] With a lion
skin over his head and draped over his shoulders, the paws tied in front
and a club over his left shoulder, and the apples of the Hesperides in his
left hand, the head of Commodus is turned to his right and the half figure

---

[195] Fejfer (2008, 259–260n104).
[196] Attanasio et al. (2018, 189, 191, fig. 6).
[197] Capitoline Museum, Rome inv. 1120; H. 1.33 m; H. head ca. 0.44 m; Hoff (2005).

Figure 3.41 Gold medallion with image of Alexander, Aboukir, Egypt, ca. 215–243 CE.

Walters Art Gallery, Baltimore, 59.1. Photo: Licensed under Creative Commons, https://art.thewalters.org/detail/21555/medallion-with-alexander-the-great/ (accessed August 21, 2020).

is mounted on an elaborate support with kneeling Amazons flanking a globe with zodiac signs; in its original context it would have been flanked by busts of marine Tritons.[198] There is nothing ordinary about the Commodus bust, but it does show that free-standing and half-figure busts can reach very large proportions; the head of Commodus is comparable in scale to the Scythopolis head.

Although there are examples of small-scale busts of Alexander in bronze,[199] and a cuirassed Alexander in bust form appears on the Aboukir medallions[200] (Figure 3.41), there are no large-scale free-standing busts of Alexander that can be identified. In each case only the head of Alexander is preserved, and it can be argued that the heads were intended for insertion into the body of a statue rather than into a bust; sometimes the bust is a modern addition.[201] If the fully modeled head of Alexander

---

[198] Hoff (2005, 122–23, Abb. 5).

[199] For example, the bronze bust in the Württemberg Landesmuseum, Stuttgart, wearing a hemhem crown (Schreiber 1903, 150, Abb. 13; Grimm 1978, 105 n22, Abb. 71; Reinsberg 2004, Abb. 23; Reinsberg 2005, 563, Kat. 133).

[200] See pp. 130, 157–59, this chapter.

[201] For example, the head of Alexander in Boston from Ptolemais Hermiou is confusingly referred to as a bust (Yalouris et al. 1980, 102, no. 8), but it was probably made for insertion into a draped statue (Stewart 1993, 334). For the Erbach Alexander from Tivoli, an ancient portrait head has been restored on a modern bust (Stewart 1993, 106–13, 421, fig. 6; Hansen et al. 2009, Kat. Nr. 2, 46, 241).

from Beth Shean is from a free-standing bust, it would almost certainly have been made in one piece with the shoulders and upper chest. There are, however, no other examples of free-standing portrait busts from Scythopolis itself, and there is a general paucity of examples from the region, documented only in Samaria-Sebaste,[202] Ascalon,[203] and Caesarea.[204] Like herms, free-standing busts seem not to have been an especially popular sculptural form in this part of the Roman Empire.

It seems most probable, therefore, that this over-life-sized Alexander portrait head from the acropolis of Scythopolis is from a standing statue. Its height can be restored to around 2.14 to 2.28 meters (7.5 to 8 times the height of the head from crown to chin)—an appropriately heroic, over-life-sized scale (Figure 3.42).[205] No other fragments of the statue have been found on the acropolis or in the lower city, and we might presume that the rest was hauled away for reuse (as building material) or destined for the lime kilns of the Byzantine period or later.[206]

In the corpus of Alexander portrait statues there are several complete or nearly complete full-scale or over-life-sized examples to cite for comparison. The Hellenistic statue identified as Alexander, found at Magnesia-by-Sipylos, measures 1.90 meters in its preserved height, lacking the lower legs.[207] An over-life-sized (H. 2.17 m) marble statue variously interpreted as Alexander, Dionysos, Helios, or a Dioscuros *in imitatione Alexandri*, probably of the Hadrianic period, was found in the Roman baths at Cyrene and was once positioned in the central niche of the Central Hall. It shows a heroic nude male with a chlamys pinned by a

---

[202] See Gersht (1996, 445–46) for a summary of Roman portraits of intellectuals from Israel. A second-century CE bust of a philosopher, identified as either Metrodoros the Younger of Lampsacus (331–278 BCE), a disciple of Epikouros, or Epikouros (341–270 BCE) himself, was found near the stadium at Samaria-Sebaste (IAA no. 35-3449, Rockefeller Museum, on display in the library; Crowfoot et al. 1957, 72–73, no. 3, pl. VII, 3–4; Richter 1965 II, 205, no. 19: Hermarchos; Kruse-Berdoldt 1975, 62ff, M10: Metrodoros; Peled 1980, 100–102, pl. XX; M. L. Fischer 1998,160, no. 186; H. 0.59; W. 0.35; Th. 0.28; P.W. base 0.22 m). Stable isotopic analysis by Ze'ev Pearl in 1989 at the Weizmann Institute indicates that the marble of this bust is from Mount Pentelikon (M. L. Fischer 1998: 249), thus likely to be a Roman copy of a Hellenistic Attic type made in an Attic workshop or by an Attic sculptor.

[203] A bust of a middle-aged female from Ascalon (M. L. Fischer 1998, 139, no. 109, for bibliography), dated ca. 245 CE.

[204] Busts of Socrates (M. L. Fischer 1998, 147, no. 139; Richter 1965 I, 127, no. 24, figs. 671, 673–674) and of Olympiodoros (M. L. Fischer 1998, 147, no. 140; Richter 1965 II, 162, figs. 894–896) were found in the same context at Caesarea.

[205] Kreikenbom (1992, 15–16, 118) includes this head in the category of "colossal," but I call it "over-life-sized" to distinguish it from the truly colossal marble fingers and from the life-sized marble hand, found in the same context. The varying scales of these fragments (and the Pentelic marble of the hand versus Aphrodisian marble for the head of Alexander) precludes the possibility that they belong to the same sculpture.

[206] See Atrash (2017, 1–2) for a Byzantine lime kiln south of Beth Shean.

[207] Stewart (1993, 335, fig. 133). Stewart questions this statue's identification.

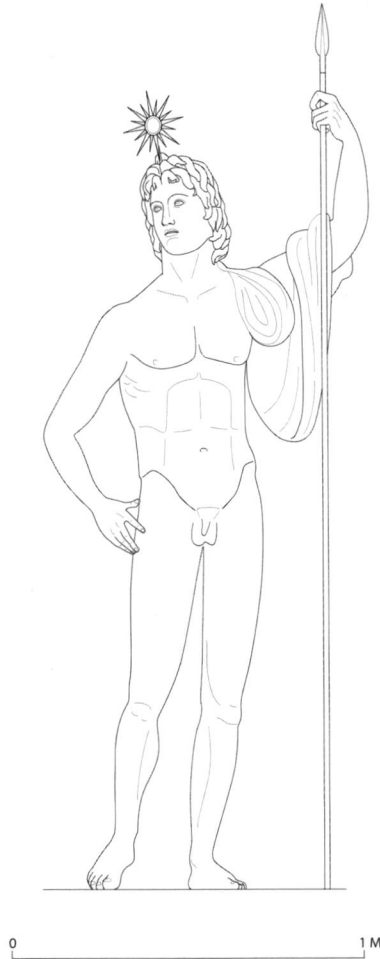

Figure 3.42 Hypothetical reconstruction of the standing statue of Alexander, Beth Shean.

Drawing: Yannis Nakas.

round fibula on his left shoulder, flanked on his left by the foreparts of a horse (if Alexander, the horse would be identified as Bucephalus) and a lance. His face is polished, and the hair is deeply drilled.[208] The fragmentary second-century CE statue of Alexander from the *scaenae*

---

[208] Ghislanzoni (1916, 105–22, figs. 47–48, 51, 54, pls. V–VI), Bagnani (1921, 237–38, pl. XVII, 1), Bieber (1949, 424, figs. 78–79; 1964, figs. 99–100). See Dorka Moreno's most recent analysis of the statue (2019b, 193–94) in which he signals its probable interpretation as a Dioscuros, though the head bears all the basic characteristics of Alexander iconography.

Figure 3.43 Roman statue of Alexander from Severan theater of Perge.

Archaeological Museum, Antalya. Photo: https://commons.wikimedia.org/wiki/File:Perge_Theater_-_Alexander_1.jpg (accessed January 9, 2023).

frons of the theater at Perge measures 3.12 meters in height. The figure's hair is long, and he is wearing laced military sandals; a short, belted tunic; and a paludamentum/himation, which acts as a backdrop for his body. His left leg is bent and he is trampling on military accoutrements, including a cuirass. His left arm is bent forward at the elbow, while the right arm is broken off at the shoulder, appearing to be raised and extended (Figure 3.43).[209]

---

[209] In the Antalya Archaeological Museum. Özgür (2008, 136–39; 2009, 36–37); see n254.

GARMENT OR CUIRASS?

The raised surface on the left side of the neck close to the bottom edge of the hair appears to be a broken remnant of a garment worn high over the left shoulder or the neck-flange of a cuirass.[210] (See Figure 3.33 for the detail of the left side of the neck.) The very presence of this detail strengthens the case for identifying this head as Alexander, rather than a deity or other hero, for Alexander is consistently shown wearing a standard Macedonian-type cloak or a *himation* or *chlamys* over the left (or sometimes right) shoulder.[211] For example, a garment is understood on the Ptolemaic/Roman alabaster statuette of Alexander-Helios in the Brooklyn Museum (in this case over the right shoulder);[212] one is well preserved on the over-life-sized marble statue from Magnesia-by-Sipylos in Istanbul (second century BCE?, cloak worn lower on the left shoulder),[213] as well as on the colossal statue from Cyrene;[214] a paludamentum/ himation is found over the left shoulder of the second-century CE colossal Alexander from the *scaenae frons* of the theater at Perge[215] (see Figure 3.43) and a partly preserved garment is shown on the left shoulder of the statuette from Priene.[216] The examples date to both the Hellenistic and Roman periods, and the identification of both the Magnesia statue and the Priene statuette as Alexander has been questioned.[217] A cloak encircling the neck and hanging on the left side or behind Alexander is also characteristic of other portraits, for example, on the Stanford bronze statuette and other examples of this type, probable Roman adaptations of a Hellenistic type.[218] The Hellenistic (ca. 125–75 BCE) Alexander-Helios from Kyme is worked with the upper edge of the cloak at the base of the neck, to be fitted into the body of a statue wearing both a cuirass and a cloak.[219] In the equestrian bronze from Herculaneum, Alexander is also wearing both a cuirass and a Macedonian cloak.[220] In

---

[210] See Cadario (2020) for a discussion of the role of the cuirass in the image-making of rulers in the Hellenistic and Roman Near East.
[211] Stewart (1993, figs. 21, 52, 59, 72, 103, 106, 144).
[212] Stewart (1993, 334–335, 427, fig. 132).
[213] Stewart (1993, 334–335, fig. 133).
[214] See pp. 113, 134, this chapter.
[215] Özgür (2008, 136–139; 2009, 36–37), found in 1992, H. 3.12 m.
[216] Stewart (1993, 335, figs. 134–35). Like the Scythopolis Alexander, the head is turned to the right.
[217] Stewart (1993, 335).
[218] Stewart (1993, 335, 429–30, fig. 39).
[219] Stewart (1993, 336, figs. 137–38).
[220] Stewart (1993, fig. 21).

the third-century CE gold medallions from Aboukir, Alexander is shown in military garb wearing a cuirass with his shield at his left front and his spear behind. In this case the upper edge of a cuirass encircles his lower neck but does not rise to his upper neck (see Figure 3.41).

If we think of the Alexander portrait from Scythopolis in its Roman setting and as a portrait made for a Roman audience, we might identify the garment as a paludamentum, a cloak fastened at the shoulders and worn by Republican Roman military commanders and Roman emperors, and thus a nod to Alexander's military heroics and emperor-like ruler status. Imperial *paludamenta* were typically crimson or purple. The faded and thin yellowish-orange pigment on the section of drapery at the left side of the neck may be a clue to the color of the original item or a faded undercoat for another color.[221]

The remnant of a garment or cuirass high on the left side of the neck of the Alexander requires that the left arm of this statue was raised. The Lysippan Alexander types, as we know them from Hellenistic and Roman copies, adaptations, and variations, show the Macedonian ruler with one arm raised holding a spear upright at either his right or left side.[222] The Fouquet type shows Alexander naked with his left arm raised with his spear and his head turned to his right, while in the Stanford type Alexander has a cloak over his left shoulder, his left arm extended forward with a sword in his hand, his right arm raised with his spear, and his head turned to the left. The Nelidow type shows Alexander naked, with his right hand on his hip, left arm raised with his spear, and head turned to the left. As Stewart points out, there are also other variations that do not conform to these.[223] The Beth Shean Alexander is likely to be an eclectic Roman version of one of these types adapted after a Lysippan portrait of Alexander of ca. 330 BCE. In this Alexander portrait, his head is turned slightly to his right, the spear would have been held in his upraised hand on the left side, and he is at least partially draped with a garment over his left shoulder or wearing a cuirass. We do not know the position of his right arm, possibly on his hip, as shown in our reconstruction in which we have chosen to show Alexander with a garment over his left shoulder.[224] (See Figure 3.42 for a hypothetical reconstruction of a standing statue of Alexander in the temple on Tel Beth Shean.)

---

[221] See pp. 120–22, this chapter, for a discussion of polychromy.
[222] Stewart (1993, 161–71).
[223] Stewart (1993, 163) with references to examples and images.
[224] Stewart (1993, 164) for the other arm position.

PORTRAIT FEATURES OF ALEXANDER THE GREAT

The various literary accounts, mostly of the Roman period, and the surviving portraits of Alexander created during his lifetime, but especially in both the Hellenistic and Roman periods, present a conflicting and romantically idealized picture of the appearance of Alexander.[225] He excelled in physical beauty (Arrian, *Alex.* 7.28.1; Aelian, *Varia historia* 12.14) and exuded charisma or a vital force. He is said to have been fair-skinned (Plutarch, *Alexander* 4.1), slight in stature (Diodorus, *Bibliotheke* 17.37.5; 17.66.3; Curtius Rufus 3.12.16; 5.2.13–15), and had the body of a man but the hair of a lion, with deep-set, melting eyes (Plutarch, *Pompey* 2.1; Plutarch, *Alexander* 4.1) of two different colors, one jet-black and one blue or grey (Pseudo-Polemon, *De physiognomonia* 14v; Pseudo-Kallisthenes, *Bios Alexandrou tou Makedonos* 1.13.3; Julius Valerius, *Res gestae Alexandri Macedonis* 1.7). He had a lofty neck, with his head turned to his left shoulder (Plutarch, *Alexander* 4.1–7) and his face gazing upward toward the sky (Plutarch, *De Alexandri Magni* 2.2 = *Moralia* 335a–b). He is described as clean-shaven (Athenaios, *Deipnosophistai* 13.565a)—a youthful feature—with a golden or tawny leonine mane of hair swept up off his forehead (*anastolé*) (Aelian, *Varia historia* 12.14; Pseudo-Kallisthenes, *Bios Alexandrou tou Makedonos* 1.13.3; Julius Valerius, *Res gestae Alexandri Macedonis* 1.7).

Andrew Stewart has marshaled the literary and epigraphical evidence, as well as the sculptural and other examples of Alexander's portraiture, and shows that the sources are varied, mostly posthumous, and that competing models or visions of him prevailed during various periods.[226] We cannot take all the information from ancient sources and mix it together to produce the quintessential portrait of Alexander. There is certainly no uniform agreement concerning the identification of many of the portraits purported to be of Alexander, and among the very large corpus there are few of marble or bronze, either large scale or statuettes, found in recoverable archaeological contexts or in controlled excavations or with identifying inscriptions. Nevertheless, there has come to be a consensus on what a portrait head of Alexander should look like—an eternally youthful (beardless), idealized ruler/warrior, turned hero, turned god with a long, leonine (god-like) coif with locks of hair rising above

---

[225] Stewart (1993, see especially Appendix 1, 341–58) for the literary testimonia on the appearance of Alexander.
[226] Stewart (1993, esp. chaps. I.1 and I.2).

his forehead (*anastolé*), his head dramatically turned to one side (usually to the left) and tipped upward toward the heavens,[227] his eyes deep-set with a longing gaze (*pothos*).

The identification of portraits of Alexander is complicated, however, by his continued popularity through the Hellenistic/Republican and imperial periods with rulers and emperors seeking to emulate him,[228] and his portrait often conflated with that of other rulers, heroes, and gods. To say that the Romans were fascinated with Alexander is an egregious understatement. In many ways the Romans created the hero/god, perpetuated his history, and embellished his mythology and legend.[229] Roman engagement with Alexander—and his image—is, thus, an especially complex matter. When Roman copies/adaptations/versions of Alexander portraits are analyzed, it is a challenge to sort out common elements of the "type," the authenticity, or direct copying of the Roman version from an earlier portrait versus a Roman creation made for a specific Roman context in which the sculptor took license to use known elements of his portraiture and create a new "look" for this famous Greek hero/god.

IDENTIFICATION OF THE PORTRAIT FROM SCYTHOPOLIS AS ALEXANDER THE GREAT
Parallels and Dating

Considering the caveats described about the security with which we can identify portraits of Alexander, it seems as clear as it can possibly be that this over-life-sized head from Scythopolis indeed represents Alexander. Various characteristics correspond to those of the surviving portraits of the Macedonian ruler that are securely identified. The portraits of Alexander dated to his lifetime are generally divided into three main types: the Erbach-Acropolis type with Alexander as the youthful Athenian ephebe;[230] the Schwarzenberg type;[231] and the Azara type (see Figure 3.40).[232] The latter type is named for and informed by the inscribed first-

---

[227] See Kiilerich (2016) for a discussion in which the notion is laid to rest that the dramatic turn of the head, right, left, or heavenward had any relationship to some medical condition Alexander had.

[228] For example, on Octavian/Augustus and Alexander, see Gruen (1998, 190–91) and O'Sullivan (2016, 340n8) for other commentary on this matter.

[229] See Gruen (1998) for an excellent and nuanced discussion of the shifting relationship of Alexander and Rome in the Republican and Augustan eras and the conclusion that the Romans used the image of Alexander not as a model to imitate but as a foil to show their superiority.

[230] Stewart (1993, 107–13, 421), Dorka Moreno (2019b, 52–56).

[231] Schwarzenberg (1976, 255–56, fig. 1), Stewart (1993, 429), and Dorka Moreno (2019b, 56–62).

[232] Stewart (1993, 423) and Dorka Moreno (2019b, 48–52, related to Zeus-Ammon).

or second-century CE herm now in the Louvre that was unearthed in the eighteenth century at Tivoli—not in Hadrian's Villa but probably in one of the other villas in the area of Tivoli, during excavations organized by Joseph Nicholas Azara, the Spanish Ambassador to the Holy See. The Azara herm portrait probably derived from the original Lysippan portrait made during Alexander's lifetime (330–320s in Egypt), though we are lacking the body type that goes with the head.[233] The herm has lost much of its surface and has been extensively recut and restored. It bears little or no relationship in style or form to our head from Scythopolis, especially not in the staid pose of its herm form, but the hair is the key element that can be compared with our head and that of other Alexander portraits.[234]

The characteristics of the hair of the Azara portrait that are close to those of the Scythopolis Alexander are the locks of the *anastolé* spurting like a fountain from the forehead;[235] a defined crown of curls behind the *anastolé*; a depression/groove separating the frontal mane of hair from the crown; the long locks on the nape of the neck; and the layered long locks on the sides of the head. There is little comparison, however, in the stylistic and technical details, as the head from Scythopolis has lively, rope- or sausage-like locks on the sides with a depth of carving and fullness lacking in the badly preserved and recut Azara head. The hair on the back of the Scythopolis head is flat and poorly finished, with only slight traces of pigment, suggesting that it was never meant to be seen. The S-shaped curls on the back of the neck are like those on the Athenian Acropolis head, which "wriggle across the surface like worms and often lack any organic connection with the skull" and on the Erbach head.[236]

The Scythopolis head is inclined to his right and tipped up, while in the traditional view, based on the literary sources and many other surviving portraits, Alexander turns to the left and looks skyward. A slight turn of the head to the right, as in the Azara herm, is also documented in other Alexander portraits of both the Hellenistic and Roman periods, including in the bronze statuette in the Louvre that is thought to best represent the full statue of the fourth-century BCE Lysippan version

---

[233] Schwarzenberg (1976, 254–55n4). See also Reinsberg (2004, 328–30), Dorka Moreno (2019b, 48–52).

[234] Paris, Louvre MR 405; Ma 436 (H. 0.68 m); Stewart (1993, 165–66, 423, with list of two other marble copies and bibliography, figs. 45–46).

[235] Though the *anastolé* is positioned just to the left of center on the Azara herm, as opposed to the Akropolis-Erbach type, where it is positioned above the right eye (Stewart 1993, 106–7), in the Scythopolis head it is right on center.

[236] Stewart (1993, 107). The dates of the Acropolis and Erbach Alexander heads are not agreed upon by all. See Stewart (1993, 107–13, 421; Dorka Moreno (2019b, 52–56).

of his portrait,[237] and in the probably Hadrianic colossal statue from Cyrene.[238]

The Scythopolis Alexander portrait has a defined, rounded brow ridge with eyes set deep beneath and relatively far apart. The face is square with broad cheeks and lacks the high, sharp cheekbones, flat cheeks, and taut skin of, for example, the Dresden copy of the type.[239] The mouth and part of the chin of the Scythopolis example are largely missing but it appears that the chin is also full. The structure beneath the skin seems soft and doughy, whereas the porcelain-like polish lends the exterior, in contrast, an almost metallic hardness. *Pathos* is lacking in this portrait, for in the turn of his head and in upward eyes he eschews engagement with the viewer. This is a cool, detached image of a youthful and idealized classical hero-god on a heroic scale—a romanticized and dramatic image of Alexander that fits well in the High Empire.

Kreikenbom cites a closeness of the Alexander from Scythopolis to the head of the over-life-sized statue found at Magnesia-by-Sipylos, now in Istanbul, especially in the curly hair and the calm visage.[240] Yet, there is little technical comparison between the two works, with the Magnesia head especially lacking the lively full hair, the drilled channels around the face, and the undercut locks that are so characteristic of the Scythopolis head. (See especially Figures 3.29 to 3.32.) An over-life-sized (H. 0.48 m) head of Carrara marble in the Museum of Fine Arts, Boston (BMFA) is usually included in the corpus of Alexander portraits, possibly in the guise of Helios, and is dated to the Antonine/Severan period; it is said to have been bought in Alexandria in the 1890s and to have come from Ptolemais Hermiou.[241] Yet, there are lingering doubts regarding its authenticity.[242] This question about authenticity highlights one of the problems with assessing the corpus of the portraiture of Alexander. Few have been found in controlled archaeological contexts, many were found so long ago that their original contexts are impossible to reconstruct, and fewer still have identifying inscriptions. Even if the BMFA head is ancient

---

[237] The Fouquet statuette in the Louvre (Stewart 1993, 425, fig. 32; Picón and Hemingway 2016, 110–11, no. 11). In the Dresden marble head (Stewart 1993, 425, fig. 9) and the Rondanini Alexander statue in Munich (Stewart 1993, 429, figs. 10, 12), the head of Alexander is also turned to the right (see Kiilerich 2016).

[238] See pp. 126–127, 129, this chapter.

[239] Stewart (1993, 44, 53, 106–07, 112–113, 169, 425, fig. 9).

[240] Kreikenbom (1992, 118); he dates the Scythopolis head to the Hellenistic period. See also Stewart (1993, 334–35, fig. 133).

[241] See Bieber (1964, 76–77n77), Stewart (1993, 333–34), Dorka Moreno (2019b, 157–59).

[242] See BMFA website where Ariel Hermann suggests it may be by Carlo Albacini and made in the nineteenth century, https://www.mfa.org/collections/object/head-of-alexander-the-great-or-helios-the-sun-god-151130.

and belongs to the Antonine or Severan period, the treatment of the hair around the face (recut in back), does not closely compare to the Beth Shean head; in the Boston head the drill is much more liberally used to give the locks a depth and chiaroscuro effect, which is lacking in the Scythopolis head. The curl lying on the right cheek and the wisps of longer curls on the sides of the BMFA face are treated quite differently than the hair along the cheek and jaw of the Scythopolis head. In addition, the round or heart-shaped face with sharp brow ridges does not compare closely to the Scythopolis head. The shape of the face, the full cheeks, and the long hair of the Alexander from Perge are more comparable to the Scythopolis head, but the hair on the Perge Alexander is even livelier with more drilled channels; ears are visible; and the eyebrows are sharp ridges. In both the Scythopolis and Perge Alexanders, the eyes are not drilled or incised (see Figures 3.31 and 3.43).[243]

The projecting arrangement of the petal-like locks around the hole in the top of the Scythopolis head is unusual in portraits of Alexander (see Figures 3.37–3.39). The only parallel with a connection to Alexander that can be cited is a bronze head from a private collection, on display in the Metropolitan Museum of Art as a loan from 2012 to 2018. In this case, the portrait may be of another hero or legendary figure using the features of Alexander. The locks of hair rise from the top of the head around a central point in a much more irregular arrangement than on the Beth Shean head, and in the example loaned to the Met, there does not appear to be a hole for an attribute.[244] One of the challenges in discussing the arrangement of locks on the top of the head is that few photographs exist showing this feature on portraits of Alexander, to be discussed further in the following text.[245]

As suggested previously, the Alexander head from Scythopolis seems to be a Roman creation based on a general knowledge of Alexander portrait elements made popular by the portraits by Lysippos. It was likely made for this particular market in the Near East during the Antonine or Severan period. Undercut locks of hair are seen in some Hadrianic sculptures, for example, in some portraits of Antinous,[246] but undercut locks

---

[243] For the Perge Alexander, see pp. 127–29, Figure 3.43, this chapter.

[244] Metropolitan Museum of Art L.2012.48: "On loan from a Private Collection, in memory of Dr. Roger Vivas, 2012," dated to the early imperial period, first–second century CE, with the addition of an inserted bronze eye with an incised pupil added later (perhaps in the fourth century). Dorka Moreno (2019a) shows, however, it is a probable forgery.

[245] An exception is Dorka Moreno (2019b, figs. 131–32) with views of the tops of (from casts) the heads of the Venice Dionysos and the Schwarzenberg Alexander.

[246] Smith and Melfi (2018, 30, fig. 13d), Antinous from Delphi.

leaving bridges or struts on the forehead, cheeks, and neck are very characteristic of Antonine workmanship, for example, on the winged figure from the pedestal of the Column of Antoninus Pius in Rome, 161 CE, or of Severan sculpture, for example, in various portraits of Septimius Severus where the corkscrew locks falling on his forehead are similarly undercut (e.g., in his portrait in the BMFA[247]). Even though we cannot assume that the sculptor was Aphrodisian because the marble is, comparisons with portraits of the Late Antonine/Severan period from Aphrodisias can be made in the treatment of the undercut hair with the struts on the brow, for example, in the portrait statue of Dometeinos found in the bouleuterion, once standing on a tall inscribed pedestal beside one of the entrances to the building, with a portrait statue of Tatiana on the other side.[248] The drilled channel that separates the hair from the face of the Alexander from Scythopolis can also be compared to the drilled groove setting off the hair along the face and neck on the head of Tatiana.[249] This treatment is certainly unlike Hellenistic works and points to an Antonine or Severan date for the head.[250]

Two other features that are worthy of note on the Scythopolis head are the lack of incising or drilling of the eyes and the summarily finished back. Typically, one would expect portraits of the Antonine or Severan periods to have the pupils drilled, with the iris rolled under the upper lid, as in the early third-century CE portrait statue of Dometeinos from Aphrodisias.[251] Yet, in classicizing, idealized works of deities or deified heroes, especially in copies or adaptations of earlier works, as is likely in this case, or in works one would describe as conservative, the eyes are often not drilled.[252] In the case of the Scythopolis Alexander, the

---

[247] MFA 60.928; Comstock and Vermeule (1976, no. 369), Vermeule and Comstock (1988, 115, additional bibliography).

[248] R. R. R. Smith (2006, 69–71, 170–176, no. 48, figs. 19, 24, pls. 40–42: Dometeinos; 216–19, no. 96: Tatiana).

[249] Her hairstyle is modeled on that of Julia Domna (R. R. R. Smith 2006, 217–18). See also R. R. R. Smith (2006, 288–89, no. 207): female head with stephane, second–third century CE, with a deeply drilled channel separating the face and neck from the hair.

[250] Stewart (1993, 338n46).

[251] Stewart (1993, 338n46) also observed that the irises of the eyes rolled up high under the upper lids is a characteristic of Severan sculpture.

[252] For example, in the head of a girl or youth, perhaps commissioned for the Baths of Caracalla in Rome, and variously dated to the Late Antonine to Early Severan period (Marvin 1983, 364–65, pl. 50, figs. 14–15) or the head of Sarapis from Corinth dated to the Early Severan period (Milleker 1985, 132–35, pls. 28–29a). See also R. R. R. Smith (2006, 60, nos. 3, 55, and 59), which should be dated by context to the Antonine period but are lacking drilled eyes and thus are described as possibly technically conservative works (or moved to the Agora Gate from elsewhere). Conservatism and continuity of styles and techniques was a trend in early third century portraiture in Aphrodisias (R. R. R. Smith 2006, 69).

eyes were painted, as is clear from the surviving red pigment, and in certain light it is possible to detect the painted ghost of semi-circles for the irises tucked under the eyelids. We can compare the treatment of the eyes of the colossal Alexander statue, likely of the Antonine or Severan period, from the theater at Perge where the eyes are also not drilled and bear the traces of a red pigment.[253]

The lack of fine, finished details on the back of the Scythopolis head (see Figure 3.34) is a characteristic of many Roman sculptures from Scythopolis, described previously, and is also generally characteristic of Roman portraiture of the Antonine period, continuing into the Severan period,[254] though not exclusively so. It also suggests that the setting of this image precluded any necessity for finishing the back. The general appearance of the head, including the pigment on the hair contrasting with the polished skin, fits closely with other sculptures assigned to the Antonine or Severan period at Scythopolis, including the Athena head, made of Thasian marble[255] (see Figure 3.19) and the Aphrodite with Eros, also probably of Aphrodisian marble (see Figure. 3.17).[256]

Even though the Alexander head and other sculptures from Scytho-polis are made of marble from Aphrodisias, as stated previously, we cannot definitively confirm that Aphrodisian sculptors were responsible for their manufacture, especially without signatures.[257] Yet, it is worth examining this possibility. There is a well-published sculptors' workshop excavated in Aphrodisias, active from the Severan period into Late Antiq-uity and specializing in portrait sculptures and mythological works, espe-cially copies or adaptations of Hellenistic statues, though there are no male heads from this area that can be compared.[258] The late fourth–early fifth-century shield portrait of Alexander from the apsidal court of the

---

[253] A full publication of the Perge Alexander has not yet appeared, and it is not clear to which phase of the theater's *scaenae frons* the statue belongs, the Late Antonine/Early Severan phase or to the Early to Middle Severan (Akçay-Güven 2018, 366–67), or if it was reused in the fourth quarter of the 3rd century (Öztürk 2009, 92–93). Özgür (2008, 139) suggests the statue belongs to the Hadrianic period and was moved from another location in the city to the *scaenae frons* in the Severan period (222–238 CE). The Late Antonine seated statue of Dionysos from the Perge *scaenae frons*, a probable adaptation of a Hellenistic work, also does not have drilled or incised eyes (Özgür 2008, 118–21).

[254] Fittschen and Zanker (1985, I:70–71, nos. 65–66, 68–71, 80–85).

[255] See pp. 88–92, this chapter.

[256] See pp. 88–89, this chapter.

[257] See Goette (2019), for example, for a bust identified as Hadrian, made of Göktepe marble from the neighborhood of Aphrodisias, sculpted in Rome by Athenian sculptors. There is one sculpted image of Alexander from Aphrodisias, a Late Antique marble shield portrait (R. R. R. Smith 1990, 135–38, Pls. VIII–IX, 1–3).

[258] Van Voorhis (2018, 31–36).

Atrium House at Aphrodisias is far removed from the Beth Shean Alexander in date, technique, and style.[259]

That Aphrodisian sculptors were generally in demand abroad in the early second century CE, however, is shown by the signatures on at least two portrait busts in Rome.[260] Highly skilled Aphrodisian sculptors, familiar with the properties of the abundant and varied marble supplies found nearby their city, were sought for commissions of sculptural works for many centers, including in Rome, especially in Göktepe marble. This very fine, statuary-quality white marble from the quarries 40 km southwest of Aphrodisias has been shown to be preferred for the highest quality imperial portraits from the early second century until Late Antiquity. The use of this marble reached its apogee in the Antonine and Severan periods. There is a strong correlation, based on signatures, that in the earliest period of its use, Aphrodisian sculptors can be identified as the craftsmen of these works in Göktepe marble, but later the material was exported and used by other sculptors.[261] Our head and the colossal fingers are not made of Göktepe marble, however. The marble is from white marble quarries within two to four kilometers of the city. The excavators at Aphrodisias have suggested that the export of large unworked blocks of white Aphrodisian marble suitable for over-life-sized statues to workshops outside the city of Aphrodisias was not a factor in the Roman economy of the city.[262] Yet, R. R. R. Smith observes that the heads of statues found in the city of Aphrodisias created of local marble were rarely separately made and that the marble supplies around the city of Aphrodisias must have been sufficiently abundant to support large-scale works.[263] In the future as more Roman sculpture is scientifically tested, it may be clearer whether the white marble quarries of Aphrodisias, as opposed to its marble workshops, specialized in orders of unworked blocks transported to sculptors' workshops outside their own city.[264] The marble

---

[259] See R. R. R. Smith (1990, 135–38, no. 2, pl. 8-9.3; 1991b, 147, fig. 3; 148, 158) with evidence for decapitation.

[260] R. R. R. Smith (2006, 29n97).

[261] Attanasio et al. (2008, 2009, 2012, 2018).

[262] Long concluded that there is little clear evidence for the export of the white marbles from the nearby city quarries of Aphrodisias, that it was mostly used for local projects, and did not play a significant role in the local economy (2012, 165, 167, 181, 191–93). See also "Aphrodisias Excavations Project" 2019 ("Quarries"). Yet, an inventory of sculptures and architectural projects of Aphrodisian marble found outside Aphrodisias has not been carried out, except for the recent work on Göktepe marble, discussed on pp. 120n179, 124, this chapter.

[263] R. R. R. Smith (2006, 30). See also Rockwell (1991, 129–30).

[264] This is a suggestion by Van Voorhis to explain the lack of unworked or partially worked quarry blocks in the sculptors' workshop in Aphrodisias (2018, 39). See Rockwell (1991) for his observations on local Aphrodisias workmanship (ca. third–fourth century CE) based on the unfinished sculptures from a sculptor's studio.

trade was brisk and profitable in the Roman world, with the raw material shipped around the Mediterranean, and with secondary and tertiary markets of marble dealers in various centers.[265] We must leave open both possibilities for the portrait head and full statue of Alexander in Scythopolis: It may have been made in Aphrodisias by an Aphrodisian sculptor or the block of white Aphrodisias marble used for the statue could have been transported from the quarries of Aphrodisias to a dealer specializing in marble supplies or to a marble workshop, then imported to Scythopolis in a semi-finished or, more likely, finished state, for there is only limited evidence of local sculptors at Scythopolis working in marble.[266] In either case, the identification of the marble of this head (and of the colossal fingers) as deriving from the Aphrodisian quarries is extremely important evidence for its post-Hellenistic date.

IMITATIO ALEXANDRI

The posthumous portraiture of Alexander is difficult to interpret in the Hellenistic and Roman periods when many divine, heroic, or ruler images were created using the model of Alexander, or vice versa, with Alexander in the guise of another hero or a god. Trofimova traces the ancient sources concerning heroes and gods *in imitatione Alexandri*, especially Achilles, Herakles, and Dionysos, as well as the merging of the characteristics of Alexander's portraiture in images of other gods, such as Dionysos, Helios, Apollo, and the Dioscuri.[267] In a more nuanced and methodologically sound analysis, Dorka Moreno recently published a monograph focused on the issues surrounding *imitatio Alexandri* paying attention to both theoretical points of view and individual Alexander portraits types and examples; he studied the questions surrounding the linking of Alexander with heroes, such as Achilles and gods, including Herakles, Helios, Sol, the Disokouroi, Dionysos, and Apollo Karneios.[268]

When we examine the motivation for erecting a statue of Alexander on the acropolis of Scythopolis in the Antonine/Severan period, we should entertain the possibility that the image might not have represented Alexander but a god *in imitatione Alexandri*. That is, could this portrait of

---

[265] See Long (2017) for the factors in the pricing of various marble varieties.

[266] See Romano and Fischer (2009, 392–95): marble (probably both Proconnesian and greyish Dokimeion) "peopled" scrolls for the Severan Theater at Beth Shean may have been finished on site from pattern books, with the carving roughed-out in advance.

[267] Trofimova (2012, esp. chap. V on Dionysos where the Beth Shean Alexander is shown).

[268] Dorka Moreno (2019b).

Alexander the Great be of a god in his guise or a conflation of Alexander
with a divine figure? In examining these possibilities, the interpretation
of the attribute inserted in the hole on top of the head is critical, for it
would have been one aspect of the statue that conveyed the message of
a union of Alexander with another hero or god and signaled the meaning
of the image in this context, including a possible association with imperial
rulers.

HEADDRESS/ATTRIBUTE

Thus, one of the important questions about this head, indeed a key to its
appearance and interpretation, lies in the (probably bronze) headdress or
attribute that would have been inserted in the single hole on top of
the head (see Figures 3.37–3.39).[269] Other portraits of Alexander or
of Alexander-like heads, especially marble and bronze statuettes from
Egyptian contexts dating both to the Hellenistic and Roman periods, bear
holes in their heads for attributes, though it is difficult to be exhaustive
in citing examples since there is often no mention of these holes in
the published accounts, and photographs often neglect the top view.[270]
Nevertheless, the third–second century BCE gilded marble head, probably
from Hermopolis (according to the dealer in Egypt), now in the Princeton
Art Museum, has a hole (Diam. 1.5 cm) drilled on top of the second row
of locks of hair.[271] A single hole behind the *anastolé* is also found in
the top of each of the following heads: a marble head from a statuette
in the J. Paul Getty Museum, of unknown provenience and dated to the
second century BCE;[272] a bronze statuette of Alexander or a ruler or
divinity in the guise of Alexander in the pose derived from the Lysippan
prototype with his right hand on his hip and left raised to hold a lance,
of unknown provenience in the J. Paul Getty Museum;[273] the Hellenistic

---

[269] See Ridgway (1990) for a discussion of Archaic *meniskoi* and their meaning as divine attributes,
rather than as protectors from bird droppings. However, the hole is located far too forward on the cranium
of this head for it to be associated with a meniskos.

[270] For a list of some of them see Bergmann (1998, 80n479).

[271] Princeton Art Museum 2008-330, formerly in the private collection of Wilhelm Horn, Berlin. Parian
marble: H. 0.184 m; Gebauer (1938/39, 85, K5), Yfantidis (1984, 294, Nr. 164), Bianchi (2010, see fig.
4 for the hole), Blume (2015, Kat. 80, 271–72). For the Hellenistic marble "Nahman Alexander" (H.
0.28 m), also said to have come from Hermopolis and now in a private American collection, Bianchi
describes a channel for a diadem and suggests the presence of a hole for a headdress, but this hole is
not visible in the photos of the head and no dimensions are provided (Bianchi 2007, 33–34).

[272] 78.AA.317; Grossman (2001, 56, no. 3, figs. 3a and 3b. H. 9.9 cm).

[273] 96.AB.153, formerly in the Fleischman collection: True and Hamma (1994, 215–16, no. 106; late
Hellenistic), Grossman (2001, 73, no. 2, figs. 37a–b). For additional bibliography, see http://www.getty
.edu/art/collection/objects/29596/unknown-maker-statuette-of-a-ruler-or-divinity-greek-125-1-bc/ (accessed January 15, 2023). The hole in the top of the head is not mentioned in its previous publications.

or Roman "Fouquet" bronze statuette from Lower Egypt in the Louvre;[274] a small Hellenistic marble head in Leipzig of unknown provenience, in which a star is conjectured for the attribute;[275] a small marble head in Alexandria, dated to the later Hellenistic period;[276] a small marble head collected by Ernst von Sieglin in Alexandria in 1899, now in Stuttgart, dated to the second half of the second to first century BCE;[277] and a second- to third-century CE marble head identified as that of Alexander from the collection of Christos Bastis, possibly from Egypt.[278]

The number of examples, especially in small scale, of images of Alexander with holes for additional attributes that are from Egypt (or said to be from Egypt), leads one to ask what the impact of the Ptolemaic conception of Alexander might have been in the imperial period, inside and outside of Egypt, and what the historical, religious, or social rationale might have been for an Alexander image with possible Egyptian elements at Scythopolis in the Antonine/Severan period.[279] Of course, Beth Shean was an Egyptian imperial center in the Late Bronze Age, but there is no evidence that there was any memory of this in the second–third centuries CE, and there is little rationale for commemorating this period. The Ptolemaic presence at Scythopolis was very short-lived, and we cannot place Alexander himself at the site. Nevertheless, we know that the mythic status of the hero/ruler Alexander was very popular in the Roman East, and his associations with Egypt were strong in all periods in the Hellenistic and former Hellenistic worlds, because of his campaigns, his visit to the Siwa oasis, the founding of Alexandria, and the site of his burial. Egypt has long been associated with Alexander's lasting legacy.

Yet, in addition to any possible Egyptian connections with this head of Alexander, we should examine other possibilities for the headdress/attribute of the Scythopolis head. We can eliminate those that cover part of the head or that would be attached in multiple places on or around the head, such as a helmet, the lion-skin of Herakles, the sun rays of Helios,[280] a diadem/taenia/wreath, an elephant scalp, or the horns of Zeus

---

[274] See pp. 130, 134n237, this chapter, and Reinsberg (2004, 334, fig. 22) for a photo montage of the Fouquet statuette with a hemhem crown.

[275] Gebauer (1938/39, 42–43, no. K17, Taf. 10, 11, 1–2, University of Leipzig Museum of Antiquities, Inv. 99.037), Bergmann (1998, 81, Taf. 15.3, top of head).

[276] Gebauer (1938/39, 45, no. K26, Taf. 12, 3–4).

[277] Stuttgart, Inv. 1.1; Laube (2012, 128–30, no. 44). The hole is 0.8 cm across and 1.9 cm deep. Laube suggests a kalathos or a hemhem crown as possible attributes.

[278] Von Bothmer and Mertens (1982, 20, no. S66): The authors speculate that the attachment may have been a sun-disk with rays.

[279] See Bergmann (1998, 21–22, 67) for methodological difficulties in interpreting images of Hellenistic and Roman rulers with Egyptian attributes.

[280] For a thorough analysis of crowns of sun rays, see Bergmann (1998).

Ammon. We must consider only those attributes that rise from a central position on top of the head and that would have been rather small to be attached using such a small and shallow hole. We must think about any symbols that would link Alexander with another god or hero, especially the two who are well attested at Scythopolis: Dionysos, though the most obvious Dionysiac headgear, the ivy or grape wreath, is certainly not present, and Zeus, or with the Antonine or Severan emperors who were enamored with Alexander.

SYMBOLS OF ZEUS

Considering epigraphical evidence for the presence of Zeus Akraios and Zeus Olympios at Scythopolis and the likelihood that the temple in which the Alexander portrait was erected was dedicated to Zeus, we might examine the possibility of attributes that link Alexander with Zeus. The Macedonians, of course, had a strong preference for Zeus, who was worshiped in the important sanctuary of Zeus Hypsistos at Dion in the shadows of Mount Olympus.[281] Controversially, Alexander made claims to be the son of Zeus, partly through his mother's Epirote heritage and partly from divine intervention, the latter confirmed when he sought the priests at the oracular shrine of Ammon at Siwa in 331 BCE (Arrian, *Anabasis* 3.3.1–4; Curtius Rufus 4.7.8–9, 30–31).[282] His mother's family was patron of the most important sanctuary in Epirus, that of Zeus at Dodona (e.g., Hyperides, *Eux.* 24–6), where the oracle was supposed to have been inspired by that of the Egyptian Ammon/Amun (Herodotus 1.182, 2.42, 4.181). Apelles is said to have created a painting of Alexander with the thunderbolt of Zeus in the Artemision at Ephesos (Cicero, *In Verrem* 4.60.135; Pliny, *NH* 35.92; Plutarch, *Moralia* 335a, 360a; Plutarch, *Alexander* 4.1).[283] On coins minted in Alexander's lifetime the seated Zeus from Olympia appears on the reverse of the silvers, and Alexander laid claim to Zeus as his own god, his special protector.[284] Thereafter, on Hellenistic coins Alexander is often shown with the horns of Zeus-Ammon.[285]

---

[281] Pandermalis (2003/2005, 2016).

[282] Stewart (1993, 95–102), Bergmann (1998, 23–25).

[283] Stewart (1993, 363–64, T 59–62), Trofimova (2012, 24–25).

[284] Stewart (1993, 93, 159–60).

[285] Stewart (1993, 231), Grimm (1978, 106–09) for the relationship of and conflation of Ammon and Zeus.

Yet, an image of Zeus *in imitatione Alexandri* is not obvious since the youthful, unbearded Alexander is simply not compatible with an image of the mature god Zeus, who is always shown bearded.[286] Moreover, if Alexander is being associated with Zeus in this image, we must consider attributes or headgear worn by Zeus. The kalathos/modius of Zeus/Serapis comes to mind,[287] but the hole and petal-like locks around the hole on the top of the Scythopolis head do not seem compatible with an attribute that would have been set on the head.[288] Alexander, as the son of Zeus-Ammon, might have worn a crown of sun rays,[289] but that, too, would not fit for this head. The hemhem crown, discussed later in the text and seen on many Ptolemaic and Roman bronzes of Zeus-Ammon, is a possibility for an attribute of Zeus, but one would have to argue that Alexander is being shown as the son of Zeus-Ammon.[290] In addition, there is no epigraphical, numismatic, or other archaeological evidence for Zeus being worshiped in Scythopolis in his Egyptian guise.

EGYPTIAN ATTRIBUTES

If Alexander was shown with an Egyptian attribute on this head in Scythopolis in the later second or third century CE, it may be explained, as mentioned, by a wider Egyptianizing tendency first fostered by Alexander in his acceptance of Egyptian gods, Graeco-Egyptian syncretism promoted by the Ptolemies, and its continuation in the Roman period, found useful for the purposes of legitimization by Roman emperors.[291] Trofimova suggests that the attribute on the Scythopolis head was a uraeus,[292] but the uraeus typically rises from above the forehead and not from the top of the head. Andrew Stewart suggests that a hemhem crown— an ornate triple *atef* rising from two corkscrew sheep horns and usually

---

[286] See Dorka Moreno (2019b, 48–52) for the relationship of the hair of the Azara type to Zeus (Zeus-Ammon).

[287] In Graeco-Roman Egyptian iconography the modius (with the lotus blossom in relief) is found on the head of Hermanubis, e.g., Laube (2012, 315, no. 169): a fragment of a votive relief dating to the second century CE, now in Dresden (Inv. ZV 2600/A 134). In this case, the head of the figure bears elements of Alexander portraiture, including the *anastolé* hair. See also the bronze statuette of Hermes with the portrait features of Alexander, holding a caduceus and in the garb of Hermes (Schreiber 1903, 145–47, Abb. 12: from a private collection in Alexandria, lacking provenience).

[288] See Laube (2012, 76–79, nos. 9 and 10) for two examples of statuettes of Serapis with large holes in a prepared surface on the tops of their heads for the added modius.

[289] Bergmann (1998, 49).

[290] Grimm (1978, Abb. 91–95).

[291] Koulakiotis (2006, 190–91).

[292] Trofimova (2012, 96–97).

two uraei—was the possible headdress for the Scythopolis head.[293] Alexander the Great is shown wearing such a crown, among others, in the more than fifty reliefs in the shrine for the sacred barque of Amun in the Luxor Temple, a project undertaken during the reign of Alexander as pharaoh (ca. 330–325 BCE).[294] Variations of the hemhem crown were especially popular in the Ptolemaic period, sometimes worn by rulers and sometimes by deities, such as Harpokrates, Isis, and Zeus-Ammon, as mentioned previously.[295] The bronze statuette in a private collection in Düsseldorf that Thomas identifies as Ptolemy IV, in the guise of the nude god Dionysos, wears a complicated headdress of many elements with a hemhem crown as its core with a lotus flower below.[296]

The hemhem crown makes infrequent appearances in the Roman period, mostly associated with Harpokrates, the Graeco-Roman version of Horus, the god of the rising sun, representing rebirth/resurrection, and is seen, for example, on the reverse of a bronze dichalkon of Trajan minted in Alexandria in 113–114 CE.[297] In a small Roman bronze bust in Stuttgart, Alexander is shown wearing a hemhem crown, an attribute that links him with Zeus-Ammon or Horus and connotes connections to the Egyptian pharaohs.[298] On the painted wooden tondo from Antinoupolis, dated ca. 130–150 CE, a standing figure of Alexander as Osiris/Antinous is shown above the right shoulder of one of the brothers.[299] If Alexander is wearing a hemhem crown in this portrait from Scythopolis, whom would he be representing or associated with: Zeus-Ammon, Osiris, Horus, or Dionysos?

There is a technical argument, however, against such a hemhem headdress appearing on this head. Typically, a hemhem crown rises from two uraei or two sheep horns, which would generally require a larger base or wider hole for mounting, rather than a small hole, as on this head (Diam. 0.015; Max. Depth [at back] 0.03 m). In addition, the pattern of carved locks of hair around the hole would be obscured or rendered unnecessary by a broad-based attribute such as a hemhem crown.

---

[293] Stewart (1993, 338n46).

[294] Stewart (1993, 173–78, 427, figs. 53–54), Bosch-Puche (2014, esp. 61n16).

[295] Grimm (1978, Abb. 91–95), see Thomas (2004) for a bronze statuette of a Ptolemaic ruler.

[296] Thomas (2000, 2002, 2004, esp. fig. 8, for a drawing that clarifies the various elements of the headdress, which include grapes in front of the ears, floral rosettes, a diadem, a lotus flower above the diadem, a hemhem crown, and the horns of Ammon to the right and left of the head). She dates it to the period of Ptolemy V, between ca. 197–180 BCE and argues that the complicated headdress contains symbols of various gods, including Dionysos and Zeus, but above all relates to the god Osiris.

[297] Dattari (1901, 1721–22), Milne (1933, 720). See also Powers et al. (2018) on an Antinous in San Antonio where a hemhem crown is suggested.

[298] Grimm (1978, 105n22, Abb. 71), Reinsberg (2004, 335, fig. 23; 2005, 563, Kat. 133).

[299] Stewart (1993, 164, 169n43, 425, fig. 33: Cairo, Egyptian Museum CG 33267).

LOTUS FLOWER

The presence of a lotus flower with the hemhem crown on the Ptolemaic statuette in Düsseldorf and the arrangement of locks of hair around the hole, which looks very much like flower petals, lead us to consider what we know about a flower as an attribute of Alexander. On the head of a second-century CE standing bronze statuette from Alexandria in the Getty (and on a similar one in Alexandria), Alexander in the guise of Hermanubis wears a kalathos/modius with a lotus flower in relief.[300] A flower, however, is not a well-known attribute of Alexander, and the one ancient source on this subject is Nikandros (*apud* Karystios of Pergamon; second century BCE) who is quoted in Athenaios (*Deipnosophistai* 15.684e; early third century CE), who records that a flower called *ambrosia* (ἀμβροσία) grows out of the head of a statue of Alexander on Kos.[301] It is not clear which plant this is, for Pliny tells us that the name *ambrosia* is a vague term that might be assigned to a branchy shrub-like plant, sometimes called *artemisia* (*NH* 27.11, 27.31). Elsewhere Pliny calls a variety of grape *ambrosia* (*NH* 14.4).

There are two Nilotic lotus species, commonly called *water lilies*, that are native to ancient Egypt, the white and blue lotus. Another, the pink lotus (*Nelumbo nucifera*) with its distinctive petals, probably introduced from Persia,[302] seems to be the species most often depicted in Ptolemaic and Roman Egyptian iconography. Both the blue and pink lotus have psychotropic properties, and either is the possible species that had a soporific effect in the famous lotus-eaters incident, the λωτοφάγοι, in the *Odyssey* (9.82ff). Pliny mentions that lotus is one of the ingredients of a "royal unguent" of the Parthian kings (*NH* 13.2). This flower is also a sacred symbol in Hinduism, Buddhism, and other Eastern religions, and represents divine beauty, eternity, fertility, and ever-renewing youth.[303] And, in the art of these Eastern regions that Alexander con-

---

[300] Schreiber (1903, 145–46, Abb. 12), Svenson (1995, 74, Abb. 171–72), Grossman (2001, 60–61, no. 6; figs. 6a–c) Agathodaimon, see Bricault (2018: Getty acc. no. 81.AB.66 and other examples of Hermanubis; H. 12.3 cm). For Agathodaimon, see Dunand (1981). See also Hansen et al. (2009, Kat. Nr. 328, 397) for a first- or second-century CE bronze bust of Hermes in the form of a balsamarium(?) found in Begram, Afghanistan, wearing a kalathos/modius with a lotus petal on the front. It is possibly an import from an Alexandrian workshop.

[301] Stewart (1993, 401, T128).

[302] The lotus blossom used in Persian royal costume and iconography, for example, in the depiction of Xerxes on the palace reliefs in Persepolis (Paetz gen. Schieck 2009, Abb. 1 and 7).

[303] Mukherjee et al. (2010). See Ignatiadou (2008, 329–31) for a discussion of the appearance and psychotropic properties of the white and blue lotus in Persian, Egyptian, and Greek iconography.

quered, the lotus flower plays a prominent role, as, for example, among the motifs on some of the Kushan period (first or second century CE) Begram ivories from Bactria.[304]

In ancient Egyptian iconography, the lotus, in general, connotes rebirth or regeneration as the flower opens with the light and closes as the sun is setting. The land of Egypt is also represented as a lotus, with its stem as the ribbon of the Nile and its open flower as the Delta region.[305] The lotus is a common attribute of Nefertem, the beautiful, youthful god who is the son of the creator god Ptah and of the lioness goddess Sekhmet. Nefertem was born from the sweet-smelling blue lotus at the beginning of creation and wears the lotus on a stem on his head, representing sunrise and rebirth.[306] The lotus is an attribute of Isis,[307] as well as of Horus/ Harpokrates, who is shown wearing a lotus on his head or sitting in one.[308] There are various examples of Ptolemaic ruler portraits from Egypt, both in marble and bronze, with lotus blossoms as part of the headdress.[309]

The flowering lotus is also associated with Dionysos and his nymphs, especially the nymph Lotis, and his eastern travels.[310] Dionysos's birthplace was said to be on Mt. Nysa, which is variously identified in ancient sources with Boeotia, as well as with many Eastern holy mountains in Phoenicia, Egypt, Arabia, and India. The mountain Nysa became personified as the nymph Nysa who nursed Dionysos and who, according to Pliny, was buried by Dionysos at this very site, which was supposedly named, in part, after her as Nysa-Scythopolis (*NH* 5.16).[311] On the coins of Scythopolis Tyche and Nysa are syncretized, and by the Severan period Nysa appears as Tyche-Nysa, seated on a high-backed throne nursing the infant Dionysos and wearing the typical high crown.[312]

---

[304] For example, see Hansen et al. (2009, Kat. Nr. 316–19, 390–91).

[305] Witt (1971, 14).

[306] Hart (1986, 130).

[307] Witt (1971, 14, 23, 32, 55, 71, 83, 177, 213–36, 259, pls. 23, 52).

[308] Jucker (1961, 178–95), Witt (1971, 212–13), Merkelbach (2001, 90–92, 188–89, Abb. 122–24, 128, 143).

[309] In addition to the bronze statuette in a private collection in Düsseldorf, see Thomas (2004, 841n100) for other examples of images in marble and bronze, identified as Ptolemaic rulers (mostly Ptolemy III), with lotus blossoms on their heads; all are from Egypt or probably from Egypt, except one from Dodona (Svenson 1995, Kat. 183, Taf. 29). See also Svenson (1995, Kat. 184–86). For associations with Hermes, see Thomas (2004, 832–35), Foerster (1914), Kyrieleis (1975, 36, 170, C14, pl. 19, 3–4; C15, pl. 26, 6–8, pl. 27, 1–4 [Ptolemaic bronze statuettes of Hermes with wings and a lotus petal at the front of his head]).

[310] Iles (2005–23).

[311] See Chapter 2, pp. 25n22, 28, 30, for more on the site name of Nysa.

[312] On the coins from Scythopolis from the Severan period to Gordian III (238–244), a seated female figure with a turret crown cradling or nursing the infant Dionysos is shown on the reverse (Barkay 2003, nos. 50, 60 74, 79–84) or standing, on some issues in a Corinthian tetrastyle temple (e.g., Barkay 2003,

Could a lotus flower on this Roman head of Alexander from Scythopolis possibly refer to the nymph Nysa or be a symbol of Alexander's
half-brother Dionysos—a divinely beautiful, youthful demi-god, who had
adventures in the East, in Egypt and Libya, Syria and Phoinikia, Phrygia
and Anatolia, and traveled to the distant reaches of India, entering the
pantheon once his earthly wanderings were complete?[313] Writing ca.
217–238 CE, just after the time of the suggested manufacture of this
head of Alexander in Scythopolis, Philostratos, in his *Life of Apollonius
of Tyana* (2. 6–10) makes the connection among Dionysos, Mt. Nysa in
India, and Alexander, and says Alexander made sacrifices at the base of
Mt. Nysa.[314] The accuracy of these accounts and others that link Alexander
with Dionysos and his travels and the motivations of the writers are, of
course, to be questioned.[315] Yet, posthumous portraits of Alexander might
likewise be regarded as concoctions of the imagination of artists and/or
their patrons, a kind of facsimile of the god-like man whose portrait
was variously used and manipulated for political, social, or religious
purposes.[316] In addition to the associations of the lotus with Dionysos
and Nysa, we might think about the lotus in reference to Alexander—
his general Egyptian connections, the founding of Alexandria, or with
his campaigns to the east and his confrontation with Eastern peoples and
their religions, including Zoroastrianism.

If we restore a lotus flower on the head of Alexander from Scythopolis, a visualization of what such an attribute might have looked like
comes from the so-called Braschi Antinous, a heavily restored acrolithic
statue of Antinous as Dionysos-Osiris from a villa near Praesente in

nos. 49, 53, 61, 67, 97) holding a scepter in her right hand and a cornucopia of the infant Dionysos in
her left (Barkay 2003, nos. 39, 44 49, 54, 61). She is alternately identified as Tyche or Nysa, or Nysa
in the guise of Tyche (Barkay 2003, 138–40). In the second century BCE clay sealings for papyri (bullae)
from Tel Iztabba show a standing draped female (with no head attribute) cradling an infant. These may
be evidence of a cult of Nysa and Dionysos in this locale already by the Ptolemaic period (Mazor 2015,
358; Mazor and Atrash 2018b, 139–40; Ovadiah 1975; Ovadiah and Mucznik 2015, esp. 393–94 for
epigraphical evidence.) See also Chapter 2, pp. 25n22, 28, 30, for a discussion of the origins of the
myth and name of Nysa.
[313] Ovid, *Metamorphoses* 4. 605 ff. (trans. Melville): "[Dionysos], conqueror of India, worshipped in
the new-built shrines of Greece … was placed among the gods of heaven." For a discussion of Alexander
and his close mythological associations with Dionysos, see Djurslev (2016) on Nonnus's *Dionysiaca* in
the fifth century CE but looking back to earlier Greek and Latin sources.
[314] *… and that it was there that Alexander held his orgies. But the inhabitants of Nysa deny that
Alexander ever went up the mountain, although he was eager to do so, being an ambitious person and
fond of old-world things; but he was afraid lest his Macedonians, if they got among vines, which they
had not seen for a long time, would fall into a fit of home-sickness or recover their taste for wine, after
they had become accustomed to water only. So, they say he passed by Nysa, making his vow to Dionysos,
and sacrificing at the foot of the mountain* (Philostratos, *Life of Apollonius of Tyana* [2. 6–10]).
[315] See Nock (1928, 22–25).
[316] Schwarzenberg (1976, 236). See also Boardman (2002, 124–25).

which he wears an elaborate crown of ivy leaves and berries and a diadem, above which would originally have been an added metal attribute. The current restoration of the statue (including the headdress), however, was done by Giovanni Pierantoni (1742–1817) and shows a lotus bud set into a cavity that had traces of bronze.[317] In at least one local representation from Scythopolis, on a locally made, limestone, figured capital of the Severan period, we see a head of Dionysos with a floral wreath and large open flower on his head, though we cannot identify it as a lotus flower.[318] The latter example suggests, however, that, along with the ivy and grape crown, as seen on other statues from Scythopolis, a floral attribute is also associated with Dionysos in this city and allows us to ask whether Alexander with a lotus flower might be syncretized with Dionysos in this portrait (see Figure 3.22C).

The foundation legend of Scythopolis and the connection to Dionysos were important in the city's self-representation and civic identity. Thus, if we can identify in this portrait of Alexander some elements of Dionysos-Alexander syncretized with the god wearing a Dionysiac attribute, albeit not his easily recognizable crown of grapes and ivy—we might be viewing the city's "founding fathers," each of them *ktistes*.[319] Though Dionysos was the well-known mythical founder of Scythopolis, Alexander was being promoted in the region in the Antonine and Severan periods as the founder of other Decapolis cities. Scythopolis, as the leading center of the league, might also have participated in this "Alexander mania."

ALEXANDER AS THE NEW DIONYSOS

In ancient mythology Dionysos and Alexander were half-brothers, both born from Zeus in miraculous fashion—Dionysos came from the thigh of Zeus and Alexander was born of Olympias, who was impregnated by Zeus in the form of a snake (Plutarch, *Alex.* 2). Like Zeus, Dionysos was particularly venerated in Macedonia and nearby Thrace and was worshiped by the Macedonian royal family (Athenaios, *Deipnosophistai* 14.659ff.).[320] Arrian (*Anabasis Alexandri* IV.8.1) says the Macedonians

---

[317] Vatican Museums, Sala Rotonda, inv. 540; Clairmont (1966, 47, Nr. 27, Taf. 21), Meyer (1991, 88–91, no. I67) suggests an Egyptian hemhem crown (89–90), Smith and Melfi (2018, 82–85).
[318] See pp. 96–99, Figure 3.22C, this chapter.
[319] An honorific monument in Ephesos set up by Plancia Magna around 122 CE included at least seven heroic founders of the city, each of them called *ktistes* on their statue bases (Ng 2016, 15, fig. 8.1).
[320] Trofimova (2012, 81–82).

kept a special day on the calendar for Dionysos, and Alexander worshiped the god annually on that day. In Alexandria, on the occasion of the great festival in honor of Ptolemy II in 275/274 BCE, statues of Alexander and Ptolemy with golden ivy crowns, Dionysos's most recognizable attribute, were carried in procession with Dionysos recumbent on an elephant, a tableau representing his Indian triumph (Athenaios, *Deipnosophistai* 5.201d–e; 202a = *FGrHist* 627 F2).

Whether historically factual or not, Plutarch (*Moralia* 332a) promotes the idea in the second century that Alexander consciously followed in the footsteps of Dionysos. Strabo also mentions the eastern campaigns of Alexander and links them to Dionysos (11.5.5). The elephant scalp and tusk on coins or gems were a reminder of Alexander's journey to the East, the triumphant Dionysos-Alexander.[321] During the Hadrianic and Antonine periods, Roman emperors, in general, were worshiped as *Neoi Dionysoi*.[322] To Pliny, Alexander walked in the footsteps of Herakles/Hercules and Liber Pater (*NH* 4.17.39), the Italic god of wine and fertility, who came to be associated with Dionysos. Liber Pater and Hercules were the patron deities of the Severan dynasty.[323]

Yet, in the end, there is little confirmable archaeological/iconographic evidence of visual assimilation of Alexander with Dionysos in the Hellenistic or Roman periods.[324] This seems surprising given the biographical/mythological details of their lives that intersect, especially promoted in Roman sources. Both were youthful heroes/gods claimed to be sons of Zeus, who traveled to the East, and had a significant impact on Greek culture. In looking for possible sculptural images that might be identified as evidence of this link, a Roman (second-century CE) male head in Venice wearing grape bunches in his hair has been suggested as an assimilation between Dionysos and Alexander,[325] but Dorka Moreno's analysis shows that the conclusion that it represents Alexander as Dionysos or vice-versa is flawed.[326] Trofimova discusses *imitatio Alexandri* in detail, Alexander's imitation of Dionysos, the similar biographies of these two heroes/gods, and provides some sculptural and numismatic depictions in which Dionysos and Alexander (or Hellenistic monarchs) are

---

[321] Schwarzenberg (1976, 257–58).

[322] See Nock (1928, 34–38), Beaujeu (1955, 172, 307–11), Augé (1986) for the iconography of Dionysos in the Near East, including in Palaestina under the Antonines and Severans; see especially no. 3a for a gem from Jerusalem with a nude Dionysos wearing a headdress with triple projections. Belayche (2001, 266).

[323] Rowan (2012, 41–45).

[324] See Dorka Moreno (2019b, 200–08) for a case study of a marble head of Dionysos in Venice.

[325] Venice, Archaeological Museum, Inv. Nr. 127 B.

[326] Dorka Moreno (2019b, 200–08).

syncretized. She cites this Alexander head from Scythopolis as evidence of iconographic syncretism.[327] Yet, in toto the visual record is overwhelmingly weak for Alexander-Dionysos or Dionysos in the guise of Alexander.

STAR OR SUN

The presence of a single hole in the top of the Scythopolis head of Alexander eliminates a crown of sun rays as the attribute, though a metal disk with a sunburst or star in relief on a rod or, more likely, a metal star on a rod rising from the hole are possibilities. The solar disk has strong Egyptian connotations as the symbol of the sun god Ra, worn on top of his hawk head and typically with a snake wrapped around its base. The starburst or sunburst was also prominently employed as an emblem on Macedonian coinage,[328] as well as on top of perhaps the most famous example, the golden larnax from Tomb II at Vergina containing the cremated remains of a Macedonian royal.[329] Symbols of the sun have specific associations with the Greek sun god Helios for whom Alexander is reported to have held special reverence, especially in his quest to conquer Helios's eastern domain (Diodorus, *Bibliotheke* 17.89.3; Curtius Rufus 9.1.1; Plutarch, *Moralia* 330D; Philostratos, *Life of Apollonios of Tyana* 2.24).[330] One of Alexander's titles was *Helios,* and images of Alexander as Helios with a crown of sun rays are well documented.[331]

The star attribute is also associated with the Dioscuri, divine astral twins, gods of the dawn and dusk, and the imagery of Alexander and the Dioscuri is often conflated during the Hellenistic and Roman period.[332] There are many bronze statuettes, especially from Egypt, of a youthful figure with an Alexander-like head crowned by a star, draped with a chlamys, or naked, holding a sword or hand on his hip and lance in the other hand. [333] A hexagonal disk bearing a star of six rays is preserved on the head of a small Hellenistic bronze statuette from Macedonia in the Allard Pierson Museum in Amsterdam, interpreted alternately as

---

[327] Trofimova (2012, 81–101, esp. 96 [Beth Shean head]).

[328] American Numismatic Database (numismatics.org): On the reverse of bronze and silver triobols from the Orthagoreia mint, ca. 380–320 BCE, where a Macedonian helmet is surmounted by a star (Gaebler 4); and bronzes from the Pella mint, ca. 187–131 BCE, on the reverse of which a star with eight rays appears above Nike driving a biga (Gaebler 2).

[329] Yalouris et al. (1980, cat. no. 172, 34–35, 186–87, fig. 17, color pl. 32). See also the gold disks from the same tomb embossed with the star emblem (cat. no. 161, 183, color pl. 29).

[330] See Green (1991, 411), Stewart (1993, 178–80, T 127).

[331] See Bergmann (1998, 73–79), Trofimova (2012, 103–13), and Dorka Moreno (2019b, 149–75) for the image of Helios in relation to Alexander.

[332] Bergmann (1998, 81), Trofimova (2012, 119–23), Dorka Moreno (2019b, 177–98).

[333] Bergmann (1998, 79–84).

Alexander or a Dioscuros in the guise of Alexander.[334] The figure is nude and standing in the pose of a Hellenistic ruler, the so-called Nelidow Alexander type with his weight on his right leg, right hand on his hip, left arm raised with a spear, head turned to the left,[335] though in this case Alexander's head is turned to the right. A first-century CE bronze statuette of a nude Dioscuros in the guise of Alexander, with a fragment of reins in his right hand, also bears a five-rayed disk on his head, made in one piece with the head.[336] A similar attribute has been suggested for several Alexander portraits from Egypt, including the one in the Bastis collection.[337] Also, a marble bust once on the London art market and now in a private collection, probably from Egypt, shows Alexander with a semi-circle on his head bearing a star in relief.[338]

A head vase from Amisos on the Black Sea, now in Brussels, depicts a Hellenistic Pontic ruler in the guise of Alexander with astral attributes: on his head are a large half-moon with a star in relief and two smaller flanking disks with stars.[339] Various dates have been assigned to the vase, but it most likely belongs in the first century BCE or first century CE.[340] A gold applique (for a priest's crown?) from Pontic Gorgippia, possibly from the same period, depicts a ruler figure in the guise of Alexander standing in a chariot and with a large disk bearing a starburst above his head.[341] In these cases, the portrait of Alexander as ruler of the universe, *kosmokrator*, has been appropriated for these Eastern ruler figures. Cosmological symbols, especially the sun, are also prominent in the iconography of the Severan emperors, discussed in the following section.[342]

THE ALEXANDER RENAISSANCE IN THE ANTONINE/SEVERAN PERIOD AND SOCIAL MEMORY

In order to try to answer the question of the attribute we might address how we should understand this portrait of Alexander in the context of

---

[334] Gulick (1940, 17, no. 27, pl. 9), Bergmann (1998, 80n479, pl. 15.5).

[335] Stewart (1993, 163–71, 427–28).

[336] Trofimova (2012, 120–21, fig. 132 [12.7 cm]): from Alexandria(?), in the Hermitage, St. Petersburg, acquired in 1887 from the Golitsyn collection (B 730).

[337] Von Bothmer and Mertens (1982, 20, no. S66).

[338] Parlasca (2004, 340–41, fig. 1, 360n7 [H. 36.2 cm]).

[339] Trofimova (2012, 113, fig. 121), Bergmann (1998, 81–84, pl. 16.1-2), Hansen et al. (2009, Kat Nr. 7, 38–39, fig. 1, 243).

[340] Before 72 BCE, according to Bergmann (1998, 82); late Hellenistic or Roman, according to Will in Hansen et al. (2009, 39); Trofimova puts it in the second century CE (2012, 113).

[341] Bergmann (1998, 83, Taf. 16.4).

[342] See pp. 156–60, this chapter, in connection with the Aboukir medallions.

Antonine/Severan Scythopolis—in light of theories of collective or social memory.[343] Memories of the Greek past of Scythopolis—or Roman cities in the East, in general—are especially embodied in the vocabulary of the city's sculptural corpus and the uses to which it is put (the "materiality of memory"[344]). There are layers upon layers of memories that could be peeled away or evoked or revived in the display of sculptures, and a portrait of Alexander is particularly explicable in the Antonine or Severan period in a city of the Decapolis as material evidence of social memory. Rather than remaining in the memory of the peoples of Scythopolis since the age of Alexander, it is more likely that Alexander's memory was revived in this period for a particular purpose. Who would have been interested in evoking these memories? To what purpose?

During the Second Sophistic when Greek rhetoric and oratory flourished and the glories of the Greek past were highlighted, if not exaggerated in a kind of cultural antiquarianism, it is typically the Classical period of ancient Athens at its height, and not especially the age of Alexander and the Diadochi, that is celebrated.[345] Classical Greece was looked upon in the Roman East as *the* authoritative and most esteemed source of cultural values, yet Alexander must have been included in this grab bag of "Greekness," for there is a resurgence of interest in Alexander in the Roman East, especially in the later second and third centuries CE.

Several cities of Transjordan alleged Alexander as their founder in this period, a time when cults of the founders developed and it was popular for cities to claim some divine or heroic Greek founding.[346] For instance, on a coin issue of Kapitolias (east of the Jordan River, identified with the modern village of Beit Ras in northern Jordan, and recorded in

---

[343] Though theoretical discussions of social memory were already rife in the 1980s, 1990s, and earlier, it was Alcock's application of this scholarship to Roman history and archaeology, beginning in the early 2000s, that propelled these concepts into the realm of classical archaeological discourse (Alcock 2001, 2002, 2016). Alcock mostly focuses on Roman Greece and Asia Minor, not on the Roman Near East, yet her theoretical arguments are valid for this case in which Scythopolis regarded itself as a Greek city. For a summary see Ng (2016, 2–5).

[344] Alcock (2001, 2002, especially 24–28).

[345] Alcock (2002, 38) and Whitmarsh (2005, esp. 3–22). See also Ng (2016, 5n21) for other relevant references.

[346] See Dahmen (2007, 52–55) for the general phenomenon of claims of Alexander as *ktistes* for cities, which reaches a highpoint from the Antonine (ca. 180s) through the Severan periods, ending with the death of Alexander Severus, as witnessed in the numismatic evidence. See also Wallace (2018, 167–68n18). Di Segni points out that seeking origins of one's city in the Greek past is a particular characteristic of the second century in Syria Palaestina, beginning in the time of Hadrian, when he encouraged a panhellenic policy in the East, and it is in this period when we see the *ktistes* cults emerging (1997, 148–61). See also Slavazzi (2007) for examples of second-century CE public monuments in cities of Asia Minor where portraits of elite citizens and emperors were set up alongside representations of legendary city founders, *ktistai*, and the city's patron deities.

Figure 3.44 Bronze coin of Gerasa, minted under Elagabalus (r. 218–222 CE). *A (Obverse)*: Elagabalus. *B (Reverse)*: **Diademed bust of Alexander and the legend "Alexander of Macedon."**

Photos: American Numismatic Society, New York, of coin in the Sofaer Collection, Israel Museum, Jerusalem. Collection of Israel Antiquities Authority. Reproduced with permission.

some lists among the Decapolis cities) from the reign of Commodus (r. 177–180 CE) the reverse bears the Greek legend ΚΑΠΙ[ΤΩΛΕΙΟΝ] ΑΛΕΞ[ΑΝΔΡΟΣ] ΜΑΚΕ[ΔΩΝ].[347] Alexander was also claimed as the founder of Gerasa (Jerash in NW Jordan), just 47 miles from Scythopolis and another city of the Decapolis. Under the Severan emperor Elagabalus (r. 218–222 CE) there is a minted bronze issue bearing the legend: ΑΛΕ[Ξ ΑΝΔΡΟΣ] ΜΑΚ[ΕΔΩΝ] ΚΤΙ[ΣΤΗΣ] ΓΕΡΑΣ ("Alexander of Macedon founder of Gerasa") beneath the diademed bust of Alexander (Figure 3.44).[348] There is no comparable coin issue for Scythopolis or other specific evidence, other than this head of Alexander, demonstrating an interest in the Macedonian ruler in this city, but to judge from the numismatic evidence there is a case to be made for a kind of general "Alexandrolatry" in Decapolis cities and among other cities of the Near East as well as in Greece, including Thessalonike,[349] Asia Minor, and Egypt, during the Antonine and Severan periods.[350] This interest in nam-

---

[347] Cohen (1998, 96).

[348] Seyrig (1965, 25–28) and Stewart (1993, 419 and fig. 111). This is a very rare issue and the examples that survive are in very poor condition. In other issues of this period from Gerasa, Alexander of Macedon is mentioned without the label "founder."

[349] Several Severan period inscriptions on statue bases from near Thessalonike record dedications to Alexander *basileus*, son of Zeus, and his family, referring also to a priest of Alexander, indicating a cult (*SEG* XLVII 960; *IG* X.2 (1), l. 1–3; Wallace 2018, 187).

[350] Cohen (1995, 104, 317; 1998, 96–97). Cohen also explains the unlikely possibility that this Alexander on the coins may be a prominent citizen claiming descent from the Hellenistic settlers of the city (1995, 318).

ing Alexander as founder of various cities in Roman Syria in the late second and early third centuries would explain the presence of a statue of Alexander on the acropolis of Scythopolis during the Late Antonine and Severan periods.

The Severan dynasty, which began with such promise, especially in the Near East, ended as a family in turmoil, ruling at the precipice of the downfall of the Roman Empire.[351] The dynastic head, Septimius Severus (r. 193–211 CE), was an outsider in Rome, born in Leptis Magna in Tripolitania, and married to a woman of the Near East, Julia Domna (160–217 CE), who hailed from a distinguished Syrian family of priests of Elagabalus in Emessa. The Syrian region was thus of special interest to Septimius, and it benefited greatly from the patronage of the Severans.[352] From a time of relative stability during Severus's rule, the succeeding years were marred by eccentric and unstable leadership and marked the beginning of the end of an empire that was already weakened by civil war, invasions, military discontent, plague, financial ruin, and imperial family intrigue.

Caracalla (r. 198–217 CE) assassinated his younger brother and co-emperor Geta soon after the death of Severus. Despite Caracalla's cruelty, megalomania, and inept administrative skills, his sole rule was in some ways transformative, especially when in 212 CE the emperor's edict granted Roman citizenship to all freeborn individuals (and, under certain conditions, to slaves at manumission and auxiliary soldiers after discharge). According to Cassius Dio (77.9–10) this was done principally to increase tax revenues, but also to appear to be magnanimous to his subjects.[353] Suddenly, the advantages of Roman citizenship, including protections under Roman law, were open to nearly all, and cities throughout the empire were impacted by the increased numbers of citizens participating in aspects of Roman life, including erecting self-representations or honorific portrait sculptures.[354]

Memories of Severan ties to Syrian cults were evoked in the posthumous naming of Marcus Aurelius Antoninus (Caracalla's names) as Elagabalus (r. 218–222), a young priest of the Syrian cult whose grandmother was Julia Maesa, the sister of Julia Domna. Elagabalus especially pro-

---

[351] See Kulikowski (2019, 98–116) for a discussion of the later Severans.

[352] See Bowersock (1983, 110–22).

[353] Garnsey (2006, 133–49) and Imrie (2018), especially chapter 4 concerning Alexander's influence on the *Constitutio Antoniniana*.

[354] R. R. R. Smith (2006, 69) points out that many honorific statues in Aphrodisias and elsewhere of governors, imperial figures, and notable citizens were made in the period from 200 to 250 CE, followed by a sharp drop off.

moted the cult of the Syrian sun god, Elagabal, renamed for popular Roman consumption Deus Sol Invictus, with himself as high priest. Following his assassination, his 14-year-old cousin Marcus Aurelius Severus Alexander Augustus (Alexander Severus) was engineered as emperor and became the last of the emperors (r. 222–235 CE) in this dynastic line. His names invoked the memory of a more stable time of the Pax Romana during the rule of Marcus Aurelius; of Severus, the dynastic founder; and, of course, of the Greek military hero Alexander the Great.

Among the Severan emperors, however, Caracalla was the one who took a passionate interest in Alexander the Great, as well as in Egypt and Egyptian religion, especially the cults of Isis and Serapis.[355] Caracalla's pathological cultivation and idolization of Alexander resulted in his self-identification as Alexander, according to Cassius Dio (77.9, 77.18.1, 78.7–9).[356] We are told by ancient sources that Caracalla made a voyage/campaign through the East in 214/215 CE, at least in part, as an *imitatio Alexandri* and that he visited sites where Alexander had been, most importantly Alexandria, perhaps also in imitation of Augustus's journey *in imitatione* of Alexander's. The exact nature of that journey, its route and its purpose have been debated, since the literary sources for this recreation are very late and we are reliant on the numismatic evidence.[357] From an anonymous *Epitome de Caesaribus Sexti Aureli Victoris* (21.4) of the fourth century CE we are told that "after Caracalla inspected the body of Alexander of Macedon, he ordered that he himself should be called 'Great' and 'Alexander' for he was led on by the lies of his flatterers to the point here, adopting the ferocious brow and neck tilted toward the left shoulder that he had noted in Alexander's countenance, he persuaded himself that his features were truly very similar."[358] Cassius Dio (78.7–8) also suggests that bringing elephants along on Caracalla's campaign was a part of this *imitatio* and that he might also seem in this way to be imitating Dionysos. Caracalla imagined himself a great hero like Alexander, both sons of great military men,[359] and set up portraits of Alexander in Rome (Herodian 4.8.1). He further developed Alexander's persona by using military equipment and cups that were thought to have

---

[355] Witt (1971, 237–38).

[356] For Caracalla and his Alexander-mania, see Baharal (1994, 1996, Appendix I, 69–83), Rowan (2012, 152–63), Kovacs (2015, 60–69 [analysis of the elements of Caracalla's portraiture in relation to Alexander]), Castritius (1988 [discussion of Cassius Dio's passages on Caracalla and Alexander]).

[357] Levick (1969, 440–45). Johnston (1983) thoroughly evaluates the numismatic evidence for Caracalla's journey and takes issue with some of Levick's conclusions. See Hekster and Kaizer (2012, 95nn27–28) for relevant bibliography, and Molina Marin (2015) for an examination of the sources on this matter.

[358] Stewart (1993, 348, T21).

[359] Kemezis (2014, 76).

been used by his hero. Herodian (4.8.2) recounts that there were "some ridiculous pictures of Alexander and Caracalla with two half-heads sprouting from a single body," perhaps referring to double herms.[360]

Material evidence of Caracalla's obsession with Alexander comes from a now lost cameo from a Polish collection depicting a youthful emperor, probably Caracalla, radiant, in the guise of Alexander.[361] Coins bearing the image of Caracalla as Alexander were struck in various cities of the empire during this period, in Philippopolis, in Thrace—where the Pythia Alexandreia games were celebrated[362]—and in Apollonia Mordiaeum in Pisidia, where Alexander is called *ktistes* on the coins.[363] Rather than simply civic pride, these claims on Alexander by various cities might also be interpreted as attempts to flatter Caracalla and show support for his "Alexander-mania."[364] As far as we know, Caracalla never went to Scythopolis or made a dedication to Alexander there; in fact, it seems unlikely given the information we have about his journeys in the East.[365] Nevertheless, Caracalla rejuvenated Alexander the Great and stimulated his memory in the Severan period, using the invocation of the Macedonian-Greek ruler-hero, along with various deities, to help legitimize his rule.[366]

ATTRIBUTE OF ALEXANDER PORTRAIT FROM SCYTHOPOLIS AND MOTIFS OF SEVERAN EMPERORS

The Aboukir medallions (and another group from Tarsos) provide more material evidence of the popularity of Alexander in the period of Caracalla's successors. The Aboukir series is part of a hoard of twenty Alexander medallions, 600 or more Roman aurei (ten dating between the reigns of Alexander Severus and Constantius I), and eighteen to twenty gold bars found in Aboukir in the Egyptian Delta in 1902.[367] Caracalla appears on

---

[360] Stewart (2003, 61).

[361] Stewart (1993, 246, fig. 82; 2003, 61, fig. 15, 61n70).

[362] Rowan (2012, 155–57).

[363] Aulock (1979, 53, no. 9, pl. 1).

[364] Dahmen (2007, 54).

[365] There are two dedicatory inscriptions for monuments (statues?) of Septimius Severus and Caracalla found in the lower city of Scythopolis, both of which use the same formulaic beginning (Ὑπὲρ σωτηρίας Αὐτοκράτορος θεοῦ), but have not been published (Mazor 2015, 375).

[366] Rowan (2012, 157–63), especially Asclepius, Apollo, Serapis, Liber Pater, and Hercules.

[367] Dahmen (2013, 10) indicates that some of the images of Alexander are similar to those of images minted by the koinon of the Macedonians during the period from Elagabalus to Philip the Arab (218–249 CE). He is shown with the horns of Ammon, a diadem, and an Attic helmet.

Figure 3.45 Gold medallion with image of Caracalla, Aboukir, Egypt, ca. 215–243 CE.

Walters Art Gallery, Baltimore, 59.3. Photo: Licensed under Creative Commons, https://art.thewalters.org/detail/3501/medallion-with-roman-emperor-caracalla/ (accessed August 21, 2020).

three of these medallions—in busts cuirassed and laureate, with a shield at his side and spear behind, his cuirass decorated with a head of Medusa (Figure 3.45).[368] In the middle of Caracalla's shield is a head of the diademed Alexander, with a small rider above engaged in a lion hunt. Alexander's portrait is shown variously on the obverses of seven medallions (with various reverse types), all in profile except one; he wears the horns of Ammon, or a diadem, or an Attic helmet. In the scenes of Alexander's life, he is fighting a boar, or in front of Bucephalus and Alexander's armor, or riding Bucephalus (see Figure 3.41).[369] On the medallion he is depicted wearing a barely visible diadem; he also wears a cuirass and has a shield at his left side with a spear behind.[370] The shield decoration comprises a female bust with a mantle over her head (Gaea?) encircled by six stars; facing her are the profile heads of Helios

---

[368] Dahmen (2013, 34, no. 10).

[369] On another medallion (Dahmen 2013, 36–37, no. 11) with a laureate head of Apollo on the obverse, Alexander is shown on the reverse seated with Nike to his left supporting her shield with a representation of Achilles slaying Penthesilea.

[370] Dahmen (2013, no. 5), same die as Dressel (1906, C and K).

and Selene, and along the rim of the shield are five zodiac signs (Aries, Taurus, Gemini, Cancer, Leo), establishing the time of the year (March 21–August 23).[371] On Alexander's cuirass, a giant and Athena with her spear, aegis, shield, and plumed helmet appear.

The earliest objects in the hoard, as well as stylistic and historical criteria, exclude a date for the Aboukir hoard earlier than the accession of Septimius Severus,[372] and suggest a date within the reigns of Elagabalus or, more probable, of Alexander Severus.[373] Portraits of Alexander, Caracalla (on the obverse of three), and Alexander Severus appear on these medallions. This portrait type of Caracalla is one that is common during his sole reign from December 211 to April 217 CE, thus we should assume that these represent a posthumous resurrection of the type (see Figure 3.45). Scholars have long considered the medallions from Aboukir (as well as others from Tarsos and other specimens) as prize money, so-called *Niketeria*, distributed, presumably by the Roman emperors who paid for the games, to the victors of athletic and other competitions in games honoring Alexander the Great.[374] This interpretation of the medallions remains unresolved, and others see these as commemoratives given by an emperor as patronage gifts.

No matter their purpose, the Aboukir and Tarsos medallions are evidence of the continued link between Caracalla and Alexander in the period of Caracalla's successors. The construct of Caracalla *as* Alexander continued to be cultivated by members of the Severan family, especially Alexander Severus, who took the Macedonian hero's name and had direct engagement in the region of Macedonia, restoring privileges to the Macedonians in 231 CE.[375] Alexander Severus was said to have been born on the day of Alexander's death in one of his temples by a mother who was descended from Alexander. He installed Alexander's statue in his lararium as one of his ancestors, and he is said to have minted coins with an image of himself in the guise of Alexander (*Historia Augusta, Severus Alexander* 5.1–2; 13.1–4; 25.9; 35.4; 50.4: late fourth century CE).[376] Both Elagabalus and Alexander Severus made claims to be sons

---

[371] Dahmen (2013, 24). Cassius Dio 76.111 for a description of the zodiac painted on the vaulted ceiling in the palace of Septimius Severus.

[372] Dressel (1981).

[373] Dahmen (2008).

[374] For example, Newell (1910, 128–30); see also Stewart (1993, 50n23).

[375] Stewart (2003, 61–63), Rösger (1988) for Alexander Severus's enthusiasm for Alexander (*Historia Augusta, Severus Alexander* 5.1–2, 25.9, 35.4, 50.4). For the problems with the *Historia Augusta* source, see Baharal (1989, 572nn25–26).

[376] Stewart (2003, 61–62); see also Rösger (1988) for the link between Alexander Severus and Alexander the Great.

Figure 3.46 Reconstruction of portrait head of Alexander the Great, Beth Shean (IAA 1931-7) with a star attribute.

Drawing: Yannis Nakas.

of Caracalla and wanted to stress their close relationship with Caracalla, especially by highlighting his hero, Alexander, through such commemorative medallions.

Thus, it is worth considering whether any Severan period motifs, including those on the shield of Alexander on the Aboukir medallions, give us clues to the attribute that might have been inserted in the hole on top of the head of the Scythopolis marble portrait of Alexander. As we have seen, a diadem, the horns of Ammon, the lion skin, and a helmet can be eliminated because they are not compatible with the finished hair on top of the head and a single hole. A star or another astrological symbol, however, are strong possibilities, signifying the universal power of the *kosmokrator* (Figure 3.46).[377] The imagery of *kosmokrator* is utilized in Septimius Severus's colossal statue among the seven planetary deities in the monumental façade to his palace on the Palatine, the Septizodium (*Historia Augusta, Septimius Severus* 19.5, 24.3).[378] The Severans had strong associations with the cult of the sun god at Emesa in Syria, and Severus himself is depicted as Sol on a coin issue of 197–198.[379] Caracalla venerated the sun god, and he appears on his coins crowned with the rays of the sun;[380] Elagabalus and Alexander Severus both take a special interest in the cult of the sun god and appear with crowns of sun rays.[381]

SUMMARY OF THE ATTRIBUTE ON THE HEAD OF ALEXANDER FROM SCYTHOPOLIS

Although we cannot be definitive in reconstructing the missing attribute worn on the head of the statue of Alexander from Scythopolis, we can summarize the most likely possibilities, given the single hole and its position, the probable date of the head in the Antonine/Severan period, the parallels for attributes known to have been worn by Alexander, by the deities identified in Scythopolis and with whom Alexander might be syncretized, or by the emperors. The possibilities are: (1) the least likely, a hemhem crown, given its breadth and weight and the size of the hole, in which case Alexander would be shown syncretized with Zeus-Ammon, Horus, or Dionysos, and Alexander's historical Egyptian links would be celebrated; (2) a lotus flower or bud with references to Egypt, Dionysos, his nymph Nysa, and the eastern journeys of both Alexander and Dionysos, thus defining Alexander as the New Dionysos; or (3) the most likely, a cosmological symbol, either a sun or star, rising from a rod in the top of the head, signaling Alexander as *kosmokrator*, linking this hero/god with Severan rulers for whom the symbolism of the universal ruler held special importance in their fraught dynastic rule.

---

[377] Dahmen (2013, 24) describes the shield of the zodiac on Roman coins of the second century CE and its meaning related to the rule of the universe, *kosmokrator*. See also Stewart (2003, 63, fig. 16).

[378] Platner and Ashby (1929, 473–75), L'Orange (1947, 79–86), and Nash (1968, 302–05).

[379] Bergmann (1998, 10, 270–71, Taf. 52.2).

[380] Bergmann (1998, 274, 280–81).

[381] Bergmann (1998, 274, 122, 281).

Even though Alexander the Great would have been a very familiar figure to Roman viewers, it is worth questioning whether Scythopolitans would have understood the multivalent symbolism of the attribute without a label on the statue's base to assist in its interpretation. We might consider the following inscriptions:
ΜΕΓΑΣ ΑΛΕΞΑΝΔΡΟΣ ΝΕΟΣ ΔΙΟΝΥΣΟΣ ΚΤΙΣΤΗΣ or
ΜΕΓΑΣ ΑΛΕΞΑΝΔΡΟΣ ΚΟΣΜΟΚΡΑΤΩΡ ΚΑΙ ΚΤΙΣΤΗΣ.

MAKING GOOD USE OF THE LEGEND OF ALEXANDER BY ONE AND ALL[382]

For Caracalla, Elagabalus, and Alexander Severus, it would have made good sense to highlight, wherever it was possible, the Severan dynasty's lineage by evoking its connections to Alexander the Great. By association with the memory of the long-gone, famed, youthful, heroic Macedonian ruler/victor who spread Greek ideals and culture across a vast empire, the Severan rulers used Alexander to legitimize their rule and emphasize their own lineage in *aemulatio* and *comparatio* of Alexander.[383] There is nothing very innovative about this, for centuries after his death rulers made use of the legend and image of Alexander to advance their own causes and position.[384] To the Romans of the Severan period, Alexander was not just any ruler—he was *the* quintessential Greek military hero, conqueror, and absolute imperial ruler. If there was any tentative relationship with or mixed reception of Alexander by the Romans,[385] in the Roman East, Alexander was *the* universal ruler, par excellence.

Unlike in the Roman Near East, in Roman Asia Minor there are many well-preserved public monuments, and it was not uncommon for these monuments to include portraits of elite citizens, set up alongside images of the legendary city founder, the emperor, a city's patron deity, and/or the monument's donor.[386] The portrait of Alexander from Scythopolis was not from such a public monument, but was almost certainly erected inside the Roman temple on the acropolis. We might consider, however, who paid for and who chose to erect the image of Alexander and the other sculptures on the acropolis and who was their primary

---

[382] With acknowledgment to Dahmen (2007, 48–55) for borrowing part of the title of her chapter 3.
[383] See Green (1978), in reference to Alexander and Caesar Augustus.
[384] See Dahmen (2007, 48–55, Chapter 3: "Making Good Use of a Legend"); for a list of sources on the image of Alexander and its use in imperial image-making see Wallace (2018, 162–63n2, 181–82).
[385] Gruen (1998).
[386] Slavazzi (2007).

audience—the city's Hellenophile elite, other local people, or the emperor and his imperial administration? The issue of the reception of the statue and its use(s) by subjects of the Roman Empire, cities, and individuals, and by the imperial rule is of great interest. Roman Scythopolis certainly projected itself as a Greek city, a *Hellenis polis*, and by erecting this image of a Greek hero, elite Scythopolitans would have been choosing to remember the city's purported Greek past and to highlight their identity as Greeks in relation to their Roman imperial overlords.[387] Alexander must have held some meaning for Scythopolitans, a city whose earliest Greek connections were to the successors of Alexander, even if those connections and that period are poorly represented in the archaeological record. Nevertheless, Scythopolis, as a self-styled Hellenic city, was keen to maintain its Hellenic identity—the Greek language, its founding Greek god, and other Greek cults—in the face of Roman cultural forces and possibly with anxiety about their local Christian, Jewish, and Samaritan populations.[388]

At the same time, setting up such an image could be viewed as a prudent and politically savvy act on the part of the city's elites to curry special status from the emperor at a time when Alexander was in great favor among certain emperors, especially Caracalla and his successors, or even to hold onto this "trading card" with hopes of gaining possible future favors and status. There would have been no objection among the local elites to this statue's presence, for such an image fit perfectly within their vision of Scythopolis as a *Hellenis polis* and could be appreciated and made use of by one and all, elites and local people alike, for various purposes—religious, social, as well as financial—including as a possible tourist attraction in a world where Alexander's celebrity was something of a "cash cow."[389]

---

[387] Alcock (2001, 323–30). See Chrubasik (2017) for a discussion of the adoption of Greek culture among Eastern cities (in fourth-century Caria and pre-Maccabean Judaea) as a political tool for elites to strengthen their position among local people. He is discussing cities of the Near East in the later Hellenistic period but this interpretation could also extend to "Hellenic cities" of the Roman period, though the process of "Hellenization," its cultural or mythical elements and its motivations, become even more complex—and possibly dangerous—under the imperial umbrella. Chrubasik (87) rightly points out that the perspective of "Greekness" was mostly a local one with local adaptations of Greek cultural, social, religious, or political vocabularies for local purposes. See Hölscher (2018) for the role images played in the lives of inhabitants of Greek cities, standing in place of ancestors and deities in community gathering. He is discussing Greek sculpture, but these ideas can equally be applied to Roman cities.

[388] Graf (1992, 5–7) and S. Schwartz (2014, 129). For Jewish animosity toward the display of images of the emperor in Roman Palestine, see Foerster (2008, 74n18). Erlich (2018, esp. 556–57) notes that the Severan period, especially during Caracalla's rule, represented something of a high point in the relationship between the emperor and Jews.

[389] See Wallace (2018, 168–69) for other examples, including the "house of Alexander" mentioned by Pausanias (8.32.1).

A portrait of Alexander erected on the acropolis of Scythopolis, probably in the temple, during the time of the "Alexander renaissance" in the Severan period suggests that a cult for Alexander may have existed in the city. As the most important administrative center of the Decapolis, it would not be surprising that Scythopolis would be regarded as a critical place to establish such a cult. It is possible that, as a result of Caracalla's and subsequent Severan emperors' hero-worship of Alexander, the temple of Zeus on the acropolis of Scythopolis was re-dedicated in the Severan period and that a portrait of the deified hero Alexander—a universal hero who stood for universal power (*kosmokrator*)—was set up alongside a colossal acrolithic image of Zeus, his purported divine father.

Though it seems more likely that this image was a local commission of Scythopolitans who wanted to display their pride in the city's Hellenic credentials, perhaps making up for the lack of a sponsored imperial cult, a Roman emperor of this period might also have had his own objectives in erecting or certainly approving of such an image. Invoking the memory of Alexander and using him as an exemplary figure from the region's and, by extension, Scythopolis's Greek past, would serve to reinforce imperial power, legitimacy, and hegemony over the East and this particular region.[390] Alexander made an especially good role model for the Severan emperors as the ultimate absolute military monarch.[391] Ignoring any negative associations with Alexander would have been easy for the emperors in a city and region that already staked their claims to Hellenic heritage. The presence of Alexander in the form of a statue—and possibly a ruler cult dedicated to him—would have been a way of emphasizing the city's mythologized Greek heritage in an empire that needed to remain resilient and in need of positive models and memories.

THE MONUMENT LANDSCAPE ON THE ROMAN ACROPOLIS OF SCYTHOPOLIS AND ITS MEANING

How, then, did the group of sculptures (and the Hellenistic inscription)[392] retrieved by the Palestine Expedition from the cistern on the acropolis

---

[390] See Roller (2018).

[391] See Noreña (2011, 240–42, 283–97; 2016, 97) for a discussion of the "good emperor" model, replaced by the military absolutism model, for projecting the imperial image in the Late Antonine and Early Severan periods.

[392] See Chapter 2, pp. 43–48, on the later life of the Hellenistic inscription and how it contributed to keeping alive the memory of Scythopolis's Greek past.

of Roman Scythopolis "communicate" with one another and contribute collectively to reinforcing the memories of the Greek past of Scythopolis? As mentioned, we can hypothesize that both the colossal acrolithic sculpture, represented only by its surviving finger and hand fragments (see Figures 3.24–3.28), and the portrait statue of Alexander, must have stood within the temple on the acropolis, the only structure of the period that existed on the height. The fragility of the acrolithic technique, with its prominent use of wood and sometimes stucco and fabric, would have necessitated an interior location, and the well-preserved paint on the head of Alexander also suggests that it stood in a protected setting. There is little we can say about the single life-sized marble left hand (see Figure 3.23) in terms of the statue's identity, technique, or setting, for it may have been erected inside the temple or outside around it. The fragment of a limestone figured capital from the tel, possibly belonging to the temple complex in a Severan phase and preserving the head of Dionysos/ Bacchus or a satyr, mentioned previously (see Figure 3.21),[393] provides some support for the identification of at least one of the deities inside the temple as Dionysos. The other importance of the figured-capital fragment in this context is that it is made from a local stone and in a local style and, thus, emphasizes local religious and iconographic inspiration on the acropolis.

The colossus, by virtue of its impressive size, must have been the focus as the cult image in the temple. The scale of the fingers and the acrolithic technique indicate this was a seated statue, making its identification as Dionysos less likely than that of Zeus. Could the over-life-sized standing statue of Alexander, dwarfed by the scale of the acrolithic god, have shared in the religious activities in the temple? Though we cannot reject the possibility that the statue was erected in the colonnade or elsewhere in the cella, we might suggest that this image of Alexander as a deified mortal could have shared the temple and its cult activities with the main deity and flanked the cult image, thus seen as *theos paredro*s or *synnaos theos* to Zeus Olympios. Alexander may have been standing on the left side of the cult statue, turning his head to the right in Zeus's direction. Although there is evidence for Hellenistic ruler cults of Alexander in the Roman period, discussed earlier, this is the only known statue of Alexander that can plausibly be situated in a temple context (Figure 3.47).

Where does Dionysos, the founding god of Scythopolis, fit in this picture? Although speculative, Dionysos might have been represented in

---

[393] See pp. 96–99, this chapter.

Figure 3.47 Interior of the temple on tel of Beth Shean with hypothetical cult statue of Zeus, flanked by Alexander the Great and Dionysos.

Drawing: Yannis Nakas.

another standing statue, perhaps flanking the cult image of Zeus on the other side. In this case, both Alexander and Dionysos would be projected as founders, as *ktistai*, divine half-brothers, both fathered by Zeus.[394] Dionysos may have been shown as a standing god, of the same approximate height as the Alexander statue, with his thyrsos and panther, wearing a tunic and crowned by an ivy or grape wreath, another *synnaos theos* to Zeus. The portrait of Alexander might have carried a symbol of Dionysos and Nysa on its head (a lotus blossom) or, more likely, a star or sun disk, a symbol of the Severans and a reference to *kosmokrator*—the ruler, imperial conqueror, military genius who followed in Dionysos's footsteps to the east and whose conquests brought about a vast empire ruled by Greeks during a time of cosmopolitan exchange in the ancient world.

In the end, despite the close analysis of all the available evidence it is impossible to be definitive about the identification of the colossus,

---

[394] Dionysos and a god whose epiklesis is Soter, probably Zeus Akraios, are mentioned together on a second-century altar from Scythopolis as *ktistais* (Beylache 2017, 14), adding more evidence that there were multiple "founders" invoked by the Romans of this city.

the reconstruction of the critically important attribute Alexander wore on his head, the way three possible images (Zeus, Dionysos, and Alexander) would have been displayed in the temple vis-à-vis one another (or other statues), or their roles. We can only suggest some likely possibilities.

THE IMAGE OF ALEXANDER AND EVIDENCE FOR CHRISTIAN ICONOCLASM AT SCYTHOPOLIS IN THE LATE ROMAN/EARLY BYZANTINE PERIOD

The large number of cases of deliberate destruction and redeposition of Roman sculpture in the Late Roman/Early Byzantine period at Beth Shean makes it an important site for understanding the various modalities of Christian responses to pagan sculpture—especially in ancient Palestine, the very epicenter of early Christianity.[395] Caesarea Maritima was also an important center of early Christianity and is the other site in the immediate region where cases of iconoclasm are also archaeologically well documented, though Caesarea had a very different political status (*colonia*), social, and cultural makeup. At Caesarea, most marble sculptures were also found in redeposited or reused contexts with some evidence of damage.[396]

The waning of the classical world and its pagan cult practices and the rise of Christianity in the Eastern Roman Empire, especially in ancient Palestine, is a process that played out during the fourth to early sixth centuries CE. By ca. 400, as formal places of pagan worship, temples in Palestine would have been destroyed or damaged beyond their original use, though other visual manifestations of paganism, such as statues and representations in mosaics, lingered into the sixth century.[397] At Scythopolis the most precise dating for the final eradication of the symbols of paganism comes from the deposition of thirteen statues, including a nude Dionysos,[398] in the hypocaust of the Eastern Bathhouse, over which

---

[395] Kristensen shows that the responses are not uniform across the Near East and varied from locale to locale (2013, 206–11). See R. R. R. Smith (2012) for a discussion of the selective defacing of nine of the eighty relief sculptures from the Sebasteion at Aphrodisias. See Brown (2016; 2018, chap. 5) for a discussion of the sculpture in Corinth in Late Antiquity. Studies at Aphrodisias and Corinth demonstrate the kind of nuanced interpretations that can be gleaned from examining a corpus of a site or region.

[396] Gersht (2008) and Kristensen (2013, 232–46). At Corinth pagan statues marked with crosses or otherwise damaged by early Christians were redeposited in wells and drains (Brown 2016; 2018, 87, 107–08).

[397] Tsafrir (1998).

[398] See pp. 76–79, Figure 3.11, this chapter.

the Silvanus Hall was built (see Figure 3.11). The construction of the Silvanus Hall is securely dated by an inscription to 515/516 CE, thus the *terminus ante quem* for the sculptures' deposition.[399] Whether they were displayed in the Eastern Bathhouse in their mutilated form in the later years of the bath's use before being buried cannot be verified archaeologically, but it makes sense in light of the fact that parts of the statues were selectively targeted for damage, for example, the genitalia of Dionysos, incapacitating the god and rendering him risible, as discussed in the text that follows.[400]

Although imperial restrictions on polytheistic practices (sacrifice, *convivia*) became gradually stricter during the course of the fourth and early fifth centuries in the Eastern Roman Empire, there were no official imperial decrees or organized efforts on the part of the Church calling for the destruction of temples. These iconoclastic acts were largely ordered or sanctioned in specific locales by zealous bishops or recently converted Christians as proof of their commitment to Christianity.[401] Yet, Eusebius of Caesarea Maritima (260/265–339/340 CE) presents a rather extreme, anti-pagan picture of Constantine's attitudes toward pagan temples and idols in his highly propagandistic *Life of Constantine*, written ca. 314 CE. He records that in Constantinople Constantine stripped (or had stripped) temples of their doors and roofs so that the statues within were exposed to public view, thus allowing them to be mocked and afterwards moved and repurposed in secular settings. Priests of the pagan cults were ordered to bring the statues of gods out of their temples so they could be stripped of their ornamentation (including polychromy), with anything of value melted down, leaving behind the bits as shameful memories of pagan worship. Bronze statues were dragged from their bases with ropes, like captives (*Vita Constantini* III.54). Socrates Scholasticus tells us about the acts of iconoclasm of the Patriarch Theophilus of Alexandria (d. 412) who, upon discovering a hidden temple in Alexandria (in 391), brought out the pagan objects so they could be publicly mocked. A riot ensued among some pagan worshippers, with a resulting order by Theophilus to destroy the Serapeion, melt down the sacred statues of precious metals, and reuse the metal to make utensils for the church (*HE* V.16). We understand from the common elements in these two sources, no matter how biased, that it was important that the pagan images and other sacred

---

[399] Tsafrir and Foerster (1997, 129–31). The definitive publication of these sculptures is eagerly awaited.

[400] For a discussion of the rationale of carefully removing the genitalia of a drunken Dionysos in a relief of the Sebasteion at Aphrodisias, see R. R. R. Smith (2012, 307, figs. 13, 16a, b).

[401] Saradi-Mendelovici (1990, 48–49).

artifacts be viewed in their damaged or transformed state and derided by the public, thus emphasizing the ostensibly ridiculous and superstitious nature of pagan cult activities,[402] and at the same time, removing any of the latent and dangerous power in these daimones. In fifth-century Scythopolis, pagan statues seem to have remained on view lining the streets of the city in their decapitated state.[403]

This fervent anti-pagan attitude in some Christian communities and the destruction, mocking, or repurposing of statues of polytheistic gods by imperial and Church leaders stand in a seeming paradox to the continued appreciation of classical statues among Christian emperors and aristocratic collectors, as well as in some Greek cities.[404] For example, the Baths of Zeuxippos in Constantinople was among the first group of structures to be built anew for the official inauguration of the city of Constantine in 330 CE. It was decorated with a collection of some eighty Greek and Roman statues or statue groups of gods, heroes, and historical persons (though Alexander was not among them), assembled from various parts of the empire. They were admired as works of art rather than as symbols of pagan antiquity and chosen for very specific propagandistic purposes.[405] This practice of collecting classical statues continued in Constantinople for two centuries to the time of Justinian.[406] We hear of private collectors, such as Lausos, a courtier under Theodosius II in the fifth century CE, whose collection of famous appropriated Greek statues, including an Athena from Lindos, the chryselephantine Pheidian Zeus from Olympia, and the Knidian Aphrodite by Praxiteles, was destroyed in a fire in 475 CE.[407] And, during the sixth century CE, pagan sculptures in Athens were reused/reinterpreted in surprising places, especially in the churches transformed from Greek temples, some with crosses carved into the sculptures to cleanse them of pagan demons.[408]

There were various reasons why Roman statues that were subjected to some kind of deliberate damage in the Early Byzantine period were then removed from their original setting and recontextualized for public display. It seems likely that on the first level it was a public demonstration

---

[402] Saradi-Mendelovici (1990, 50).

[403] Tsafrir and Foerster (1997, 128–29).

[404] See Mango (1963) and R. R. R. Smith (2012) for a discussion of the continued life of the Sebasteion after the defacing of some of its relief sculptures.

[405] Christodoros, *Ekphrasis,* in *Greek Anthology II,* composed in the sixth century. For the sculptural program of the baths, see Stupperich (1965); for a list of the sculptures, see Bassett (2004, esp. 160–85) and Martins de Jesus (2014).

[406] Bassett (2004).

[407] Bassett (2000; 2004, 98–120, 232–37).

[408] Burkhardt (2016, 142–47).

of the power of the Church, Church leaders, and Christianity in general—
a signal of the victory of Christianity over polytheism.[409] On another
level, however, the public display of these ancient images invited the
creation or recreation of new stories and interpretations by Early Byzantine viewers,[410] some of whom must still have been of a polytheistic
persuasion. Videbech hypothesizes that a primary function of displays
of pagan sculptural collections in private settings (such as Lausos's), both
domus and villa, in Late Antiquity was to draw links to earlier periods,
to transmit traditions and memories of the past, and thereby contrast
those with contemporary values.[411] Such may also have been the case
for some public displays of reused ancient sculpture.

In the case of the image of Alexander at Scythopolis, it is clear that
it was subjected to deliberate mutilation, with its mouth and nose attacked
and possibly other parts of its face (an *anastolé* lock, eyes, eyebrows,
and throat) deliberately damaged before it was decapitated (Figure 3.48;
see also Figures 3.29 and 3.35). We do not know if or where it might
have been repositioned and displayed for the public to behold it in a
transformed, mutilated state before it was dumped into the cistern and
completely erased from memory until the twentieth century. It may have
been left in its original position, partial and damaged, from ca. 400 CE
(before it was decapitated?), then deposited in its final resting place before
the late fifth or early sixth century CE. A parallel situation may have
occurred at Caesarea where the Herodian temple (with its cult image)
was destroyed no later than ca. 400, but the octagonal church on that
same site on the hill was not built until more than a century later in the
sixth century CE (between 525 and 550 CE), reusing some of the presumably purified architectural blocks of the temple.[412] Elsewhere in Caesarea
some pagan sculptures were repurposed, even in their partially damaged
or incomplete state, in new contexts in a period when the city was
undergoing a kind of urban renewal.[413]

---

[409] Kristensen (2013, 240–42) discusses another possible reason—that of a nostalgia for and (a partial)
rehabilitation of the ancient past.

[410] Kristensen (2013, 244–46).

[411] Videbech (2015). For a discussion of other examples of the display of damaged statues, see Kristensen
(2013, 9–22, 218–32).

[412] Tsafrir (1998, 203–06) and Holum (1999, 27; 2003, 161–63). It is also in the later fifth or early sixth
century CE that the Temple of Aphrodite at Aphrodisias was converted into a church (R. R. R. Smith
2012, 318–19).

[413] For example, a decapitated porphyry seated statue that may once have represented Hadrian and a
headless marble seated statue of an emperor in the guise of Zeus/Jupiter were repositioned facing one
another in the "Byzantine Esplanade." See Holum (2003, 158–59; 2008, 544–47, 549, 551) and Kristensen
(2013, 235–40).

Figure 3.48 Portrait of Alexander the Great, Beth Shean. Detail of face.

Israel Museum, IAA 1931-7. Photo: Hans Rupprecht Goette. Collection of Israel Antiquities Authority, reproduced with permission.

There are at least three other examples of portraits of Alexander the Great from varying contexts and time periods that arguably display evidence of deliberate damage that can be linked to Christian iconoclasm. A Hellenistic (ca. second-century BCE[414]) marble head from Volantza (Alfeiousa) in Elis, now in the Museum of the Olympic Games in Olympia (H. 0.37 m), was cut from its body; the face was damaged, especially the eyes, nose, mouth, and throat, while the hair was left more or less

---

[414] Stewart (1993, 332).

intact.[415] On the over-life-sized, first-century BCE Parian marble head from the portico of the Sanctuary of Herakles at Tivoli, now in the Palazzo Massimo, Museo Nazionale Romano in Rome (with fourteen holes around the head for a metal crown), the damage is focused on the eyes, nose, mouth and chin, while the hair has been left undamaged.[416] And, the late fourth- to fifth-century CE marble shield portrait bust of Alexander that was part of a decorative ensemble of portraits of philosophers and notable Greeks in an apsidal room (a philosophical school?) at Aphrodisias was defaced. The chin, right eyebrow, nose, and mouth seem deliberately damaged, while a deep groove was cut into the neck, possibly in preparation for decapitation or as a symbolic decapitation.[417]

As a powerful—and dangerous—symbol of an ancient hero-turned god and a historical ruler of the pagan past who sometimes received religious veneration, we can understand why sculptures of Alexander would have been targeted for damage and eventual destruction by early Christian zealots. In Scythopolis the sculpture's primary context was probably in the temple alongside the colossus of a pagan god. Thus, evil daimones would have resided in both statues.[418] In 402 CE the Bishop Porphyry confronted such a demon in the nude statue of Aphrodite in Gaza, where the goddess was enjoying particular popularity among women. At the approach of the bishop and a devout group of Christians carrying crosses, the demon inhabiting the image caused the statue to fall to the ground, smashing it into pieces and slicing the head of one her pagan worshippers (Marcus Diaconus, *Vita Porphyrii* 59–61). In this case, we are to understand that the demon was exorcized by the approach of the symbols of Christianity. In general, demons embodied in some pagan images needed to be exorcized and the images purified before they were safe to be reused, displayed, or even buried at a site.[419]

The deposition of mutilated statue parts in wells, drains, and other dark, underground watery places is a characteristic of iconoclastic practices in the Late Antique period, well documented at Corinth, for example,

[415] Olympia Museum, no. Λ 246; Gebauer (1938/39, 79, 105, K80), Alscher (1957, 149–54, fig. 72), Buschor (1971, 26, 32, no. 95, fig. 23), Yalouris et al. (1980, 101–02, no. 7 and color pl. 3), and Stewart (1993, 54, 331–32, 430, fig. 127).

[416] Stewart (1993, 331–33, 429 [bibliography], fig. 126).

[417] R. R. R. Smith (1990, 136, 155; 1991b, 158). See also R. R. R. Smith (2012) for more about selective Christian iconoclasm at Aphrodisias. Pollini (2002, 39–41nn89–90) suggests that it is more likely the groove was cut to remove the head in order to replace it with another image. See also Jacobs (2010, 283–84) for interpretations of the motivations of the defacers.

[418] On the belief of demons in pagan statues in the Byzantine period, see Mango (1963, 59–64).

[419] In Gaza a Christian church was built over the ruins of a temple, only after purification ceremonies and the exorcism of the demons by removing architectural blocks from the temple and reusing them to be trodden upon as paving stones in the city (Tsafrir 1998, 203–04; Kristensen 2013, 197).

and plays a role in the purification of pagan and other images.[420] The dumping of the Alexander head and parts of other pagan sculptures in the cistern on the citadel of Scythopolis is consistent with this practice.[421] Other than their fragmentary state, there is no specific evidence for tool marks, which might prove that there was deliberate damage to the other sculptures found in the cistern. For the Alexander head, however, the mutilation is clear. It seems that sensory deprivation was critical to the cleansing of this pagan image. By striking blows to his nose and mouth, possibly damaging the proper right *anastolé* lock—representative of the leonine, divine aspect of Alexander that was possibly recognized in Late Antiquity—and the area above the left eye and scratching his throat, this demon no longer had the power to breathe or speak or transmit its evil.[422]

The image of Alexander was also decapitated, though the evidence of the underside of the neck is confusing, likely tampered with in modern times to fit a museum mount, but also clearly subjected to some deliberate, violent act. The separation of the head from the body is one of the most potent ways of erasing the power of a symbol of polytheism and the most common form of iconoclastic mutilation among free-standing sculptures of polytheistic gods and other pagan images, in general, in the Late Antique period.[423] There is a long history of decapitation of enemies in warfare and the display of the severed heads in the ancient Near East, in Mesopotamia, and Syria from the third to first millennium BCE. The meaning of such actions can be interpreted as an annihilation of the self-control of the enemy and simultaneously the rendering of the victim as anonymous.[424] There are many biblical passages that testify to the practice of decapitation of enemies, with the severing of the head of Goliath by

---

[420] Brown (2016; 2018, 85, 108–09). In the second century BCE a bronze statue of an equestrian ruler, possibly Philip V, was stripped of its gilding, dismembered, and thrown into a well in the Athenian Agora, showing that the watery grave for images of dishonored individuals is not restricted to the Late Antique period (Kousser 2015, 37–39).

[421] An Antonine period Alexander head was found in a well of a late Roman house on the Areopagus in Athens, though there is no evidence for its deliberate mutilation (Shear 1971, 273–74, pl. 58b; Athenian Agora Inv. S2356; H. 0.523). See Kristensen (2013, 26–27).

[422] Among the sculptures buried under the Silvanus Hall at Scythopolis, selective damage to the eyes, nose, and mouth is prevalent. (It is not clear whether the damage to Alexander's left eye and eyebrow was deliberate.) At least one statue of Aphrodite buried under a pavement in the Severan Theater area had her breasts mutilated, and elsewhere in Late Antique contexts, male gods were commonly castrated. For examples, see Kristensen (2013, 225–26, esp. 226n121). This damage to sexual organs almost certainly relates to Christian attitudes toward sexuality, nudity, and morality (226–27). Unlike at Corinth (and at Ephesos, Sparta, and Rhodes), where there is abundant evidence for carving crosses on pagan images (Brown 2016; 2018, 87, 107–8), this phenomenon has not been observed at Scythopolis.

[423] A similar case of mutilation of pagan figures in one phase, then later decapitation in the high-relief frieze of the Temple of Ares in the Athenian Agora have recently been well documented by Stewart et al. (2019, 688–91).

[424] Dolce (2018).

David (1 Samuel 17:50–51) as the most storied example. Near Eastern ruler statues were also targeted for decapitation and desecration. The famous bronze head of an Akkadian ruler (Sargon? who ruled from 2340 BCE) from Nineveh, now in the Iraq Museum in Baghdad, was deliberately mutilated: it was cut from its body, its left eye gouged out, the bridge and tip of the nose struck, and the ears and tips of the beard cut off, probably carried out when (or soon after) Nineveh fell to the Medes and Babylonians ca. 612 BCE.[425] Just as in many examples in Late Antiquity of the decapitation of pagan statues that were powerful symbols of the enemy of Christianity, the head of the Akkadian ruler was not completely obliterated, but disfigured as a humiliating sign of the defeat of this enemy.

In the recent, well-publicized, videotaped "performances" by followers of the Islamic State in Syria (ISIS) of the destruction of pagan sculptures in museums such as in Mosul or on archaeological sites such as Hatra, decapitation of pagan images is an action taken, though somewhat inconsistently. The decapitation and subsequent display of the head of the heroic 82-year-old Khaled Al-Asaad, director of antiquities at Palmyra from 1963 to 2003, in August of 2013, was a gruesome imitation of an ancient act.[426] The larger aim of such barbaric acts and iconoclasm by ISIS purports to be the erasure of all symbols of any culture or religion— pagan, Christian, or Muslim—that do not adhere to the beliefs of "pure Islam" from the period following Mohammad in the seventh and eighth centuries CE. The effect is to annihilate the local sense of belonging and the collective memory among local communities in a kind of cultural genocide or cleansing. The inconsistency and hollowness of their ideology, however, is revealed by the discovery that at the same time ISIS was destroying statues, archaeological sites, churches, and mosques, it was systematically using the sale of artifacts from "heretical" cultures, especially Greek and Roman antiquities, to fund its terrorist aims.[427] The contemporary parallels with iconoclastic practices in Late Antiquity can only go so far, but it is useful to remember that religious genocide and cleansing of past memories was a motive of the early Christian zealots in carrying out their destructive actions.

Alexander would surely have been a prime target for desecration as a deified mortal of great renown who prefigured the career of Jesus Christ. In addition, if early Christian viewers saw in this portrait of

---

[425] Nylander (1980).
[426] Reported in various news accounts, e.g., "ISIS Beheads Elderly Archeologist in Palmyra" (2015).
[427] Taub (2015).

Alexander or in another statue on the acropolis of Scythopolis some association with the founding god of Scythopolis, Dionysos (which would have been made clear by the attribute on his head and perhaps by an inscription on the base or pedestal), the image would also have been a special target of Christian iconoclasm. Earlier, the Christian convert Clement of Alexandria (d. 215 CE) was especially virulent on the subject of Dionysiac cults that needed to be wiped out (*Protrepticus* 12). The licentious behavior of the sexually ambivalent, rather effeminate god Dionysos/Bacchus would have been particularly seen as contrary to the new morality of Christianity (e.g., 1 Timothy 1:10; John Chrysostom, *Homily* 4. *Rom.* 1.26, 27). It would have been especially alarming for religiously conservative early Christians to witness the continued popularity of this god, especially in Scythopolis, where he was the patron and founding divinity of the city. The life-sized statue of Dionysos from under the floor of the Silvanus Hall kept his head but was perhaps made a subject of ridicule by the removal of his genitalia and the battering of his face (see Figure 3.11*A, C*).[428] The effectiveness of the altar dedicated to Dionysos in the basilica was eradicated by the removal of the upper surface on which sacrifices would have been made to the god (see Figure 3.10*A*).[429] At the same time, if the Alexander statue was still in place around 400 CE on the acropolis of Scythopolis, it might well have been viewed by early Christians in a negative light—as a symbol of an anti-Christ.

THE MODERN AFTERLIFE AND USE OF THE PORTRAIT OF ALEXANDER THE GREAT

The marble head of Alexander came to light in the excavations at Beth Shean on November 19, 1925. It remained in the excavation storage rooms until it was time for the division of the finds for the 1925 and 1926 seasons. The decision regarding the distribution of the finds was made by John Garstang (1876–1956), Director of the British School of Archaeology in Jerusalem (1919–1926) and the authorized representative of the Department of Antiquities in the British Mandate for Palestine (1920–1926).[430] We get a glimpse of the seemingly friendly archaeological protocols followed in this period through Alan Rowe's field diary,

---

[428] See pp. 76–79, this chapter.
[429] See p. 75, this chapter.
[430] Gurney and Freeman (2012).

where he briefly records that on December 6, 1926, Professor Garstang came from Jerusalem to Beisan, accompanied by Mrs. Garstang and Père Vincent (Louis-Hughes Vincent, 1872–1960, a Dominican monk and noted archaeologist at the École Biblique in Jerusalem[431]) to look over the finds and make the decisions. Rowe laconically mentions that the "division was generally satisfactory from the point of view of the Philadelphia museum" and later says, with no further comment on the matter, that the marble head was "among the articles taken for Jerusalem."[432] The head of Alexander and other finds that were designated to remain in the Mandate were transferred on the morning of December 21, 1926, into the custody of the Mandatory Department of Antiquities and sent by truck to Jerusalem.[433]

From this point forward, certain aspects of the history of the archaeological museums in Jerusalem and of geopolitics of the region can be told through the peregrinations of the head of Alexander. The finds from Beth Shean were almost certainly taken in December 1926 to the Palestine Museum of Antiquities in East Jerusalem, a short-lived, British-sponsored museum (1921–1930) housed in a building called *Way House*, north of the École Biblique, shared by the British School of Archaeology and the Mandatory Department of Antiquities.[434] It was soon clear that Way House would not be satisfactory for the size and importance of the archaeological collections from Palestine, both those older collections excavated under Ottoman rule that were housed in the Ottoman Müze-i-Hümayun (The Imperial Museum), known to the British as the "Jerusalem Government Museum" (1901–1917),[435] and the finds from excavations conducted under the Mandate, such as those arriving from Beth Shean. With a $2 million donation from John D. Rockefeller, brokered by James Henry Breasted of the Oriental Institute of the University of Chicago, the cornerstone of a new museum was laid in June of 1930 and officially opened in 1938, close to the Old City wall and Herod's Gate on land expropriated by the Mandate. The museum was called the *Palestine*

[431] Sellers (1961).

[432] Alan Rowe, Field Diary, Beth Shean 1926, 139 (Archives, University of Pennsylvania Museum of Archaeology and Anthropology). Rowe left the Palestine Expedition after the 1929 season with dissatisfaction over what he regarded as unfair partage practices on the part of Garstang's replacement (Reid 2015, 292).

[433] Alan Rowe, Field Diary, Beth Shean 1926, 139 (Archives, University of Pennsylvania Museum of Archaeology and Anthropology).

[434] See photos of the museum in Phythian-Adams and Garstang (1924; published the year before the discovery of the Alexander head). See also St. Laurent (2013, 6, 26–37, figs. 13–23) for the history of the Palestine Museum of Antiquities and references to the emerging Palestine Archaeological Museum, to be named the "Rockefeller Museum."

[435] St. Laurent (2013).

Figure 3.49 Rockefeller Archaeological Museum, Jerusalem.

Photo: I. B. Romano, 2016.

Archaeological Museum (*PAM*) and the structure would also house the Palestine Department of Antiquities (Figures 3.49 and 3.50). Designed by the British chief architect of Palestine's Public Works Department, Austen St. Barbe Harrison, the grand limestone building combined modernist, classical, and Middle Eastern/Byzantine/Islamic elements and was arranged around a central pool, surrounded by arcades and two large exhibition rooms. The walls around the central courtyard were decorated with ten reliefs by Eric Gill referencing major world cultures, and blue tiles by Armenian master potter David Ohannessian adorned the domed pavilion at the end of the central courtyard.[436]

The head of Alexander was moved to PAM by the time the museum opened in 1938. It was exhibited in South Room 4, presumably in its chronological (Hellenistic?) sequence, as all the displays were so arranged. Later it was moved for exhibition to one of the corridors around

---

[436] See Karmi-Melamede and Price (2014, 23–24, 110–29), Hoffman (2016, 164–98), and text panel in foyer of Rockefeller Museum.

Figure 3.50 Rockefeller Archaeological Museum, Jerusalem, inner courtyard.

Photo: I. B. Romano, 2016.

the reflecting pool,[437] a typical place for the display of architectural finds,

---

[437] Recorded on back of inventory card 31.7, Rockefeller Archaeological Museum, Jerusalem.

Figure 3.51 Head of Alexander the Great, Beth Shean, IAA 1931-7 in an old mount in Rockefeller Archaeological Museum, Jerusalem, date unknown.

Photo: ©The Israel Museum, Jerusalem. Collection of Israel Antiquities Authority. Reproduced with permission.

sarcophagi, and stone sculptures (Figure 3.51). From 1948 until 1967, PAM was in the Jordanian annexed area of East Jerusalem and the West Bank. Although it was known informally as "the Rockefeller Museum" or "the Rockefeller" from its inception, PAM was officially renamed the "Rockefeller Archaeological Museum" in 1967 after the Six-Day War and the annexation of East Jerusalem by Israel. In the meantime, there were several administrative arrangements for PAM: from 1938 to 1948 it was run by the Mandatory Department of Antiquities; in May of 1948 the British High Commissioner established a board of trustees composed of twelve individuals representing various international museums; and in 1966 King Hussein nationalized the museum under Jordanian control, lasting only briefly until the conclusion of the Six-Day War in the summer of 1967. Since 1968 the Rockefeller Museum has been run jointly under the administration of the Israel Museum, Jerusalem (IMJ) and the Israel Department of Antiquities and Museums (IDAM), known since 1990 as the Israel Antiquities Authority (IAA).[438] Under international law, however, the Rockefeller Museum stands in the occupied territory of East Jerusalem, leaving the status of the building, its archaeological collections, and library complicated, to state it in as simple and apolitical terms as possible.

THE ISRAEL MUSEUM AND ISRAELI NATIONAL IDENTITY

From the birth of the modern museum in the eighteenth century, one of the purposes and driving forces of public- or state-sponsored museums, in addition to being tools of Enlightenment values of egalitarian education, was to provide public spaces for the display of national pride and history. These were institutions where national identity as well as the nation's values and aspirations could be showcased.[439] By the nineteenth century Theodore Herzl articulated his vision for a museum in the Promised Land as "tangible evidence of a people."[440] Founded in 1906, the Bezalel National Museum in Jerusalem, focused on Jewish art, was the first attempt to establish such a national museum and is regarded as the forerunner of the Israel Museum, at least the part of it that encompasses the fine arts department. In addition, a 1936 bequest by Gedaliahu Morris of South Africa made possible the Museum for Jewish Antiquities on Mount Scopus. It opened in 1941 with collections on the upper floor, and the library and offices of the Department of Archaeology of the Hebrew University below. Its mission was to preserve and exhibit archaeo-

---

[438] "Museums in Jerusalem: The Rockefeller Archaeological Museum" 1998–2023. The library of the Rockefeller Museum will be moved to a new 36,000 square-meter IAA headquarters (Jay and Jeanie Schottenstein National Campus for Archaeology in Israel), designed by Israeli-born architect Moshe Safdie, with planned office, laboratory, library, storage, and exhibition space next to the IMJ, but the archaeological collections will remain in the Rockefeller Museum, according to the IAA (Hasson 2016, Pelletier 2017).

[439] See McLean (2007) for a discussion of museums and their role in constructing national identity; see also Levitt (2015), especially the Introduction, and Paul (2012) for articles on the founding and early history of many European museums.

[440] Barsky (2013, 485n1).

logical objects from the land of Israel and the Diaspora. It was not opened to the public until after 1948, housing donated collections and eventually objects from archaeological expeditions of the Hebrew University in Jerusalem, from Samaria, Tel Gerisa, and elsewhere. The building and museum collections eventually became the Institute of Archaeology of the Hebrew University.[441]

With the creation in 1948 of the state of Israel as the Jewish homeland, a national museum to showcase the breadth of the history and art of the Jewish people was a critical goal.[442] It was paramount to highlight archaeology and archaeological finds in that museum because documenting the antiquity of the Jewish people and their presence in the lands of modern Israel was—and still is—central to the raison d'être of the Jewish state in that critical place in the Middle East. The opening of the Israel Museum, Jerusalem (IMJ), however, was long in coming. Following a 1959 architectural competition,[443] it was finally inaugurated in 1965 in West Jerusalem on a parcel of land in an area called *Sheikh Badr*, now *Givat Ram*, near the Knesset building (completed in 1966) and, later, the Supreme Court of Israel (inaugurated in 1992)—just one mile from the 1949 "Green Line" or armistice line between Israel and the Hashemite Kingdom of Jordan.[444] In his speech at the opening of the IMJ, the chairman of the museum's Board of Governors and mayor of Jerusalem (1965–1993), Theodor "Teddy" Kollek, references the armistice line, nation-building, and the museum as a place for "exhibiting the sources of our own past."[445]

The IMJ houses the most important archaeological collections from Israel and the region, as well as holdings of fine arts, including Jewish art and collections telling the story of the Jewish people from the Middle Ages to the present day throughout the world. It is a museum with a strong sense of its mission to educate the public, and preserve and exhibit collections related to Israel but with a wider vision to serve as Israel's "encyclopedic museum,"[446] including holdings and exhibitions of contemporary art. Although it is possible for contemporary art exhibitions to explore issues relating to the fraught politics of the Middle East, the

---

[441] Text panels from "The Early Days," an exhibition on the seventieth anniversary of the Museum for Jewish Antiquities at the Institute of Archaeology, Hebrew University, Mount Scopus, Jerusalem, June 2016.

[442] Barsky (2013, 485) records that the Department of Antiquities maintained a small museum in Jerusalem from 1948 until the opening of IMJ in 1965.

[443] Barsky (2013, 499).

[444] "The Construction of the New Supreme Court Building" 2017N.

[445] Barsky (2013, 487).

[446] Barsky (2013, 485n6).

archaeology displays at the Israel Museum reinforce the nation-building ethos and present the Bible and the Holy Land as the core of and the rationale for the existence of modern Israel. The antiquities' collections are housed today in the Samuel and Saidye Bronfman Archaeology Wing (or Department of Archaeology) and in the Shrine of the Book, which houses the Dead Sea scrolls. The Rockefeller Archaeological Museum is described as an off-site branch of the IMJ for the antiquities excavated during the period of the British Mandate.[447] To complete the exhibition narrative, a limited number of archaeological objects have been moved from the Rockefeller Museum to the IMJ over the years—the Alexander head from Scythopolis being one such object.

The head of Alexander the Great was included in a special exhibition at the Rockefeller Museum in 1978.[448] It was sent to IMJ in 1984, possibly for a special exhibit on gods and goddesses, and was probably not returned to the Rockefeller Museum,[449] for, by the late 1980s the sculpture was incorporated into a long-term display at the IMJ.[450] In the summer of 2010 a major renovation to upgrade the IMJ complex and add new gallery space, including the Samuel and Saidye Bronfman Archaeology Wing, was completed.[451] During this renovation the head of Alexander was reinstalled in its present prominent location, taking on special meaning, both from its place of exhibition in its new museum context and from the interpretive materials (in Hebrew, Arabic, and English) associated with its display in the section of the gallery devoted to "Greeks, Romans and Jews."[452] The head is mounted on a single pedestal in front of a large picture window framing the nearby Knesset, the national parliament building (see Figure 3.1).

To the viewer's left of the sculpture is an extensive text panel focused on the Hellenistic period in which Alexander is presented, in a sense as a hero of Israel, a ruler who "laid the foundations of the Hellenistic worldview which advocated for freedom of religion and made it possible for the Jews of the Land to continue worshiping according to their beliefs," a nod to the much-disputed discussion in Josephus to Alexander's meeting

---

[447] IMJ website: https://www.imj.org.il/en/wings/archaeology (accessed November 14, 2018).

[448] Personal communication, Alegre Savariego, June 2016 and Rockefeller Museum object file.

[449] Personal communications, David Mevorach, Israel Museum, Jerusalem, and Alegre Savariego, Rockefeller Museum, June 2016.

[450] The head had already been transferred to the Israel Museum by 1989 when Ze'ev Pearl sampled the head for his (unpublished) master's thesis (Pearl 1989; M. L. Fischer 1998, 255n343, sample numbers P/MI 109–110; personal communication, M. L. Fischer, June 2016).

[451] IMJ website: https://www.imj.org.il/en/wings/archaeology (accessed November 14, 2018), Barsky (2013).

[452] See McLean (2007, esp. 247–48) on the display of cultural objects in identity politics.

with the high priest of Jerusalem and the resulting edict allowing the Jews to follow their religious practices.[453] The label on the pedestal for the sculpture records that Alexander "tried to promote cultural integration throughout his empire."[454] In the major, "coffee-table" publication of the museum's history and collections, Alexander is presented as the figure who personifies the emergence of Western culture (in the East?) and as a leader with "a vision of all people unified in one shared culture."[455] These statements about Alexander as a leader driven by his vision of a unified world echo the now widely discredited views of W. W. Tarn, who, in turn, sought confirmation, in part, in Plutarch's essays in *Moralia: On The Fortune or the Virtue of Alexander*.[456] Ernst Badian, in his insightful discussion of the history of scholarship concerning Alexander the Great, dissects and dismantles the various fanciful, romantic, and inaccurate notions regarding who Alexander was and what motivated him. In doing so, he takes on Tarn's biased and romantic, but highly influential, views of Alexander as a unifier of mankind.[457]

Just as in the late second- to early third-century CE presentation of Alexander on the acropolis of ancient Scythopolis, where the memory of the city's Greek past and Greek identity were being celebrated, the contemporary display of the head of Alexander—with its accompanying inscriptions (label and text panel) in the Israel Museum—serves as a mnemonic to evoke the memory of the Holy Land in the Late Classical and Hellenistic periods and in its ancient past, in general.[458] The portrait of Alexander is contextualized and appropriated as a vehicle in a very public setting for communal remembrance of Israel's rich cultural heritage, as well as an indirect reminder that since antiquity the land of Israel has been home to people of different faiths, even if the invocation of Alexander in this context may be viewed as incomplete or misleading.

CONCLUSIONS

Why has Alexander been such a target for idealized heroization since the fourth century BCE? And why does Alexander—his life, deeds, and

---

[453] See pp. 64–66, this chapter.

[454] Also cited in the commentary for the head of Alexander on the museum's website: https://www.imj .org.il/en/collections/222840 (accessed December 3, 2018) and the main text panel for the section on Greeks, Romans, and Jews: https://www.imj.org.il/en/wings/archaeology/archaeology-land-israel (accessed December 3, 2018).

[455] *The Israel Museum* (2005, 245).

[456] Tarn (1933; 1948; 1956, esp. 116–17, 122, 148).

[457] Badian (1976, esp. 287–96).

[458] See Chapter 2, pp. 46–48 and Noreña (2016) for a discussion of imperial "memoryscapes" and statues and inscriptions used as mnemonic devices in the service of Hellenistic rule cults in the Roman Empire.

images—keep slipping through our fingers and generating more questions than definitive answers? Should Alexander the Great be viewed as an enlightened Greek ruler or a tyrannical barbarian (βάρβαρος) monarch from a non-Greek territory on the fringes of the ancient Greek world? As a military genius and explorer of unknown lands or an obsessive sociopath who couldn't stop himself from world domination? A visionary liberator of people under the yoke of the Persian empire or an invader of territories? A founder of over seventy cities or a strategic colonizer? A man of his time and culture or a sexual predator who took advantage of the ultimate power imbalance?[459] A promoter of religious syncretism and local expressions of faith or a propagandist and opportunist? Who is the real Alexander the Great?[460] Stewart answered this best by eloquently replying, mostly with reference to his portraiture: "The 'real' Alexander cannot be recovered, for description is always partial and subjective. Since we are forever suspended uneasily between this chimerical 'real' Alexander and his interpreters, every statement made about him becomes a question about his reception among those who encountered him. Since he exists only through his public, even the simplest of 'facts' about him are charged with their judgments and their beliefs."[461]

Cultural bias over the millennia has blurred our focus of Alexander. History loves a good story of passion, fame, fortune, and an early death (at 32 years, 10 months, to be exact). Alexander's successors and especially the Romans ran with the headlines of his brief but spectacular career and turned the Macedonian ruler into the paradigmatic cultural icon for the ages.[462] We do not hear his saga from the viewpoint of the peoples whose territories Alexander conquered, except for Josephus, the Jewish historian who, writing from his vantage point in Rome, had other "fish to fry," namely, the Samaritans, and who used the probable "fake news" about Alexander and the visit to the high priest in Jerusalem to push his particular bias. Obsessive and cruel characters like Caracalla appropriated the myth of Alexander and used it for their own purposes. The stories of Alexander's fame extended far and wide, from the "Alexander Romance" of the third or fourth centuries,[463] to the later Byzantine and Western medieval worlds, the Islamic world, and India.[464] The modern

---

[459] While engaging in a homosexual relationship with Hephaisteion, Alexander had a sexual relationship with one woman and married three wives, all Persian princesses, two possibly at the same wedding, one of whom murdered the other, and left behind two sons (Carney 2003).
[460] See Naiden (2018) for a recent iconoclastic view of the life of Alexander.
[461] Stewart (1993, 72).
[462] See especially Spencer (2002) on the Roman Alexander.
[463] For a discussion of "The Alexander Romance" see Koulakiotis (2006, 189–233).
[464] See many articles and catalogue entries in Hansen et al. (2009).

Greeks feel Alexander is theirs, a favorite son of proud heritage from the Greek region of Macedonia, where he was born and raised in Pella, worshiped at Dion, and where his royal ancestors and successors were buried at Aigai (Vergina).[465]

If we turn our focus back to the subject of our study of this important and enigmatic portrait head of Alexander from ancient Scythopolis, we might summarize what the object biography approach has revealed to us. Alexander became so popular in the Roman East, especially in the second and third centuries CE, that cities of the Decapolis, including Scythopolis, who prided themselves on their Greek heritage, could not resist claiming him as their founder. Various cities in other parts of the Roman Empire established Hellenistic ruler cults to the youthful hero-turned-god,[466] and if we are right in claiming this Alexander head as belonging to an image of veneration, a *synnaos theos* to the main deity (Zeus) in the Roman temple on its acropolis, Scythopolis might be added to those cities that worshiped Alexander. The mythical life and deeds of Alexander were projected on the life of Jesus in early Christian theology,[467] yet Alexander, the quintessential *kosmokrator* in the Roman period, was an anti-Christ who threatened Christian monotheistic beliefs in the Late Roman/Early Byzantine period. Thus, in the early Christian period in Scythopolis, his statue was mutilated and decapitated, and the demons that lived within the image of Alexander were exorcized. Though his memory lived on elsewhere in the Late Antique period, at Scythopolis Alexander was laid to rest in a watery cistern, to be brought back to "life" again with the discovery of this head in 1925 during the British Mandate. It was put on display in twentieth-century Palestine and eventually displayed in the IMJ as an ancient model in the modern state of Israel.

---

[465] Although now more than forty years old, a picture of the Greek view of Alexander and his legacy was presented in the exhibition catalogue for *Search for Alexander* (Yalouris et al. 1980). In that same year, Lane Fox (1980) presents something of the complexity of Alexander's character, the responses to Alexander by his contemporaries (387–97), as well as the legacy he left (412–41).

[466] See pp. 80–81, this chapter.

[467] Amitay (2010).

Appendix

Marble Provenance Investigation of the Head of Alexander the Great and a Hand Fragment from Ancient Nysa-Scythopolis, Israel

Dimitris Tambakopoulos and Yannis Maniatis

INTRODUCTION

Two marble samples taken from two sculpture fragments from the site of Beth Shean (ancient Nysa-Scythopolis), Israel, were sent to us in 2016 by Dr. Irene Bald Romano, with the permission of the Israel Museum, Jerusalem, in order to scientifically identify the marble source(s) used for their manufacture. The aims of this study are first, to provide evidence for the origin of the marble of the sculptures; second, to provide possible evidence for their date of manufacture, if the history of the quarry/quarries is known; and, third, to clarify whether the two fragments could belong to the same statue or not, since both pieces were excavated from the same context.[1]

SAMPLES AND TECHNIQUES

The first sample (Table A.1) comes from a life-sized left hand, S.968 (Figure A.1), currently in storage in the Rockefeller Museum, Jerusalem. It was taken from the broken wrist on June 14, 2016, by conservators at the Israel Museum. The second sample (see Table A.1) was taken from an over-life-sized male head, IAA 1931-7 (Figure A.2), currently on display in the Israel Museum, Jerusalem, and identified there as a Hellenistic portrait of Alexander the Great of the third to first century BCE. In Chapter 3, Irene Romano shows that the head likely belongs to a Roman statue of Alexander the Great, probably dating to the late second or very early third century CE.

The samples were analyzed using the following techniques:[2]

1. Measurement of maximum grain size (MGS) and most frequent grain size (MFS) under a stereoscopic microscope and qualitative examination of the marble's crystalline features,
2. Electron paramagnetic resonance spectroscopy (EPR), and
3. Stable isotope analysis of carbon and oxygen using isotope ratio mass spectrometry (IRMS).

Table A.1 Archaeological Details for the Two Samples

Sample	Object	Description
1	S.968, Rockefeller Museum, Jerusalem	Life-sized left hand from ancient Nysa-Scythopolis, Tel Beth Shean
2	IAA 1931-7, Israel Museum, Jerusalem	Over-life-sized male head, portrait of Alexander the Great, from ancient Nysa-Scythopolis, Tel Beth Shean

---

[1] See Chapter 3, pp. 71n69, 94–95, and Figure 3.5, for the details of their findspot in a cistern to the south of the Roman temple on the tel.
[2] Maniatis (2004).

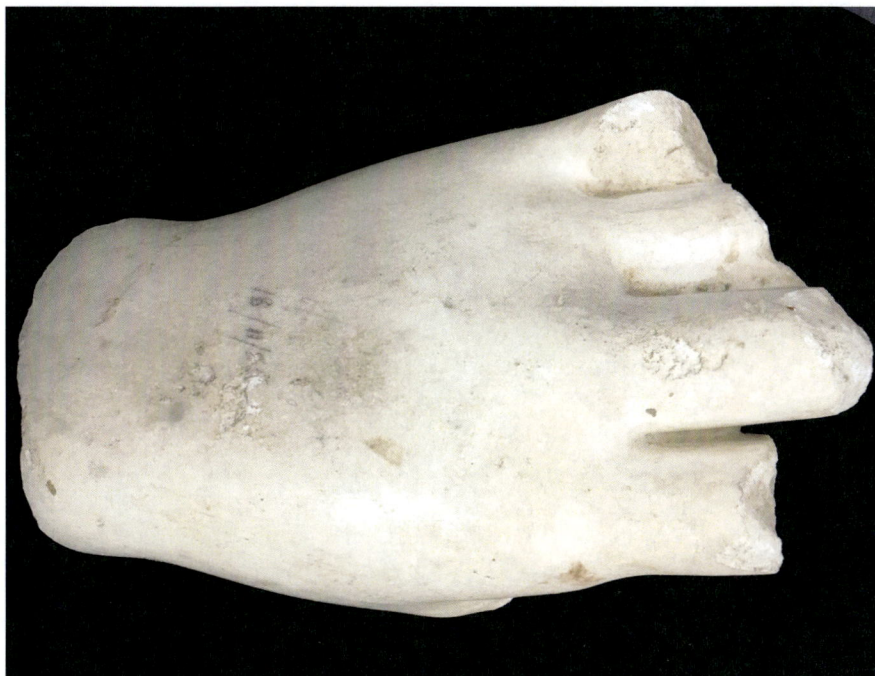

Figure A.1 Marble left hand, Tel Beth Shean. Rockefeller Archaeological Museum, Jerusalem S.968 (sample 1).

Photo: I. B. Romano. Collection of Israel Antiquities Authority. Reproduced with permission.

MGS MEASUREMENTS AND SAMPLE PREPARATION

The samples were examined using the optical microscope at the Laboratory of Archaeometry. The MGS, MFS, and the marble crystallization features were measured and assessed. Weathered layers of the samples were then mechanically removed, and a small clean sample of each was ground gently in an agate mortar and sieved to retrieve fractions between 63 and 180 μm for the EPR analysis. Fine aliquots, with particles less than 63 μm, were also collected during the sieving for the stable isotope analysis.

EPR ANALYSIS

As described in Polikreti and Maniatis,[3] three spectra were obtained for each powder sample at different operating conditions using an X-band

---

[3] Polikreti and Maniatis (2002).

Figure A.2 Over-life-sized male head from Tel Beth Shean, IAA 1931-7 (sample 2).

Photo: Hans Rupprecht Goette. Collection of Israel Antiquities Authority. Reproduced with permission.

EPR spectrometer (EPR BRUKER ER-200) operating at approximately 9.4 GHz. From these spectra we measured the height of the first peak of the Mn^{2+} sextet (parameter: Mn^{2+}) in relative units (r.u.), the percentage of dolomite in the sample from the low magnetic field peak of the sextet, the half-width at half maximum of the fifth "forbidden" peak in Gauss (parameter: width), the height of the peak with g = 14.25 in relative units (parameter: Fe^{3+}), whereas the type of marble (calcitic or dolomitic) is evaluated from the line shape of the spectrum.

STABLE ISOTOPE ANALYSIS

The isotopic ratios of carbon-13/carbon-12 (parameter $\delta^{13}C‰$) and oxygen-18/oxygen-16 (parameter $\delta^{18}O‰$) were measured at the Department for Applied Geosciences and Geophysics, University of Leoben, Austria, by Professor Walter Prochaska, using a ThermoFisher DELTA V mass spectrometer, connected online to a ThermoFisher GasBench II and a CTC Combi-Pal autosampler,[4] and compared to the international standard PDB (Pee Dee Belemnite).

DATABASES

The results of the analysis of the two samples are compared to the data for known ancient marble quarries from Greece, Turkey, Italy, Portugal, Spain, and Morocco accumulated over the last 25 years by measurements at the Laboratory of Archaeometry, National Centre of Scientific Research (NCSR) "Demokritos" in Athens[5] and by data published in the literature.[6] The EPR data from Attanasio (2003) and Attanasio et al. (2006) were integrated with our data by using as a theoretical standard the mean value of Mn^{2+} of all the Penteli samples from each laboratory, given the large number of the analyzed samples (161 for Attanasio and 277 for "Demokritos").

---

[4] Craig and Craig (1972), Allison et al. (1995), and Attanasio et al. (2006).
[5] Polikreti and Maniatis (2002), and Maniatis et al. (2012).
[6] Herz (1987), Gorgoni et al. (2002), Lazzarini and Antonelli (2003), Attanasio (2003), Attanasio et al. (2006), and Lazzarini and Malacrino (2010).

RESULTS

The results of all analyses for the two samples are listed in Table A.2. The optical examination showed that their marble is quite different. Although both are well crystallized and have a homoblastic texture, the marble of sample 1, from the hand (S.968), is fine-grained and of brilliant white color, but sample 2, from the head (IAA 1931-7), is medium-grained and whitish in color. In addition to grain sizes and color, there are significant differences in the Mn^{2+} and $\delta^{18}O$ parameters. These facts alone could suggest the marble samples are of different origin, but it is not that rare for quarries to exhibit such variations. Nevertheless, considering the diagram in Figure A.3, plotting the parameters $LnMn^{2+}$ versus LnMGS of the samples against the database of known ancient quarries, one can see that there are no common possible origins for the two samples, verifying the initial optical observation. In particular, the possible quarries for sample 1 are those of Mt. Pentelikon/Penteli and the quarries of Phrygia, Dokimeion (Afyon), and Altintas, whereas for sample 2 the possible quarries are Aphrodisias, Miletos, Proconnesos, Ephesos, Paros-Lakkoi, and Naxos-Apollon. From the diagram in Figure A.4, plotting

Table A.2 Results of the Optical, Isotopic, and EPR Analyses

Sample	Object	Marble	MGS (mm)	MFS (mm)	Mn^{2+} (r.u.)	Width (Gauss)	Fe^{3+} (r.u.)	$\delta^{18}O$ (‰)	$\delta^{13}C$ (‰)
1	S.968 (hand)	Brilliant white, fine-grained, very well crystal-lized, ho-moblastic	0.9	0.5–0.8	2061	2.39	7.44	–6.06	2.83
2	IAA 1931-7 (head)	Whitish, medium-grained, very well crystal-lized, ho-moblastic	2.0	1.0–1.5	601	2.40	11.91	-3.50	2.25

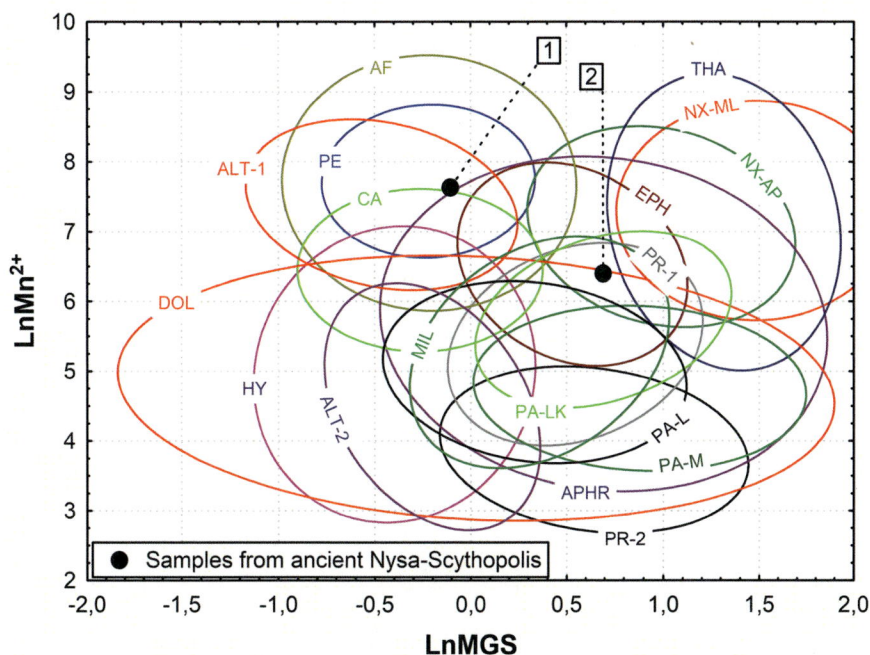

Figure A.3 Diagram of natural logarithm of the manganese (Mn^{2+}) versus the natural logarithm of the maximum grain size (MGS) for the two samples from ancient Nysa-Scythopolis and the ancient marble quarries of Dokimeion/Afyon (AF), Penteli (PE), Altintas (ALT-1, ALT-2), Carrara (CA), Hymettos (HY), Doliana (DOL), Aphrodisias (APHR), Ephesos (EPH), Miletos (MIL), Proconnesos (PR-1, PR-2), Paros (PA-LK, PA-L, PA-M), Thasos (THA), and Naxos (NX-AP, NX-ML).

Diagram: Tambakopoulos and Maniatis.

the isotopic signature of the samples against the isotopic fields of known ancient quarries, the possible quarries for sample 1 remain the same, that is, Penteli or Afyon/Altintas, but for sample 2, the possibilities are narrowed to Aphrodisias, Miletos, and Proconnesos.

To further narrow the possible quarries for each sample we performed discriminant analysis with StatSoft Statistica v.8.0.360, using more than two parameters for the possible quarries and the samples. The results are presented in the diagrams of Figures A.5 and A.6. Sample 1 falls in the middle of the Penteli distribution, but field samples from Altintas and Afyon are also close (see Figure A.5). The analysis returns the following probabilities for the origin of this sample: 95% for Penteli, 3% for Afyon, and 2% for Altintas.

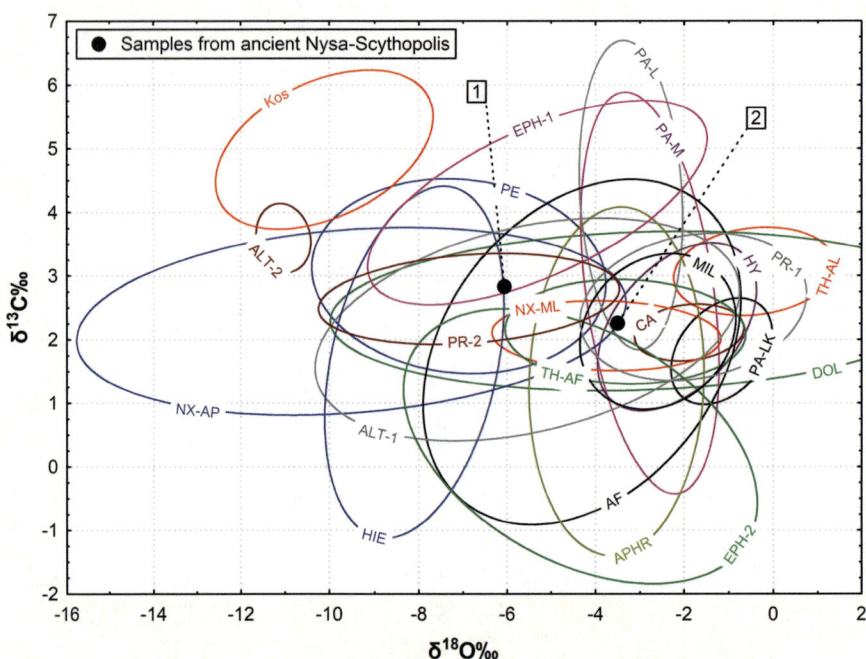

Figure A.4 Diagram of δ¹³C‰ versus δ¹⁸O‰ for the two samples from ancient Nysa-Scythopolis and the ancient marble quarries of Dokimeion/Afyon (AF), Penteli (PE), Altintas (ALT-1, ALT-2), Carrara (CA), Hymettos (HY), Doliana (DOL), Aphrodisias (APHR), Ephesos (EPH-1, EPH-2), Miletos (MIL), Proconnesos (PR-1, PR-2), Paros (PA-LK, PA-L, PA-M), Thasos (TH-AL, TH-AF), Naxos (NX-AP, NX-ML), Kos and Hierapolis (HIE).

Diagram: Tambakopoulos and Maniatis.

Sample 2, treated in the same way, falls practically outside the Proconnesos field point distribution, but inside the Aphrodisias and Miletos distributions (see Figure A.6). The calculated probabilities for sample 2 are: 61% for Aphrodisias, 33% for Miletos, and 6% for Proconnesos.

DISCUSSION

With the combined use of three techniques and statistical analysis, the marble provenance for the two archaeological objects from ancient Nysa-Scythopolis was narrowed down to three possible origins with certain probabilities assigned to each option (Table A.3).

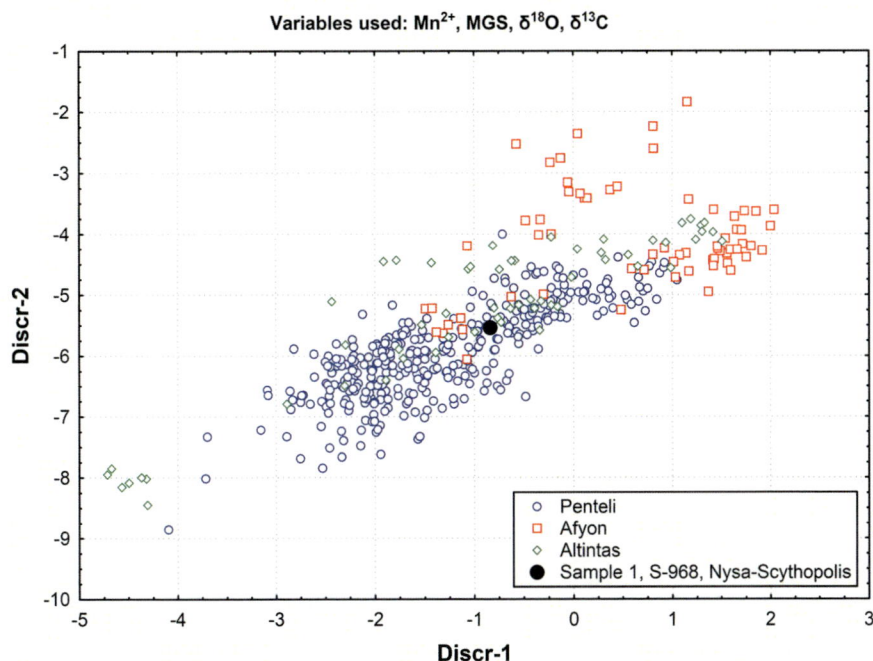

Figure A.5 Diagram of variables derived from discriminant analysis for sample 1 and its three possible quarries: Penteli, Afyon, and Altintas.

Diagram: Tambakopoulos and Maniatis.

MARBLE PROVENANCE

The marble of sample 1, an over-life-sized hand (S.968), comes almost undoubtedly from Penteli. Its crystallinity characteristics; fine-grained, well-crystallized, and homoblastic texture; as well as its brilliant-white color validate this provenance. According to its spectroscopic and isotopic parameters, there is a very small probability (5%) that it is made of marble from Afyon/Altintas in Phrygia, but the marble's crystallinity practically excludes this. The results for sample 2, an over-life-sized male head (IAA 1931-7), point to an origin of Aphrodisias, but not as confidently as the determination of Penteli as the origin for sample 1. Nevertheless, its marble characteristics—medium-grained whitish marble with very good crystallization, well-defined grains with mostly straight borders with no intermediate material in the whole fracture of the sample—strengthen further the choice of Aphrodisias as the best option. In fact, the marble of Proconnesos is quite different and can essentially be

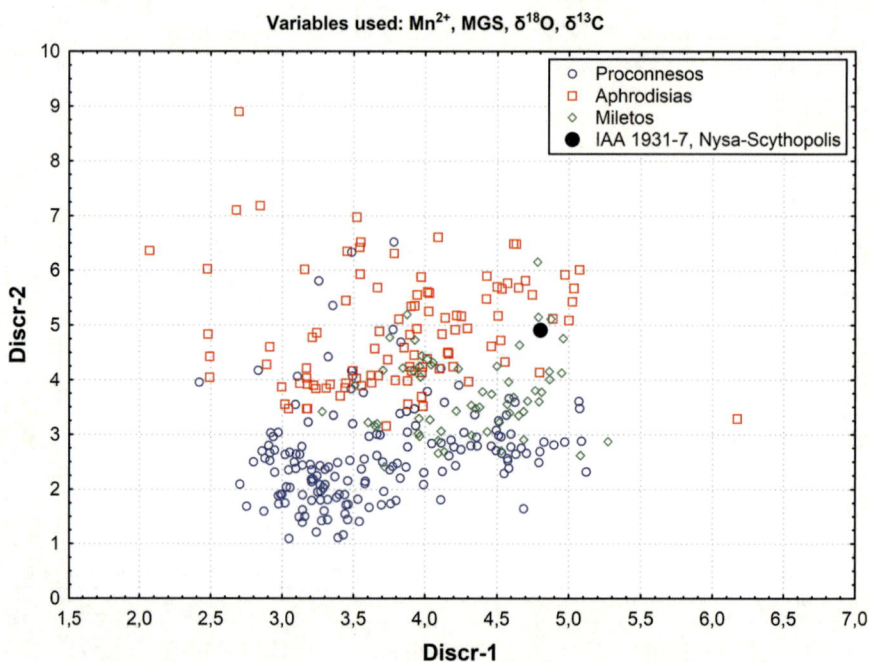

Figure A.6 Diagram of variables derived from discriminant analysis for sample 2 and its three possible quarries: Aphrodisias, Miletos, and Proconnesos.

Diagram: Tambakopoulos and Maniatis.

Table A.3 Marble Provenance for the Two Samples of Ancient Nysa-Scythopolis

Sample	Object	Arch. Description	Marble Provenance
1	S.968, Rockefeller Museum, Jerusalem	Life-sized left hand from ancient Nysa-Scythopolis, Tel Beth Shean.	**Penteli (95%)** or Dokimeion/Altintas (5%)
2	IAA 1931-7, Israel Museum, Jerusalem	Over-life-sized male head, Hellenistic portrait of Alexander the Great from ancient Nysa-Scythopolis, Tel Beth Shean.	**Aphrodisias (61%)**, Miletos (33%), or Proconnesos (6%)

excluded entirely. The marble from Miletos is described by Attanasio, et al.[7] as gray or of various shades of gray and rarely white, and basically of local use. This could further reduce the Miletos possibility, but not entirely dismiss it. Therefore, the most probable provenance of the over-life-sized male head in the Israel Museum (IAA 1931-7) is Aphrodisias, but with a limited probability of Miletos as an alternative provenance.

DATING SUGGESTIONS

Acknowledging Aphrodisias as the most likely provenance of the marble head, a few interesting clues about its dating emerge. Although Aphrodisian marble was used locally from pre-Hellenistic and early Hellenistic times, it was largely exploited only in and after the later first century BCE in Aphrodisias for the construction of the Temple of Aphrodite and other buildings in the city.[8] Therefore, it is reasonable to suggest that the marble of Aphrodisias was exported for use outside of Aphrodisias after that. Consequently, a dating later than the first century BCE for the head would be more realistic than the third to first century BCE date suggested by various sources.[9] Unfortunately, a dating suggestion for the hand cannot be provided based on the use of the quarry of origin, since the marble of Penteli was widely used from classical times and throughout antiquity. However, it was during the Roman period when Pentelic marble was widely exported outside of Greece and throughout the Mediterranean.[10]

ONE OR TWO STATUES?

Given the results just described, it is obvious that the head and the hand are not made of marble from the same origin. This strongly suggests that they belong to different statues, although there are cases in which newer additions of statue parts were made of different types of marble.[11] The difference in the scale of the two fragments (life-sized hand versus over-

---

[7] Attanasio et al. (2006).

[8] Long (2012).

[9] See Chapter 3, pp. 92, 120.

[10] Bernard (2010, Republican period in Rome), Romano et al. (2012, Domitianic Rome), Gaggadis-Robin et al. (2015, fourth-century CE sarcophagi from Vienne, France), and M. L. Fischer et al. (2018, 453–54, a second- to third-century CE (?) mutilated statue from ancient Apollonia in Israel).

[11] Darblade-Audoin et al. (2015).

life-sized head) would also suggest, however, that it is unlikely they belong to the same statue.[12]

---

[12] See Chapter 3, hand: pp. 99–101; head: pp. 108–22.

Bibliography

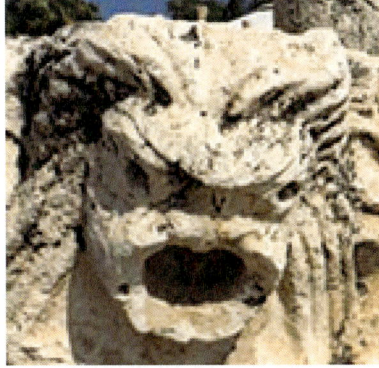

Abbe, M. B. "Recent Research on the Painting and Gilding of Roman Marble Statuary at Aphrodisias." In *Circumlitio: The Polychromy of Antique and Medieval Sculpture*, edited by V. Brinkman, O. Primavesi, and M. Hollein, 277–89. Frankfurt: Hirmer, 2010.

———. "Polychromy." In *The Oxford Handbook of Roman Sculpture*, edited by E. A. Friedland, M. G. Sobocinski, and E. K. Gazda, 173–88. Oxford: Oxford University Press, 2015.

Abel, F.-M. *Histoire de la Palestine depuis la conquête d'Alexandre jusqu'à l'invasion arabe.* Vol. 1: *De la conquête d'Alexandre jusqu'à la guerre juive.* Paris: Gabalda, 1952.

Akçay-Güven, B. "A Reworked Group of Emperor Statues from the Theatre of Perge." In *Sculpture in Roman Asia Minor*, edited by M. Aurenhammer, 365–76. Proceedings of the International Conference at Selçuk, 1st–3rd October 2013. Österreichisches Archäologisches Institut Sonderschriften Band 56. Wein: Holzhausen, 2018.

Al-Bashaireh, K. "Archaeometric Characterization and Provenance Determination of Sculptures and Architectural Elements from Gerasa, Jordan." *Applied Physics A* 124 (2018): 135–38.

Alcock, S. E. "The Reconfiguration of Memory in the Eastern Roman Empire." In *Empires: Perspectives from Archaeology and History*, edited by S. E. Alcock, T. D'Altroy, C. Sinopoli, and K. Morrison, 323–50. Cambridge, UK: Cambridge University Press, 2001.

———. *Archaeologies of the Greek Past: Landscape, Monuments and Memories*. Cambridge, UK: Cambridge University Press, 2002.

———. "Kaleidoscopes and the Spinning of Memory in the Eastern Roman Empire." In *Cultural Memories in the Roman Empire*, edited by K. Galinsky and K. Lapatin, 24–32. Los Angeles: Getty Publications, 2016.

Allison, C. E., R. J. Francey, and H. A. J. Meijer. "Recommendations for the Reporting of Stable Isotope Measurements of Carbon and Oxygen in CO2 Gas." In *Reference and Intercomparison Materials for Stable Isotopes of Light Elements, IAEA-TECDOC 825*, 155–62. Vienna: International Atomic Energy Agency, 1995.

Alscher, L. *Griechische Plastik*, vol. 4. Berlin: Deutscher Verlag der Wissenschaften, 1957.

Amelung, W., H. M. Cotton, W. Eck, A. Ecker, B. Isaac, A. Kushner-Stein, H. Misgave, J. Price, P. Weiss, and A. Yardeni, eds. *Corpus Inscriptionum Iudaeae/Palaestinae*. Vol. IV: *Iudaea/Idumaea, Part 2*, 3325–978. Berlin: De Gruyter, 2018.

Amitai-Preiss, N. "The Coins." In *Excavations at Tel Beth-Shean, 1989–1996. Vol. I: From the Late Bronze Age IIB to the Medieval Period*, edited by A. Mazar and N. Amitai-Preiss, 607–15. Jerusalem: Israel Exploration Society/Institute of Archaeology, The Hebrew University of Jerusalem, 2006.

Amitay, O. *From Alexander to Jesus*. Berkeley: University of California Press, 2010.

Andrade, N. J. *Syrian Identity in the Greco-Roman World*. Cambridge, UK: Cambridge University Press, 2013.

Aperghis, G. G. *The Seleukid Royal Economy: The Finances and Financial Administration of the Seleukid Empire*. Cambridge, UK: Cambridge University Press, 2004.

"Aphrodisias Excavations Project." Oxford: University of Oxford, 2019. http://aphrodisias.classics.ox.ac.uk/index.html (accessed January 15, 2023).

Applebaum, S. *Judea in Hellenistic and Roman Times*. Leiden: Brill, 1989.

Arav, R. "The Round Church at Beth-Shan." *Liber Annuus* 39 (1989): 189–97.

Ariel, D. T. "Two Rhodian Amphoras." *AEJ* 38 (1988): 31–35.

―――. "Stamped Amphora Handles from Bet-She'an: Evidence for the Urban Development of the City in the Hellenistic Period." In *Proceedings of the Danish Institute at Athens 5: Transport Amphorae and Trade in the Eastern Mediterranean, International Colloquium 26 September 2002*, edited by J. Lund and J. Eiring, 23–30. Aarhus: Aarhus University Press, 2004.

―――. "The Stamped Amphora Handles." In *Excavations at Tel Beth-Shean 1989–1996.* Vol. 1: *From the Late Bronze Age IIB to the Medieval Period*, edited by E. Mazar and N. Amitai-Preiss, 594–606. Jerusalem: Israel Exploration Society/The Hebrew University of Jerusalem, 2006.

Arnold-Biucchi, C. *Alexander's Coins and Alexander's Image.* Cambridge, MA: Harvard University Art Museums, 2006.

Arubas, B. "Excursus: The Impact of Town Planning at Scythopolis on the Topography of Tel Beth-Shean: A New Understanding of its Fortifications and Status." In *Excavations at Tel Beth-Shean 1989–1996.* Vol. 1: *From the Late Bronze Age IIB to the Medieval Period*, edited by E. Mazar, 48–58. Jerusalem: Israel Exploration Society/The Hebrew University of Jerusalem, 2006.

Atrash, W. "Bet She'an, El-Muntar el Abyad." *Hadashot Arkheologiyot: Excavations and Surveys in Israel* 129 (2017): 1–6.

Atrash, W., and J. A. Overman. "Monumentalizing Nysa-Scythopolis from the Late 1st – 2nd Century AD." In *Cities, Monuments and Objects in the Roman and Byzantine Levant: Studies in Honour of Gabi Mazor*, edited by W. Atrash, A. Overman, and P. Gendelman, 16–32. Oxford: Archaeopress, 2022.

Attanasio, D. *Ancient White Marbles: Analysis and identification by Paramagnetic Resonance Spectroscopy.* Rome: L'Erma di Bretschneider, 2003.

Attanasio, D., M. Brilli, and N. Ogle. *The Isotopic Signature of Classical Marbles.* Rome: L'Erma di Bretschneider, 2006.

Attanasio, D., M. Bruno, and C. Landwehr. "I marmi scultorei di Caesarea Mauretaniae (Cherchel, Algeria)." In *L'Africa romana. Trasformazione dei paesaggi del potere nell'Africa settentrionale fino alla fine del mondo antico. Atti del XIX convegno di studio. Sassari 16–19 dicembre 2010*, edited by M. B. Cocco, A. Gavini, and A. Ibba, 527–40. Rome: Carocci, 2012.

Attanasio, D., M. Bruno, W. Prochaska, and A. B. Yavuz. "Aphrodisian Marble from the Göktepe Quarries: The Little Barbarians, Roman Copies from the Attalid Dedication in Athens." *Papers of the British School at Rome* 80 (2012): 65–87.

———. "The Marble of Roman Imperial Portraits." In *ASMOSIA XI, Interdisciplinary Studies of Ancient Stone, Proceedings of the Eleventh International Conference of ASMOSIA, Split, 18–22 May 2015*, edited by D. Matetić Poljak and K. Marasović, 185–94. Split: University of Split, 2018.

Attanasio, D., M. Bruno, and A. B. Yavuz. "Quarries in the Region of Aphrodisias: The Black and White Marbles of Göktepe (Muğla)." *JRA* 22 (2009): 312–48.

Attanasio, D., M. Bruno, A. B. Yavuz, and H. Elçi. "Aphrodisias and the Newly Discovered Quarries at Göktepe." In *Roman Portraits at Aphrodisias*, edited by R. Smith and J. Lenaghan, 217–27. Istanbul: Yapı Kredi Yayınları, 2008.

Augé, C. "Dionysos in Peripheria Orientali." *LIMC III*, 1 (1986): 514–31.

Aulock, H. von. *Münzen und Städte Pisidiens II. IstMitt Beih* 22. Tübingen: E. Wasmuth, 1979.

Avi-Yonah, M. "Mount Carmel and the God of Baalbek." *IEJ* 2 (1952): 118–24.

———. "Scythopolis." *IEJ* 12 (1962): 123–34.

———. *The Holy Land*. New York: Holt, Rinehart and Winston, 1973.

Badian, E. "Some Recent Interpretations of Alexander." In *Alexandre le Grand, image et réalité*. (Entretiens Hardt XXII), edited by O. Reverdin, 279–303. Geneva/Vandoeuvres: Fondation Hardt, 1976.

Bagnani, G. "Hellenistic Sculpture from Cyrene." *JHS* 41, no. 2 (1921): 232–46.

Baharal, D. "Portraits of the Emperor L. Septimius Severus (193–211 AD) as an Expression of his Propaganda." *Latomus* 48, no. 3 (1989): 566–80.

———. "Caracalla and Alexander the Great: A Reappraisal." *Studies in Latin Literature and Roman History* VII. Brussels: *Latomus*, 1994: 524–67.

———. *Victory of Propaganda: The Dynastic Aspect of the Imperial Propaganda of the Severi, the Literary and Archaeological Evidence AD 193–235*. BAR International Series, vol. 657. Oxford: *Tempvs Reparatvm*, 1996.

Bakirtsis, X. "Περί του Συγκροτήματος της Αγοράς της Θεσσαλονίκης." In *Archaia Makedonia II: Papers Read at the Second International*

Symposium Held in Thessaloniki 19–24 August 1973. Thessaloniki: Institute for Balkan Studies, 1977: 257–269.

Barkay, R. *The Coinage of Nysa-Scythopolis (Beth Shean)*. Jerusalem: Israel Numismatic Society, 2003.

Bar-Kochva, B. *Pseudo-Hecataeus, "On the Jews": Legitimizing the Jewish Diaspora*. Berkeley: University of California Press, 1997.

Bar-Nathan, R., and W. Atrash. *Bet She'an*. Vol. 2: *Baysan. The Theater Pottery Workshop* (*IAA Reports* 48). Jerusalem: Israel Antiquities Authority, 2011.

Bar-Nathan, R., and F. Snyder. "Is the Opus Reticulatum Building at Banias a Palace of Herod the Great? New Insights after Analyzing its Opus Sectile Floor." In *Between the Sea and the Desert: On Kings, Nomads, Cities and Monks: Essays in Honor of Joseph Patrich*, edited by O. Peleg-Barkat, J. Ashkenazi, U. Leibner, M. Aviam, and R. Talgam, 23–40. Jerusalem: Kinneret Institute for Galilean Archaeology, 2019.

Barsky, V. "Mobile Truth: The Israel Museum, Jerusalem, 1965/2010." *Third Text* 27, no. 4 (2013): 485–501. https://doi.org/10.1080/09528822.2013.810888 (accessed December 3, 2018).

Bassett, S. "Excellent Offerings": The Lausos Collection in Constantinople." *The Art Bulletin* 82, no. 1 (2000): 6–25.

———. *The Urban Image of Late Antique Constantinople*. Cambridge, UK: Cambridge University Press, 2004.

Beaujeu, J. *La religion romaine à l'apogée de l'Empire. I. La politique religieuse des Antonins (96–192)*. Paris: Société d'édition les belles lettres, 1955.

Bekker, I., ed. *Georgius Cedrenus: Ioannis Scylitzae ope*, Vol 1. Bonn: Weber, 1838.

Belayche, N. *Judaea-Palaestina: The Pagan Cults in Roman Palestine (Second to Fourth Century)*. Tübingen: Mohr Siebeck, 2001.

———. "Foundation Myths in Roman Palestine. Traditions and Reworkings." In *Ethnic Constructs in Antiquity: The Role of Power and Tradition*, edited by T. Derks and N. Roymans, 167–88. Amsterdam: Amsterdam University Press, 2009a.

———. "'Languages' and Religion in Second- to Fourth-Century Palestine: In Search of the Impact of Rome." In *From Hellenism to Islam: Cultural and Linguistic Change in the Roman Near East*, edited by H. M. Cotton, R. G. Hoyland, J. J. Price, and D. J. Wasserstein, 177–202. Cambridge, UK: Cambridge University Press, 2009b.

———. "Cults in Contexts in the Hellenistic and Roman Southern Levant: The Challenge of Cult Places." In *Expressions of Cult in the Southern*

Levant in the Greco-Roman Period: Manifestations in Text and Material Culture, edited by O. Tal and Z. Weiss, 3–21. Turnhout: Brepolis, 2017.

———. "Religions de Rome et du monde romain." *Annuaire de l'école pratique des hautes études (EPHE), Section des sciences religieuses* 126 (2019): 139–48. http://journals.openedition.org/asr/2612 (accessed March 14, 2020).

Ben Shahar, M. "Jews, Samaritans and Alexander: Facts and Fictions in Jewish Stories on the Meeting of Alexander and the High Priest." *Brill's Companion to the Reception of Alexander the Great* (Brill's Companions to Classical Studies Online IV, vol. 14), 403–26. Leiden: Brill, 2018.

Ben-Yehuda, N. "The Exquisite Linen of Beth Shean." In *Papers of Ars Textrina International Textiles Conference*, 21–22 July 2005, edited by B. G. Thomas, 7–14. Leeds: University of Leeds, 2005.

Berger, E. "Ein neues Porträt Alexanders des Grossen." *Antike Kunst* 14, no. 2 (1971): 139–44.

Bergmann, M. *Die Strahlen der Herrscher. Theomorphes Herrscherbild und politische Symbolik im Hellenismus und in der römischen Kaizerzeit.* Mainz: von Zabern, 1998.

Bernard, S. "Pentelic Marble in Architecture at Rome and the Republican Marble Trade." *Journal of Roman Archaeology* 23, no. 1 (2010): 35–54.

Bernhardt, J. C. *Die jüdische Revolution. Untersuchungen zu Ursachen, Verlauf und Folgen der hasmonäischen Erhebung. KLIO. Beiträge zur Alten Geschichte.* Beihefte, neue Folge, Band 22. Berlin: De Gruyter, 2017.

Bianchi, R. S. "The Nahman Alexander." *JARCE* 43 (2007): 29–42.

———. "The Princeton Portrait of Alexander the Great." *Record of the Art Museum, Princeton University* 69 (2010): 22–29.

Bieber, M. "The Portraits of Alexander the Great." *Proceedings of the American Philosophical Society* 93, no. 5 (1949): 373–427.

———. *Alexander the Great in Greek and Roman Art.* Chicago: Argonaut, 1964.

Bietenhard, H. "Die syrische Dekapolis von Pompeius bis Traian." *ANRW* II, no. 8. Berlin: de Gruyter, 1977: 220–61.

Bikerman, E. *Institutions des Séleucides.* Paris: Librairie Orientaliste Paul Geuthner, 1938.

Blume, C. *Polychromie hellenistischer Skulptur: Ausführung, Instandhaltung und Botschaften.* Petersberg: Michael Imhof Verlag, 2015.

Boardman, J. *Alexander the Great: From His Death to the Present Day.* Princeton, NJ: Princeton University Press, 2019.

———. *The Archaeology of Nostalgia: How the Greeks Re-created Their Mythical Past.* London: Thames and Hudson, 2002.

Bosch-Puche, F. "Alexander the Great's Egyptian Names in the Barque Shrine at Luxor Temple." In *Alexander the Great and Egypt History, Art, Tradition*, edited by V. Grieb, K. Nawotka, and A. Wojciechowska, 55–87, Philippika 74. Wiesbaden: Harrassowitz Verlag, 2014.

Bothmer, D. von, and J. Mertens. *The Search for Alexander: Supplement to the Catalogue.* New York: Metropolitan Museum of Art, 1982.

Bourgeois, B., and P. Jockey. "La dorure des marbres grecs. Nouvelle enquê te sur la sculpture hellénistique de Délos." *Journal des Savants* Juillet–Décembre (2005): 253–316.

Bowersock, G.W. *Roman Arabia.* Cambridge, MA: Harvard University Press, 1983.

———. *Hellenism in Late Antiquity.* Ann Arbor: University of Michigan Press, 1990.

Bricault, L. "A Statuette of Hermanubis in the J. Paul Getty Museum." *Getty Research Journal* 10 (2018): 225–31.

Brinkmann, V., R. Dreyfus, U. Koch-Brinkmann, eds. *Gods in Color: Polychromy in the Ancient World.* Munich: Fine Arts Museum of San Francisco/Legion of Honor, 2017.

Britt, K., and R. Boustan. *The Elephant Mosaic Panel in the Synagogue at Huqoq: Official Publication and Initial Interpretations.* JRA Supplement 106. Portsmouth, RI, 2017.

Brown, A. R. "Crosses, Noses, Walls, and Wells: Christianity and the Fate of Sculpture in Late Antique Corinth." In *The Afterlife of Greek and Roman Sculpture: Late Antique Responses and Practices* , edited by T. M. Kristensen and L. Stirling, 150–76. Ann Arbor: University of Michigan Press, 2016.

———. *Corinth in Late Antiquity: A Greek, Roman and Christian City.* London/New York: Taurus, 2018.

Bruno, M., H. Elçi, A. B. Yavuz, and D. Attanasio. "Unknown Ancient Marble Quarries of Western Asia Minor." In *Interdisciplinary Studies on Ancient Stone. Proceedings of the IX ASMOSIA Conference (Tarragona 2009)*, edited by A. Gutierrez Garcia-M., P. Lapuente Mercadal, and I. Roda de Llanza, 562–72.Tarragona: Institut Català d'Arqueologia Clàssica, 2012.

Burkhardt, N. "The Reuse of Ancient Sculpture in the Urban Spaces of Late Antique Athens." In *The Afterlife of Greek and Roman Sculpture:*

Late Antique Responses and Practices, edited by T. M. Kristensen and L. Stirling, 118–49. Ann Arbor: University of Michigan Press, 2016.

Burrell, B. *Neokoroi: Greek Cities and Roman Emperors*. Leiden: Brill, 2004.

Buschor, E. *Das hellenistische Bildnis*, 2nd ed. Munich: Beck, 1971.

Butcher, K. *Roman Syria and the Near East*. London: British Museum Press, 2003.

Cadario, M. "The Image of the Rulers and the Role of the Military Costume in the Near East from the Hellenistic to the Roman Age." In *Imperial Connections. Interactions and Expansion from Assyria to the Roman Period. Proceedings of the 5th "Broadening Horizons" Conference (Udine 5–8 June 2017)*, edited by K. Gavagnin and R. Palermo, 231–58. Trieste: West and East Monografie 3, 2020.

Cahill, N., and C. H. Greenewalt. "The Sanctuary of Artemis at Sardis: Preliminary Report, 2002–2012." *AJA* 120 (2016): 473–509.

Canepa, M. "Royal Images of Persian Kingship and Persian Identity in Post-Achaemenid Western Asia." In *Persianism in Antiquity*, edited by R. Strootman and M. J. Versluys, 201–22. Stuttgart: Franz Steiner Verlag, 2017.

Carney, E. D. "Women in Alexander's Court." In *Brill's Companion to Alexander the Great*, edited by J. Roisman, 227–52. Leiden: Brill, 2003.

Castritius, H. "Caracalla, Augustus und Alexander?" In *Zu Alexander d. Gr. Festschrift G. Wirth zum 60. Geburtstag am 9.12.86.*, edited by W. Will, 879–84. Amsterdam: Verlag A.M. Hakkert, 1988.

Chankowski, A.S. "Les cultes des souverains hellénistiques après la disparition des dynasties: Formes de survie et d'extinction d'une institution dans un context civique." In *Des rois au prince, Pratiques du pouvoir monarchique dans l'Orient hellénistique et romain (IVe siècle avant J.-C.-IIe siècle après J.-C.)*, edited by I. Savalli-Lestrade and I. Cogitore. *Topoi* 17, no. 2 (2011): 271–80.

Chrubasik, B. *Kings and Usurpers in the Seleukid Empire: The Men Who Would Be King*. Oxford: Oxford University Press, 2016.

———. "From Pre-Makkabaean Judaea to Hekatomnid Karia and Back Again." In *Hellenism and the Local Communities of the Eastern Mediterranean. 400 BCE-250 CE*, edited by B. Chrubasik and D. King, 83–109. Oxford: Oxford University Press, 2017.

Chrubasik, B., and D. King, eds. *Hellenism and the Local Communities of the Eastern Mediterranean. 400 BCE-250 CE*. Oxford: Oxford University Press, 2017.

Clairmont, C. W. *Die Bildnisse des Antinoos: ein Beitrag zur Porträtplastik unter Kaiser Hadrian*. Bibliotheca Helvetica Romana 6. Rome: Schweizerisches Institut, 1966.

Claridge, A. "Ancient Techniques of Making Joins in Marble Statuary." In *Marble: Art Historical and Scientific Perspectives on Ancient Sculpture*, edited by M. True and J. Podany, 135–62. Papers delivered at a symposium organized by the Departments of Antiquities and Conservation and held at the J. P. Getty Museum April 28–30, 1988. Malibu: J. Paul Getty Museum, 1990.

Cohen, G. M. *The Hellenistic Settlements in Europe, the Islands and Asia Minor*. Berkeley: University of California Press, 1995.

———. "The Letters IAAΓ on Some Coins of Abila and Gadara." *American Journal of Numismatics* 10 (1998): 95–102.

———. *The Hellenistic Settlements in Syria, the Red Sea Basin, and North Africa*. Berkeley, Los Angeles, and London: University of California Press, 2006.

———. "Did Alexander the Great Visit Jerusalem?" Unpublished text from lecture at University of Arizona, March 26, 2012.

Comstock, M. B., and C. C. Vermeule. *Sculpture in Stone: The Greek, Roman and Etruscan Collections*. Boston: Museum of Fine Arts, 1976.

———. *Sculpture in Stone and Bronze: Additions to the Collections of Greek, Etruscan, and Roman Art 1971–1988*. Boston: Museum of Fine Arts, 1988.

"The Construction of the New Supreme Court Building." The State of Israel. The Supreme Authority, 2017. https://supreme.court.gov.il/sites/en/Pages/HistoricalBG.aspx (accessed November 15, 2018).

Cotton, H. M., and M. Wörrle. "Seleukos IV to Heliodoros: A New Dossier of Royal Correspondence from Israel." *ZPE* 159 (2007): 191–205.

Craig, H., and V. Craig. "Greek Marbles: Determination of Provenance by Isotopic Analysis." *Science* 176, no. 4033 (1972): 401–3.

Crowfoot, J. W., G. M. Crowfoot, and K. M. Kenyon. *Samaria-Sebaste III. The Objects from Samaria*. London: Palestine Exploration Fund, 1957.

Daebritz, R. "Herakleides Lembos." In *RE* VIII, 1, edited by W. Kroll, 488–91. Stuttgart: J. B. Metzlersche Verlagsbuchhandlung, 1912.

Daehner, J., and K. Lapatin. *Power and Pathos: Bronze Sculpture of the Hellenistic World*. Los Angeles: J. Paul Getty Museum, 2015.

Dahmen, K. *The Legend of Alexander the Great on Greek and Roman Coins*. London: Routledge, 2007.

————. "Alexander in Gold and Silver: Reassessing Third Century A.D. Medallions from Aboukir and Tarsos." *American Journal of Numismatics* 20, 2008: 493–546.

————. *Medallions from Aboukir in the Calouste Gulbenkian Museum.* Lisbon: Calouste Gulbenkian Foundation, 2013.

Danforth, L. M. "Alexander the Great and the Macedonian Conflict." In *Brill's Companion to Alexander the Great*, edited by J. Roisman, 347–64. Leiden: Brill, 2003.

Darblade-Audoin, M. P., D. Tambakopoulos, P. Vassiliou, and Y. Maniatis. "Provenance Investigation of Roman Marble Sculptures from the Gallo-Roman Museum of Lyon." In *Interdisciplinary Studies on Ancient Stone, ASMOSIA X, Proceedings of the Tenth International Conference of ASMOSIA*, Rome, Italy, 21–26 May 2012, edited by P. Pensabene and E. Gasparini, 503–12. Rome: L'Erma di Bretschneider, 2015.

Dattari, G. *Catalogo completo della collezione Dattari. Numi Augg. Alexandrini.* Cairo: Forni Editore Bologna, 1901; reprinted Trieste: Giulio Bernardi, 1999.

Dayagi-Mendels, M., and S. Rozenberg, eds. *Chronicles of the Land: Archaeology in The Israel Museum Jerusalem*, 3rd ed. Jerusalem: Israel Museum Jerusalem, 2013.

Debord, P. "Le culte royal chez les Séleucides." *Pallas* 62 (2003): 281–308.

Del Chiaro, M. A. *Classical Art: Sculpture.* Santa Barbara: Santa Barbara Museum of Art, 1984.

Despinis, G. I. *Συμβολὴ στὴ μελέτη τοῦ ἔργου τοῦ Ἀγορακρίτου.* Athens: Hermes, 1971.

————. *Ἀκρόλιθα. ArchDelt Demosieumata* 21. Athens: Greek Ministry of Culture, 1975.

————. "Το Αντίγραφο της Αθηνάς Medici του Μουσείου Θεσσαλονίκης." In *Archaia Makedonia II: Papers Read at the Second International Symposium Held in Thessaloniki 19–24 August 1973*, 95–102. Thessaloniki: Institute for Balkan Studies, 1977.

————. "Neues zu einem alten Fund." *AM* 109 (1994): 173–98.

————. "Ακρόλιθα αγάλματα των ρωμαϊκών χρόνων." In *Κλασική παράδοση και νεωτερικά στοιχεία στην πλαστική της ρωμαϊκής Ελλάδας, Thessaloniki, 7–9 May 2009*, edited by T. Stefanidou-Tiveriou, P. Karanastasi, and D. Damaskos, 19–34. Thessaloniki: University Studio Press, 2012.

Despinis, G. I., T. Stefanidou-Tiveriou, and E. Voutiras. *Catalogue of Sculpture in the Archaeological Museum of Thessaloniki*, vol. 1. Thessaloniki: Cultural Foundation of National Bank of Greece, 1997.

Dindorf, W., ed. *Georgius Syncellus et Nicephorus Cp., Corpus Scriptorum Historiae Byzantinae*. Bonn: Weber, 1829.

Dirven, L. "The Imperial Cult in the Cities of the Decapolis, Caesarea Maritima and Palmyra: A Note on the Development of Imperial Cults in the Roman Near East." *ARAM* 23 (2011): 141–56.

Di Segni, L. "A Dated Inscription from Beth Shean and the Cult of Dionysos Ktistes in Roman Scythopolis." *Scripta Classica Israelica* 16 (1997): 139–61.

Di Segni, L., and B. Y. Arubas. "An Old-New Inscription from Beth Shean." In *Man Near a Roman Arch: Studies Presented to Prof. Yoram Tsafrir*, edited by L. Di Segni, Y. Hirshfeld, J. Patrich, and R. Talgam, 115–124. Jerusalem: Israel Exploration Society, 2009.

Di Segni, L., G. Foerster, and Y. Tsafrir. "A Decorated Altar Dedicated to Dionysos, the 'Founder', from Bet Shean (Scythopolis)" [Hebrew]. *ErIsr* 25 (1996): 336–50.

———. "The Basilica and an Altar to Dionysos at Nysa-Scythopolis." In *The Roman and Byzantine Near East*. Vol. 2: *Some Recent Archaeological Research*, edited by J. H. Humphrey. *JRA* (1999): 59–75.

Djurslev, C. T. "The Figure of Alexander the Great and Nonnus' Dionysiaca." In *Alexander the Great and the East: History, Art, Tradition*, edited by K. Nawotka and A. Wojciechowska Philippika, 103, 213–21. Wiesbaden: Harrassowitz Verlag, 2016.

———. Review of *Arrian the Historian: Writing the Greek Past in the Roman Empire*, by D. W. Leon, Austin: University of Texas Press, 2021. *Bryn Mawr Classical Review* 2023.01.03. https://mailchi.mp/bmcreview.org/bmcr-20230103djurslev-onleon-arrian-the-historian-writing-the-greek-past-in-the-roman-empire?e=48a31a1b8a (accessed January 15, 2023).

Dolce, R. *"Losing One's Head" in the Ancient Near East: Interpretation and Meaning of Decapitation. Studies in the History of the Ancient Near East*. London: Routledge, 2018.

Dorka Moreno, M. "15 Minuten Ruhm: Eine Notiz zu einem (falschen?) Alexanderporträt aus Bronze in New York." *Göttinger Forum für Altertumswissenschaft* 22 (2019a): 83–115.

———. *Imitatio Alexandri? Ähnlichkeitsrelationen zwischen Götter— sowie Heroenbildern und Porträts Alexanders des Großen in der griechisch-römischen Antike*. Tübingen: Verlag Marie Leidorf, 2019b.

Dressel, H. "Fünf Goldmedaillons aus dem Funde von Abukir." In *The Coinages of Alexander the Great*, edited by S. Gardiakos, 1–130. Chicago: Obol International, 1981. Reprinted from Berlin: Abhandlungen der Königlich Preussischen Akademie der Wissenschaften, 1906.

Dunand, F. "Agathodaimon." *LIMC* I (1981): 277–82.

Ebeling, P., M. Edrey, T. Harpak, A. Lichtenberger, and O. Tal. "Field Report on the 2019 German-Israeli Tell Izṭabbā Excavation Project (Beth She'an), Israel." *Zeitschrift des Deutschen Palästina-Vereins* 136, no. 2 (2020): 176–90.

———. "Field Report on the 2020 German-Israeli Tell Izṭabbā Excavation Project (Beth She'an), Israel." *Zeitschrift des Deutschen Palästina-Vereins* 137, no. 1 (2021): 60–74.

Eck, W. "The Bar Kokhba Revolt: The Roman Point of View." *JRS* 89 (1999): 76–89.

———. "The Language of Power: Latin Reflected in the Inscriptions of Judaea/Syria Palaestina." In *Semitic Papyrology in Context: A Climate of Creativity*, edited by L. H. Schiffman, 125–44. Leiden: Brill, 2003.

———. "The Presence, Role and Significance of Latin in the Epigraphy and Culture of the Roman Near East." In *From Hellenism to Islam: Cultural and Linguistic Change in the Roman Near East*, edited by H. M. Cotton, R. G. Hoyland, J. J. Price, and D. J. Wasserstein, 15–42. Cambridge, UK: Cambridge University Press, 2009.

———. "Statuenehrungen als Zeugnis für den Einfluss römischer Amtsträger im Leben einer Provinz." In *Aspects of Ancient Institutions and Geography: Studies in Honor of Richard J.A. Talbert*, edited by L. L. Brice and D. Slootjes, 145–60. Impact of Empire 19. Leiden: Brill, 2014.

Edrey, M., P. Ebeling, T. Harpak, A. Lichtenberger, and O. Tal. "Back to Bet She'an: Results of the 2019–2020 Fieldwork of the German-Israeli Tell Izṭabbā Excavation Project." In *Cities, Monuments and Objects in the Roman and Byzantine Levant: Studies in Honour of Gabi Mazor*, edited by W. Atrash, A. Overman, and P. Gendelman, 2–15. Oxford: Archaeopress, 2022.

Ehling, K. *Untersuchungen zur Geschichte der späten Seleukiden (164–63 v. Chr.): Vom Tode des Antiochos IV. bis zur Einrichtung der Provinz Syria unter Pompeius*. Stuttgart: Franz Steiner Verlag, 2008.

Eisenberg-Degen, I. Peretz, and E. Jakoel. "Identifying a Dionysian Community in Ashkelon's Eastern Cemetery." *NEA* 82, no. 2 (2019): 102–13.

El Fakharani, F. "The Library of Philadelphia (?) or, The So-called Temple on the Citadel Hill in Amman." *Wissenschaftliche Zeitschrift der Universität Rostock* 24, no. 6 (1975): 533–54.

Erickson, K. "Seleucus I, Zeus and Alexander." In *Every Inch a King: Comparative Studies in Kings and Kingship in the Ancient and Medieval Worlds*, edited by L. Mitchell and C. Melville, 109–27. Leiden: Brill, 2013.

———. "Where Are the Wives: Royal Women in Seleucid Court Documents." In *Rome and the Seleukid East. Select Papers from Seleukid Study Day V, Brussels, 21–23 August 2015, Collection Latomus* 360, edited by A. Coskun and D. Engels, 135–58. Leuven: Peeters, 2019.

Erlich, A. *The Art of Hellenistic Palestine*. British Archaeological Reports International Series 2010. Oxford: Archaeopress, 2009.

———. "The Patriarch and the Emperor: The Elephant Mosaic Panel in the Huqoq Synagogue Reconsidered." *JRA* 31 (2018): 542–58.

Fejfer, J. *Roman Portraits in Context*. Berlin: de Gruyter, 2008.

Finkielsztejn, G. "The Amphora Stamps." In *Hellenistic Nysa-Scythopolis. The Amphora Stamps and Sealings from Tel Iztabba. IAA Reports,* No. 62: *Bet She'an Archaeological Project 1986–2002. Bet She'an IV*, edited by G. Mazor, W. Atrash, and G. Finkielsztejn, 13–126. Jerusalem: Israel Antiquities Authority, 2018.

Fischer, M. L. *Das korinthische Kapitell im Alten Israel in der hellenistischen und römischen Periode*. Mainz: von Zabern, 1990.

———. "Figured Capitals in Roman Palestine. Marble Imports and Local Stones: Some Aspects of 'Imperial' and 'Provincial' Art." *AA* (1991): 119–44.

———. *Marble Studies: Roman Palestine and the Marble Trade. Xenia* 40. Konstanz: UVK Universitätsverlag, 1998.

———. Review of *Beth She'an*. Vol. 1: *Nysa-Scythopolis: The Caesareum and the Odeum*, by G. Mazor and A. Najjar. *IAA Reports* 33. Jerusalem, 2007. *AJA* 114, no. 1 (2010). http://www.ajaonline.org/online-review-book/669 (accessed January 15, 2023).

Fischer, M. L., and T. Grossmark. "Marble Import and Marmorarii in Eretz Israel." In *Classical Studies in Honor of David Sohlberg*, edited by R. Katzoff, 320–52. Ramat-Gan: Bar-Ilan University, 1996.

Fischer, M. L., and Z. Pearl. "Excursus III: Provenance of marble imported to Roman Palestine: A geochemical, petrographic and artistic analysis." In M. L. Fischer, *Marble Statues*, 247–61.

Fischer, M. L., D. Tambakopoulos, and Y. Maniatis. "Recycling of Marble: Apollonia/Sozousa/Arsuf (Israel) as a Case Study." In *ASMOSIA XI, Interdisciplinary Studies on Ancient Stone, Proceedings of the XI ASMOSIA Conference*, Split 18–22, 2015, edited by D. Matetić Poljak and K. Marasović, 443–56. Split: University of Split, 2018.

Fischer, M. L., and Y. Tepper. "A Group of Pilaster Capitals from Shivta: Marble Import in the Byzantine Negev." *Palestine Exploration Quarterly* 154 (2022): 35–51. https://doi.org/10.1080/00310328.2020 .1866328 (accessed 15 January 2023).

Fischer, T. "Ein Bildnis des Tryphon in Basel?" *Antike Kunst* 14 (1971): 56.

———. "Tryphons verfehlter Sieg von Dor." *ZPE* 93 (1992): 29–30.

Fisher, C. S. "BethShean: Excavations of the University Museum Expedition, 1921–1923." *MusJ* XIV, no. 4 (1923): 227–48.

Fittschen, K. "Zur Panzerstatue aus Samaria Sebaste." In *What Has Athens to Do with Jerusalem: Essays on Classical, Jewish, and Early Christian Art and Archaeology in Honor of Gideon Foerster*, edited by L. V. Rutgers, 9–17. Leuven: Peeters, 2002.

Fittschen, K., and P. Zanker. *Katalog der römischen Porträts in den Capitolinischen Museen und den anderen kommunalen Sammlungen der Stadt Rom* I. Vol. 1, Kaiser- und Prinzenbildnisse. Beiträge zur Erschließung hellenistischer und kaiserzeitlicher Skulptur und Architektur 3. Mainz: von Zabern, 1985.

Fitzgerald, G. M. *The Four Canaanite Temples of Beth Shan – The Pottery*. Philadelphia: University Museum/University of Pennsylvania Press, 1930.

———. *Beth Shean Excavations 1921–1923: The Arab and Byzantine Levels*. Philadelphia: University Museum/University of Pennsylvania Press, 1931.

———. "Excavations at Beth-Shan in 1931." *Palestine Exploration Fund, Quarterly Statement* (July 1932): 138–48.

———. "Excavations at Beth-Shan in 1933." *Palestine Exploration Fund, Quarterly Statement* (January 1934): 123–34.

Foerster, G. "A Cuirassed Statue of Hadrian." *IMN* 16 (1980): 107–10.

———. "A Cuirassed Bronze Statue of Hadrian." *'Atiqot* 17 (1985): 139–57.

———. "A Modest Aphrodite from Bet Shean." *Israel Museum Studies in Archaeology* 4 (2005): 3–21.

———. "Marble Sculptures of the Roman Period in the Near East and Its Hellenistic Origins." In *The Sculptural Environment of the Roman Near East: Reflections on Culture, Ideology and Power*, edited by Y. Z. Eliav, E. A. Friedland, and S. Herbert, 69–90. Leuven: Peeters, 2008.

Foerster, G., and Y. Tsafrir. "Nysa-Scythopolis: A New Inscription and the Titles of the City on its Coins." *Israel Numismatic Journal* 9 (1986–87): 53–58.

————. "The Bet Shean Project." *Excavations and Surveys in Israel* 6 (1987–88): 7–45.

————. "Bet Shean Project—1988: Hebrew University Expedition." *Excavations and Surveys in Israel* 7, no. 8 (1988–89): 15–22.

————. "A Statue of Dionysus as a Youth Recently Discovered at Beth-Shean" [Hebrew]. *Qadmoniot* 89–90 (1990): 52–54.

————. "Nysa-Scythopolis in the Roman Period: 'A Greek City of Coele Syria' – Evidence from the Excavations at Bet Shean." *ARAM* 4 (1992): 117–38.

————. "City Center (North) – Excavations of the Hebrew University Expedition." *Excavations and Surveys in Israel* 11 (1993): 3–32.

Foerster, R. "Hermes mit Lotosblatt." *RM* 29 (1914): 168–85.

Fogelin, L., and M. B. Schiffer. "Rites of Passage and other Rituals in the Life Histories of Objects." *Cambridge Archaeological Journal* 25, no. 4 (2015): 815–27.

Friedland, E. A. "Visualizing Deities in the Roman Near East: Aspects of Athena and Athena Allat." In *The Sculptural Environment of the Roman Near East: Reflections on Culture, Ideology, and Power*, edited by Y. Z. Eliav, E. A. Friedland, and S. Herbert, 315–50. Leuven: Peeters, 2008.

————. *The Roman Marble Sculptures from the Sanctuary of Pan at Caesarea Philippi/Panias (Israel).* Boston: American Schools of Oriental Research, 2012.

————. "Beth She'an 'Beauties': An Introduction to the Sculptures from Roman and Byzantine Nysa-Scythopolis." In *Cities, Monuments and Objects in the Roman and Byzantine Levant: Studies in Honour of Gabi Mazor*, edited by W. Atrash, A. Overman, and P. Gendelman, 48–58. Oxford: Archaeopress, 2022.

Friedland, E. A., and R. H. Tykot. "The Quarry Origins of Nine Roman Marble Sculptures from 'Amman/Philadelphia and Gadara Qays." *Annual of the Department of Antiquities of Jordan* 54 (2010): 177–87.

Fuks, G. "Scythopolis – A Study of a Greek City in the Near East." D. Phil. thesis. Oxford: University of Oxford, 1976.

————. "The Foundation of Scythopolis." [Hebrew]. *Cathedra* 8 (1978): 3–11.

————. "Antiochus son of Phallion." *IEJ* 31 (1981): 237–38.

————. "The Jews of Hellenistic and Roman Scythopolis." *Journal of Jewish Studies* 83 (1982): 407–16.

————. *Scythopolis—A Greek City in Eretz—Israel* [Hebrew]. Jerusalem: Yad Yitsḥak Ben-Tsvi, 1983.

Gaebler, H. *Die antiken Münzen Nord-Griechenlands*. Bd. III: Makedonia und Paionia. Berlin: Druck und Verlag von Georg Reimer, 1906.

Gaggadis-Robin, V., J.-L. Prisset, D. Tambakopoulos, and Y. Maniatis. "Provenance Investigation of Some Funeral Marble Sculptures from Ancient Vienne (France)." In *Interdisciplinary Studies on Ancient Stone, ASMOSIA X, Proceedings of the Tenth International Conference of ASMOSIA*, Rome, Italy, 21–26 May 2012, edited by P. Pensabene and E. Gasparini, 725–38. Rome: L'Erma di Bretschneider, 2015.

Garnsey, P. "Roman Citizenship and Roman Law in the Late Empire." In *Approaching Late Antiquity: The Transformation from Early to Late Empire*, edited by S. Swain and M. Edwards, 133–55. Oxford: Oxford University Press, 2006.

Gasparri, C., and A. Veneri. "Dionysos." *LIMC* III (Zurich/Munich 1986): 414–514.

Gebauer, K. "Alexanderbildnis und Alexandertypus." *AM* 63/64 (1938/39): 1–106.

Gergel, R. "The Tel Shalem Hadrian Reconsidered." *AJA* 95 (1991): 231–51.

Gersht, R. "Roman Copies Discovered in the Land of Israel." In *Classical Studies in Honor of David Sohlberg*, edited by R. Katzoff, 433–50. Ramat-Gan: Bar-Ilan University, 1996.

———. "Caesarean Sculpture in Context." In *The Sculptural Environment of the Roman Near East: Reflections on Culture, Ideology, and Power*, edited by Y. Z. Eliav, E. A. Friedland, and S. Herbert, 509–38. Leuven: Peeters, 2008.

Ghislanzoni, E. "Gli scavi delle Terme Romane a Cirene." *Notiziario archeologico del Ministero delle Colonie* 2 (1916): 7–126.

Gitler, H. "New Aspects Concerning the Dionysiac Cult in Nysa-Scythopolis." *SNR* 70 (1991): 23–29.

Goette, H. R. "Fragment of a Newly Discovered Portrait of Hadrian in Budapest." *Mouseion* (Museum of Fine Arts, Budapest) 3 (2019): 2–16.

Gorgoni, C., L. Lazzarini, P. Pallante, and B. Turi. "An Updated and Detailed Mineropetrographic and C-O Stable Isotopic Reference Database for the Main Mediterranean Marbles Used in Antiquity." In *ASMOSIA 5: Interdisciplinary Studies on Ancient Stone – Proceedings of the Fifth International Conference of the Association for the Study of Marble and Other Stones in Antiquity. ASMOSIA V, Museum of Fine Arts, Boston, 12–15 June 1998,* edited by J. Herrmann, N. Herz, and R. Newman, 115–31. London: Archetype Publications, 2002.

Gosden, C., and Y. Marshall. "The Cultural Biography of Objects." *World Archaeology* 31, no. 2 (1999): 169–78.

Graf, D. "Hellenisation and the Decapolis." *ARAM* 4 (1992): 1–48.

Graf, F. "Theoi Soteres." *ARG* 18 (2017): 239–54.

Grainger, J. D. *A Seleukid Prosopography and Gazetter*. Leiden: Brill, 1997.

Green, P. "Caesar and Alexander: aemulatio, imitatio, comparatio." *AJAH* 3 (1978): 1–26.

———. *Alexander of Macedon, 356–323 B.C.: A Historical Biography*. Berkeley: University of California Press, 1991.

Grimm, G. "Die Vergöttlichung Alexander des Grossen in Ägypten und ihre Bedeutung für den ptolemäischen Königskult." In *Das Ptolemäische Ägypten: Akten des Internationalen Symposions 27–29 Sept. 1976, Berlin*, edited by H. Maehler and V. M. Strocka, 103–9. Mainz: von Zabern, 1978.

Grossman, J. "Images of Alexander the Great in the Getty Museum." *Studia Varia from the J. Paul Getty Museum*, vol. 2. *Occasional Papers on Antiquities* 10 (2001): 51–78.

Gruen, E. S. "Rome and the Myth of Alexander." In *Ancient History in a Modern University: The Ancient Near East, Greece, and Rome*, vol. I, edited by E. A. Judge and T. Hillard, 178–91. Grand Rapids: W. B. Eerdmans Publishing Co., 1998.

———. "Jews and Greeks." In *A Companion to the Hellenistic World*, edited by A. Erskine, 264–79. Malden, MA: Blackwell, 2003.

———. *Constructs of Identity in Hellenistic Judaism*. Berlin: De Gruyter, 2016.

Guarducci, M. "Le Impronte del *Quo Vadis* e Monumenti Affini, Figurati ed Epigrafici." *Rendiconti della Pont. Accad. Rom. d'Arch.* 19 (1942–43): 305–44.

Guldager Bilde, P., and M. Moltesen. *In the Sacred Grove of Diana: Finds from a Sanctuary at Nemi*. Copenhagen: Ny Carlsberg Glyptotek, 1997.

Gulick, H. C. van. *Catalogue of bronzes in the Allard Pierson Museum. Archaeologisch-historische bijdragen* 7. Amsterdam: Noord-hollandsche uitgevers-mij., 1940.

Gurney, O. R., and P. W. M. Freeman. "Garstang, John (1876–1956)." *Oxford Dictionary of National Biography*. Oxford: Oxford University Press, 2012. https://doi.org/10.1093/ref:odnb/33341 (accessed November 9, 2018).

Habicht, C. *Athens from Alexander to Antony*, trans. D. L. Schneider. Cambridge, MA: Harvard University Press, 1997.

———. *The Hellenistic Monarchies: Selected Papers*. Ann Arbor: University of Michigan Press, 2006.

Hadley, R. A. "Royal Propaganda of Seleucus I and Lysimachus." *JHS* 94 (1974): 50–65.

Hannestad, L. "The Economy of Koile-Syria after the Seleukid Conquest: An Archaeological Contribution." In *The Economies of Hellenistic Societies, Third to First Centuries BC*, edited by Z. H. Archibald, J. K. Davies, and V. Gabrielsen, 251–79. Oxford: Oxford University Press, 2011.

Hannestad, N. "The Marble Group of Daidalos: Hellenism in Late Antique Amman." *Studies in the History and Architecture of Jordan* 7 (2001): 513–19.

Hansen, S., A. Wieczorek, and M. Tellenbach. *Alexander der Grosse und die Öffnung der Welt*. Regensburg: Schnell and Steiner, 2009.

Hart, G. *A Dictionary of Egyptian Gods and Goddesses*. London: Routledge & Kegan Paul, 1986.

Hasson, N. "Group Challenges Plan to Move Archaeological Relics from East Jerusalem." *Haaretz*, May 6, 2016. https://www.haaretz.com/israel-news/.premium-plan-to-move-relics-from-east-jlem-challenged-1.5380294 (accessed November 14, 2018).

Hekster, O., and T. Kaizer. "An Accidental Tourist? Caracalla's fatal trip to the temple of the Moon at Carrhae/Harran." *Ancient Society* 42 (2012): 89–107.

Herz, N. "Carbon and Oxygen Isotopic Ratios: A Data Base for Classical Greek and Roman Marble." *Archaeometry* 29, no. 1 (1987): 35–43.

Heyden, K. "Beth Shean/Scythopolis in Late Antiquity: Cult and Culture, Continuity and Change." In *One God—One Cult—One Nation*, edited by R. G. Kratz and H. Spieckermann, 301–37. Berlin: De Gruyter, 2010.

Hezser, C., ed. *The Oxford Handbook of Jewish Daily Life in Roman Palestine*. Oxford: Oxford University Press, 2010; online edition, Oxford Academic, September 18, 2012. https://doi.org/10.1093/oxfordhb/9780199216437.001.0001 (accessed January 11, 2023).

Hölscher, T. *Die Geschöpfe des Daidalos: Vom sozialen Leben der griechischen Bildwerke*. Heidelberg: Verlag Antike, 2018.

Hoff, R. von den. "Commodus als Hercules." In *Meisterwerke der antiken Kunst*, edited by L. Giuliani, 114–35. München: Beck, 2005.

Hoffman, A. *Till We Have Built Jerusalem: Architects of a New City*. New York: Farrar, Straus and Giroux, 2016.

Holum, K. G. "The Temple Platform: Progress Report on the Excavations." In *Caesarea Papers* 2, edited by K. G. Holum, A. Raban, and J. Patrich, 12–34. Portsmouth, RI: JRA, 1999.

———. "The Christianizing of Caesarea Palaestinae." In *Die spätantike Stadt und ihre Christianierung. Symposion vom 14. bis 16. Februar 2000 in Halle-Saale*, edited by G. Brands and H.-G. Severin, 151–64. Wiesbaden: Reichert Verlag, 2003.

———. "Caesarea's Fortune: Ancient Statuary and the Beholder in a Late Antique City." In *The Sculptural Environment of the Roman Near East: Reflections on Culture, Ideology and Power*, edited by Y. Z. Eliav, E. A. Friedland, and S. Herbert, 539–58. Leuven: Peeters, 2008.

Hoover, O. D. "Ceci n'est pas l'autonomie. The Coinage of Seleucid Phoenicia as Royal and Civic Power Discourse." In *Le roi et l'economie, Autonomies locales et structures royales dans l'économie de l'empire séleucide*, edited by V. Chankowski and F. Duyrat. *Topoi* Supplement IV, 484–507. Lyon: Société des Amis de la Bibliothèque Salomon-Reinach, 2004.

Ignatiadou, D. "Psychotropic Plants on Achaemenid-Style Vases." In *Ancient Greece and Ancient Iran: Cross-Cultural Encounters*, edited by S. M. R. Darbandi and A. Zournatzi, 327–37. Athens: National Hellenic Research Foundation, 2008.

Iles, L. "The Lotus in Ancient Egypt." In *Isis, Lotus of Alexandria Lyceum*, 2005–2023, edited by L. Iles. https://sites.google.com/site/isislotusofalexandrialyceum/the-lotus-in-ancient-egypt?pli=1 (accessed January 15, 2023).

Imrie, A. *The Antonine Constitution: An Edict for the Caracallan Empire. Impact of Empire* 29. Leiden: Brill, 2018.

İnan, J. "Der Bronzetorso im Burdur-Museum aus Bubon und der Bronzekopf im J.-Paul-Getty-Museum." *IstMitt* 27/28 (1977/1978) (1979): 266–87.

———. "Neue Forschungen zum Sebasteion von Bubon und seinen Statuen." In *Akten des II. Internationalen Lykien-Symposions Vienna, 6.–12. Mai 1990*, edited by J. Borchardt and G. Dobesch, 213–39. Vienna: Österreichische Akademie der Wissenschaften, 1993.

Isaac, B. "Latin in the Cities of the Roman Near East." In *From Hellenism to Islam: Cultural and Linguistic Change in the Roman Near East*, edited by H. M. Cotton, R. G. Hoyland, J. J. Price, and D. J. Wasserstein, 43–72. Cambridge, UK: Cambridge University Press, 2009.

"ISIS Beheads Elderly Archeologist in Palmyra, Syrian Official Says." *Huffington Post*, August 18, 2015, Updated August 19, 2015. https://www.huffpost.com/entry/isis-beheads-archeologist-palmyra_n_55d3a125e4b055a6dab1da13 (accessed January 15, 2023).

The Israel Museum. Jerusalem/New York: Abrams, 2005.

Issawi, D. "Alexander Had a Great Hairdo, Too." *The New York Times* (print edition), November 11, 2021: D5; online edition. https://www.nytimes.com/2021/11/11/todayspaper/quotation-of-the-day-alexander-had-a-great-hairdo-too.html (accessed November 12, 2021).

Jacobs, I. "Production to Destruction? Pagan and Mythological Statuary in Asia Minor." *AJA* 114 (2010): 267–303.

James, F. "Beth-Shean." In *Encyclopedia of Archaeological Excavations in the Holy Land* [Hebrew], 63–76. Jerusalem: Israel Exploration Society and Masada Ltd., 1970.

Johnston, A. "Caracalla's Path: The Numismatic Evidence." *Historia* 32 (1983): 58–76.

Jones, A. H. M. *The Cities of the Eastern Roman Provinces*, 2nd ed. Oxford: Oxford University Press, 1971.

Joy, J. "Reinvigorating Object Biography: Reproducing the Drama of Object Lives." *World Archaeology* 41, no. 4 (2009): 540–56.

Jucker, H. *Das Bildnis im Blätterkelch: Geschichte und Bedeutung einer römischen Porträtform.* Bibliotheca Helvetica Romana, 3. Olten: URS Graf-Verlag, 1961.

Kanellopoulos, C. *The Great Temple of Amman. The Architecture.* Amman: American Center of Oriental Research, 1994.

Kansteiner, S. "Teil-Imitationen antiker Statuen: Apollon Typus Centocelle und Silen Orsini." In S. Kansteiner, *Pseudoantike Skulptur* 1. *Fallstudien zu antiken Skulpturen und ihren Imitationen*, 25–44. Berlin: De Gruyter, 2016.

Karmi-Melamede, A., and D. Price. *Architecture in Palestine During the British Mandate, 1917–1948.* Jerusalem: Israel Museum, Jerusalem, 2014.

Kasher, A. *Jews and Hellenistic Cities in Eretz-Israel: Relations of the Jews in Eretz-Israel with the Hellenistic Cities during the Second Temple Period (332 BCE–70 CE).* Tübingen: J. C. B. Mohr, 1990.

Kastritsis, D. "The Trebizond Alexander Romance (Venice Hellenic Institute Codex Gr. 5): The Ottoman Fate of a Fourteenth-Century Illustrated Byzantine Manuscript." *Journal of Turkish Studies* 36 (2011): 103–31.

Kemezis, A. M. *Greek Narratives of the Roman Empire under the Severans: Cassius Dio, Philostratus and Herodian.* Cambridge, UK: Cambridge University Press, 2014.

Kiilerich, B. "The Head Posture of Alexander the Great." *Acta ad archaeologiam et artium historiam pertinentia* 29 (2016): 1–22. http://dx.doi.org/10.5617/acta.6074 (accessed January 15, 2023).

Kislev, M. E., O. Simchoni, Y. Melamed, and L. Maroz. "Flax Seed Production: Evidence from the Early Iron Age Site of Tel Beth-Shean, Israel and from Written Sources." *Veget Hist Archaeobot* 20 (2011): 579–84.

Koçak, M., and D. Kreikenbom, eds. *Sculptures from Roman Syria (SFRS) II: The Greek, Roman and Byzantine Marble Statuary.* Mainz: De-Gruyter, 2023.

Koepp, F. *Über das Bildnis Alexanders des Großen.* Berlin: Reimer, 1892.

Kokkinia, C., ed. "Survey Results in Boubon (Cibyratis, Northern Lycia) 2004–2006: The Sebasteion." KERA: Institute for Greek and Roman Antiquity, updated 2021: https://boubonkera.eie.gr/sebasteion.asp (accessed January 15, 2023).

Kopytoff, I. "The Cultural Biography of Things: Commoditization as Process." In *The Social Life of Things: Commodities in Cultural Perspective,* edited by A. Appadurai, 64–91. Cambridge, UK: Cambridge University Press, 1986.

Kosmin, P. *The Land of the Elephant Kings: Space, Territory, and Ideology in the Seleucid Empire.* Cambridge, MA: Harvard University Press, 2014.

Koulakiotis, E. *Genese und Metamorphosen des Alexandermythos im Spiegel der griechischen nichthistoriographischen Überlieferung bis zum 3. Jh. Nach Christus.* Xenia Heft 47. Konstanz: UVK, 2006.

Kousser, R. "Monument and Memory in Ancient Greece and Rome: A Comparative Perspective." In *Cultural Memories in the Roman Empire,* edited by K. Galinsky and K. Lapatin, 33–48. Los Angeles: Getty Publications, 2015.

Kovacs, M. "Imitatio Alexandri – Zu Aneignungs- und Angleichungsphänomenen im römischen Porträt." In *Imitatio heroica. Heldenangleichung im Bildnis von der Antike bis zum Ende des 18. Jahrhunderts,* edited by R. von den Hoff and A. Schreurs-Moret, 47–83. Würzburg: Ergon, 2015.

———. *Vom Herrscher zum Heros. Die Bildnisse Alexander des Grossen und die Imitatio Alexandri.* Unpublished Habilitationsschrift, Freiburg University. Freiburg, 2017.

Kreikenbom, D. *Griechische und römische Kolossalporträts bis zum späten ersten Jahrhundert nach Christus. (JdI-EH 27).* Berlin: de Gruyter, 1992.

Kreikenbom, D., and T. Sharvit. "3.8.5 Skythopolis/Nysa/Beisan/Bet She'an." In Koçak and Kreikenbom, *Sculptures from Roman Syria (SFRS),* 389–411.

Kristensen, T. M. *Making and Breaking the Gods: Christian Responses to Pagan Sculpture in Late Antiquity.* Aarhus: Aarhus University Press, 2013.

Kristensen, T. M., and L. Stirling, eds. *The Afterlife of Greek and Roman Sculpture: Late Antique Responses and Practices.* Ann Arbor: University of Michigan Press, 2016.

Kropp, A. J. M. *Images and Monuments of Near Eastern Dynasts, 100 BC–AD 100.* Oxford: Oxford University Press, 2013.

Kruse-Berdoldt, V. "Kopienkritische Untersuchungen zu den Porträts des Epikur, Metrodor und Hermarch." PhD diss., University of Göttingen. Göttingen, 1975.

Kulikowski, M. *The Triumph of Empire: The Roman World from Hadrian to Constantine.* Cambridge, MA: Harvard University Press, 2019.

Kyrieleis, H. *Bildnisse der Ptolemäer. Archäologische Forschungen* 2. Berlin: Gebr. Mann, 1975.

Laflı, E., and E. Christof. "A Niche with Nymphs from Kulu in Galatia." In *Sculpture in Roman Asia Minor. Proceedings of the International Conference at Selçuk, 1st–3rd October 2013, Österreichisches Archäologisches Institut, Sonderschriften* 56, edited by M. Aurenhammer, 319–28. Vienna: Österreichisches Archäologisches Institut, 2018.

Landau, Y. H. "A Greek Inscription from Acre." *IEJ* 11 (1961): 118–26.

———. "A Greek Inscription Found Near Hefzibah." *IEJ* 1 (1966): 54–70.

Lane Fox, R. *The Search for Alexander.* Boston: Little, Brown, 1980.

La Rocca, E., C. P. Presicce, A. Lo Monaco, C. Giroire, and D. Roger. *Augusto.* Milan: Mondadori Electa, 2013.

Laube, I. *Thorakophoroi: Gestalt und Semantik des Brustpanzers in der Darstellung des 4. bis 1. Jhs. v. Chr.* Rahden: Verlag Marie Leidorf, 2006.

———. *Expedition Ernst Von Sieglin: Skulptur des Hellenismus und der Kaiserzeit aus Ägypten. Die Sammlungen in Dresden, Stuttgart und Tübingen.* Munich: Hirmer, 2012.

Lazzarini, L., and F. Antonelli. "Petrographic and Isotopic Characterization of the Marble of the Island of Tinos (Greece)." *Archaeometry* 45, no. 4 (2003): 541–52.

Lazzarini, L., and C. G. Malacrino. "The White Marble of Kos, Its Quarries and Archaeometric Characterisation." *Marmora* 6 (2010): 57–70.

Leon, D. W. *Arrian the Historian: Writing the Greek Past in the Roman Empire.* Austin: University of Texas Press, 2021.

Levick, B. "Caracalla's Path." In "Hommages à Marcel Renard," edited by J. Bibauw, special issue, *Latomus* 102 (1969): 426–46.

Levitt, P. *Artifacts and Allegiances: How Museums Put the Nation and the World on Display*. Berkeley: University of California Press, 2015.

Lichtenberger, A. *Kulte und Kultur der Dekapolis. Untersuchungen zu numismatischen, archäologischen und epigraphischen Zeugnissen. Abhandlungen des Deutschen Palästina-Vereins* 29. Wiesbaden: Harrassowitz, 2003.

———. "Artemis and Zeus Olympios in Roman Gerasa and Seleucid Religious Policy." In *The Variety of Local Religious Life in the Near East in the Hellenistic and Roman Periods*, edited by T. Kaizer, 133–53. Leiden: Brill, 2008.

Lichtenberger, A., C. Meyer, and O. Tal. "Magnetic Prospecting at Nysa-Scythopolis (Tell Iẓṭabba): Deciphering Urban Planning at a Newly Founded Hellenistic Town of the Decapolis." *Strata: Bulletin of the Anglo-Israel Archaeological Society* 38 (2020): 45–70.

Lichtenberger, A., and O. Tal. "A Hoard of Alexander II Zabinas Coins from Tell Iẓṭabba (Beth She'an), Israel." *Israel Numismatic Research* 15 (2020): 45–59.

Lifshitz, B. "Der Kult des Zeus Akraios und des Zeus Bakchos in Beisan (Skythopolis)." *ZDPV* 77 (1961): 186–90.

———. "Beiträge zur palästinischen Epigraphik." *Zeitschrift des Deutschen Palästina-Vereins* 78, no. 1 (1962): 64–88.

———. "Sur le culte dynastique des Séleucides." *Revue Biblique* (1946–) 70 (1963): 75–81.

———. "Scythopolis. "L'histoire, les institutions et les cultes de la ville à l'époque hellénistique et impérial." *ANRW* II, no. 8 (1977): 262–94.

Long, L. E. "The Regional Marble Quarries." In *Aphrodisias V, The Aphrodisias Regional Survey*, edited by C. Ratté and P. D. De Staebler, 165–202. Mainz: von Zabern, 2012.

———. "Extracting Economics from Roman Marble Quarries." *Economic History Review* 70, no. 1 (2017): 52–78.

"Lotis." In *Theoi Greek Mythology*, edited by A. J. Atsma. Netherlands/New Zealand, 2000–2019. https://www.theoi.com/Nymphe/Nymphe-Lotis.html (accessed January 15, 2023).

Lundgreen, B. "Use and Abuse of Athena in Roman Imperial Portraiture: The Case of Julia Domna." In *Proceedings of the Danish Institute at Athens* IV, edited by J. Eiring and J. Mejer, 69–91. Athens: Aarhus University Press, 2004.

Mango, C. "Antique Statuary and the Byzantine Beholder." *DOP* 17 (1963): 55–75.

———. "Septime Sévère et Byzance." *Comptes rendus des séances de l'Académie de Inscriptions et Belles-Lettres* 147, no. 2 (2003): 593–608.

Maniatis, Y. "Scientific Techniques and Methodologies for the Provenance of White Marbles." In *Physics Methods in Archaeometry. Proceedings of the International School of Physics "Enrico Fermi," Varenna on Como Lake, Villa Monastero, Societa Italiana di Fisica, 17–27 June 2003*, edited by M. Martini, M. Milazzo, and M. Piacenntini, 179–202. Amsterdam: Ios Press, 2004.

Maniatis, Y., D. Tambakopoulos, B. D. Wescoat, and D. Matsas. "The Sanctuary of the Great Gods on Samothrace: An Extended Marble Provenance Study." In *Interdisciplinary Studies on Ancient Stone, Proceedings of the IX Association for the Study of Marbles and Other Stones in Antiquity Conference. Documenta 23, ASMOSIA IX, Tarragona, Spain, 8–13 June 2009*, edited by A. Gutiérrez Garcia-M., P. Lapuente Mercadal, and I. Roda de Llanza, 263–78. Tarragona: Institut Català d'Arqueologia Clàssica, 2012.

Martins de Jesus, C. A. "The Statuary Collection Held at the Baths of Zeuxippus (*Ap* 2) and the Search for Constantine's Museological Intentions." *Synthesis* 21 (2014): 1–16. https://www.synthesis.fahce.unlp.edu.ar/article/view/SYNv21a02 (accessed January 15, 2023).

Marvin, M. "Freestanding Sculptures from the Baths of Caracalla." *AJA* 87 (1983): 347–84.

Mattusch, C. C. *Pompeii and the Roman Villa: Art and Culture Around the Bay of Naples*. Washington, DC: National Gallery of Art, 2008.

Mazar, A. "Beth-Shean from the Late Bronze Age IIB to the Medieval Period: A Summary." In *Excavations at Tel Beth-Shean, 1989–1996*. Vol. I: *From the Late Bronze Age IIB to the Medieval Period*, edited by A. Mazar and N. Amitai-Preiss, 26–47. Jerusalem: Israel Exploration Society and Institute of Archaeology, The Hebrew University of Jerusalem, 2006.

———. "Tel Beth-Shean: History and Archaeology." In *One God, One Cult, One Nation. Archaeological and Biblical Perspectives*, edited by R. G. Kratz and H. Spieckermann, *Beihefte zur Zeitschrift für die alttestamentliche Wissenschaft* 405 (2010): 239–71.

———. "The Egyptian Garrison Town at Beth Shean." In *Egypt, Canaan and Israel: History, Imperialism, Ideology and Literature: Proceedings of a Conference at the University of Haifa, 3–7 May 2009*, edited by S. Bar, D. Kahn, and J. J. Shirley, 155–89. Leiden: Brill, 2011.

————. *Excavations at Tel Beth-Shean, 1989–1996.* Vol. 4: *The Fourth and Third Millennia BCE.* Jerusalem: Israel Exploration Society/ Institute of Archaeology, The Hebrew University of Jerusalem, 2012.

Mazar, A., and N. Amitai-Preiss, eds. *Excavations at Tel Beth Shean 1989–1996.* Vol. 1: *From the Late Bronze Age IIB to the Medieval Period.* Jerusalem: Israel Exploration Society/Institute of Archaeology, The Hebrew University of Jerusalem, 2006.

Mazar, A., and R. Mullins, eds. *Excavations at Tel Beth-Shean, 1989–1996.* Vol. 2: *The Middle and Late Bronze Age Strata in Area R.* Jerusalem: Israel Exploration Society/Institute of Archaeology, The Hebrew University of Jerusalem, 2007.

Mazar, A., G. Mazor, B. Arubas, G. Foerster, Y. Tsafrir, and J. Seligman. "Beth Shean." In *The New Encyclopedia of Archaeological Excavations in the Holy Land*, vol. 5, edited by E. Stern, A. Lewinson-Gilboa, and J. Aviram, 1616–44. Jerusalem: Israel Exploration Society and Biblical Archaeology Society, 2008.

Mazor, G. "The Hellenistic to Early Islamic Periods: The Israel Antiquities Authority Excavations." In *The New Encyclopedia of Archaeological Excavations in the Holy Land*, vol. 5, edited by E. Stern, A. Lewinson-Gilboa, and J. Aviram, 1623–36. Jerusalem: Israel Exploration Society/Biblical Archaeology Society, 2008.

————. "The Visits of St. Sabas to Beth Shean." *Expedition* 55 (2013): 43–48.

————. "The Imperial Cult in the Decapolis: Nysa-Scythopolis as a Test Case." In *Viewing Ancient Jewish Art and Archaeology: Essays in Honor of Rachel Hachlili. Supplement to the Journal for the Study of Judaism*, vol. 172, edited by A. Killebrew and G. Fassbeck, 355–83. Leiden: Brill, 2015.

Mazor, G., and W. Atrash, eds. *Bet She'an Archaeological Project 1986–2002. Bet She'an III: Nysa-Scythopolis: The Southern and Severan Theaters, Part 1: The Stratigraphy and Finds (IAA Reports 58/1).* Jerusalem: Israel Antiquities Authority, 2015.

————. "Introduction." In *Hellenistic Nysa-Scythopolis. The Amphora Stamps and Sealings from Tel Iztabba. IAA Reports,* No. 62: *Bet She'an Archaeological Project 1986–2002. Bet She'an IV,* 1–11. Jerusalem: Israel Antiquities Authority, 2018a.

————. "The Sealings." In *Hellenistic Nysa-Scythopolis. The Amphora Stamps and Sealings from Tel Iztabba. IAA Reports,* No. 62: *Bet She'an Archaeological Project 1986–2002. Bet She'an IV,* edited by G. Mazor, W. Atrash, and G. Finkielsztejn, 127–68. Jerusalem: Israel Antiquities Authority, 2018b.

Mazor, G., W. Atrash, and G. Finkielsztejn, eds. *Hellenistic Nysa-Scytho-polis. The Amphora Stamps and Sealings from Tel Iztabba. IAA Reports,* No. 62: *Bet She'an Archaeological Project 1986–2002. Bet She'an IV.* Jerusalem: Israel Antiquities Authority, 2018.

Mazor, G., and A. Najjar, eds. *Nysa-Scythopolis: The Caesareum and the Odeum, Bet-Shean.* Jerusalem: Israel Exploration Society and Biblical Archaeology Society, 2007.

McDowell, R. H. *Stamped and Inscribed Objects from Seleucia on the Tigris.* Ann Arbor: University of Michigan Press, 1935.

McLean, F. "Museums and the Construction of National Identity: A Review." *International Journal of Heritage Studies* 3, no. 4 (2007): 244–52. https://www.tandfonline.com/doi/pdf/10.1080/13527259808722211 (accessed November 15, 2018).

Merkelbach, R. *Isis Regina – Zeus Serapis: Die griechisch-ägyptische Religion nach den Quellen dargestellt.* Munich/Leipzig: K. G. Sauer, 2001.

Meyer, H. *Antinoos: Die archäologischen Denkmäler unter Einbeziehung des numismatischen und epigraphischen Materials sowie der literarischen Nachrichten. Ein Beitrag zur Kunst- und Kulturgeschichte der hadrianisch-frühantoninischen Zeit.* Munich: Wilhelm Fink, 1991.

Millar, F. "The Problem of Hellenistic Syria." In *Hellenism in the East: The Interaction of Greek and non-Greek Civilizations from Syria to Central Asia after Alexander,* edited by A. Kuhrt and S. Sherwin-White, 110–33. Berkeley: Duckworth, 1987.

Milleker, E. J. "Three Heads of Sarapis from Corinth." *Hesperia* 54 (1985): 121–35.

Milne, J. G. *Catalogue of Alexandrian Coins. Ashmolean Museum.* Oxford: University of Oxford, 1933, reprinted with addenda, 1971.

Molina Marin, A. I. "Desmontando un tirano perfecto: Caracalla y la imitatio Alexandri." *Studia Historica. Historia Antigua* 33 (2015): 223–50.

Mørkholm, O. *Antiochus IV of Syria* (Classica et Mediaevalia Dissertationes 8). Copenhagen: Gyldendal, 1966.

Mouterde, P. Review of *The Topography and History of Beth-Shan,* by A. Rowe. Philadelphia: University of Pennsylvania Press, 1930. *Mélanges de l'université Saint-Joseph* (1933): 180–84.

Mukherjee, D. K., D. Mukherjee, A. K. Maji, S. Rai, and M. Heinrich. "The Sacred Lotus (Nelumbo nucifera): Phytochemical and Therapeutic Properties." *Journal of Pharmacy and Pharmacology* 61, no. 4

(2010). https://onlinelibrary.wiley.com/doi/full/10.1211/jpp.61.04
.0001 (accessed January 15, 2019).

"Museums in Jerusalem: The Rockefeller Archaeological Museum." In
Jewish Virtual Library. American-Israeli Cooperative Enterprise,
1998–2023. https://www.jewishvirtuallibrary.org/the-rockefeller
-archaeological-museum (accessed November 14, 2018).

Nabel, J. "The Seleucids Imprisoned: Arsacid-Roman Hostage Submis-
sion and Its Hellenistic Precedents." In *Arsacids, Romans, and Local
Elites: Cross-Cultural Interactions of the Parthian Empire*, edited by
J. M. Schlude and B. B. Rubin, 25–49. Oxford: Oxbow Books, 2017.

Naiden, F. S. *Soldier, Priest, and God: A Life of Alexander the Great*.
Oxford: Oxford University Press, 2018.

Najjar, M. "Rabbath Ammon—Philadelphia—Amman." In *Gadara—
Gerasa und die Dekapolis*, edited by A. Hoffmann and S. Kerner,
88–97. Mainz: von Zabern, 2002.

Nash, E. *Pictorial Dictionary of Ancient Rome*, rev. ed. London: Thames
and Hudson, 1968.

Nawotka, K. *The Alexander Romance by Ps.-Callisthenes: A Historical
Commentary. Mnemosyne Supplements* 399. Leiden: Brill, 2017.

Neto-Ibáñez, J.-M. "The Sacred Grove of Scythopolis (Flavius Josephus,
Jewish War II 466–471)." *IEJ* 49 (1999): 260–68.

Newell, E. T. "The Gold Medallions of Abukir." *AJN* 44 (1910): 128–
30.

———. *The Seleucid Mint of Antioch*. New York: The American Numismatic Society, 1918.

Ng, D. Y. "Monuments, Memory, and Status Recognition in Roman Asia
Minor." In *Memory in Ancient Rome and Early Christianity*, edited
by K. Galinsky, 235–62. Oxford: Oxford University Press, 2016.
http://www.oxfordscholarship.com/view/10.1093/acprof:oso/
9780198744764.001.0001/acprof-9780198744764-chapter-9 (accessed January 10, 2019).

Nocera, D. "The Round Church at Beth Shean." *Expedition* 55 (2013):
16–20.

Nock, A. D. "Notes on Ruler—Cult I-IV: I. Alexander and Dionysus."
JHS 48 (1928): 21–30.

Noreña, C. F. *Imperial Ideals in the Roman West: Representation, Circu-
lation, Power*. New York: Cambridge University Press, 2011.

———. "Ritual and Memory: Hellenistic Ruler Cults in the Roman
Empire." In *Cultural Memories in the Roman Empire*, edited by K.
Galinsky and K. Lapatin, 86–100. Los Angeles: Getty Publications,
2016.

Nygard, T., and V. Tomasso. "Andy Warhol's "Alexander the Great" : An Ancient Portrait for Alexander Iolas in a Post-modern Frame." *Classical Receptions Journal* 8, no. 2, (2016): 253–75.

Nylander, C. "Earless in Nineveh: Who Mutilated 'Sargon's' Head?" *AJA* 84 (1980): 329–33.

Opper, T. *Hadrian: Empire and Conflict.* London: The British Museum, 2008.

L'Orange, H. P. *Apotheosis in Ancient Portraiture.* Oslo: Aschehoug & Co., 1947.

O'Sullivan, L. "Augustus and Alexander the Great at Athens." *Phoenix* 70 (2016): 339–60.

Ousterhout, R. "Beth Shean Revisited: Reexamining a Late Antique City in Transition." *Expedition* 55 (2013): 8–15.

Ovadiah, A. "Greek Cults in Beth Shean-Scythopolis in the Hellenistic-Roman Period" [Hebrew]. *ErIsr* 12 (1975): 116–24.

Ovadiah, A., and S. Mucznik. "Dionysos in the Decapolis." *Liber Annuus* 65 (2015): 387–405.

Ovadiah, A., and Y. Turnheim. *"Peopled" Scrolls in Roman Architectural Decoration in Israel: The Roman Theater at Beth Shean/Scythopolis.* Rome: Bretschneider, 1994.

Özgür, M. E. *Sculptures of the Museum in Antalya*, rev. 3rd ed. Ankara: Dömnez, 2008.

———. *Marble Reflections: Antalya Museum Selection, A Photographic Essay.* Ankara: Dömnez, 2009.

Öztürk, A. *Die Architektur der Scaenae Frons des Theaters in Perge.* DAI Denmäler Antiker Architektur Band 20. Berlin: De Gruyter, 2009.

Paetz gen. Schieck, A. "Alexander der Grosse und das Ornat des persischen Grosskönigs." In *Alexander der Grosse und die Öffnung der Welt*, edited by S. Hansen, A. Wieczorek, and M. Tellenbach, 105–9. Regensburg: Schnell and Steiner, 2009.

Palagia, O. "Imitation of Herakles in Ruler-Portraiture: A Survey from Alexander to Maximinus Daza." *Boreas* 9 (1986): 137–51.

Pandermalis, D. "Ζευς Ὑψιστος και άλλα." *AEMΘ* 17, no. 2003 (2005): 417–24.

———, ed. *Gods and Mortals at Olympus: Ancient Dion, City of Zeus.* New York: Onassis Foundation, 2016.

Panitz-Cohn, N. "The History of Excavations at Tel Bet She'an and the Regional Surveys of the Bet She'an Valley." In *Archaeology in the 'Land of Ruins': A History of Excavations in the Holy Land Inspired by the Photographs and Accounts of Leo Boer*, edited by B. Wagemakers, 234–44. Oxford: Oxbow Books, 2014.

Panitz-Cohn, N., and A. Mazar. *Excavations at Tel Beth-Shean, 1989– 1996,* vol. 3: *The 13th–11th centuries BCE (Areas S and N).* Jerusalem: Israel Exploration Society/Institute of Archaeology, The Hebrew University of Jerusalem, 2009.

Parker, R. *Greek Gods Abroad: Names, Natures, and Transformations* (*Sather Classical Lectures* 72). Oakland: University of California Press, 2017.

Parker, S. T. "The Decapolis Reviewed." *Journal of Biblical Literature* 94 (1975): 437–41.

Parlasca, K. "Alexander Aigiochos: Das Kultbild des Stadtgründers von Alexandria in Ägypten." In *Fremdheit – Eigenheit. Ägypten, Griechenland und Rom. Austausch und Verständnis. Symposium des Liebieghauses 28–30 November 2002 und 16–19 Januar 2002,* edited by P. C. Bol, G. Kaminski, and C. Maderna, 340–62. *Städel-Jahrbuch* 19. Munich: Städel Museum, 2004.

Paul, C., ed. *The First Modern Museums of Art: The Birth of an Institution in 18th- and Early-19th Century Europe.* Los Angeles: The J. Paul Getty Museum, 2012.

Pearl, Z. "Archaeological Marble in Israel: Chemical and Mineralogical Analysis." Master's thesis, Rehovot: Weizmann Institute of Science, 1989.

Pearl, Z., and M. Magaritz. "The Marble Source of the Tel-Naharon-Scythopolis Heads." *'Atiqot* 20 (1991): 46–48.

Peled, R. "Two Roman Sculptures." *'Atiqot* 14 (1980): 99–102.

Peleg, O. "A Roman Intaglio and a Roman Gypsum Cast." In *Excavations at Tel Beth-Shean, 1989–1996.* Vol. I: *From the Late Bronze Age IIB to the Medieval Period,* edited by A. Mazar and N. Amitai-Preiss, 638–42. Jerusalem: Israel Exploration Society/The Hebrew University of Jerusalem, 2006.

Pelletier, M. "Where Do Israel's Antiquities Belong?" *Apollo Magazine* June 26, 2017. https://www.apollo-magazine.com/where-do-israels-antiquities-belong/ (accessed November 14, 2018).

Pensabene, P., L. Lazzarini, and B. Turi. "New Archaeometric Investigations on the Fragments of the Colossal Statue of Constantine in the Palazzo dei Conservatori." In *Interdisciplinary Studies on Ancient Stone, ASMOSIA 5,* edited by J. J. Herrmann, N. Herz, and R. Newman, 250–55. London: Archetype Publications, 2002.

Pfeiffer, S. "The Ptolemies: Hellenistic Kingship in Egypt." In *Oxford Handbooks Online,* 2016. https://www.oxfordhandbooks.com/view/

10.1093/oxfordhb/9780199935390.001.0001/oxfordhb-9780199935390-e-23 (accessed January 15, 2023).

Phythian-Adams, W. J., and J. Garstang. *Guidebook to the Palestine Museum of Antiquities*. Jerusalem: Department of Antiquities by the Greek Convent Press, 1924.

Pickett, J. "Contextualizing Penn's Excavations at Beth Shean (1921–1933)." *Expedition* 55, no. 1 (2013): 12–15.

Picón, C. A., and S. Hemingway. *Pergamon and the Hellenistic Kingdoms of the Ancient World*. New York: Metropolitan Museum of Art, 2016.

Piejko, F. "Ptolemies in a List of Deified Seleucids from Teos, *OGIS* 246." *ZPE* 49 (1982): 129–31.

Plantzos, D. "Archaeopolitics: The Second Lives of Statues." *CAS Sofia Working Paper Series* 14 (2023): 72–102. https://www.ceeol.com/search/article-detail?id=1121876 (accessed June 4, 2023).

Platner, S. B., and T. Ashby. *A Topographical Dictionary of Ancient Rome*. London: Oxford University Press/H. Milford, 1929.

Polikreti, K., and Y. Maniatis. "A New Methodology for the Provenance of Marble Based on EPR Spectroscopy." *Archaeometry* 44, no. 1 (2002): 1–21.

Pollini, J. "A New Portrait of Octavia and the Iconography of Octavia Minor and Julia Maior." *RM* 109 (2002): 11–42.

Powers, J., M. Abbe, M. Bushey, and S. H. Pike. "New Evidence for Ancient Gilding and Historic Restorations on a Portrait of Antinous in the San Antonio Museum of Art." In *ASMOSIA XI Interdisciplinary Studies of Ancient Stone, Proceedings of the Eleventh International Conference of ASMOSIA, Split, 18–22 May 2015*, edited by D. M. Poljak and K. Marasović, 783–92. Split: University of Split, 2018.

Prentice, W. K. *Greek and Latin Inscriptions from Northern Central Syria, Palmyra and the Region of the Hauran*. New York: The Century Co., 1908.

Price, S. R. F. *Rituals and Power: Roman Imperial Cult in Asia Minor*. Cambridge, UK: Cambridge University Press, 1984.

Reid, D. M. *Contesting Antiquity in Egypt: Archaeologies, Museums, and the Struggle for Identities from World War I to Nasser*. Cairo: American University in Cairo, 2015.

Reinsberg, C. "Alexanderbilder in Ägypten: Manifestation eines neuen Herrscherideals." In *Fremdheit – Eigenheit. Ägypten, Griechenland und Rom. Austausch und Verständnis. Symposium des Liebieghauses 28–30 November 2002 und 16–19 Januar 2003*, edited by P. C. Bol, G. Kaminski, and C. Maderna, 319–41. *Städel-Jahrbuch* 19. Munich: Städel Museum, 2004.

————. "Alexanderporträts." In *Ägypten – Griechenland – Rom. Abwehr und Berührung. Ausstellungskatalog Städelsches Kunstinstitut und Städtische Galerie Frankfurt, 26.11.2005–26.2.2006*, edited by H. Beck, 216–34. Frankfurt: Städtische Galerie, 2005.

Reisner, G. A., C. S. Fisher, and D. G. Lyon. *Harvard Excavations at Samaria 1908–1910*. Cambridge, MA: Harvard University Press, 1924.

Renault, M. *Fire from Heaven*. New York: Pantheon/Random House, 1969.

————. *The Persian Boy*. New York: Pantheon Books, 1972.

————. *Funeral Games*. New York: Pantheon Books, 1981.

Retzleff, A., and A. Majeed Mjely. "Seat Inscriptions in the Odeum at Gerasa (Jerash)." *BASOR* 336 (2004): 37–48.

Richter, G. M. A. *The Portraits of the Greeks*. 3 vols. New York: Phaidon, 1965.

Ridgway, B. S. "Birds, 'Meniskoi,' and Head Attributes in Archaic Greece." *AJA* 94 (1990): 583–612.

Rigsby, K. J. "Seleucid Notes." *TAPA* 110 (1980): 233–54.

Robert, J., and L. Robert. "Bulletin épigraphique, no. 316." *REG* 75 (1962): 207.

————. "Bulletin épigraphique, no. 281." *REG* 76 (1963): 180–81.

Robinson, B. A. *Histories of Peirene: A Corinthian Fountain in Three Millennia*. Princeton, NJ: American School of Classical Studies at Athens, 2011.

Rockwell, P. "Unfinished Statuary Associated with a Sculptor's Studio." In *Aphrodisias Papers 2: The Theater, a Sculptor's Workshop, Philosophers, and Coin-types*, edited by R. R. R. Smith and Kenin T. Erim, 127–43. *Journal of Roman Archaeology Supplement, series 2*. Ann Arbor, MI: *Journal of Roman Archaeology*, 1991.

Rösger, A. "Severus Alexander und Alexander der Große." In *Zu Alexander d. Gr. Festschrift G. Wirth zum 60. Geburtstag am 9.12.86*, edited by W. Will, 885–906. Amsterdam: Verlag A. M. Hakkert, 1988.

Roller, M. B. *Models from the Past in Roman Culture: A World of Exempla*. Cambridge, UK: Cambridge University Press, 2018.

Romano, I. B. "The Archaic Statue of Dionysos from Ikarion." *Hesperia* 51 (1982): 398–409.

————. *Classical Sculpture: Catalogue of the Cypriot, Greek, and Roman Stone Sculpture in the University of Pennsylvania Museum of Archaeology and Anthropology*. Philadelphia: University of Pennsylvania Museum, 2006.

―――. "A Colossal Roman Acrolith from Scythopolis." In *ΣΠΟΝΔΗ - Αφιέρωμα στη μνήμη του Γιώργου Δεσπίνη.* 10⁰ Παράρτημα, edited by A. Delivorrias, N. Kaltsas, I. Trianti, E. Vikela, and A. Zarkadas, 941–54. Athens: Benaki Museum, 2020.

Romano, I. B., and M. L. Fischer. "Roman Marble and Limestone Sculpture from Beth Shean, Israel." In *Les Ateliers de sculpture régionaux: techniques, styles et iconographie, Actes du X Colloque International sur l'art provincial romain.* Arles/Aix-en-Provence, May 21–23, 2007, edited by V. Gaggadis-Robin, A. Hermary, M. Reddé, and C. Sintes, 391–400. Arles: Centre Camille Jullian (CNRS), 2009.

Romano, I. B., S. Pike, and E. Gazda. "The Use and Symbolism of Pentelic Marble in Domitianic Rome." In *Interdisciplinary Studies on Ancient Stone, Proceedings of the IX Association for the Study of Marbles and Other Stones in Antiquity Conference. Documenta* 23, ASMOSIA IX, Tarragona, Spain, 8–13 June 2009, edited by A. Gutierrez Garcia-M., P. Lapuente Mercadal, and I. Roda de Llanza, 772–79. Tarragona: Institut Català d'Arqueologia Clàssica, 2012.

Romano, I. B., D. Tambakopoulos, and Y. Maniatis. "A Roman Portrait of Alexander the Great from Beth Shean: The Most Important Hellenistic Sculpture Found in the Holy Land." *Israel Museum Studies in Archaeology* 10 (2020–2021): 2–28.

Rose, C. B. *Dynastic Commemoration and Imperial Portraiture in the Julio-Claudian Period.* Cambridge, UK: Cambridge University Press, 1997.

Rosenbaum, E. *A Catalogue of Cyrenaican Portrait Sculpture.* London: British Academy/Oxford University Press, 1960.

Rostovtzeff, M. "ΠΡΟΓΟΝΟΙ." *JHS* 55 (1935): 56–66.

Rowan, C. *Under Divine Auspices: Divine Ideology and the Visualisation of Imperial Power in the Severan Period.* Cambridge, UK: Cambridge University Press, 2012.

Rowe, A. "The 1927 Expedition at Beisan: Final Report." *Museum Journal* 19 (1928): 144–69.

―――. *The Topography and History of Beth-Shan.* Philadelphia: University of Pennsylvania Press, 1930.

―――. *The Four Canaanite Temples of Beth-Shan: The Temples and their Cult Objects* (*Beth-Shan* II/1). Philadelphia: University of Pennsylvania Press, 1940.

Sachs, A. J., and H. Hunger. *Astronomical Diaries and Related Texts from Babylonia.* Vol. 3. *Diaries from 164 B.C. to 61 B.C.* Vienna: Austrian Academy of Sciences, 1996.

Saradi-Mendelovici, H. "Christian Attitudes Toward Pagan Monuments in Late Antiquity and Their Legacy in Later Byzantine Centuries." *DOP* 44 (1990): 47–61.

Sartre-Fauriat, A., and M. Sartre. *Inscriptions grecques et latines de la Syrie. Tome XVI – L'Auranitide.* Vol. 1: *Qanawāt (Canatha) et la bordure nord-ouest du Jebel al-'Arab, N°s 1 à 303 (BAH 219).* Beyrouth: Presses de l'Ifpo, 2020.

Savalli-Lestrade, I. "Usages civiques et usages dynastiques de la damnatio memoriae dans le monde hellénistique (323-30 av. J.-C.)." In *Mémoires, partagées, mémoires disputées, écriture et réécriture de l'histoire*, edited by S. Benoist, A. Daguet-Gagey, Chr. Hoët-van Cauwenberghe, and S. Lefebvre, 127–158. Metz: Centre régional universitaire lorrain d'histoire, 2009.

Schäfer, P. *The History of the Jews in the Greco-Roman World.* London: Routledge, 2003.

Schiffer, M. B., and A. R. Miller. *The Material Life of Human Beings: Artifacts, Behavior, and Communication.* London: Routledge, 1999.

Schreiber, T. *Studien über das Bildniss Alexanders des Großen.* Leipzig: Teubner, 1903.

Schürer, E., G. Vermes, F. Millar, and M. Black, eds. *The History of the Jewish People in the Age of Jesus Christ (175 B.C.–A.D. 135)*, rev. ed. London: T&T Clark, 1973.

Schwartz, J. "Note complémentaire (à propos d'une inscription grecque de St. Jean d'Acre)." *IEJ* 12 (1962): 135–36.

Schwartz, S. *Imperialism and Jewish Society, 200 BCE to 640 CE.* Princeton, NJ: Princeton University Press, 2014.

Schwarzenberg, E. "Der lysippische Alexander." *BonnJhb* 167 (1967): 58–118.

———. "The Portraiture of Alexander." In *Alexandre le Grand: Image et Réalité*, edited by E. Badien, 223–78. Geneva: Fondation Hardt. Entretiens sur L'Antiquité Classique 22, 1976.

Schwemmer, M. "Review of *Imitatio Alexandri* in Hellenistic Art by A. A. Trofimova." https://www.sfb948.uni-freiburg.de/de/publikationen/ejournal/ausgaben/1.1.2013/helden.heroes.heros.2013-01-11 (accessed January 15, 2023).

Search for Alexander Supplement to the Catalogue. Art Institute of Chicago, May 16–September 7. Chicago: The Art Institute of Chicago, 1981.

Search for Alexander Supplement to the Catalogue. San Francisco: Fine Arts Museums of San Francisco/M.H. de Young Memorial Museum,

February 20–May 16, 1982. San Francisco: The Fine Arts Museums of San Francisco, 1982.

Segal, A. "Temples for the Imperial Cult in the Roman East: The Architectural Aspect." In *Cities, Monuments and Objects in the Roman and Byzantine Levant: Studies in Honour of Gabi Mazor*, edited by W. Atrash, A. Overman, and P. Gendelman, 103–19. Oxford: Archaeopress, 2022.

Segal, D. "The Roman Quarries in the Area of Beit-Shean: The Stone Origins of the Roman-Byzantine City of Nyssa-Scythopolis; Regional Research of Quarries." Poster presented at Conference of the Association for the Study of Marble and Other Stones in Antiquity (ASMOSIA). Aix-en-Provence, 12–18 June 2006.

Sellers, O.R. "Louis-Hughes Vincent, in Memoriam." *The Biblical Archaeologist* 24, no. 2 (1961): 62–64.

Seyrig, H. "Antiquités Syriennes." *Syria* 39 (1962): 193–211.

———. "Alexandre le Grand, fondateur de Gérasa." *Syria* 42 (1965): 25–28.

Sharvit, T. "Three Marble Statues from The Severan Theater." In *Bet She'an III, Nysa-Scythopolis: The Southern and Severan Theaters Part 2: The Architecture* (*IAA Reports* 58/2), edited by G. Mazor and W. Atrash, 613–24. Jerusalem: Israel Antiquities Authority, 2015.

Shayegan, M. "On Demetrius II Nicator's Arsacid Captivity and Second Rule." *Bulletin of the Asia Institute*, n.s. 17 (2003): 83–103.

Shear, T. L. "The Athenian Agora: Excavations of 1970." *Hesperia* 40 (1971): 241–79.

Skupinska-Løvset, I. *Funerary Portraiture of Roman Palestine: An Analysis of the Production in its Culture-Historical Context*. Gothenburg: Åström, 1983.

———. *Portraiture in Roman Syria: A Study in Social Regional Differentiation within the Art of Portraiture*. Lodz: Wydan, 1999.

Slavazzi, F. "Uso dei modelli e recupero del passato nei programmi scultorei ufficiali di età antonina in Asia Minore." In *Arte e memoria culturale nell'età della Seconda Sofistica*, edited by O. Cordovana and M. Galli, 123–36. Catania: Edizioni del Prisma, 2007.

Smith, H. "Macedonia statue: Alexander the Great or a warrior on a horse." *The Guardian* August 14, 2011. https://www.theguardian.com/world/2011/aug/14/alexander-great-macedonia-warrior-horse (accessed January 17, 2019).

Smith, R. R. R. *Hellenistic Royal Portraits*. Oxford: Clarendon Press, 1988.

————. "Late Roman Philosopher Portraits from Aphrodisias." *JRS* 80 (1990): 127–55.

————. *Hellenistic Sculpture*. London: Thames & Hudson, 1991a.

————. "Late Roman Philosophers." In *Aphrodisias Papers 2: The Theater, a Sculptor's Workshop, Philosophers, and Coin-types*, edited by R. R. R. Smith and K. T. Erim, 144–58. *Journal of Roman Studies Supplement, series 2*. Ann Arbor, MI: *Journal of Roman Studies* 1991b.

————, *Roman Portrait Statuary from Aphrodisias. Aphrodisias: Results of the Excavation at Aphrodisias in Caria II*. Mainz am Rhein: von Zabern, 2006.

————. "Defacing the Gods at Aphrodisias." In *Historical and Religious Memory in the Ancient World*, edited by B. Dignas and R. R. R. Smith. Oxford: Oxford University Press, 2012. https://oxford.university presssscholarship.com/view/10.1093/acprof:oso/ 9780199572069.001.0001/acprof-9780199572069-chapter-13 (accessed January 15, 2023).

————. *The Marble Reliefs from the Julio-Claudian Sebasteion*. Aphrodisias VI. Darmstadt: von Zabern, 2013.

Smith, R. R. R., and M. Melfi. *Antinous: Boy Made God*. Oxford: Ashmolean Museum, University of Oxford, 2018.

Spencer, D. *The Roman Alexander: Reading a Cultural Myth*. Exeter: University of Exeter Press, 2002.

Stewart, A. *Faces of Power: Alexander's Image and Hellenistic Politics*. Berkeley: University of California Press, 1993.

————. "Alexander in Greek and Roman Art." In *Brill's Companion to Alexander the Great*, edited by J. Roisman, 31–66. Leiden: Brill, 2003.

————. *Art in the Hellenistic World: An Introduction*. Berkeley/New York: University of California/Cambridge University Press, 2014.

Stewart, A., and R. S. Martin. "Hellenistic Discoveries at Tel Dor, Israel." *Hesperia* 72 (2003): 121–45.

Stewart, A., E. Driscoll, S. Estrin, N. J. Gleason, E. Lawrence, R. Levitan, S. Lloyd-Knauf, and K. Turbeville. "Classical Sculpture from the Athenian Agora, Part 2: The Friezes of the Temple of Ares (Temple of Athena Pallenis)." *Hesperia* 88 (2019): 625–705.

St. Laurent, B. "The Imperial Museum of Antiquities in Jerusalem, 1890–1930: An Alternative Narrative." *Jerusalem Quarterly* 55 (2013): 6–45.

Stoneman, R. *Alexander the Great: A Life in Legend*. New Haven, CT: Yale University Press, 2008.

Stoneman, R., and K. Erickson, eds. *The Alexander Romance in Persia and the East*. Groningen: Barkhuis Publishing/Groningen University, 2012.

Stoneman, R., K. Nawotka, and A. Wojciechowska, eds. *The Alexander Romance: History and Literature. Ancient narrative. Supplementum 25*. Groningen: Barkhuis/Groningen University Library, 2018.

Stupperich, R. "Das Statuenprogramm in den Zeuxippos-Thermen." *Ist-Mitt* 32 (1965): 210–35.

Svenson, D. *Darstellungen hellenistischer Könige mit Götterattributen*. Frankfurt: Peter Lang, 1995.

Tal, O. "'Hellenistic Foundations' in Palestine." In *Judah between East and West: The Transition from Persian to Greek Rule (ca. 400–200 BCE), A Conference Held at Tel Aviv University, 17–19 April 2007 Sponsored by the ASG (the Academic Study Group for Israel and the Middle East) and Tel Aviv University*, edited by L. L. Grabbe and O. Lipschits, 242–54. London: T&T Clark International, 2011.

———. "Arsinoë II Philadelphia at Philoteria/Bet Yeraḥ (Israel)." *ZPE* 209 (2019): 181–94.

Tarn, W. W. *Alexander the Great and the Unity of Mankind*. London: Humphrey Milford, 1933.

———. *Alexander the Great*. Vol. I, Narrative; Vol. II, Sources and Studies. Cambridge, UK: Cambridge University Press, 1948.

———. *Alexander the Great*, paperback reprint. Boston: Beacon Press, 1956.

Taub, B. "The Real Value of the ISIS Antiquities Trade." *The New Yorker* December 4, 2015. http://www.newyorker.com/news/news-desk/the-real-value-of-the-isis-antiquities-trade (accessed January 10, 2019).

Tcherikover, V. *Die hellenistischen Städtegründungen von Alexander dem Grossen bis auf die Römerzeit, Philologus* Suppl. 19, no. 1. Leipzig: Arno Press, 1927.

Themelis, D. "The Cult of Isis at Ancient Messene." *Bibliotheca Isiaca* II (2011): 97–109.

Thiel, W. "Überlegungen zur Kultur- und Religionspolitik König Antiochos' IV. Epiphanes am Beispiel der Entwicklung des Heiligtums des Zeus Olympios/Akraios von Nysa-Skythopolis." In *Kult und Kommunikation. Medien in Heiligtümern der Antike*, edited by C. Frevel and H. von Hesberg, 121–63. Wiesbaden: Reichert Verlag, 2007.

Thiersch, H. "Ein hellenistischer Kolossalkopf aus Besan." *Nachrichten der Göttinger Gesellschaft der Wissenschaften Philolog-Hist. Klasse* (1932): 52–76.

Thomas, R. "Bemerkungen zu einer Ptolemäerstatuette mit Hm-Hm-Krone." In *Antike Bronzen. Werkstattkreise, Figuren und Geräte. Akten des 14. Internationalen Kongresses für Antike Bronzen*, Köln 21.–24. September 1999, edited by R. Thomas, 85–89. *KölnJb* 33. Cologne: Gebr. Mann, 2000.

————. *Eine posthume statuette Ptolemaios IV und ihr historischer Kontext. Zur Götterangleichung hellenistischer Herrscher. Trierer Winckelmannsprogramme* 18. Mainz: von Zabern, 2002.

————. "Herrscher und Gott. Zur Götterangleichung in hellenistischen Herrscherdarstellungen." In *Studi di archeologia in onore di Gustavo Traversari* 2, edited by M. Fano Santi, 829–48. Rome: Bretschneider, 2004.

Thompson, R. W. *Moses Khorenats'i: History of the Armenians.* Cambridge, MA: Harvard University Press, 1978.

Thurn, I., ed. *Ioannis Malalae Chronographia. Corpus Fontium Historiae Byzantinae* 35. Berlin: Walter de Gruyter, 2000.

Toma, N. "Aphrodisias and the Regional Marble Trade. The Scaenae Frons of the Theater at Nysa." In *ASMOSIA XI: Interdisciplinary Studies of Ancient Stone, Proceedings of the 11th International Conference of ASMOSIA, Split, 18–22 May 2015*, edited by D. M. Poljak and K. Marasovic, 513–21. Split: University of Split, 2018.

Trofimova, A. *Imitatio Alexandri in Hellenistic Art: Portraits of Alexander the Great and Mythological Images. Studi Archaeologica* 187. Rome: Bretschneider, 2012.

True, M., and K. Hamma, eds. *A Passion for Antiquities. Ancient Art from the Collection of Barbara and Lawrence Fleischman.* Malibu: J. Paul Getty Museum, 1994.

Trümper, M. Review of *Beth She'an.* Vol. 1: *Nysa-Scythopolis: The Caesareum and the Odeum* G. Mazor and A. Najjar. *IAA Reports* 33. Jerusalem, 2007 *BASOR* 354 (2009): 95–97.

Tsafrir, Y. "Further Evidence of the Cult of Zeus Akraios at Beth Shean (Scythopolis)." *IEJ* 39, 1989: 76–78.

————. "The Fate of Pagan Cult Places in Palestine: The Archaeological Evidence with Emphasis on Bet Shean." In *Religious and Ethnic Communities in Later Roman Palestine* (*Studies and Texts in Jewish History and Culture* 5), edited by H. Lapin, 197–218. Bethesda: Meyerhoff Center for Jewish Studies, University of Maryland, 1998.

Tsafrir, Y., and G. Foerster. "Bet Shean Excavation Project: 1988/1989." *Excavations and Surveys in Israel 1989–1990* 9 (1989–90): 120–28.

————. "Excavations of the Hebrew University Expedition at Bet Shean, 1980–1994" [Hebrew]. *Qadmoniot* 27, nos. 107–8 (1994): 93–116.

————. "Urbanism at Scythopolis—Bet Shean in the Fourth to Seventh Centuries." *DOP* 51 (1997): 85–146.

Turnheim, Y., and A. Ovadiah. "Dionysos in Beth Shean." *Rivista di Archeologia* 18 (1994): 105–14.

van Groningen, B. A. *A Family-Archive from Tebtunis (P. Fam. Tebt.).* Leiden: Brill, 1950.

Van Nuffelen, P. "Un culte royal municipal de Séleucie du Tigre à l'époque séleucide." *Epigraphica Anatolica* 33 (2001): 85–87.

————. "Le culte royal de l'empire des Séleucides: une réinterprétation." *Historia* 53 (2004): 278–301.

Van Voorhis, J. *The Sculptor's Workshop. Aphrodisias 10.* Wiesbaden: Reichert Verlag, 2018.

Vermeule, C. C. "The Late Antonine and Severan Bronze Portraits from Southwest Asia Minor." In *Eikones, Studien zum Griechischen und Römischen Bildnis, Hans Jucker zum Sechzigsten Geburtstag Gewidmet,* edited by R. A. Stucky and I. Jucker. *Antike Kunst,* Beiheft 12 (1980): 185–90.

Vermeule, C. C., and K. Anderson. "Greek and Roman Sculpture in the Holy Land." *The Burlington Magazine* 123, no. 934 (1981): 7–19.

Vermeule, C. C., and M. B. Comstock. *Sculpture in Stone and Bronze: Additions to the Collections of Greek, Etruscan, and Roman Art 1971–1988 in the Museum of Fine Arts, Boston.* Boston: Museum of Fine Arts, 1988.

Videbech, C. "Private Collections of Sculpture in Late Antiquity: An Overview of the Form, Function and Tradition." In *Tradition: Transmission of Culture in the Ancient World. Acta Hyperborea: Danish Studies in Classical Archaeology* 14, edited by J. Fejfer, M. Moltesen, and A. Rathje, 451–79. Copenhagen: Tusculanum Press/University of Copenhagen, 2015.

Vincent, L. H. "Chronique, L'année archéologique 1923 en Palestine." *Revue Biblique* 33 (1924): 420–37.

Vitto, F. "Two Marble Heads of Goddesses from Tel Naharon-Scythopolis." *'Atiqot* 20 (1991): 33–45.

Vlachogianni, E. "Kosmetai and Ephebes" and "The Diogeneion and the Herms of the 'Kosmetai'." In *Hadrianus–Ἀδριανός. Hadrian, Athens and the Gymnasia,* edited by M. Lagogianni-Georgakarakos and E. Papi, 158–65. Athens: National Archaeological Museum/Scuola Archeologica Italiana di Atene, 2018.

Waddington, W. H. *Inscriptions grecques et latines de la Syrie. Recueillies et expliquées.* Paris: F. Didot, 1870.

Wallace, S. "Metalexandron: Receptions of Alexander in the Hellenistic and Roman Worlds." In *Brill's Companion to the Reception of Alexander the Great. Brill's Companions to Classical Studies Online* IV, vol. 14, edited by K. R. Moore, 162–96. Leiden: Brill, 2018. https://doi.org/10.1163/9789004359932_008 (accessed June 1, 2023).

Watzinger, C. *Denkmäler Palästinas* II. Leipzig: Hinrichs'sche Buchhandlung, 1935.

Waywell, G. B. "Athena Mattei." *BSA* 66 (1971): 373–82.

Weber, T. M. *Gadara Decapolitana. Abhandlungen des Deutsches-Palästina-Vereins* 30 (*Gadara-Umm Qês* I). Wiesbaden: Harrassowitz, 2002.

———. "Odeion and Imperial Cult at Scythopolis." Review of *Beth She'an.* Vol. 1: *Nysa-Scythopolis: The Caesareum and the Odeum* by G. Mazor and A. Najjar. *IAA Reports* 33. Jerusalem, 2007. *JRA* 22 (2009): 745–51.

———. "Near East." In *Oxford Handbook of Roman Sculpture*, edited by E. Friedland and M. G. Sobocinski, 569–86. Oxford: Oxford University Press, 2015.

Weber-Karyotakis, T. M. "The Sculptures from the Eastern Great Baths: Old and New Finds." In *The Eastern Great Baths at Gerasa/Jerash: Preliminary Report on the 2016 Campaign*, edited by T. Lepaon, N. Turshan, and T. M. Weber-Karyotakis, 1–54. Düsseldorf: Edit. Digitale Publikation, Gerda Henkel Stiftung, 2017. https://edit.gerda-henkel-stiftung.de/gerasa/the-eastern-baths-at-gerasa-jerash (accessed January 15, 2023).

Welles, C. B. "Inscriptions." In *Gerasa: City of the Decapolis. An Account Embodying the Record of a Joint Excavation Conducted by Yale University and the British School of Archaeology in Jerusalem (1928–1930), and Yale University and the American Schools of Oriental Research (1930–1931, 1933–1934)*, edited by C. H. Kraeling, 355–494, 573–616. New Haven, CT: Yale University Press, 1938.

Welles, C. B., R. O. Fink, and J. F. Gilliam, eds. *The Excavations at Dura-Europos conducted by Yale University and the French Academy of Inscriptions and Letters*, Final Report V, Part I, *The Parchments and Papyri.* New Haven: CT, Yale University Press, 1959.

Wenning, R. "Hellenistische Skulpturen in Israel." *Boreas* 6 (1983): 105–18.

"What in the World." *Archaeology* 6 (1954): 18–23.

Whitmarsh, T. *The Second Sophistic. Greece and Rome: New Surveys in the Classics* 35. Cambridge, UK: Cambridge University Press, 2005.

Williams, A. R. "Explore This Mysterious Mosaic—It May Portray Alexander the Great." *National Geographic* September 9, 2016. https://www.nationalgeographic.com/history/article/mysterious-mosaic-alexander-the-great-israel (accessed January 15, 2023).

Witt, R. E. *Isis in the Graeco-Roman World*. London: Thames and Hudson, 1971.

Worthington, I., ed. *Brill's New Jacoby*. Leiden: Brill, 2006–2023, https://scholarlyeditions.brill.com/bnjo/.

Yalouris, N., M. Andronikos, K. Rhomiopoulou, A. Herrmann, and C. Vermeule. *The Search for Alexander: An Exhibition*. New York/Athens: Greek Ministry of Culture and Sciences, 1980.

Yfantidis, K. "Die Polychromie der Hellenistischen Plastik." PhD diss., Johannes Gutenberg-Universität Mainz. Mainz, 1984.

Youtie, H. C., and C. Bonner. "Two Curse Tablets from Beisan." *TAPA* 68 (1937): 43–77, 128.

Zuwiyya, D. *A Companion to Alexander Literature in the Middle Ages*. Brill: Leiden, 2011.

Index

Page numbers in *italics* refer to illustrations.

A

Aboukir medallions, 125, *125*, 156–59; *see also* Tarsos medallions

acrolithic statue, 23, 43, 44, 101–8, 147, 163, 164

Afyon, 59, 120, 190–93; *see also* marble

Alexander Balas, 19, 31, 32, 33, 36, 38; *see also* Late Seleucid kings

Alexander II Zabinas, 8, 19, 31, 32, 36, 37, 40, 42
  coins of, 8, 24, 42

Alexander III, the Great, 1, 38, 43, 44, 46, 48, 155
  Alexander *in imitatione*, 61, 62, 126, 139–40, 143, 155; *see also imitatio Alexandri*
  as anti-Christ, 184
  Azara portrait, 133
  anastolé, 57, 57n8, 109, 114, 115, 131, 132, 133, 133n23, 140, 143n287, 169, 172
  bronze statuettes of, 125, 129, 131, 133, 140–41, 145, 150
  busts of, 62, 113, 122–28, 171
  on bronze coin, *153*
  of Dionysos, 98

Alexander III, the Great (*continued*)
  free-standing statuettes, 123, 124, 126
  on gold medallion, *125*
  half-figure, 123
  colossal ruler portraits, 58
  cults of, 164
  temple statue, 164, *165*
  as deified mortal, 164
  depicted with horns of Zeus-Ammon, 141, 142, 156n367, 157, 159
  as Dionysos, 59, 98, 139, 148, 149, 160
  divine aspect of, 172
  fascination with, 63–64
  games honoring, 158
  golden hair of, 121, 131
  as Helios, 126, 129, 134, 139, 141, 150
  historical interpretation of, 64, 183
  as *kosmokrator*, 151, 160, 163, 165, 184
  as *ktistes*, 165
  legend of, 161–63
  as Osiris, 144
  portrait head of Alexander, 1, 10, 15, 23, 43, 55, *56*, 58, 62, 82, 95, 108, *110*, 122, 125, 126, 134, 139, 147, 164, 169, 171, *178*, 184, 186, *188*, 193, 194

Alexander III, the Great
(*continued*)
and *anastolé*, 57, 109, 110,
114, 115, 131, 132,
133, 140, 143n287,
169, 172
as archaeological find, 14–15
attribute, 115, 140–42, 143,
145, 147, 148, 150,
156–61, 166
hole for, 62, 115, *118, 119,*
150
interpretation of, 140–42
missing, 62, 160
significance of lotus flower,
147
star or sun, 127, 150–51,
159, 160, 165
of Zeus, 143, 144n296
bronze coin of Gerasa, *153*
and contents of the cistern,
94–95
dating of, 43
Hellenistic period, 59, 60,
71
drilled pupils, 118, 136
Egyptian connection, 141
excavation of, 174–79
exhibition of, 62, 181, 182
garment, 109, 113, 121, 122,
129–30
cuirass, 109, 122, 129–30
himation, 86, 128, 129
hypothetical reconstruction,
15, *127,* 130, *159,* 166
identification as Alexander
the Great, 132–39
marble provenance, 90, 185–
96
samples, 185, 186, 187,
189, 190–92

Alexander III, the Great
(*continued*)
modern history of, 174–79
and Rockefeller Archaeo-
logical Museum,
Jerusalem, 176–79, 178,
181
mutilation of, 17, 59, 62, 169,
170, 172
and Palestine Expedition, 1,
94
pigment/paint, 92, 120–22,
130, 133, 137, 164
placement in temple of Zeus,
142–43, 165
previous scholarship, 55–64
reconstruction drawing, 119,
165
as representation of Dionysos,
47n130, 142
portrait from theater of Perge,
128, 135, 137
portraiture of, 61, 62, 126, 133,
157, 170
features of, 131–32, 135
Lysippan Alexander, 57, 58,
130, 133, 134, 140
Nelidow Alexander type, 130,
151
Schwarzenberg Alexander,
123, 135n245
presence in Scythopolis, 5, 64,
66, 161
renaissance, 151–56, 163
during Severan dynasty, 161
as son of Zeus, 142, 143,
153n349
with symbols of Zeus, 142–43
veneration of, 58
Alexander Jannaeus, 11

Alexander Severus, 49, 152, 155,
156, 158, 160, 161; *see
also* Caracalla, Geta,
Severan Dynasty,
Septimius Severus
reign of, 156, 158
Alexandria, Egypt, 30, 64, 81,
134, 141, 144, 145,
149, 155
founding of, 147
hidden temple, 167
Allard Pierson Museum, 150
Altintas, 190, 191, 192, 193; *see
also* marble
quarries, 190–94
Amarna tablet EA 289, 5n5
anastolé motif, 109; *see also*
Alexander III the Great
Antinous Braschi, 147
Antioch, 46
Antiocheia-Gadara, 10, 29
Antiocheia-Gerasa, 10, 29
Antiocheia-Hippos, 10, 29
Antiocheia-in-Persis, 26
Antiochene revolt, 39
Antiochos III, 8, 9n23, 19, 26, 49
Antiochos IV Epiphanes, 7n10, 8,
9, 10, 19, 25n23, 26–
30, 33, 37n75, 38, 43,
46n123, 47, 57
as Dionysos-Alexander-Zeus,
57
Antiochos VI Dionysos, 31, 32,
33, 35n66, 37, 38; *see
also* Late Seleucid
kings
coinage of, 38
Antiochos VII Sidetes, 19, 20, 31,
32, 33n58, 35, 36, 37,
40, 41, 42, 65n53; *see*

Antiochos VII Sidetes (*continued*)
also Late Seleucid
kings
anabasis, 40
bronze coins of, 42
Antiochos VIII Grypos, 8, 20, 31,
32, 36, 37, 40, 41,
42n93; *see also* Late
Seleucid kings
Antiochos IX Kyzikenos, 9, 11,
20, 30, 31, 32, 41, 42;
see also Late Seleucid
kings
bronze coins of, 42
Antonine era, 48, 61, 83, 92, 107,
120, 120n79, 134–35,
136, 137, 139, 141,
142, 148, 149, 160, 172
marble use in, 138
Antonine workmanship, 85, 136
Antoninus Pius, 24, 66, 69n66,
74, *74*, 78, 83, 94, 123,
136
Apameia, 33, 35, 37
Treaty of, 19
Apelles, 142
Aphrodisian marble, 101,
104n161, 120, 120n179,
124, 126n204, 137,
138, 138n262, 139
export of, 195
Aphrodisian sculptors, 120, 136,
137, 138–39
Aphrodisias, 59, 62n41, 88, 92,
101, 104, 120, 124,
136, 137, 138, 139,
154n354, 166n395, 167,
169n412, 171, 190,
191, 192, 193, 194,
195; *see also*

Aphrodisias (*continued*)
  Aphrodisian marble,
    marble
Aphrodite, 25n22
  Knidian, 168
  statue with Eros in Eastern
      Bathhouse, Scythopolis,
      88, *89*, 92, 137,
      172n422
  statue from Gaza, 171
  statue from the Severan
      Theater, Scythopolis,
      87–88, 172n422
  temple at Aphrodisias,
      169n412, 195
Apollo, 37–38n77, 38, 86, 139,
      156n366, 157n369
  Centocellle type, 86
  and *Theoi Soteres*, 26
Apollo Karneios, 139
Archelaos, 27
Artemis, 25n22, 37, 38n77, 92
  temple of, in mythical
      Trikomis, 10n26
  and *Theoi Soteres*, 26
Arubas, Benjamin, 66
Astarte-Atargatis, 25, 74
  temple of, 5, 74n74
asylia, 29
Athena, 93, 158
  cult of in Scythopolis, 25n22
  sculpture from Tel Naharon,
      88–91, *91*, 120n180,
      137
Athenas of the Ince type, 90
Athens, 28, 101, 120, 122, 123,
      152, 168, 189
Attalos II, 33
attributes, 76, 95n144, 174, *see
      also* Alexander III, the
      Great

attributes (*continued*)
  of Alexander, 62, 145, 147,
      151, 156–61
  Egyptian, 143–44
  flower, 145, 146, 148
  ivy as, 149
  lotus, 145–48
    significance of, 147
  star, 150–51, *159*
Azara, Joseph Nicholas, 133
  Azara herm, 123, *124*, 132, 133

B
Baal, 27
Bar Kokhba Revolt, 69n61, 85
Bargylia (Caria), 81
basalt, use of in Scythopolis, 8,
      24, 83
Baths of Caracalla, Rome,
      136n252
Baths of Zeuxippos,
      Constantinople, 168
Battle of Pelusion, 30
Bay of Naples, 122
Begram, Afghanistan, 62n41, 145
  ivories, 146
Beth Shean/Tel Beth Shean/
      Scythopolis/Nysa-
      Scythopolis, 1, *2, 3, 6,*
      15, 29, 30, *68*, 146,
      185, 192
  acropolis, 15, 57, 62, 69, 71,
      74, 76, 77, 95, 99, 102,
      126, 139, 154, 163,
      174, 182
  Bronze Age of, 2, 4, 141
  burial place of Nysa, 75
  Christian iconoclasm in, 15,
      109, 166–74
  cistern on the tel, 10, 15, 23,
      25, 43, 44, 45, 58, 62,

Beth Shean/Tel Beth Shean/
     Scythopolis/Nysa-
     Scythopolis (*continued*)
     66, *70*, 72, 73, 76, 77,
     80, 93, 94, 98, 102,
     172, 184
  colossal acrolithic statue in,
     23, 43–44, 57, 95, 101–
     8, 164
    colossal marble fingers
       found in, 23, 44, 58,
       60n32, 61, 71n69, 93,
       95n145, 99–101, 102,
       102n158, 103, *104*,
       105, 106, 107, 108,
       126n205, 138, 164
  column drums, 24, 43, *71*, 72
  Corinthian figured capital, 24,
     61, 69, *72*, 76, 91n126,
     99
  debris of, 23, 43, 45, 71n69,
     95, 99
  as findspot, 28, 30, 71n69,
     186n1
  life-sized marble hand, 99–
     101, *102, 187*
  limestone figured-capital
     fragment, 96, 97, 98
  limestone stele fragment, 10,
     18, 20n7, *22*, 23,
     23n11, 24, 25, 43, 44,
     45, 48, 66, 77; *see also*
     Supplementum
     Epigraphicum Graecum
     (*SEG*) 8 33
  marble head, 108–22, 169,
     172, 184; *see also*
     Alexander III, the Great
  plan of, *6, 67*
  and sculptural fragments, 15,
     62, 71n69, 80, 94–96,
     163, 169, 172

Beth Shean/Tel Beth Shean/
     Scythopolis/Nysa-
     Scythopolis (*continued*)
  coins of mint, *74*, 81
  destruction of pagan
     sanctuaries, 44, 45
  Dionysos and, 99, 107, 142,
     146, 148; *see also*
     Dionysos
  flax production and, 12
  foundation legend of, 146, 147,
     148
  Hellenistic period, 3, 5–12, 14,
     17–43, 46, 47, 49, 56,
     57, 58, 59, 60, 61, 66,
     71, 83, 94 95, 120, 121,
     129, 131, 132,
     134n240, 139, 140,
     141, 149, 150, 152–53,
     181
    Catalogue of priests of, 17–
       54, *see SEG* 8 33
    Greek inscriptions from,
       49–54
  numismatic evidence, 11,
     12n41, 25n22, 78, 79,
     80, 143, 152n346, 153,
     155
  history, 1–15, 141, 166
  Neolithic period, 4
  imperial period, 9, 12–14, 18,
     19n2, 20, 23, 24, 26,
     43, 47, 48, 49, 66–69,
     79, 84, 120, 130, 140,
     141, 151, 162, 163–64
  ideology, 48
  and monument erasure, 48
  portrait sculptures of, 83, 93,
     94, 105, 123, 124, 130,
     132, 138
  limestone sculptures, 13, 23,
     50, 51, 52, 69, 78, 83,

Beth Shean/Tel Beth Shean/
    Scythopolis/Nysa-
    Scythopolis (*continued*)
    93, 94n138, 95, 96–99,
    107, 148, 164
  marble sculpture found in, 139,
    185–87, 189–95
  monument landscape, 163–66
  and over-life-sized marble head,
    55, 108, 143
  Penn Museum excavation, 1, 2,
    8, 14, 30, 56, 174, 175
  Roman acropolis (tel) of, 6, 15,
    62, 69–73, 163–66
    temple on, 19, 24, 25, 56, 61,
      69–82, 108, 161, 163,
      184
      building materials, 24, 69
      and octagonal limestone
        altar, 25, 76
    Zeus and, 25–30, 78, 142–43
Bishop Porphyry, 171
bol, 121
Breasted, James Henry, 175
British Mandate for Palestine, 1,
    102n158, 174, 181, 184
British Museum, London, 56
British School of Archaeology,
    Jerusalem, 174, 175
Brooklyn Museum, 129
Bucephalus, 127, 157

C
Caesarea Maritima, 83, 97, 99,
    106n165, 126, 166,
    167, 169
Canatha, 12
Caracalla, 13, 46n120, 51, 84,
    154–55, 160, 183; *see
    also* Alexander Severus,

Caracalla (*continued*)
    Geta, Septimius
    Severus, Severan
    dynasty
  as Alexander, 65n53, 156
  bronze coin, *81*
  bronze portrait, 81
  and Dionysos, 155
  gold medallion, *157*, 158
  interest in Alexander the Great,
    155–56, 158, 159, 162
  and Severan Dynasty link to
    Alexander, 161
  sons of, 158–59
Carrara, 82, 82n102, 134, 191,
    192; *see also* marble
Cassius Dio, 154, 155
chlamys, 86, 126, 129
  and garment of Alexander, 129,
    150
Christian iconoclasm, 86, 88–89,
    166–74
  and Christian zealots, 86, 92,
    109, 112, 171, 173
  and portrait mutilation, 59, 72,
    89, 112, 166, *170*
cistern on the tel, *see* Beth Shean
Classical Greece, 152
Clement of Alexandria, 174
cloak, 129; *see also* chlamys
colossal Alexander portrait, 137
colossal ruler portraits of
    Alexander, 58
colossal statue from Cyrene, 129
Commodus, 49, 153
  as Hercules, 124–25
  reign of, 153
Constantine the Great, 14, 105,
    167, 168
  treatment of pagan temples, 167

Constantinople, 167, 168
Corinthian column capitals, 24,
    61, 70, *72*, 96
Corinthian columns, 24
cosmological symbols, 151, 160
crown, 146, 148; *see also*
        attributes
    hemhem, 125, 141n277, 143,
        144, 145, 160
    and portrait head of Alexander,
        116, 143, 144, 150, 151
cuirass, 65n53, 83, *85*, 109, 121,
        122, 128, 129–30, 157,
        158
    statue from Samaria Sebaste, 82
cults
    activities, 14, 166, 168
    of Alexander, 15, 44, 47–48,
        81, 152, 163, 164
    during imperial period, 9,
        25n22, 44, 45, 80
        at Scythopolis, 25, 47n127,
            48, 62, 108
        Seleucid, 9, 10, 20, 26–30,
            29, 45–46, 58
    of Zeus Olympios, 17, 19n2,
        26–30, 108, 164–65,
        165

D
damnatio memoriae, 10, 20, 36,
        48, 66
Dead Sea scrolls, 181
decapitation, 172–73; *see also*
        iconoclasm
    of pagan statues, 171, 173
Decapolis, 12, 18, 163
    cities, *13*, 26, 28, 29, 61, 148,
        152, 153, 184
    cults in, 29, 59

deliberate destruction, 8, 11, 44,
        59, 167; *see also*
        Christian iconoclasm,
        damnatio memoriae
    of sculpture, 92, 112, 166, 168–
        69, 171, 173
Demeter, 9n23, 25n22, 47n130,
        50, 52
    temple of, in Cyrene, 123
Demetrios I Soter, 23, 30, 31, 33
Demetrios II Nikator, 8, 10, 17,
        19–20, 20n7, 22n9, 23,
        26n29, 30–33, 35–37,
        39–43, 48, 49, 66; *see
        also* Kleopatra Thea
    bronze coin of, 42
    reign of, 32, 48, 49
    on stele, 30, 43, 48
"Demokritos" Laboratory, Athens,
        101, 120, 189
Department of Antiquities in the
        British Mandate for
        Palestine, 2, 99n156,
        174–76, 178, 179
Diadochi, 8, 152
Diodotos Tryphon, 19, 31, 32,
        33–38, 47n130, 51
Dion, Decapolis, 12; *see also*
        Decapolis
Dion, Macedonia, 27, 142, 184
Dionysos/Bacchus, 19n2, 25, 38,
        44n104, 46, 57, 74–75,
        78, 86, *96*, 99, 126,
        139, 142, 166, 174
    Alexander as, 44, 148–50, 160
    altars dedicated to, 50, 51, *75*,
        165n394
    coins of, 107, 108n170
    and double-headed herms, 76,
        80

Dionysos/Bacchus (*continued*)
 and flowering lotus, 146–47,
  148, 166
 as founder of Nysa-Scythopolis,
  3, 4, 9, 19, 25, 47, 50,
  85, 93, 107, 142, 144,
  164, 174
 imagery, 9
 and *imitatio Alexandri*, 139
 and inscription on stele, 46, 47
 and limestone head on
  Corinthian capital, 23,
  43, 76, 95, *96–98*, 96–
  99, 148, 164
 and Nysa, 9–10, 13, 60, 146,
  147n312
 portrait head as, 57–59, 60n32,
  126
 on reverse of bronze coin, *74*
 and Roman temple in
  Scythopolis, 74, 76, 78,
  82, 108, 164, *165*
 statue from Sylvanus Hall, *77–
  79*, 166, 167, 174
 treatment in Scythopolis, 74–
  82, 146–50
Dionysos Ktistes, 46, 47nn129–
  130, 50
Dionysos-Alexander, 148, 149
Dionysos-Osiris, 147
Dioscuri, 26, 38, 139, 150
Doliana, 191, 192; *see also*
  marble
dolomitic marble, 89, 189; *see
  also* marble
Dometeinos, 136
double-headed herms, 76, 156;
  see also herm
Dura Europos, 26, 29, 45, 46

E
Early Byzantine period, 13, 15,
  62, 75, 166, 168, 169,
  184
Early Christian period, 59, 184
 zealots, 86, 109, 171, 173, 174
Early Iron Age, 2, 5, 69, 72
earthquake
 of 363 CE, 13, 45, 52
 of 749 CE, 13n47, 14, 46, 86
Eastern Bathhouse, Beth Shean
 excavation of, 88
 fountain of, 88
 hypocaust of, 88, 166
 statue of Aphrodite with Eros,
  89
 statue of a nymph with shell,
  90, 92
 and Sylvanus Hall, 167
Eastern Roman Empire, 45, 48,
  166, 167
École Biblique, Jerusalem, 175
Egyptian attributes, 143–44; *see
  also* Alexander III, the
  Great
Egyptian iconography, 143n287,
  145, 146
Egyptian pharaohs, 144
Elagabal, 155
Elagabalus, 13, 46n120, 49, 51,
  79,108n170, 153, 154,
  158, 160, 161
 bronze coin of, *153*
electron paramagnetic resonance
  spectroscopy, 104n161,
  120, 186
Ephesos, 81, 142, 148n319,
  172n422, 190, 191,
  192; *see also* marble

Epikrates, 11, 30; *see also SEG* 8 33

Erlich, A., 59, 65n53, 162n388

Eudoxia, 46, 52

Eumenes II, 28

Eusebius of Caesarea Maritima, 167

F

Fischer, Moshe, 58, 59, 70, 82n102, 120

Fisher, Clarence, 2

Fitzgerald, Gerald M., 2, 57, 94n139

Flavius Josephus, 7, 10, 11, 28n46, 35n66, 65, 74n75, 181, 183

fountain
  of Eastern Bathhouse, Beth Shean, 88
  of Peirene, Corinth, 88

Fundilia Rufa, statue of, Nemi, 122

Fundilius Doctus, statue of, Nemi, 123

funerary portraits, 51, 94

G

Gabinius, 12, 25n22, 44

Garstang, John, 174

Geta, 49, 154; *see also* Alexander Severus, Caracalla, Septimius Severus, Severan dynasty

gilding of ancient marble statuary, 121; *see also* polychromy
  gilded marble head of Alexander, 140

gilding of ancient marble statuary (*continued*)
  gold leaf or golden-yellow pigment, 122, 140

Gill, Eric, 176

golden larnax, Vergina, 150

Gordian III, 25n27, 44n104, 74, 78, 79, 108n170, 146n312
  bronze coin of, *74*

Graeco-Egyptian syncretism, 143

Graeco-Roman Egyptian iconography, 143n287

H

Hadrian, 50, 85, 152n346
  bronze torso of, 84
  rule of, 69n61
  and Scythopolis, 84

Hadrianic sculptures, 84n109, 134, 135,137n257, 169n413

Harpokrates/Horus, 144, 146, 160

Hasmonean rulers, 43, 44
  takeover of Judaea, 7, 10, 11, 59

Helios, 126, 141, 150, 157
  Alexander as, 129, 134, 139, 150

Hellenis polis, 12, 46, 162

Hellenistic coins, 7n10, 9, 24, 38, 39, 42–43, 142, 153n350, 156, 158, 160
  Ptolemaic coin hoard, 7, 11, 24
  Seleucid hoard, 7, 8, 30, 42

Hellenistic portraits of Alexander, 58, 61, 121, 134n240, 140, 141

Hellenistic ruler cults, 17–49, 184

Hellenistic sculpture in Israel, 58
"Hellenization," 162n387
hemhem crown, 125n190, 141,
143, 144, 144n296,
145, 160; *see also*
Alexander III, the
Great; crown
Herakleides, son of Sarapion, 30,
30n55
Herakleides Lembos, 30
Herakles/Hercules, 149
cult of, 25n22
and *imitatione Alexandri,* 139
Sanctuary of at Tivoli, 171
Herakles-Melqart, 39
herm, 122–28
of Alexander, 62, 122
Azara, 123–24, *124*, 132–33
double-herm of Dionysos and
Ariadne, 76, *80*
herm head of Fundilia Rufa,
122–23
Herodian, 156, 169
Herzl, Theodore, 179
High Priest Jonathan, 33, 35
himation, 86, 129
hoard
and Aboukir medallions, 156,
157, 158
Ptolemaic, 7, 11, 24
Seleucid, 7, 8, 30, 42
Holy Land, 57, 181, 182
Homer's *Odyssey*, 46, 145
Hymettos, 191, 192; *see also*
marble

I
iconoclasm, *see* Christian
iconoclasm, 167
iconoclastic mutilation, 89, 167,
171–73

Idealplastik, 93
imitatio Alexandri, 60, 139–40,
149, 155; *see also*
Alexander *in imitatione*
imperial cults in the Decapolis,
25n22, 59, 80
Institute of Archaeology of the
Hebrew University,
Jerusalem, 180
interpretatio Graeca, 27
Isis, 25n22, 144
cult of, 155
lotus as attribute, 146
Islamic State in Syria (ISIS), 173
Israel, 178, 179, 182
state of, 62, 180, 181, 182, 184
Israel Antiquities Authority
(IAA), 42, 82n99, 120,
179
Israel Department of Antiquities
and Museums, 179
Israel Museum, Jerusalem, 55, *56*,
60, 62, *75*, 76n82, *77*,
80, 84n109, *85, 87, 89,
90, 91, 95, 110, 111,
112, 113, 114, 115,
116, 117, 118, 119,
153, 170, 178*, 179,
185, 186, 195
and Israeli national identity,
179–82
Samuel and Saidye Bronfman
Archaeology Wing, 181

J
Jerusalem, 107
Alexander's travels to, 65,
65n53, 66, 183
annexation of East Jerusalem,
178, 179

Jerusalem (*continued*)
  excavated objects sent to,
      99n56, 175
  Rockefeller Achaeological
      Museum, 95, 104, 110,
      176, 177, 178, 181, 186
Jewish homeland, 180
Jews, 9, 46n123, 162n388
  and Alexander, 9, 65, 181
  persecution of, 9
John Hyrkanos, 11, 30, 44
Jordan, 12, 153, 180
Jordan River, 3, 7n11, 152
Jordan Valley, 12
Judaea, 12, 33, 35, 64, 84,
      162n387
  and persecution of Jews in, 9
Julia Domna, 136n249, 154
Julia Maesa, 154
Jupiter Capitolinus, 28

K
kalathos/modius, 141n277, 143,
      145, 145n300
Kapitolias, 12, 28, 29n49
  coin issue of, 152
Khaled Al-Asaad, 173
King Hussein, 179
Kleopatra Thea, 8, 20, 31, 33, 35,
      40, 41, 42, 42n93
Kleopatra II, 36
Kleopatra III, 11, 36
Kos, 58, 145, 192; *see also*
      marble
kosmetai, 122, 123
  Athenian herms, 122n184, 123
kosmokrator, 150, 151, 159, 160,
      163, 165, 184; *see also*
      Alexander III, the Great
Kovacs, Martin, 61

Kreikenbom, D., 58, 134
ktistai/ktistes, 46, 47nn129–130,
      58, 148, 152n345, 156,
      165
  Alexander as, 61, 148, 156,
      165
  Dionysos as, 46, 47nn129–130,
      50, 60, 148, 165

L
Late Antiquity, 137, 138, 169,
      172, 173
Late Antonine/Severan period, 48,
      136, 137n253,
      163n391
Late Roman/Early Byzantine
      period, 15, 62, 172n421
      184
  and Christian iconoclasm, 15,
      83, 86, 88, 166–74
Late Seleucid kings, 14, 31, 43
Latin, 12
Latin inscriptions, 12n44, 13n48,
      52, 85
Liber Pater, 149, 156n156
Lichtenberger, A., 8, 29, 59, 78
Lifshitz, B., 26, 57
limestone, 24, 83, 91n126, 94, 96,
      99
  figured-capital fragment, 95,
      96, *96–98*, 98; *see also*
      Dionysos
  funerary bust, 13, *93*, 94
  hexagonal altar, 46n124,
      47n129, 50, 51, *75*, 76,
      79n93
  octagonal altar, 25, 51, 76
  stele, 10, 20n7, 23
Lotis, 146
lotus, 144, 145, 146-48; *see also*
      attributes

lotus (*continued*)
  and Alexander, 145, 147
  as attribute of Horus/
        Harpokrates and Isis,
        146
  iconography, 143, 146, 147,
        148, 160, 165
  and Isis, 146
  pink (*Nelumbo nucifera*), 145
  and Ptolemaic rulers, 146n309
  significance of, 147
  white, 145
Lucius Aninius Rufus, 123
Lucius Verus, 69n66, 81,
        108n171
  coins, 24

M
Maccabean Revolt, 9
Macedonia
  and Alexander, 64n50, 158, 184
  and Dionysos, 148
  statuary from, 64n50, 150
Macedonian coinage, 150
Manasseh, 5
Maniatis, Yannis, 59, 61, 101,
        120
marble
  Afyon, 59, 120, 190, 191, 192,
        193
  Alexander portrait, 59, 185–87,
        193–95
  Altintas, 190, 191, 192, 193
  analysis of, 59, 86, 101, 104,
        120, 187, 189–92
  Aphrodisias, 88, 92, 104, 120,
        124, 126n204, 136,
        138, 139, 190, 191, 192
  of Asia Minor, 86, 92, 104, 120
  Carrara, 82, 82n102, 134, 191,
        192

marble (*continued*)
  calcitic white, 104, 189
  crystallization, 187, 193
  dating issues and, 60, 69
  Dokimeion/Afyon, 59, 120,
        190, 191, 192, 193
  Doliana, 191, 192
  Ephesos, 81, 142, 148n319,
        172n422, 190, 191, 192
  Göktepe, 120n179, 124,
        137n257, 138
  grain size, 104n161, 186, 191
  in Greece and Asia Minor, 86,
        92, 101n161, 189
  Hymettos, 191, 192
  imported, 60, 82, 83, 92, 107
  isotope analysis, 120, 187, 189
  isotope ratio mass spectrometry,
        186
  Kos, 58, 192
  Miletos, 190, 191, 192
  Mount Gilboa, 23, 83
  Naxos-Apollon
    marble samples, 189, 190,
        191, 192, 193, 194
  Parian, 83n102, 121n182,
        140n271, 171
  Paros I, 105n164
  Paros-Lakkoi, 190–192
  Penteli/Mount Pentelikon, 101
    marble samples, 189, 191,
        192, 193, 194
  polish and pigment, 120–22,
        124, 138
  Proconnesos, 86, 190, 191, 192
  sculptors, 91n126, 92, 139
  Thasos, 89, 90, 92, 137, 191,
        192
  trade, 120n79, 139
  use in Hellenistic sculpture, 59,
        88, 89, 91, 131, 140,
        141, 146, 166

Marcus Aurelius Antoninus, 13,
    20n5, 46, 51, 66, 81,
    83, 94, 108n171, 123,
    154
Marcus Aurelius Severus
    Alexander Augustus
    (Alexander Severus),
    49, 155
medallions, *see* Aboukir
    medallions, Tarsos
    medallions
Miletos, 190, 191, 192, 194, 195;
    see also marble
    quarries
military garb, 130; *see also*
    cuirass
Morris, Gedaliahu, 179
Mount Nysa, 146
Mount Olympus, 142, 147n314
Museum for Jewish Antiquities,
    179
mutilation, *see* Christian
    iconoclasm

N
Nachleben of *SEG* 8 33, 18, 43–
    49
Nahal Ḥarod, 7, 9
naiskos, 24, 71
Naxos-Apollon, 189, 190, 191,
    192, 193, 194; *see also*
    marble
Nefertem, 146
Neoi Dionysoi, 149
neokoros, 79, 80n95, 108n171
Nikandros, 145
Nikanor, 45
Nikatoreion, 46
Nike, 25n22, 150n328, 157n369
Nike acroterion, 59n26,
Niketeria, 158; *see also* Aboukir
    medallions

Nysa, 9, 10n26, 74, 146, 147,
    160; *see also* Mount
    Nysa
cult of, 25n22, 147n312
as nurse of Dionysos, 9, 10, 13,
    60, 75, 146
and Scythopolis, 3, 28, 30
symbol of, 160, 165
worship of, 9
Nysa-Scythopolis, *see* Beth Shean

O
object biography, 62, 184
octagonal limestone altar, Beth
    Shean, 25, 51, 75, 76;
    see also limestone
Ohannessian, David, 176
Old Testament, 5
Olympias, 148
Osiris, 144

P
pagan cults, 25, 167
    practices, 166, 168
pagan inscriptions, 45
pagan sanctuaries, 11, 43n102,
    44, 45
pagan sculptures, 168, 169, 172,
    173; *see also* Christian
    iconoclasm
    deliberate mutilation of, 59, 62,
    109, 112, 166, 168,
    169, 170, 172
Palaestina Secunda, 14; *see also*
    Scythopolis
Palestine, 184
    ancient, 5, 58, 59, 60, 166
    archaeological collections from,
    175
    Roman Palestine, 9, 12, 15,
    80n95, 82, 96, 162

Palestine (*continued*)
  map of, *4*
Palestine Archaeological
    Museum, Jerusalem,
    102n158, 175n434,
    176; *see also*
    Rockefeller
    Archaeological
    Museum
Palestine Expedition, 1, 94, 163
Palestine Museum of Antiquities,
    Jerusalem, 175; *see*
    also Palestine
    Archaeological
    Museum
paludamentum/himation, 128,
    129, 130
Paros-Lakoi, 105n164, 190, 191,
    192; *see also* marble
Parthia, 19n3, 32n57, 35
Patriarch Theophilus of
    Alexandria, 167
  and iconoclasm, 167
Pax Romana, 66, 155
Penteli, 189, 190, 191, 192, 193,
    194, 195; *see also*
    marble
peripteral temple, Beth Shean,
    69–73
Philadelphia (Amman, Jordan),
    12, 29, 61, 106n165
Philadelphia, PA, 2, 95, 101,
    102n158
Philistines
  Beth Shean and, 5
Philostratos, 147
Phraates II, 35, 40
Pierantoni, Giovanni, 148
Pliny the Elder, 3, 12, 75, 145,
    146, 149

Plutarch, 142, 182
polychromy, 121, 122, 167
polytheism, 72, 169, 172
portraits of Alexander of the
    Hellenistic period, 57,
    58, 121, 131
posthumous portraiture of
    Alexander, 56, 58, 121,
    131, 139, 147
Princeton Art Museum, 121, 140
Proconnesos, 86, 92, 190, 191,
    192, 193, 194; *see also*
    marble
Ptah, 146
Ptolemaic coin hoard, 7, 9, 29, 24
Ptolemaic conception of
    Alexander, 141
Ptolemaic presence at
    Scythopolis, 7, 28–30,
    36, 141
Ptolemais, Palestine, 8, 35, 40, 41
  bronze coin of, 42
Ptolemais Hermiou, 134
Ptolemies, 5, 9, 33, 36
Ptolemy II, 5, 7
  festival of, 149
Ptolemy III, 28
Ptolemy IV, 144
Ptolemy V, 8
Ptolemy VI, 26n29, 30, 33, 36,
    37n75, 38
Ptolemy VIII Physkon, 36

Q
quadriporticus, 68, 69

R
Ra, 150
religious syncretism, 183
Rhodogune, 35, 39

Rockefeller, John D., 175
Rockefeller Archaeological
        Museum, Jerusalem, 95,
        104, 110, *176*, *177*,
        178, 181, 186; *see also*
        Jerusalem, Rockefeller
        Archaeological
        Museum
Roman Asia Minor, 105, 161
Roman East/Near East, 12, 14,
        48, 62, 106, 123, 129,
        141, 152, 161, 184
Roman Empire, 45, 62, 88, 126,
        154, 162, 166, 167,
        182n458, 184
Roman Palestine, *4*, 12, 15, 82,
        123
Roman Syria, 58, 154; *see also*
        Roman East/Near East
Round Church, Beth Shean,
        11n37, 23n11, 24, 43,
        45, 72, 95
    plan of, *73*
Rowe, Alan, 2, 22, 71, 175,
        175n432
    and *SEG* 8 33, 23, 25, 57

S

Samaria, 9, 26, 29, 32, 64, 82, 94,
        126, 180
    and *SEG* 8 96, 23, *34*
Scythians, 9, 10n26
Scythopolis, *see* Beth Shean
Sekhmet, 146
Selene, 158
Seleucid coins, 8, 11, 30, 42, 43
    hoard of, 42
Seleucid royal cult, 10, 20, 26,
        27, 29n51, 45–46
Seleukeia-in-Pieria, 25, 26, 27,
        29, 33, 46

Seleukos I Nikator, 25, 26n29,
        27, 43, 44–46
    cult of, 46
Seleukos IV, 19, 25n28, 28,
        29n51, 30
Semele, 78
Septimius Severus, 44n104, 51,
        79, 81, 84, 108n170,
        136, 154, 156n365,
        158, 160
Serapis, 143, 155, 156n366
Severan dynasty, 149, 154, 161;
        see also Alexander
        Severus, Caracalla,
        Geta, Septimius
        Severus
Severan period, 48, 66, 107, 124,
        134–37, 139, 141, 156,
        161, 163
    motifs, 159
Severan Theater, Beth Shean, 68,
        83, 87, 98, 172n422
    excavations of, 86
    frieze, *84*, 98
    statue of Tyche/Fortuna, *87*
Silvanus Hall, Beth Shean, 83,
        86, 167, 172, 174
    statue of Dionysos, *77*
Smith, R. R. R., 58, 138
Sol, 139, 155, 160
Solinus, 3, 75
Stewart, Andrew, 60, 61, 130,
        131, 143, 183
*Supplementum Epigraphicum
        Graecum* (*SEG*) 8 33,
        17, *18*, 19, 20–21, *22*,
        23, 24, 25–33, 36, 37,
        38, 42
    Catalogue of priests of Zeus
        Olympios, 17, 49

Supplementum Epigraphicum Graecum (SEG) 8 33 (*continued*)
   erasure on the stele, 14, 20, 32, 36–37, 39, 40–42, 48, 66
   found in Beth Shean, 8, 9, 11, 25, 28, 39, 66
   Hellenistic inscription on stele, 1, 17, 20–49, 163
   importance of, 14–15
   historical analysis, 17–43, 79, 167
   Nachleben, 43–49
Supplementum Epigraphicum Graecum (SEG) 8 96, 23, 29n51, 32, 40n90
   Catalogue of priests of Zeus Olympios, *34*
   erasure on the stele, 37, 42
   historical analysis, 32
Supplementum Epigraphicum Graecum (SEG) 19 904/20 413, 40, *41*
Supplementum Epigraphicum Graecum (SEG) 44 1332, 37, 38
synnaos theos, 44, 164, 165, 184
Syria, 12, 35, 37, 40, 64, 147, 172
   cults of, 19n2, 154, 155, 160
   Roman, 58, 82n99, 154
Syria Palaestina, 84, 106, 152n346

T
Tambakopoulos, Dimitris, 59, 61, 101, 120

Tarsos medallions, 156, 158; *see also* Aboukir medallions
Tel Beth Shean, *see* Beth Shean
Tel Dor, 35–36, 59
Tel Iztabba, Beth Shean, 7, 8, 9, 11, 28–30, 42, 49, 51, 59, 147n312
   excavation of, 7, 8, 42, 82, 82n102, 99n156, 174
   general plan of, *6*
   remains of settlement, 7, 11n37, 28, 49, 51, 54, 59
Tel Shalem, 13n48, 84, 85
temenos, Beth Shean, 12, 24, 46, 71
Temple of Aphrodite, Aphrodisias, 195
Temple of Demeter, Cyrene, 123
Teos, 26
terminus ante quem, 88, 167
terminus post quem, 61, 82
Thasos, 89, 92, 191, 192; *see also* marble
Theoi Soteres, 9, 17, 20n7, 22, 23, 26, 27, 28, 29, 32, 49, 66
theos synnaos/theoi synnaoi, 82, 108, 164
theos paredros, 164
theos synnaos, 108, 164
Thiersch, H., 57
Thrace, 148, 156
Tiglath-Pilaser III, 5
Treaty of Apameia, 19
Trofimova, Anna, 60, 139, 143, 149
Tyche, 9, 19n2, 25n22, 93, 146
Tyche/Fortuna, 86, *87*

Tyche-Nysa, 9, 74, 79, 146,
          147n312
Tyre, 33, 36, 39, 64, 65

U
University of Pennsylvania
          Museum of
          Archaeology and
          Anthropology (Penn
          Museum), 1, 2, 21, 95
    and Beth Shean excavation,
          2n1, 10, 21, 71n68, 95,
          103, 104; *see also*
          Palestine Expedition
uraeus, 60n32, 143

V
Venus Pudica, 88; *see also*
          Aphrodite
Vincent, Louis-Hughes (Pére
          Vincent), 175

W
Walters, H. B., 56
Watzinger, Carl, 57
Wenning, Robert, 58, 59

Z
Zeus, 12, 18, 26, 27, 44, 46, 47,
          57, 79, *81*, 144, 148,
          149
    attributes for, 140, 143-44, 166
    cult of, 19n2, 25n22, 78
    epithets of, 26, 77
    seated image, 44, 93, 108, 142,
          143, 164, *165*

Zeus (*continued*)
    shrine on Tel Beth Shean, 71
    symbols of, 74, 142–43
    temple of, 36, 44, 50, 76, 82,
          163, 184
Zeus Akraios, 19n2, 25, 26, 27,
          47, 50, 51
    cult of, 27n37
    and presence in Scythopolis,
          60, 142
Zeus Akraios (*continued*)
    seated image of, 108
    and temple on Tel Beth Shean,
          25, 61, 76
Zeus-Ammon, 64, 142, 143, 144,
          160
Zeus Bacchus, 78, 108
Zeus Hypsistos, Dion, 142
Zeus Kasios, 27
Zeus Koryphaios, 27
Zeus Megistos, 26
Zeus Olympios, 26, 27, 46, 47,
          78, 108, 142, 168; *see
          also SEG* 8 33, *SEG* 8
          96
    Catalogue of priests, 17, 20–22,
          23, 32, 49, 66
    cults of, 9, 19n2, 28, 29, 30,
          78n92,
    seated image of, 44, 108, 164
    temple of, 19, 28, 44n108, 76,
          142, 164
Zeus/Serapis, 143
Zoroastrianism, 147